This is a collection of recent revisionist essays on the economic and social history of seventeenth-century Castile by Spanish historians. Since the 1970s an explosion of historical scholarship in Spain, employing new techniques, approaches and sources, has transformed our knowledge of the Castilian past. Hardly any of this research has been absorbed into non-specialist scholarship outside Spain, thereby diminishing the value of any analysis of European economic development that fails to take account of it.

The major areas of current historiographical interest and debate are covered: demography, agriculture, pastoralism, the Indies trade, industrial decline, deurbanisation, taxation and the fiscal system, reseignorialisation, and the politics of redistribution. Developments in Castile are related to the issue of the general crisis of the European economy in the seventeenth century, a crisis which is itself not properly intelligible without an understanding of the Castilian experience.

The essays are important in showing the apparently monolithic seventeenth-century depression in Castile to have been far from uniform in intensity, chronology or space, and in their emphasis on responses to the crisis and on explanations for failure to recover from crisis which was decisive for Spain's divergence from other Western European developments.

Past and Present Publications

The Castilian crisis of the seventeenth century

Past and Present Publications

General Editor: PAUL SLACK, *Exeter College, Oxford*

Past and Present Publications comprise books similar in character to the articles in the journal *Past and Present*. Whether the volumes in the series are collections of essays – some previously published, others new studies – or monographs, they encompass a wide variety of scholarly and original works primarily concerned with social, economic and cultural changes, and their causes and consequences. They will appeal to both specialists and non-specialists and will endeavour to communicate the results of historical and allied research in the readable and lively form.

For a list of titles in Past and Present Publications, see end of book.

The Castilian crisis of the seventeenth century

New perspectives on the economic
and social history of seventeenth-century Spain

Edited by

I. A. A. THOMPSON
University of Keele

and

BARTOLOMÉ YUN CASALILLA
University of Valladolid

Published in association with the
Instituto de Estudios Fiscales, Madrid

CAMBRIDGE
UNIVERSITY PRESS

Published by the Press Syndicate of the University of Cambridge
The Pitt Building, Trumpington Street, Cambridge CB2 1RP
40 West 20th Street, New York, NY 10011–4211, USA
10 Stamford Road, Oakleigh, Melbourne 3166, Australia

© Cambridge University Press 1994

First published 1994

Printed in Great Britain at the University Press, Cambridge

A catalogue record for this book is available from the British Library

Library of Congress cataloguing in publication data

The Castilian crisis of the seventeenth century: new perspectives on the economic
and social history of seventeenth-century Spain / edited by I. A. A. Thompson and
Bartolomé Yun Casalilla.
    p.   cm. – (Past and present publications)
ISBN 0 521 41624 8
1. Spain – Economic conditions. 2. Agriculture – Economic aspects – Spain –
History – 17th century. 3. Spain – Social conditions.
I. Thompson, I. A. A. II. Yun Casalilla, Bartolomé
HC384.C34   1994
330.946'051 – dc20   93–27991   CIP

ISBN 0 521 41624 8 hardback

Contents

List of figures   *page* ix
List of tables   x
Acknowledgements   xii
List of abbreviations   xiv

Introduction   1

1 Castile 1580–1650: economic crisis and the policy of 'reform'   13
ANGEL GARCÍA SANZ

2 The plague in Castile at the end of the sixteenth century and its consequences   32
VICENTE PÉREZ MOREDA

3 The agrarian 'depression' in Castile in the seventeenth century   60
GONZALO ANES

4 Castilian agriculture in the seventeenth century: depression, or 'readjustment and adaptation'?   77
ENRIQUE LLOPIS AGELÁN

5 Wool exports, transhumance and land use in Castile in the sixteenth, seventeenth and eighteenth centuries   101
L. M. BILBAO and E. FERNÁNDEZ DE PINEDO

6 Andalusia and the crisis of the Indies trade, 1610–1720   115
A. GARCÍA-BAQUERO GONZÁLEZ

7 The textile industry in the economy of Cordoba at the end of the seventeenth and the start of the eighteenth centuries: a frustrated recovery   136
JOSÉ IGNACIO FORTEA PÉREZ

8 Credit procedures for the collection of taxes in the
   cities of Castile during the sixteenth and seventeenth
   centuries: the case of Valladolid   169
   FELIPE RUIZ MARTÍN

9 Urbanisation and deurbanisation in Castile,
   1500–1800   182
   JUAN E. GELABERT

10 Fiscal pressure and the city of Cordoba's communal
    assets in the early seventeenth century   206
    JOSÉ MANUEL DE BERNARDO ARES

11 Medina del Campo 1500–1800: an historical account
    of its decline   220
    ALBERTO MARCOS MARTÍN

12 'Refeudalisation' in Castile during the seventeenth
    century: a cliché?   249
    IGNACIO ATIENZA HERNÁNDEZ

13 The Castilian aristocracy in the seventeenth century:
    crisis, refeudalisation, or political offensive?   277
    BARTOLOMÉ YUN CASALILLA

14 Spain and the seventeenth-century crisis in Europe:
    some final considerations   301
    BARTOLOMÉ YUN CASALILLA

Index   322

Figures

1.1 Baptisms, 1580–1690   *page* 16
1.2 Grain tithes, 1580–1649   18
1.3 Grain tithes, 1580–1649   19
1.4 Wheat prices, 1580–1649   20
1.5 Wheat prices, 1580–1649   21
1.6 Merino wool prices in Segovia   23
1.7 Mutton prices, 1580–1649   25
1.8 Donations of Segovia Guilds to cathedral building   26
2.1 Mortality 1580–1610   42
2.2 Intensity of general mortality crises in Interior Spain   45
2.3 Demographic effects of 1599 plague in Chiloeches   48
4.1 Grain production in the archdiocese of Toledo   100
5.1 Exports of Castilian wool, 1561–1796   106
5.2 Prices of wool and wheat of the Monastery of Paular   107
5.3 Value of pasturage leases   108
6.1 Total tonnage of merchant shipping, 1600–1720   117
6.2 Total shipping movements, 1600–1720   119

Map 2.1 The Plague of 1596–1602   35

ix

Tables

2.1	Pauper deaths in Vitigudino, 1599	*page* 40
2.2	Plague victims by sex and age	41
2.3	Plague mortality, increase in deaths around 1599	44
2.4	Mean annual number of baptisms	53
2.5	Mean annual number of marriages	54
4.1	Grain production in the archdiocese of Toledo	96
4.2	*Tercias reales* of city and region of Trujillo	96
4.3	Price ratios: wheat and barley	97
4.4	Price ratios: wheat and wine	97
4.5	Price ratios: wheat and oil	98
4.6	Price ratios: wheat and wool	98
4.7	Price ratios: wheat and meat	99
4.8	Price ratios: livestock and wheat	99
5.1	Wool exports, 1561–1796	102
5.2	Transhumant sheep	103
5.3	Land use	112
5.4	Income from pasture	112
6.1	Bullion imports, 1601–1700	121
6.2	Exports to the Indies, 1650–1699	123
App. 7.1	Types of silk looms in use in Cordoba between 1690 and 1776	168
9.1	The deurbanisation process in 11 provinces of Castile, 1591–1750	190
12.1	Noble titles, 1520–1700	255
12.2	Members of the Council State in the reign of Philip IV	257
12.3	Representative offices in Italy	257
App. 12.1	Creation of titles during the reign of Philip III	271

App. 12.2 Annual revenues of Dukes (sixteenth and
       seventeenth centuries)   274
App. 12.3 The top ten ducal revenues (sixteenth and
       seventeenth centuries)   276

Acknowledgements

Chapter 1 is a revised version of 'Castilla 1580–1650: crisis económica y política de "Reformación"', in J. H. Elliott and A. García Sanz (eds.), *La España del Conde Duque de Olivares* (Valladolid, 1990), pp. 495–515. Chapter 2 is a modification of sections 2–4 of chapter 12 of Vicente Pérez Moreda's *Las crisis de mortalidad en la España interior. Siglos XVI–XIX* (Siglo XXI, Madrid, 1980), pp. 257–93. Chapter 3 was first published as 'La "Depresión" agraria durante el siglo XVII en Castilla', in *Homenaje a Julio Caro Baroja* (Madrid, 1978), pp. 83–100. Chapter 4 is based on Documento de Trabajo 8601 of the Facultad de Ciencias Económicas y Empresariales, Universidad Complutense de Madrid, developing the same author's article, 'El agro castellano en el siglo XVII: ¿Depresión o "reajustes y readaptaciones"?', *Revista de Historia Económica* 4:1 (1986), 11–37. Chapter 5, 'Exportación de lanas, trashumancia y ocupación del espacio en Castilla durante los siglos XVI, XVII y XVIII', in P. García Martín and J. M. Sánchez Benito (eds.), *Contribución a la historia de la Trashumancia en España* (Madrid, 1986), pp. 343–59, was first given as a paper at the Eighth International Economic History Congress in Budapest, 1982, in Section B8, Migrations, Population and Occupation of Land (Before 1800). Chapter 6, 'Andalucía y la crisis de la Carrera de Indias (1610–1720)', is chapter 3 of García-Baquero's *Andalucía y la Carrera de Indias (1492–1824)*, (Andaluzas Unidas, Seville, 1986), pp. 87–114. Chapter 7 originally appeared as 'La industria textil en el contexto general de la economía cordobesa entre fines del Siglo XVII y principios del XVIII: Una reactivación fallida', in *Andalucía Moderna. Actas II Coloquios Historia de Andalucía* (Cordoba, 1983), I, pp. 443–65, and chapter 8 as 'Procedimientos crediticios para la recaudación de los tributos fiscales en las ciudades castellanas durante los siglos XVI y XVII: el caso de Valladolid', in Alfonso Otazu (ed.), *Dinero y crédito (siglos XVI al XIX)* (Madrid, 1978), pp. 37–47. Chapter 9 is a substantially modified version of 'Il declino della rete urbana nella Castiglia dei secoli XVI–XVIII', *Cheiron* 11 (1989–90), *Crescità e declino delle città nel'Europa Moderna (secoli XIV–XIX)*, ed. Marco Belfanti, pp. 9–46. The original of chapter 10 is 'Presión fiscal y bienes de propios a principios del siglo XVII', *Axerquia. Revista de Estudios Cordobeses* 2 (1981), 131–42. Chapter 11 is a reworking, specially prepared for this volume, of 'Medina del Campo en la época moderna: del florecimiento a la decadencia', in E. Lorenzo Sanz (ed.), *Historia de Medina del Campo y su Tierra. Vol. II Auge de las Ferias, Decadencia de Medina* (Valladolid, 1986), pp. 481–634. Chapter 12 was first published as '"Refeudalización" en Castilla durante el Siglo XVII: ¿Un tópico?', *Anuario de Historia del Derecho Español* 56 (1986), 889–920, and chapter 13 as 'La aristocracia castellana en el seiscientos. ¿Crisis, refeudalización u ofensiva política?', *Revista Internacional de Sociología*, 2nd series, 45 (1987), 77–104.

The initial translation of chapters 1, 2, 4–8, and 10–13 was undertaken by the Instituto de Estudios Fiscales, Madrid. Chapters 3, 9 and 14 were translated by the editor.

Abbreviations

ADV	Archivo Diocesano de Valladolid
AGS	Archivo General de Simancas
AHN	Archivo Histórico Nacional (Madrid)
AHP	Archivo Histórico Provincial
AP	archivo parroquial
BN	Biblioteca Nacional (Madrid)
CJH	Consejo y Juntas de Hacienda
CODOIN	*Colección de Documentos Inéditos para la Historia de España*, 113 vols., Madrid 1842–95
DGT	Dirección General del Tesoro
leg.	*legajo*
M y P	Mercedes y Privilegios

Introduction

The seventeenth century has long been established as a key moment in the economic development of modern Europe, a period of crisis, which was decisive for the transformation of the European economy and its differentiation into Atlantic, Mediterranean and Eastern models, for the transition from 'feudal' to 'capitalist' economic formations, and for the subsequent genesis of the industrial revolution.[1] Yet, in the now extensive economic historiography of this crucial period, the marginalisation of Spain is one of the most striking and most deplorable failings. It is enough to examine the bibliographical references of scholars, such as Hobsbawm, North and Thomas, Wallerstein, Brenner, De Vries, or Kriedte, among others, for whom the seventeenth century is central to their depiction of Europe's long-term economic development, to recognise how unsatisfactory is their treatment of metropolitan Spain.[2]

Yet Spain's role in early-modern Europe was pivotal. The economy of Castile, which was four parts or more of Spain in terms of manpower and wealth, was in many ways the hub of the entire economy of Europe. Not only did it sustain, as long as it was able,

---

[1] See the now classic exposition of these themes by E. J. Hobsbawm, 'The overall crisis of the European economy in the seventeenth century', *Past and Present* 5 & 6 (1954).

[2] D. C. North and R. P. Thomas, *The Rise of the Western World* (Cambridge, 1973); I. Wallerstein, *The Modern World-System*, 2 vols. (New York and London, 1974–80); J. de Vries, *The Economy of Europe in an Age of Crisis, 1600–1750* (Cambridge, 1976); P. Kriedte, *Peasants, Landlords and Merchant Capitalists. Europe and the World Economy 1500–1800* (Leamington Spa, 1983), original German edition, Göttingen 1980; T. H. Aston and C. H. E. Philpin (eds.), *The Brenner Debate. Agrarian Class Structure and Economic Development in Pre-Industrial Europe* (Cambridge, 1985).

1

the military and political hegemony of the Spanish monarchy, which was itself the *raison d'être* of so much of Europe's international finance and exchange, it was also the link between North and the Mediterranean and between Europe and America, a key market for grain, naval stores, copper, woollens, silks and linen, an important supplier of raw wool and the main source of Europe's precious metals. The performance of the Castilian economy was thus a crucial factor in the performance of all the other major European economies. For the first three-quarters or more of the sixteenth century Castile's population multiplied, the arable was extended, agricultural production increased, the level of urbanisation rose, the manufacture of silks and woollens flourished in the great textile centres of Toledo, Granada, Segovia and Cordoba; wool exports remained buoyant until the 1560s, foreign trade until the 1590s, and traffic with the Indies until the 1610s. In the last quarter of the sixteenth century this expansion first petered out and then fell back on itself. The progressive downturn of the Castilian economy was arguably one of the triggers of the general crisis of the European economy in the seventeenth century, the mark of the shift of economic preponderance from the Mediterranean to the Atlantic, and the archetypical model of the 'failed' economy.

The experience of Spain is thus one of the keys to an understanding of the dynamics of the early-modern European economy. Yet the economic history of Spain is perhaps the worst known of all the major economies of sixteenth and seventeenth-century Europe among early-modern historians. This ignorance is undoubtedly related to the paucity of information that has been available until quite recently, as well as to the limited accessibility of original Spanish work to non-Spanish historians. In 1958, in a review of the recent historiography of early-modern Spain, the authors, Jaime Vicens Vives, Joan Reglà and Jordi Nadal, drew attention to the enormous gaps in our knowledge of Spanish economic history.[3] Like J. H. Elliott in his celebrated article on the decline of Spain three years later,[4] they pointed to the excessive concentration of historians on external influences on the Spanish economy and the

---

[3] J. Vicens Vives, J. Reglà, J. Nadal, 'L'Espagne aux XVIe et XVIIe siècles', *Revue Historique* ccxx (1958).
[4] J. H. Elliott, 'The Decline of Spain', *Past and Present* 20 (1961).

relative neglect of internal factors. Agrarian conditions, land
holding, methods and techniques of cultivation, crops, yields and
returns, regional differences, population structure and change, the
organisation of manufacturing activity, of the trades and crafts,
investment, markets, the structure of demand were all key areas of
the economy about which solid knowledge was almost totally
lacking; there was no adequate modern study of any industry, nor a
substantial piece of recent research on any local or urban economy.
That lack they attributed in large part to the domination of Spanish
economic history by foreign scholarship with its own concerns and
preoccupations, which both skewed work in the direction of commerce, foreign trade, monetary flows and the international credit
system, and filtered the explanation of the 'decline of Spain' through
national and religious prejudices and the interlocking prisms of
Protestant individualism, political liberty, freedom of thought and
expression, and the teleological perspectives of industrialisation and
modernisation. Thus the failure of the Spanish economy has in a
long tradition that extends from the seventeenth century to the
second half of the twentieth been explained in terms of arbitrary
government, a bad religion, the tyrannical Inquisition, reactionary
hidalgo values, the wretched laziness of the people, the absence of a
capitalist and entrepreneurial spirit and other failings of the
national character, as much as in terms of objective economic
analysis.[5]

Although it would be wrong to suggest either that all those gaps
have been plugged, or that none of the orthodoxies of the early
sixties has survived, a great deal has changed since then. Alongside
the continuing contributions of foreign scholars, there has been a
veritable explosion of historical scholarship in Spain since the
1970s. Not only has the factual information available to us been
multiplied enormously, but by their openness to the methodological
and interdisciplinary influences of recent French and Anglo–
American historiography and by seeking out new sources in tithe,
fiscal, parish and municipal records and subjecting them to new
methods of quantitative and comparative analysis, the new
generation of Spanish historians has both invalidated many of the

5 For an early and trenchant expression of many of these prejudices see Francis
Willughby, 'A relation of a voyage made through a great part of Spain' (1664) in
J. Ray, *Travels through the Low Countries* (London, 1738), I, pp. 339–428; Pedro

conclusions of their predecessors and pursued lines of investigation into the social relations of power and the economy hitherto unexplored.

As Angel García Sanz points out in chapter 1 in this volume, economic history now has a much wider and more solid evidential basis. In 1958 historians were still very much reliant on normative, descriptive and anecdotal sources – legislation, the debates and petitions of the Cortes, the frequently propagandist treatises of the *arbitristas*, the accounts of travellers, often lacking in chronological and geographical perspective. Hamilton's price data published in 1934 was the only major continuous quantitative series available on which solid argument could be established.[6] The completion in 1959 of the massive study of H. and P. Chaunu,[7] with its painstaking, if not always uncontentious, evaluations of the tonnages of shipping engaged in the American trade between 1504 and 1650, gave a new statistical basis to the curve of the fortunes of the Spanish economy in the sixteenth and seventeenth centuries, but at the same time reinforced that over-concentration on external influences that Elliott wanted redressed. During the 1960s, however, as the influence of the materialism of the *Annales* school and its methodologies penetrated into Spain – mediated through Catalan history and historians as a covert expression of a more diffuse, soft Marxist, intellectual opposition to the cultural and spiritual underpinnings of the Franco regime – demographers and economic historians began to exploit parish registers, tithe returns and the immense wealth of the records of the royal fisc in Simancas in an entirely new and systematic way. Then, from the mid-1970s, the regional sentiment and the political and academic decentralisation of the 'España de las autonomías', released with the ending of Franco's Spain, had a profound effect on the orientation and the local funding of historical studies. There is now hardly a major provincial capital that has not commissioned its own multi-volumed history, organised its own historical conferences, published its own local journal, and reprinted its classic histories. The regions have established their own universities and the historical research they conduct is overwhelm-

Sainz Rodríguez, *Evolución de las ideas sobre la decadencia española* (Madrid, 1962), is still the fullest general survey of the subject.

[6] E. J. Hamilton, *American Treasure and the Price Revolution in Spain, 1501–1650* (Cambridge, MA, 1934).

[7] H. and P. Chaunu, *Séville et l'Atlantique (1504–1650)*, 8 vols. (Paris, 1959).

ingly focused on the region. The result has been a huge acceleration of output, remarkable in both quantity and quality, represented by a series of local demographic studies, urban histories, and regional monographs in the elaboration of which Spanish scholars have been in the forefront. As yet, however, hardly any of this impressive and wide-ranging research has been absorbed into the wider non-specialist scholarship outside Spain, or into general surveys of the European economy. The ignorance of this work outside Spain is not only an injustice, it also diminishes the value of any analysis of European economic development that fails to take account of it.

It is the purpose of the present collection to make available to an English-speaking readership some of the most important of the radically new perspectives on seventeenth-century Castilian economic and social history that have been opened up in the last twenty years or so by this new generation of Spanish historians that has flourished since the end of the Franco regime. The seventeenth-century crisis, so long abandoned to polemicists of 'decline', has been 'rediscovered' as the crucible of modern Spain and, perhaps even more important, of modern Castile. It is one of the areas in which Spanish historians have been able to break ground untilled or left fallow by their predecessors, and to reinsert Spain into the mainstream of European historiography, which in political, as well as in historical terms, means both to accept Europe into Spain and to restore Spain to Europe.

In view of the important political, social and structural differences between the Castilian core and the Galician, Cantabrian, Basque and Aragonese peripheries, it has seemed sensible to retain some measure of coherence by limiting the selection of material to the Crown of Castile and to economic and social aspects of the crisis in Castile. The essays have been chosen in order to provide a broad overall coverage of the main themes of Castilian economic and social history, population, agriculture, pastoralism, the Indies trade, manufacturing, urban decline and seignorial reaction, as well as a discussion of some of the key concepts around which the debate on the nature of the Castilian crisis is being structured, concepts such as dependence, peripheralisation, deurbanisation, oligarchisation, refeudalisation, which, as the different points of view expressed in these essays reveal, are themselves subjects of contention among Spanish historians.

In chapter 1, García Sanz presents a succinct overview of the advances in knowledge and the major changes in interpretation of the seventeenth-century crisis and Castilian 'decadence' that have taken place since the 1960s. These revisions amount to a breaking-up of the monolithic 'seventeenth-century depression' into two distinct regional patterns, interior and coastal, with different chronologies and intensities. Indeed, in some regions the seventeenth century was actually positive and can be regarded as the starting point of the growing gap in modern Spain between centre and periphery which reversed the economic balance of the fifteenth and sixteenth centuries and persisted into the twentieth century. García Sanz also draws attention to the way the new revisionism is presenting a less passive view of the Castilian past, a recognition that the seventeenth century evinced an ability to react to depression, and to readjust, shifting cereal production from bread grains to fodder to promote livestock, moving to the manufacture of lower quality textiles, and responding to lower rents by increased land concentration and the strengthening of seignorial rights.

The perspectives of current Spanish historiography are thus significantly different from those which informed Vicens Vives's influential *Economic History of Spain*, a work which when it was first published in 1955 was a synthesis of the state of the art at the time.[8] Vicens Vives saw plague as decisive in the evolution of population; the expulsion of the *moriscos* and the privileges of the Mesta as crucial in the collapse of agriculture; wage-price differentials as central to an explanation of industrial failure. He gave a major role to economic policy, to the burden of taxation, currency manipulations, price fixing, monopolies, government and guild regulations, as well as to the administrative structure of the state. He also put considerable emphasis on traditional explanations of Spanish economic failure, theological prejudices against commerce, indiscriminate charity, the *hidalgo* mentality, the lack of a capitalist spirit, rentism, parasitism, the 'puerile pride in indolence'. Little of this survives, and where it does it is formulated in very different terms from those employed by Vicens. Plague, as Pérez Moreda shows in an innovatory work which deploys a wide range of historical demographic techniques to challenge the resident orthodoxy (chapter 2), cannot be demonstrated to have had a decisive role in

---

[8] J. Vicens Vives, *Historia económica de España* (Barcelona, 1955); English translation, *An Economic History of Spain* (Princeton, NJ, 1969).

the history of population in the seventeenth century; the expulsion of the *moriscos*, whatever its consequences for Valencia and Aragon, was of marginal, or at best of local importance in the Crown of Castile; the Mesta was really no more than a bit-player on the agricultural scene compared with the changes in land use and control that were operating at the local level. There is a new sophistication of agrarian analysis, a greater attention to 'the social relations of production', the proletarianisation of the smallholder, the extension of rent, the privatisation of the commons. There is a different approach to the burden of the fisc, which is understood not simply as extraction, but as a system of redistribution of the social product through the oligarchisation of taxation and credit. The Europeanisation of the seventeenth-century Castilian crisis has also had the effect of shifting the focus of interest from explanations of the 'crisis' itself, which was a phenomenon common to Europe, to explanations of the failure to recover from the crisis, which was not, but which was decisive for Spain's divergence from the western European path. That has meant an increased concern with responses to the crisis, which is now seen much more as a series of readjustments, or shifts between public and private, centre and locality, town and country, arable and pasture, peasant and lord, consumer and producer, manufacture and commerce.

The concept of 'readjustment' was first applied to the agrarian crisis of seventeenth-century Castile by Gonzalo Anes in the pathbreaking article, originally published in 1978, which is printed here as chapter 3. His analysis of tithe returns, relative price movements and baptismal records questioned the previously unchallenged reality of a general agrarian depression in the seventeenth century. What he saw was a quasi-Malthusian crisis in the sixteenth century, which disrupted the equilibrium between arable, pasture and woodland, resolved by the establishment of a new balance leading to increased productivity and therefore greater *per capita* income, together with a shift in output from wheat and barley to rye, wine, oil, wool and meat. 'The depression of the seventeenth century consisted (in Castile, Extremadura and Andalusia) of a series of readjustments and adaptations ... to harmonise food production with population.' The stimulus Anes gave to looking anew at the Castilian agrarian economy is evidenced in the response of Llopis Agelán in chapter 4. Llopis's arguments for an absolute deterioration of *per capita* agricultural incomes lead not to a return to a static view of the agrarian economy but, in seeking to reconcile his conclusions with those of Anes, to a different emphasis on change. The agrarian balance was not simply a neo-Malthusian relationship between population and resources, but a more complex relationship between arable and pasture in which the vicissitudes of population and urban demand played their part but within a framework of political and social domination which had as much to do with the determination of land use and the distribution of the surplus product of agriculture as straightforward market forces. The increased supply of land in the seventeenth century went hand in hand with a process of privatisation and enclosure which transferred the usufruct of the commons from the peasant to the local bosses. What was critical about the seventeenth century, Llopis argues, was the rise of the 'poderosos' and the appearance of a distinct, truly landless, rural class.

The concept of 'dependence', applied to the Castilian economy by Henry Kamen in his challenge to the very notion of a 'decline of Spain',[9] is another key issue which has informed the current debate about the nature of the Spanish economy. It is addressed directly (though not always explicitly) in these essays. In chapter 5, Bilbao and Fernández de Pinedo argue, though without actually using Wallerstein's terms, that the 'dependence' of the economy of the Castilian 'semi-periphery' on the requirements of the 'core' economies of France, England and the Low Countries, was a crucial determinant of land use and hence of agrarian prosperity. The combination of the vicissitudes in European demand for Spanish wool with the control of the land by sheep and pasture owners first rendered the relative abundance of pasture in the seventeenth century nugatory and then deprived the farmer of the full benefits of the expanding demand for arable products after 1670. However, whether the fate of the Castilian economy can be satisfactorily explained by this concept of 'dependence' is questioned in chapter 6 by García-Baquero's examination of the links between the Indies trade and the Andalusian economy. His conclusions, though cautious and tentative, not only underline the lack of uniformity in the behaviour of the various sectors of the Andalusian economy in the seventeenth century and the important chronological disphase

[9] H. Kamen, 'The Decline of Spain: an historical myth?', *Past and Present* 81 (1978).

between north and south, where the crisis was limited to the second half of the century, but they bring us back to re-emphasising internal causes of both the expansion of the regional economy in the sixteenth century and its crisis in the seventeenth. The process of ruralisation, which was the common experience of most European economies in the seventeenth century, also characterised the economy of Castile. The breakdown of the extended networks of the sixteenth century and of the historic symbiosis of town and country, and the regression to forms of local economic autarky are major themes in the essays of Gelabert, Marcos Martín and Fortea. Ruiz Martín, in a short but seminal essay on the civic debt of the city of Valladolid, identifies the transfer to the municipalities of responsibility for underwriting the public debt as one of the crucial elements in that process. Gelabert, developing this theme in the broader perspective of urban decline in Castile, focuses on the shift of the fiscal burden to the towns and on the disadvantaged state of the royal municipalities, as compared with those in seignorial jurisdictions and in the privileged, non-Castilian kingdoms, as the key to the long-term deurbanisation of Castile. Bernardo Ares's close analysis of one particular transaction between Crown and city, however, raises the possibility that it was the cities rather than their rural districts which were the beneficiaries of such fiscal bargains with the Crown. The urban/rural, sectoral and regional incidence of taxation is something about which we are still too ignorant for sound conclusions, but the ruralisation of population and the economy throughout the interior between the sixteenth and eighteenth centuries is undoubted. It is an aspect of the crisis of fundamental long-term importance for the shaping of modern Castile, the explanation of which calls for bold general hypotheses, such as that of Gelabert, or Ringrose's thesis concerning the distorting effect of Madrid on the Spanish economy,[10] as well as for specific illustrations of the process, such as that provided by Marcos Martín in his subtle analysis of the long-term transformation of the famous fairs-city of Medina del Campo from an international commercial centre to a small, provincial market town.

From the perspective of the history of industrialisation, the

[10] David R. Ringrose, *Madrid and the Spanish Economy, 1560–1850* (University of California Press, 1983).

collapse of commerce and manufacturing in the seventeenth century has always been regarded as the central feature of Spain's economic 'failure'. Until current work in progress on the textile industries of Toledo and Segovia is completed, Fortea's original and detailed examination of the decline of textile manufacturing in Cordoba and, even more important, of its failure to recover, is almost unique as a contribution to the problem of the long-term de-industrialisation of the Castilian economy. In the conclusion of his illuminating survey of the various unsuccessful projects for the regeneration of Cordoba's manufactures, Fortea hints at social-structural rigidities and cultural conservatism as the underlying inhibitors of modernisation and successful economic adaptation in Castile. The same theme is central to Marcos Martín's account of the provincialisation of Medina del Campo. The reinforcement of the traditional social structure, with its implications for the distribution of the social product, the composition of the market, the employment of capital and the control of the means of agricultural production, has come to be seen as one of the determining responses to the crisis in Castile. The most characteristic form of that reinforcement was what is often described as 'aristocratic reaction', or as 'refeudalisation'.

Whether the reaction of the aristocracy to the economic crisis of seignorialism in the seventeenth century is properly to be understood as a form of 'refeudalisation', a privatisation of public functions and a real increase in the effective power of the nobility, and, therefore, how the economic crisis affected the distribution of power within the state, is the issue which divides Atienza and Yun in the final section of the volume. For Atienza, 'we can speak bluntly of "refeudalisation"'. For Yun, what has the appearance of 'refeudalisation' takes place within the framework of the state, is effected through the authority of the Crown not through the power of the lord, and implies neither a fragmentation of the political system nor a diminution of royal power. For both, however, the crisis of the seventeenth century reinforced the bonds between state and aristocracy and thus strengthened the grip of the extracting classes on the economy and on the distribution of the national wealth. All these themes are developed by Bartolomé Yun in his concluding observations and brought together in an overview which places Castile within the broader framework of the debate about the General European Crisis of the Seventeenth Century.

The essays in this collection give some indication, therefore, though by no means a complete one, of the directions of current research into Spanish social and economic history in the early-modern period. They also reveal – by the absence of what has not been available for inclusion – some of the lines of research which present-day scholars are showing little inclination to pursue, yet which will surely need to be revived if a comprehensive understanding of the nature and development of modern Spain and hence of the origins of industrial society in general is to be achieved. The concentration on agrarian, urban and fiscal history is clearly preponderant, but price history has not really advanced since Hamilton, despite Le Flem's work on the Segovia *mercurial* and some unsystematic use of local price series; and, apart from Garzón Pareja's study of the Granadan silk industry and Alcalá Zamora's of the Cantabrian cast-iron cannon factories,[11] there has been so far no significant research published on manufacturing and industry, or on the trades and crafts, the internal market and domestic demand. Nor has there been any interest at all in the ideological, cultural, intellectual and psychological characteristics which have in the past been given such a prominent – if frequently perverse – role in explanations of Spain's decline. None of these subjects can be approached seriously without attempting to exploit the vast buried wealth of the wills, entails, marriage settlements, inventories, contracts and bills of sale lying deep in the mountainous documentation of the still barely explored notarial archives. The notarial archives remain one of the great frontiers which, though some have crossed, most researchers have been understandably reluctant to traverse; yet the potential rewards are immense. Finally, if from one point of view the regionalisation of historical research has been salutory both in redressing a long-standing historiographical imbalance and in beginning to provide us with the detailed studies upon which a more solid overall assessment can be constructed, at the same time the abandonment of research into national history, or better into history from the perspective of the centre, has discouraged work on the macro-economy and on international and even interregional topics, and has rather knocked the bottom out of 'economic policy' as an issue. This is a new

---

[11] M. Garzón Pareja, *La industria sedera en España. El arte de la seda de Granada* (Granada, 1972); J. Alcalá Zamora, *Historia de una empresa siderúrgica española: los altos hornos de Liérganes y La Cavada, 1622–1834* (Santander, 1974).

imbalance which needs rapidly to be corrected. It is to be hoped that both the strengths and the limitations demonstrated in this collection will encourage greater interest not only in the excellent work that has already been done, but also in the vast amount there is still to do.

1. *Castile 1580–1650: economic crisis and the policy of 'reform'*

ANGEL GARCÍA SANZ

EVIDENCE FOR ECONOMIC CRISIS IN CASTILE[1]

For the last ten years or so in Spanish historiography the concepts of 'general crisis' and 'decadence', traditionally held to be characteristics applicable to the Spanish economy in the seventeenth century, have been undergoing revision. The extraordinary advances in historical research during the past decades, due in great part to the utilisation of new sources of a quantitative nature (parish records of tithes, rents, prices, revenues, etc.), which permit a greater degree of precision than the qualitative sources almost exclusively employed until recently (*arbitrista* texts, reports and debates of the Cortes, contemporary literary accounts, etc.), have made it possible to reconstruct a new, more detailed and reliable picture than that afforded by the concepts of 'general crisis' and 'decadence'.

This historiographic revisionism has made three basic contributions. The first is the establishment of a precise chronology of the economic situation throughout the seventeenth century, which has shown that the effects of the economic depression were felt only during the first half of the century, and in certain areas only during the first thirty years. In the second half of the century the greater part of the country experienced a period of recovery, although its intensity varied from region to region and from district to district. Thus the seventeenth century is no longer in its entirety negative from an economic point of view.

[1] I wish to express my gratitude to Alberto de Miguel Hidalgo, my colleague at the Faculty of Business and Economics at Valladolid, who generously and whole-

Secondly, the revision has shed light on the regional contrasts in demographic and economic evolution during the seventeenth century, pointing out the inconsistency of a global evaluation and of the very concept of a 'Spanish economy'. In fact, it becomes more and more apparent that there coexisted two patterns of development: on the one hand, that of the interior of the Peninsula, and on the other, that of the coastal areas. Although there is proof in both the interior and the coastal areas of a decline in economic activity from the last decades of the sixteenth century and throughout the first thirty years of the next (in some areas, for the whole of the first half of the seventeenth century), the last fifty years of the century present a picture of contrasts. While in the interior, population and economic activity stagnated at a low level, or made a modest recovery, which in no case brought about a restoration of the situation that prevailed in 1580, in the coastal regions there was a definite revival which amply surpassed the greatest achievements of the sixteenth century. The best-known case of demographic and economic recovery in the coastal areas during the second half of the seventeenth century is that of the Cantabrian coast, from Galicia to the Basque country, where the introduction and cultivation of maize greatly contributed to the very positive results. This contrast between the economic and demographic behaviour of the interior and the coastal areas during the second half of the seventeenth century can be regarded as the starting point of the growing gap in economic development and wealth between the different regions of Spain. This gap continued to widen throughout the eighteenth and nineteenth centuries to the present day, with the end result that is exactly the opposite of the situation in the fifteenth and sixteenth centuries, when the interior was the richest, most developed part of the country. But the interesting point to be made here is that, as a consequence of this historiographic revision, the seventeenth century cannot be seen as economically regressive in all areas of Spain; in certain regions it was actually positive.

The third contribution of this reappraisal of the seventeenth century in Spain has been to underline the capacity of the economic and social actors to respond effectively to the depression, not resigning themselves to the role of victims of adverse circumstances,

---

heartedly placed at my disposal his computer skills in the analysis and graphic representation of the historical data.

but setting in motion a series of mechanisms ('readjustments') which were intended to make the best of the situation. Thus, in the agricultural sector it can be shown that the cultivation of cereals for fodder, rather than for bread production, encouraged livestock farming. As for the textile industry, the manufacture of middling and poor quality goods became increasingly important in an effort to adapt supply to a less demanding market. In the distribution of agricultural profits (which has social as well as economic aspects) the cereal growers benefited from lower land rents, a fact which did not, however, spell ruin to the landowners, since they were favoured by a process of land concentration and the strengthening of their seignorial rights of jurisdiction, which enabled them to make up for the fall in rents by an increase in the numbers of their tenants.

After this brief reference to the contribution made by recent research on the seventeenth century in Spain, we shall now consider in some detail the case of the interior of the Peninsula, the central lands of the old kingdom of Castile, concentrating on the interesting period between 1580 and 1650.

(a) The fall in population

The most conclusive evidence on this point has been published by Jordi Nadal.[2] Figure 1.1 shows the evolution of baptisms in sixty-four parishes in Extremadura, León, Old Castile and New Castile. It shows clearly how during the first half of the seventeenth century the rural population (which made up at least 80 per cent of the total population) fell in the interior of the Peninsula, a fall which in some regions (Extremadura and Old Castile) was particularly dramatic. In the second half of the century, in almost all the interior regions, population revived, but in no case did it completely recover from the injuries inflicted on it between the last decades of the sixteenth century and the middle years of the seventeenth century.

As Vicente Pérez Moreda has shown, it was not catastrophic mortality which accounted for the population loss in the interior in the seventeenth century, but emigration to other parts of the

[2] Jordi Nadal, *La población española (siglos XVI a XX)* (Barcelona, 1984), corrected and augmented edition, pp. 78–80.

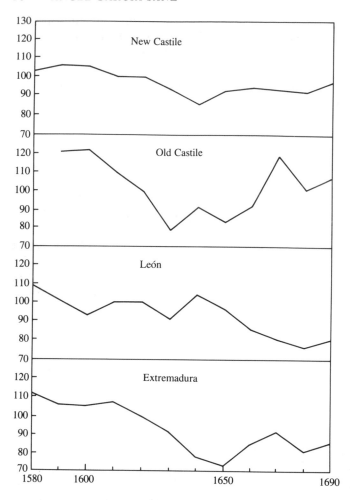

Figure 1.1 Index numbers of baptisms, 1580–1690 (index on base 1610–1619)
Source: J. Nadal, *La población española (siglos xvi–xx)* (Barcelona, 1984)

country and overseas, a migratory movement spurred on by the growing economic deterioration.[3] Even the blow struck by the plague of 1596–1602, traditionally held to be the main cause of

[3] Vicente Pérez Moreda, *Las crisis de la mortalidad en la España interior, siglos XVI–XIX* (Madrid, 1980).

the process of 'decadence', was comparatively harmless and easily overcome, as recent research proves.

Madrid, a town which became the capital of the realm in 1561, underwent a demographic development which, as might be expected, contrasts radically with that of the interior as a whole. Its population increased by 100,000 between 1561 and the 1630s (i.e. from approximately 30,000 to 130,000 inhabitants). This spectacular growth in the population of Madrid was fed by immigrants from the surrounding areas, who flocked to the Court in the hope of better prospects; but it is obvious that the population increase in Madrid in no way made up for the demographic losses which the rest of the interior suffered.[4]

(b) The fall in agricultural production

Thanks to excellent information on the evolution of tithes (which includes tithes in kind rather than money rents and revenues), we are reasonably familiar with the evolution of harvests in a wide, representative area of the interior of the Peninsula. Here we can show (a) the wheat tithes collected by the Chapter of the Cathedral of Segovia in twenty parishes in the province of Segovia itself, situated in the northern submeseta;[5] (b) the 'bread' tithes (wheat and barley) levied by the Cathedral of Toledo in the parishes of the twenty archdeaconries in the archbishopric, which consisted of the greater part of the southern submeseta and included certain lands in Extremadura.[6] The results of the elaboration of data on tithes are shown in Figures 1.2 and 1.3. In Figures 1.4 and 1.5, we see the evolution of wheat prices based on statistics published by Hamilton for Old Castile, León and New Castile.[7] The chief conclusions that we can arrive at are as follows:

---

[4] On the economic impact of Madrid upon the interior regions of Spain, see David R. Ringrose, *Madrid and the Spanish Economy, 1560–1850* (Berkeley and Los Angeles, 1983). On population growth see Maria F. Carbajo, *La población de la villa de Madrid* (Madrid, 1987).

[5] I made a study of tithes in Segovia in *Desarrollo y crisis del antiguo régimen en Castilla la Vieja. Economía y sociedad en tierras de Segovia, 1500–1814* (Madrid, 1977), 2nd edn, 1986.

[6] The tithe figures in Toledo were published, archdeaconry by archdeaconry, by Jerónimo López-Salazar and Manuel Martín Galán in 'La producción cerealista en el Arzobispado de Toledo, 1463–1699', *Cuadernos de historia moderna y contemporánea* 2 (1981).

[7] Earl J. Hamilton, *American Treasure and the Price Revolution in Spain, 1501–1650* (Cambridge, MA, 1934).

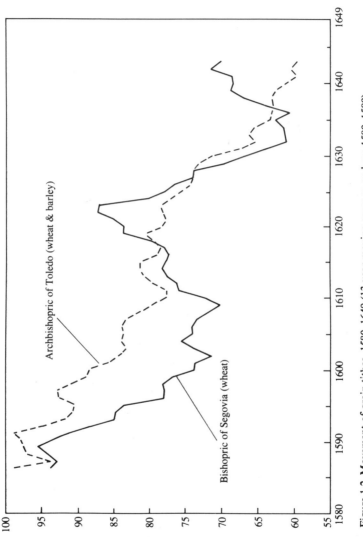

Figure 1.2 Movement of grain tithes, 1580–1649 (13-year moving average on base 1580–1589)
Source: As for figure 1.1

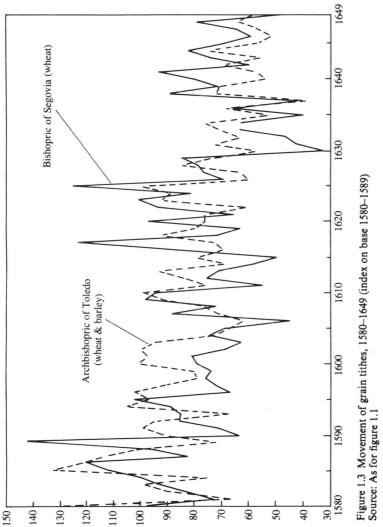

Figure 1.3 Movement of grain tithes, 1580–1649 (index on base 1580–1589)
Source: As for figure 1.1

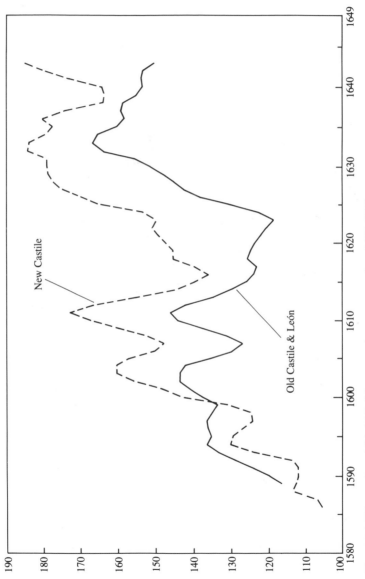

Figure 1.4 Wheat prices, 1580–1649 (13-year moving average on base 1580–1589)
Source: As for figure 1.1

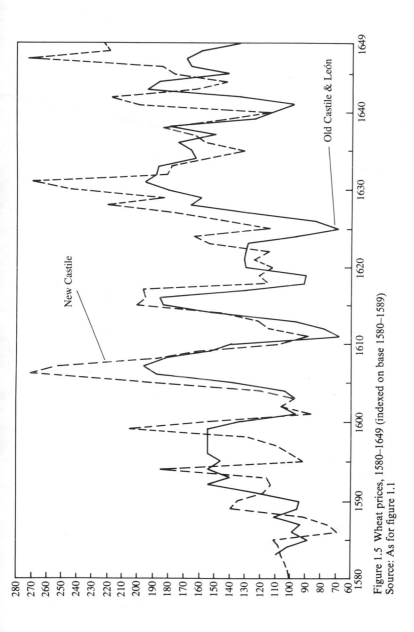

Figure 1.5 Wheat prices, 1580–1649 (indexed on base 1580–1589)
Source: As for figure 1.1

1. There is evidence in Castile as a whole of a sharp drop in the production of the most important cereals (wheat and barley) between the 1580s, the period of greatest agricultural expansion in that century, and the 1630s. The fall in cereal production can be set at almost 40 per cent.[8]

2. The rhythm of this fall in production was irregular throughout the period, with three distinct phases: (a) 1586–1606: twenty years of sharp decline, of genuine collapse, particularly in the northern submeseta. (b) 1606–28/9: approximately two decades when the decline is halted, and in the northern submeseta during 1615–25 recovery takes place. (c) 1628/29–1637: a decade of total collapse; the depression reaches rock bottom.

3. The movement of wheat prices was inversely related to the trend of production (the former rose while the latter fell), which proves that prices were more affected by irregularity of supply than by monetary factors (debasement of the coinage caused by the growing use of *vellón* and manipulation of the face value of coins).[9] In fact, the periods of sharp rises in prices (from 1585 to 1606 and from 1625 to 1631) coincide with spells of prolonged decline in production, while the opposite occurs in those periods when prices were low (1618–25, for example).

The rising trend in crop prices was not enough to slow down the process of depression and bring about a recovery *before* 1650, since the principal crisis factors in rural areas were less economic than social: pressure of land rents and taxes, privatization of common municipal land, growing concentration of landed property, etc.

(c) The livestock crisis

Though less is known about livestock than about arable production, there is evidence that at least until the 1630s livestock production

---

[8] Our information on the evolution of harvests in the important cereal-producing region of Tierra de Campos and in the northern submeseta, coincides with that of Segovia. On this point, see Bartolomé Yun, *Sobre la transición al capitalismo en Castilla. Economía y sociedad en Tierra de Campos (1500–1830)* (Salamanca, 1987), p. 425 in particular.

[9] On the dominant role of production as opposed to monetary policy in the determination of prices, see Fernando Urgorri Casado in his interesting and pioneering study 'Ideas sobre el gobierno económico de España en el siglo XVII. La crisis de 1627, la moneda de vellón y el intento de fundación de un banco nacional

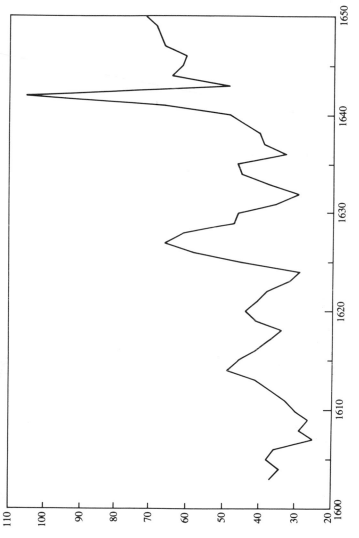

Figure 1.6 Merino wool prices in Segovia, 1600–1650 (*reales/arroba*)
Source: As for figure 1.1

was also severely depressed. This conclusion is based not only on the repeated complaints about the scarcity of animal products (meat, skins, wool) which came before the Cortes of Castile, and on reliable reports on the subject written by certain contemporaries (the best known of them being Miguel Caxa de Leruela in his *Restauración de la Antigua Abundancia de España*, published in Naples in 1631),[10] but also on quantifiable data, of which we can highlight three items. The first is the fall in the number of sheep in the transhumant flocks (from approximately 2.5 million in the mid-sixteenth century to approximately 1.6 million in the 1630s). The second is the broad stability of the price of fine merino wool, an important export item, during the first forty years of the seventeenth century. Only in 1626, 1627 and 1628 did prices rise above 50 *reales* per *arroba*. See Figure 1.6, elaborated from figures taken from the Libros de Menudos in the archives of the Cathedral of Segovia, which shows the evolution of wool prices in the city of Segovia, the most representative fine wool market in the interior, since the greatest of the Mesta's itinerant flocks were shorn in the nearby rural areas. Third is the constant increase in mutton prices from the later years of the sixteenth century, in both the northern and southern submesetas (cf. Hamilton's figures in Figure 1.7). The first two factors argue in favour of a reduction in foreign demand for fine wool, which is corroborated by figures available for taxes on wool exports; the third factor suggests increasing pressure from internal demand for meat, in spite of the previously mentioned reduction in population.

From the middle of the seventeenth century on, sheep farming was to be the focus of one of the 'readjustments' taking place in response to the agrarian slump: the growth of sedentary flocks benefited from the abandonment of unprofitable arable land.

(d) The decadence of the centres of industry

Segovia and Toledo were in the second half of the sixteenth century the most flourishing industrial centres in the interior, both specialising in textile manufactures. These two cities exemplify the down-

---

exclusivo', *Revista de la Biblioteca, Archivo y Museo del Ayuntamiento de Madrid* 19–60 (1950), pp. 123–230.
[10] There is a recent edition by Jean Paul Le Flem, Instituto de Estudios Fiscales, Madrid, 1985.

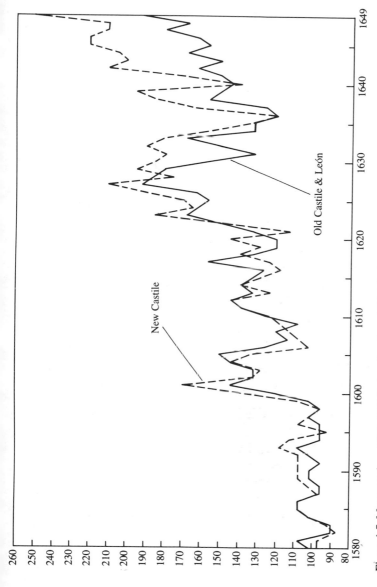

Figure 1.7 Mutton prices, 1580–1649 (indexed on base 1580–1589)
Source: As for figure 1.1

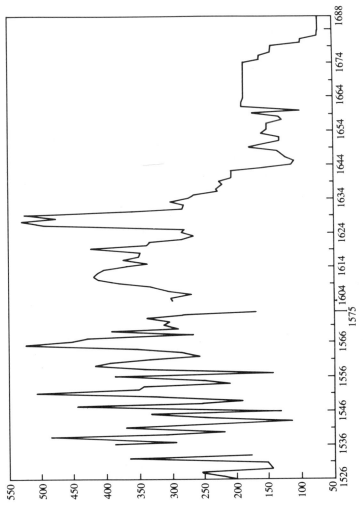

Figure 1.8 Contributions of Segovia guilds to cathedral building (in 1000s *maravedís*)
Source: As for figure 1.1

turn which industry suffered. Segovia had over 25,000 inhabitants around 1580, 76 per cent of whom were employed in domestic industries (60 per cent in the manufacture of relatively high-quality woollen cloth). But industrial activity began to decline from the 1580s, although the slump was not fully felt until after the 1620s. Figure 1.8 shows indirectly the evolution of industrial activity in this city, as reflected in the donations which the artisans of Segovia made towards the building of the cathedral between 1526 and 1690, according to the Libros de Fábrica in the archives of the Chapter. It clearly shows a sharp fall in donations from 1630 onwards. It is no coincidence that the Libros de Acuerdos of the city council confirm that in that year 'more than 4,000 souls are missing from the said city, forced by necessity', clearly the necessity of emigrating. In the mid-seventeenth century, when the city must have had only about half its population of 1580, the craftsmen presented several reports in which they accused the former merchants (manufacturers who employed the putting-out system) of having lost interest in production and having transferred their interests and money to the export of raw wool, in preference to cloth manufacture.

Toledo underwent a slump similar to that of Segovia, in spite of its having a greater diversity of industry (woollen cloth, silks, tanneries, etc.). The 60,000 inhabitants of which it boasted in 1571 were reduced to 20,000 in 1631. Madrid was a decisive factor in the economic decline of Toledo, drawing off population and economic resources, especially from 1606 on, when the Court was finally reestablished in Madrid, after a brief sojourn in Valladolid from 1601 to 1606.

(e) The decline of the centres of commerce

Burgos and Medina del Campo were in the mid-sixteenth century flourishing centres of commercial and financial activity, the residence of a prosperous middle class on whose business a vigorous body of craftsmen depended.

Burgos was a meeting point for the export and import exchanges which took place between the northern submeseta and the western seaboard of Europe. In Medina del Campo were held internationally renowned fairs at which, apart from the contracting of merchandise, payments were effected which facilitated the commercial traffic passing through Burgos. These two economic centres underwent a period of severe decline which began with the rebellion of the Low Countries against Spanish rule in the 1560s. An indication of this decadence is the spectacular drop in their populations. Burgos had around 20,000 inhabitants in 1561, only 12,000 by 1591, and less than 5,000 in 1646. Medina fell from 15,000 inhabitants in 1561 to a mere 5,373 in 1626.[11]

THE DEPRESSION AND THE POLICY OF 'REFORM'

The government was aware of the economic depression which from the 1580s had hung over the central lands of the Kingdom of Castile. Madrid made a fine vantage-point. The proctors in the Cortes, for their part, were constantly denouncing the difficult situation and presenting the king with reports full of complaints and demanding solutions to the evils which threatened. Not only that, many of those who worried most about the national welfare took it upon themselves to set down in writing their particular view of the situation and its causes, and to propose *arbitrios* (projects) which would halt the process of decline and restore the 'former abundance'. These writers formed the '*arbitrista* movement', which came to be a literary genre in its own right and which flourished particularly from 1615 to 1625, that is, in the later years of Philip III's reign and at the beginning of Olivares's period in the royal favour.[12] Olivares himself, at the beginning of his mandate, followed the *arbitrista* line in many aspects of his ministry.

But the ministry became aware of the economic depression in the interior mainly through the realities of taxation (budgeted revenues which they were unable to collect, more and more petitions from the towns claiming insolvency, increasing resistance to the imposition of new taxes or the raising of old ones). In fact, for the government the anti-depression policy of 'reform' became, until the end of the 1620s, a necessary means of improving the economic situation, the main aim of which was to augment the national revenues and thus the tax contributions. With this in mind, in 1618 a special body was set up, the Junta de Reformación, charged with the elaboration of

[11] For the demography of Medina del Campo see Alberto Marcos Martín, *Auge y declive de un núcleo mercantil y financiero de Castilla la Vieja* (Valladolid, 1978).

[12] On 'arbitrismo', see Jean Vilar's interesting study *Literatura y economía. La figura satírica del arbitrista en el Siglo de Oro* (Madrid, 1973).

reform projects which were to affect not only the economy, but also public morality and the national way of life.[13] From 1627 onwards, when this attempt to improve the economy with the object of increasing the national income and 'redeeming the monarchy' had failed, what was proposed was no longer a policy of 'arbitrism', but an openly fiscalist policy, that is, one which sought to obtain increased revenues by direct and immediate taxation, although this would mean not only sacrificing any plans of economic reform, but would also aggravate the depression; 1627 marks the point of transition from 'reform' to 'fiscalism'.[14]

That there was such enthusiasm for 'reform', from about 1615 to 1625, seems to be linked to the fact that during this period harvests were particularly good (cf. Figure 1.2, 1.3, 1.4 and 1.5). The depressive trend in agricultural production was halted; even in the northern submeseta there was a prolonged recovery; and the prices of staple foods were low. Taking into account the undeniably positive and stimulating effects of these figures on the rest of the economy, it is easy to imagine that people at the time thought with reason that a general economic revival was possible, that all was not lost, and that the bad times of the past had been merely a hiatus after which prosperity would return. In order for these hopes to become reality all that was needed was for the proper 'reform' policy to be put into practice. The objective conditions in agriculture were, in fact, the breeding-ground for reformism, although we should not wish to minimise the important role of the political factors which contributed to the promotion of 'reform' measures.

The fact that from about 1627 economic reform was abandoned and an exclusively fiscalist policy adopted is also linked to the economic situation. A continuous drop in harvests from 1626 on, with the worst harvest in 1630, and the spectacular rise in prices which followed, as the graphs show, meant a return to sad reality and put an end to the last hopes of a revival. In the case of the textile industry in Segovia it was in these years that the final crash came, if we are to believe the indications of Figure 1.8. From then on it was

---

[13] On this Junta's activities, Angel González Palencia, *La Junta de Reformación* (Valladolid, 1932).

[14] John H. Elliott, 'El programa de Olivares y los movimientos de 1640', in *La España de Felipe IV, El Gobierno de la Monarquía. La crisis de 1640 y el fracaso de la hegemonía europea*, vol. XXV of *La Historia de España* founded by Ramón Menéndez Pidal and directed by José María Jover Zamora (Madrid, 1982), p. 413.

clear that, if tax revenues were to be increased, rapid action was called for and all ideas of 'reform' were laid aside, a course which was to exacerbate the effects of the economic crisis.

The 'reform' measures proposed for agriculture are a good example of the degree to which economic policy was influenced by specific circumstances. Thus the famous pragmatic of 29 March 1594, which improved the lot of farmers in debt to money-lenders and authorised them to sell part of their crop as bread (*panadear*), and not only as grain, must be understood as a measure intended to encourage arable cultivation, the decline of which had been evident for a decade or so. We must consider in the same light the raising in 1600 of the legal price maxima for wheat and barley (*tasa*) from 476 and 238 *maravedís* to 612 and 306 *maravedís* respectively. In 1619, farmers were legally freed from observing the *tasa* on the sale of the cereals they had grown themselves. This was a brave decision and doubtless should have benefited the producers, but it was adopted at a moment when there was little risk that the removal of the *tasa* would provoke an uncontrolled rise in prices; market prices had been dropping rapidly since 1617 and would remain low until 1625 (see Figure 1.5). As a consequence of this, cereal producers were unable to take advantage of this ruling. When, after 1625, prices again rose because of bad harvests, this price freedom was again withdrawn from the farmers, in 1628, just when it might have been of use to them. Farmers were once more permitted freedom of pricing in 1632, but by then prices were falling again, which meant that they did not reach the legal maxima which the non-producing cereal merchants were obliged to respect. It is clear that behind this apparent mockery of the cereal growers' interests lies nothing less than the absence of a firm and decided commitment on the part of the government to agricultural recovery, and that, if this commitment had been firm and decided, they would have been prepared to ignore the dissatisfaction and protests of the urban consumers. But the political price of such a brave stance seemed too high and they preferred a less risky solution, although that implied the perpetuation of the depressed state of the rural areas.

I believe that the behaviour of the ministry in the matter of the grain *tasa* is an indication of the attitude they adopted in other affairs. They were accustomed to giving way and renouncing 'reform', if standing by their reformist decisions meant a high political cost. In fact, the economy was at the service of the political interests of the monarchy. This is the ultimate explanation of why, after 1627, a purely fiscal policy was adopted, at the sacrifice of economic, and also social and moral, reform in Spain.

The pragmatic of 4 March 1633 confirmed unequivocally the privileges of sheep-breeders, especially those of the transhumants associated with the Mesta, whose privileges had been eroded during the high-point of the expansion of arable farming in the second half of the sixteenth century, and afforded them fresh advantages. With this ordinance, which doubtless was influenced by the writings of the pro sheep-rearing *arbitrista*, Miguel Caxa de Leruela, the government did nothing but succumb passively to the pressure of circumstances. The drop in population, the fall in urban demand for staple foods, and the abandonment of arable lands, all argued for the promotion of an extensive form of land use whose products (merino wool above all) could count upon a safe demand from overseas.

2. The plague in Castile at the end of the sixteenth century and its consequences

VICENTE PÉREZ MOREDA

Plague is the dominant feature of catastrophic mortality throughout the sixteenth century in Castile, although its importance would appear to increase as the century progresses, since the period ends with the most serious epidemic of all those that had affected the interior of Castile since the time of the Black Death.[1] In effect, these crises were 'mixed crises' in the sense that they were a result of the combined effect of poor harvests, plague and infectious and contagious diseases such as typhus, which was to become more important during the seventeenth century, as well as influenza, malaria, smallpox, and diphtheria. From 1590 mortality figures began to announce the widespread aggravation of crises involving all the above factors, which was to culminate in the outbreak of the epidemic of 1599.

The purpose of this chapter is to examine the extent of the epidemic, combining reports and literary sources with analysis of the most important demographic variables. This analysis will be followed by a study of the morphology of the epidemic, and will conclude with consideration of its effects on the process of medium-term demographic decline recorded in the interior of the Spanish peninsula during the first decades of the seventeenth century.

This chapter is an abridged version of Chapter 12 of Vicente Pérez Moreda's *Las crisis de mortalidad en la España interior, siglos XVI-XIX* (Madrid, 1980). The first part of the original chapter, relating to disease and crises throughout the sixteenth century, has been almost completely eliminated, and the second part, on the geographical spread of the epidemic, has been summarised. The third and fourth parts have been retained almost in their entirety. The figure showing the intensity of the general mortality crises in the interior of Spain, which appears in an earlier chapter of the above-mentioned work on p. 122, has also been included. Eds.

[1] See more fully, Pérez Moreda, *Las crisis de mortalidad*, pp. 245–56.

I. THE GEOGRAPHICAL SPREAD OF THE EPIDEMIC OF
1596–1602

Bartolomé Bennassar has provided the fullest overview of the
plague epidemic in Castile between 1596 and 1602.[2] The importance
of this epidemic was, of course, already well known, as is clear from
the many references contained in the work of Villalba, who in turn
based his data on the local chroniclers and on the medical literature
of the time, or more recently in that of Domínguez Ortiz.[3] Bearing in
mind that Bennassar presented his work as a preliminary study for
subsequent correction and expansion, what is there to be said about
the spread of the epidemic?

We have carefully mapped all the places affected according to the
information provided in Bennassar's work, both the areas where the
spread of the epidemic is certain and those in which its presence is
only probable, insofar as the present state of research allows. We
have also added other places revealed by our own data.

There are two large areas that appear to have suffered most from
the epidemic. Firstly, the Cantabrian coast, from Santander to the
French border, and its hinterland, that is, the region of the Montaña
and all the Basque provinces, as well as the neighbouring areas of
Logroño and Navarre; secondly, the entire central region, within a
circular area comprising parts of Valladolid, Madrid and Toledo,
and centred on the entire provinces of Avila and Segovia. These two
large areas were connected by a narrow belt made up of the central
part, running from north to south, of the province of Burgos and a
parallel strip of the province of Palencia. This map clearly reveals
one of the routes taken by the plague, as Bennassar noted,[4] in its
descent from the Cantabrian coast, through Burgos and Aranda,
spreading out across Old Castile, and crossing the central range
over the Somosierra pass to invade Madrid and the entire central
area of the north of New Castile.

The references to the spread of the plague through Asturias
(evidenced by the case of Oviedo in 1598) and Galicia, as well as into
a small section of Valencia in the area of Alcoy and Onteniente, on

[2] Bartolomé Bennassar, *Recherches sur les grandes épidémies dans le Nord de
l'Espagne à la fin du XVIe siècle* (Paris, 1969).
[3] A. Domínguez Ortiz, *La sociedad española en el siglo XVII*, I (Madrid, 1963),
pp. 68–70.
[4] *Ibid.*, p. 43.

the border between Valencia and Alicante, are less numerous and less reliable.[5] Although other evidence may give credibility to the existence of the epidemic in Galicia, such as its Atlantic nature and references in other Spanish documentary sources,[6] the mention by a Valencian historian of an epidemic crisis very localised in extent does not necessarily prove the existence of a Mediterranean phase of the same epidemic, even though the term 'plague' may be used to describe it. However, the references to the outbreaks recorded in Seville, Jaén and Lisbon are entirely reliable.[7] Furthermore, the work of Bernard Vincent leaves no room for doubt concerning the spread of the disease throughout Andalusia, and in particular across western Andalusia, southern Portugal and possibly certain parts of southern Extremadura.[8]

In the case of Andalusia, and certainly in the case of Portugal, the epidemic could have been more or less independent of that which spread across the north and centre of the Peninsula. Its early appearance, it was first recorded in Lisbon in 1597, and the fact that the areas affected were coastal areas, important ports connected with the North Atlantic trade, are factors which tend to place these outbreaks within the orbit of the epidemics that affected a large part of the Atlantic area during the same period. Indeed, during these same years the international nature of the plague became very clear, with the notable difference that it had abandoned its traditional centre in the Mediterranean and was spreading with great virulence towards central and Atlantic Europe. Hamburg and Lübeck, Dunkirk in Flanders, and Brittany and Normandy, as well as the

[5] According to references in G. Escolano, *Décadas de la historia de la insigne y coronada Ciudad y Reino de Valencia* (Madrid and Valencia, 1880 ed), III, pp. 685–6.
[6] In October 1598 the municipal authority of Talavera de la Reina received news that many parts of Galicia were suffering from the plague, and as from that date 'large numbers of homeless people and many people who have travelled from the kingdom of Galicia and from many other parts to this city' began to be recorded; M. del C. González Muñoz, *La población de Talavera de la Reina (Siglos XVI–XX)* (Toledo, 1975), p. 176.
[7] Documented in the work of A. de Freylas, *Conocimiento, curación y preservación de la peste* (Jaén, 1605); see G. García Sedeño, 'La epidemia de peste que padeció la ciudad de Jaén en el año 1602', *Seminario Médico* 1 (1953), 86–93; Bennassar, *Recherches sur les grandes épidémies*, pp. 28, 41, 101. According to Joaquin de Villalba, *Epidemiología española, o historia cronológica de las pestes, contagios y epizootias que han acaecido en España* (Madrid, 1803), 'Portugal suffered the same disease as both Old and New Castile.'
[8] Bernard Vincent, 'La peste atlántica de 1596–1602', *Asclepio* 28 (1976), 5–25; especially the map of the areas affected by the plague.

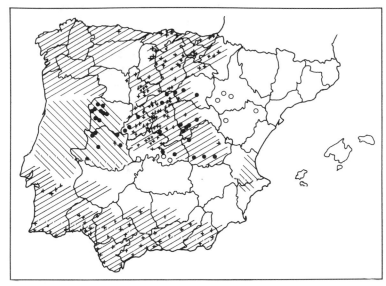

/// areas where epidemic confirmed

\\\ areas where epidemic probable

+ places affected by plague

● places in the sample, plague-affected or with large abnormal mortality

○ places in the sample with no evidence of abnormal mortality

Map 2.1 The Plague of 1596–1602

Cantabrian coast in Spain, Portugal and western Andalusia were all directly affected,[9] and in 1603 a violent outbreak of the plague hit London.[10] The epidemic may even have extended to the Swedish coast in the north and to Bordeaux on the French Atlantic coast to the west. Even further south in Morocco, the Canary Islands and the Azores, virulent outbreaks were recorded, lasting perhaps, as they did in other parts of Europe, until 1607–8,[11] when France, Poland, the coastal and inland regions of Germany, Ireland and central Russia were also affected.[12]

[9] Bennassar, *Recherches sur les grandes épidémies*, pp. 35, 63.
[10] M. F. and T. H. Hollingsworth, 'Plague-mortality rates by age and sex in the parish of St. Botolph's without Bishopsgate in London, 1603', *Population Studies* 25 (1971), 131–46. Also T. R. Forbes, *Chronicle from Aldgate. Life and death in Shakespeare's London* (New Haven and London, 1971), pp. 131–2.
[11] Vincent, 'La peste atlántica', pp. 5, 10–11.
[12] P. Goubert, *The Ancien Régime* (London, 1973), I, p. 54; E. Keyser, 'Die Pest in Deutschland und ihre Erforschung', *Actes du Colloque International de Démogra-*

As for the spread of the plague in the Iberian peninsula, we have taken various soundings at the edges of the map drawn up by Bennassar to see whether or not his frontiers were reflections of his sources rather than of the real limits of the epidemic.[13] These soundings show that the plague spread to Extremadura, the province of Salamanca and areas on the Portuguese border, although the latter may have been the result of contagion from Lisbon. It is also clear that the epidemic spread across the provinces of Soria, Guadalajara, Cuenca and part of Albacete, and although there is no proof that it spread from the south of Toledo and Cuenca to join up with the centres of infection in Andalusia, it is clear that the extent was greater than that revealed in earlier studies.[14] (See Map 2.1)

2. DEMOGRAPHIC ANALYSIS OF THE CRISIS

In the same way as the other great catastrophe at the beginning of the century, the epidemic of 1507, which was undoubtedly attributable to the plague, the epidemic of 1596–1602 was preceded and accompanied by numerous reports of agrarian crisis which added to the deplorable picture of the state of public health. In both cases everything suggests that to a certain extent, and even taking into account its high specific mortality, plague required, or at least induced, a marked deterioration in the economy.[15]

The first point to be made in this respect is that, as in the case of the crisis of 1591–5, it was not only a question of plague. The tragic and revealing connection between famine and typhus was also present, and in many places typhus appeared as the principal disease

phie Historique, Liège, 18–20 April, 1963: Problèmes de mortalité (Paris, 1965), p. 374; T. H. Hollingsworth, 'Population crises in the Past', in B. Benjamin, P. R. Cox, and J. Peel (eds.), Resources and Population (New York, nd), pp. 99–108.
[13] Bennassar used, on an illustrative and provisional basis, the correspondence between the Court of Madrid and the corregidores of various towns affected by the plague in 1599. This correspondence is held in the Estado Section of the Archivo General de Simancas.
[14] [For a more detailed discussion see Las crisis de mortalidad, pp. 261–5; eds.]
[15] Nevertheless, J. N. Biraben explicitly denies the existence of a direct causal relationship between food shortages and the plague, although he does admit that scarcity and famine may be effects deriving from the presence of the epidemic and that the epidemic may spread more easily due to an increase in the number of persons and grain on the move in times of shortage, Les Hommes et la peste en France et dans les pays européens et méditerranéens, (Paris, 1975), I, pp. 147–53.

that preceded the plague. Together with other less frequent cases of tertian fever,[16] pneumonia and influenza, it was almost always typhus that punished the population in the winter and spring immediately preceding the outbreak of the plague.

In the most significant places included in our sample a seasonal analysis of mortality rates has been made, and in the majority of cases the summer–autumn pattern of the plague is clearly visible, although in places there seems to have been a substantial increase in mortality in certain periods of the spring. Winter crises are much less frequent and manifest the greatest divergence from the seasonal pattern that is typical of the bubonic plague. However, such cases, in addition to being insignificant in terms of the total picture, are almost all located very close to the border with Portugal. That means we cannot rule out the possibility that the high mortality rates may be due to a combination of factors, particularly the agricultural crisis, independently of the possible, or probable incidence of the plague.

Bennassar presented few rural examples of the typical seasonal pattern of the plague (Pomar de Valdivia, Oña, Sandoval), but his urban examples are unanimous in fixing the seasonal nature of the epidemic in all the towns and cities of Castile in the last months of the summer and the first months of the autumn of 1599, in Valladolid, Burgos, Segovia, Madrid, etc.[17] In Bennassar's opinion, a relatively large number of cases in the central area of the interior of Spain diverge from the summer–autumn pattern.[18] This could be explained by the possible existence of pulmonary complications, which would, if it were so, make the epidemic recorded in Castile during this period one of the strangest cases in the history of the plague in Europe in modern times. This explanation would also resolve in part the question of the spread of the disease in rural areas, since it generally spread by means of personal

---

[16] Domínguez Ortiz claimed that 'an epidemic of acute malaria could be traced' by means of cases of tertian fever that were so widespread in the summers of both 1598 and 1599 that, according to Mariana, 'the crops were lost in the fields because the workers did not have the strength to gather them', *La sociedad española en el siglo XVII*, p. 69. The reports of the *corregidores* to the Court also denounced the presence of tertian fever in Avila, Aranda de Duero and Arévalo, Bennassar, *Recherches sur les grandes épidémies*, p. 46.

[17] Bennassar, *Recherches sur les grandes épidémies*, pp. 18–9, 171.

[18] *Ibid.*, pp. 40, 64.

contagion,[19] which on other occasions has been assumed to be limited to densely populated urban areas. In any case, the presence of other diseases, such as typhus, which has been sufficiently well documented, must not be ruled out in any attempt to find an explanation for the more discordant seasonal patterns. It should help to highlight food shortages among the causes of the crisis, as well as the circumstances of contagion, accidental or not, in the original centre of the epidemic, and also its sea-borne origins.[20]

There is plenty of evidence on the grave economic situation of the humble masses of the population of Castile, some of which is very moving. Famine and disease became synonymous, and for all the writers of the time, informants to the Crown, physicians, municipal authorities, local chroniclers and parish priests, the victims of the plague were to be counted mainly or exclusively among the starving population. In the view of the *corregidor* of Toledo, famine was a second disease, not to be dismissed lightly; whilst for Tomás de Mercado it was one of the principal causes of the disaster.[21] A few years later Colmenares was to describe the situation as follows: 'There was a great shortage of bread due to the poor harvest of August 1598 when a *fanega* of wheat came to be sold in the fields for thirty *reales*;[22] and because of dearth and malnourishment, the epidemic increased in strength.'[23] According to Pérez de Herrera, the plague appeared 'among the poor who lacked all means of subsistence'.[24]

[19] Nevertheless rats, acting as passive carriers in the transport of cereals, goods and foodstuffs of all kinds made in times of economic crisis, and particularly in ships, may have been one of the principal vehicles of contagion. Transmission by fleas, by virtue of the movements of the fleas' habitual carriers, must have had a greater effect than the movements of persons (tramps, mendicants, travellers and merchants), and the role of direct contagion is reduced merely to the much less probable forms of pulmonary plague.

[20] Strictly speaking, the increase in grain movements by sea that preceded and accompanied the epidemic should not be considered to be a factor of chance, since in this manner we could relate the food crisis to the strictly epidemic crisis.

[21] Bennassar, *Recherches sur les grandes épidémies*, p. 69.

[22] [A *fanega* was a measure of capacity that differed according to the different regions.]

[23] Diego de Colmenares, *Historia de la Insigne Ciudad de Segovia*, new edn, 2 vols. (Segovia, 1970), II, p. 364. In Villacastín, where mortality was not very high, 'very few people died of the plague because great care was taken of those suffering from the disease and prayers were offered up to Our Lord'. Indicating the causes of the disaster, the parish priest adds, 'In 1599 there was plague and famine throughout Spain', Libro 1 de Defunciones, vol. 46, folio 74.

[24] Pierre Vilar, 'The Age of Don Quixote', in P. Earle (ed.), *Essays in European Economic History* (Oxford, 1974), p. 101.

If famine was neither the principal factor nor the immediate cause of the crisis, it may certainly have increased both the rhythm and the intensity of mortality. The large number of references to the desperate food situation following the disastrous harvest of 1598 coincides with the peaks on Hamilton's price graphs, at least for Andalusia and New Castile in 1598–9.[25] There are a number of cases in the southern part of our sample with extremely high mortality that could be due primarily to the food crisis. The deplorable agricultural situation, particularly in those southern areas, together with the plague that originated in Cantabria at the end of the decade, justified the view of Mateo Alemán, so often quoted, that the centre of Castile marked the dramatic meeting point of 'the famine travelling up from Andalusia' and 'the plague travelling down from Castile'.[26]

The plague of 1596–1602 resulted, therefore, in a socially selective rise in mortality. It was as if the rats and fleas had held back in the face of wealth and social standing, a point which may in fact be true if account is taken of factors such as the level of personal hygiene, the quality of habitat, or the possibilities of isolation and escape, the best and almost the only effective remedy against the plague at that time. The victims were, therefore, almost exclusively the 'poor and badly nourished', those 'impoverished persons who neither have nor have had the means with which to feed themselves'.[27] If the parish records used in this study were fuller, we could no doubt have established statistically the selective nature of the mortality. Unfortunately the death certificates at this time do not generally record the trade or occupation of the deceased; this information is provided in some cases but it is irregular and is not sufficient to serve as a basis for statistical analysis. Nor do these certificates generally offer any other items of information that could reveal the wealth or social status of the deceased. Notes made by the parish priests in the margins recording if the deceased was a 'pauper' are useful, although in times of crisis levels of real poverty will be much higher than what is normally regarded as such. Nevertheless, the analysis

[25] Earl J. Hamilton, *American Treasure and the Price Revolution in Spain, 1501–1650* (Cambridge, MA, 1934), p. 200.
[26] Mateo Alemán, *Guzmán de Alfarache* (1599), II, ch. 2.
[27] Reports from Aranda de Duero and Sepúlveda, respectively, Bennassar, *Recherches sur les grandes épidémies*, pp. 110, 171.

Table 2.1. *Pauper deaths in Vitigudino, 1599*

Month	Total	'Paupers'
January	10	6
February	1	–
March	5	3
April	6	5
May	4	2
June	3	2
July	11	5
August	25	12
September	60	31
October	29	13
November	15	6
December	5	2

of socially differential mortality can achieve a certain degree of accuracy. The figures in Table 2.1 give the number of 'absolute paupers' (*pobres de solemnidad*) listed among the total number of adult deaths in Vitigudino in 1599.

Conclusions as to the mortality rate by age and sex are, however, much less clear-cut. Bennassar aimed to show, on the basis of his data, the groups that were most at risk: in short, there was a higher rate of mortality among females and infants. However, he only had three examples of the former, Pamplona, Fuenterrabía and Toledo, where the mortality rate among females was, respectively, 50.7, 175 and 45.6 per cent higher than among males. As to the disproportion in infant mortality rates, his evidence does not confirm, save in certain isolated cases, the conclusions he comes to in various parts of his book,[28] as Appleby's criticism noted.[29] Infant mortality, together in certain cases with child mortality up to 10, or even up to 16 years of age, represented in almost all cases less than half of total mortality, and fluctuated most frequently around one-third of the total. Although the records used in this study do not contain many references to infants during this period, I have four examples from different areas of the sample. Table 2.2 shows a summary of the data

---

[28] *Ibid.*, pp. 18, 70.
[29] Andrew B. Appleby, 'Disease or famine? Mortality in Cumberland and Westmorland, 1580–1640', *Economic History Review*, 2nd series, 26 (1973), p. 407.

Table 2.2. *Plague victims by sex and age*

Location	Adults M	Adults F	Total adults	Child mortality	Total mortality	% child
Pamplona	75	113	188	88	276	31.9
Madrid			169	88	257	34.2
Fuenterrabía	36	99	135	84(^{a})	219	38.4
Toledo	57	83	140	104	244	42.6
Aranda de Duero			159	150(^{a})	309	48.5
Gutierre Muñoz	4	8	12	20(^{b})	32	62.5
Pomar de Valdivia			31	63	94	67
Santo Tomé del Puerto			55	150(^{b})	205	73.2
Almazán (San Andrés)			28	13	41	31.7
Chiloeches			164	79	243	32.5
Retortillo (1599)			20	13	33	39.4
Retortillo (1601)			34	23	57	40.4
Collado de Contreras			29	38	67	56.7

(^{a}) Less than ten years of age.
(^{b}) Less than sixteen years of age.

compiled by Bennassar, together with those derived from our own investigations.[30]

As can be seen from Table 2.2, the parish records also show a predominance of adult mortality. Only in Collado de Contreras do infant deaths represent more than half the total, whereas in all the other cases they are of the order of one-third of total deaths. Nor do the conclusions drawn by Bennassar concur with the specialist evidence presented by Appleby that the age groups most severely punished by the bubonic plague in the early modern period were those between 10 and 35, that is, neither the very young nor the old.[31]

It is very likely that it will never be possible to establish a chronology of mortality that will enable us to trace the chain of contagion and the itinerary of the epidemic across the different regions of Spain, since the crisis may appear in an apparently spontaneous manner in any area because of chance circumstances or very localised factors, either before an entire area becomes affected

---

[30] Bennassar, *Recherches sur les grandes épidémies*, pp. 18, 50, for the data corresponding to the first group of locations. The data corresponding to the second group are taken from the records used exclusively for this study.
[31] Appleby, 'Disease or famine?', p. 407.

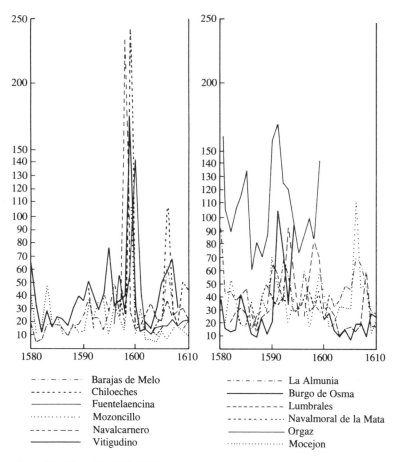

Figure 2.1 Mortality 1580–1610
Source: Vicente Pérez Moreda, *Las crisis de mortalidad en la España interior, siglos xvi–xix* (Madrid, 1980)

or following the most serious phase of the epidemic when the area appeared to be free. Thus, it appeared in Vitigudino in the summer and autumn of 1599 when the highest mortality rates in the neighbouring district of El Abadengo and the rural areas of Ciudad Rodrigo had been recorded in the years immediately before. On the other hand, the high point of the plague in the heart of the interior as it descended from Cantabria after 1596 can be definitively dated to the summer and autumn of 1599.

It should also be clear that the crisis reached its maximum intensity in the central area, and that its incidence was practically total around the year 1599; whereas on the margins of the interior, on the edges of the area chosen for this study, neither the intensity of the crisis nor its generality would appear to be located in the last years of the century. The most important fact to emerge from Figure 2.1 is the sharp rise in the number of deaths recorded between 1598 and 1600 in a sample of places in the provinces of Madrid, Segovia and Guadalajara and in the diocese of Salamanca, whereas the figures relating to areas further from the centre, such as Aragon, Soria, Ciudad Rodrigo and Extremadura, do not show such a uniform rise in those years, and where there is a rise, mortality does not reach the levels recorded during the earlier part of the 1590s. In the interior of the Peninsula the plague produced a general mortality crisis in and around 1599, but the crisis was at its most acute, with very high death rates, in the central areas.

Following all that we have said about the exceptional nature of the demographic crisis that occurred at the end of the sixteenth century and its importance compared with the other crises that have affected the interior of Spain in the early modern period, statistical analysis of the data confirms the impressions that we have been given by essentially descriptive evidence. By adapting Hollingsworth's formula to the Spanish sources, we have already noted the high values obtained because of the intensity of the crisis in certain rural centres of the interior, values which are much higher in relative terms than those recorded in the various towns and cities of Castile. These figures demonstrate the widespread nature of the epidemic, which was by no means limited to the urban centres. In general, the intensity of this crisis was considerably greater than that of any of the crises recorded in the interior of Spain during subsequent centuries, irrespective of whether the calculation is made on the basis of Hollingsworth's formula, or by using the methods of M. W. Flinn.[32] Table 2.3 also permits comparison with the high level of mortality that was general during the first years of the decade, calculated in this case as the simple percentage increase in the number of deaths recorded compared with the mean mortality rate in a recent base period: Table 2.3.

[32] See Figure 2.2. [For development of this point and the method of calculation applied, see Pérez Moreda, *Las crisis de mortalidad*, ch. 7: eds.]

Table 2.3. *Plague mortality, increase in deaths around 1599*

Location	Date	Base period	% increase
Vitigudino	1599	1581–1590	574.4
Vitigudino	1599	1601–1610	917.5
Navalcarnero	1598	1593–1600	644.3
Navalcarnero	1598	1601–1610	786.8
Fuentelaencina	1600	1601–1610	290.2
Chiloeches	1599	1603–1610	539.5
Arévalo (San Martín)	1599	1580–1589	306.9
Arévalo (San Juan)	1599	1600–1607	278.9
Collado de Contreras	1599	1586–1594	262.2
Acebo	1599	1600–1609	148.7
Torre de D. Miguel	1599	1590–1600	131.4
Torrejoncillo	1597	1591–1596	171.3
Belmonte	1599	1601–1610	109.5
Barajas de Melo	1601	1590–1599	153.3
Fuenterrebollo	1599	1600–1607	528.6
Mozoncillo	1599	1590–1600	366.1
Mozoncillo	1599	1600–1609	733
Almazán (San Andrés)	1599	1600–1609	197.1
Almazán (N.Sra. Campanario)	1599	1590–1598	91.4
Castillejo de Robledo	1600	1581–1590	733.3
Lumbrales	1598	1582–1589	233.7
Fuente de San Esteban	1598	1590–1600	339
Villar de la Yegua	1597	1581–1590	110.3
Retortillo	1601	1602–1610	428.9
Ciudad Rodrigo (San Andrés)	1598	1581–1590	227

The majority of the locations in the area analysed have percentages that are significantly higher than those found by Bennassar in cases where he was able to consult parish records. This would lead one to believe that the crisis may possibly also have been less severe to the north of the central area, in León, Burgos and Valladolid. According to the data compiled by Bennassar, a large number of villages in Valladolid record death rates of barely 10 per cent of the estimated population, and only in very few cases are figures of 15, 20 or 30 per cent recorded. In the first case, an 'anomalous' annual death rate of the order of 100 per 1,000 is only slightly more than double the ordinary death rate. The really significant cases, of which there are many examples in the previous table, are those in which the normal mean mortality rate increases fivefold or more in the year of the crisis, representing a gross mortality rate of the order of at least 200 per 1,000. Looked at the other way round, we can estimate, for

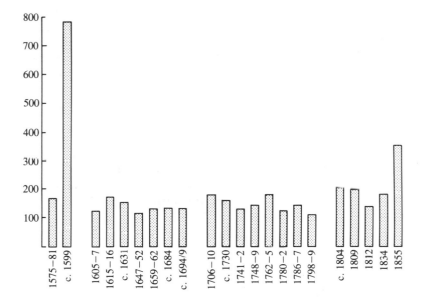

Figure 2.2 Intensity of general mortality crises in interior Spain, 1575-1855
Source. As for figure 2.1

those areas that do not have records of deaths for the years immediately before or after the crisis, that if the epidemic represented a loss of approximately 40 per cent of the population, as was the case in Cantalejo or in Berninches, the death rate for that year would be approximately ten times higher than the mean rate in a base period of ordinary mortality.

Calculated in this basic way, the crisis reached its peak intensities in the central area of our study, namely Madrid, Guadalajara, Segovia, Avila and Salamanca, in contrast with the lower percentages in Soria, Cuenca, Ciudad Rodrigo and Cáceres. Moreover, the earlier increases recorded at the beginning of the decade in the areas located on the edge of our interior zone, in Cáceres, Toledo and Aragon, were in every case very much lower than those experienced in the central area around 1599. The intensity of this crisis means that it must be placed among the great European epidemics of the early modern period, and it was perhaps more serious in the interior of Spain than it was anywhere else in these years, England in 1598, for example,[33] or France in 1590–2 and 1595–7.[34] However, the crisis was not especially catastrophic, save in certain localised cases, if it is compared with other outbreaks of the plague in Italy, England, or France during the seventeenth century.[35] Nevertheless, despite this, and precisely because a large part of the rural population of Castile was involved, the total mortality figures suggested at the time by some contemporary writers and accepted by modern historians should not be rejected out of hand. These figures indicate a total of approximately 600,000 victims,[36] which would be equivalent to less than 10 per cent of the population of the Peninsula as a whole, which at that time would be less than 8 million,[37] and around 10 per cent if we are considering the kingdom of Castile alone. On the basis of Hollingsworth's index, the intensity of the crisis would, however, be rather greater than the other major epidemic of the mid-seventeenth century, the plague of 1647–52, which was typically Mediterranean and was, therefore, limited to the coastal area of the Spanish Levant and to Andalusia.

The mortality rates recorded as a consequence of the epidemic on this occasion would also appear to be within the levels that may be considered normal for the bubonic plague. It is estimated that in the European epidemics of the fourteenth to the seventeenth centuries the mean mortality rate during the entire course of an epidemic

[33] Appleby, 'Disease or famine?', passim.
[34] According to Dupâquier and Demonet, cited by J. N. Biraben, 'Crises de mortalité: conséquences démographiques', Colloque International de Démographie Historique (Montreal, 1975), pp. 11–12.
[35] This derives from application to our data of the Hollingsworth index, as above. The Dupâquier method has also been applied, resulting in levels of 'great crisis' only in certain isolated cases (in Navalcarnero, for example), although unfortunately the sources do not permit application of this method in other cases that are assumed to have a similar degree of intensity, whereas in no case as a result of application of this method are the levels estimated as 'catastrophic' obtained. However, it must also be indicated that in a study of fourteen parishes in the area of Nantes between 1576 and 1600, a 'great crisis' level was only obtained in one case and a 'catastrophic' crisis was never revealed using this procedure, in this or in any other region of France analysed by Dupâquier and Demonet, in the seventeenth and eighteenth centuries, Biraben, 'Crises de mortalité'.
[36] Bennassar, Recherches sur les grandes épidémies, p. 11, and Domínguez Ortiz, La sociedad española en el siglo XVII, p. 70, who include, respectively, the views of Francisco Ruiz y Porcerio and Cabrera de Córdoba. In the view of Bernard Vincent, the figure of half a million dead is 'somewhat underestimated', 'La peste atlántica', p. 11.
[37] Compare the latest estimates made by A. Domínguez Ortiz, El Antiguo Régimen: los Reyes Católicos y los Austrias (Madrid, 1973), p. 76.

would be in the region of 60 per cent of the persons who suffered
from the plague, the figures ranging from 90 per cent of the earliest
cases to 30 per cent at the end of the epidemic. Although very
partial, there is some data available for death rates in hospital cases;
these rates are considerably below the norm, providing evidence for
the effectiveness of some health care and possibly even certain
surgical practices. In 1599, for example, the number of cured
patients leaving San Antón Hospital in Madrid and San Lázaro
Hospital in Segovia is equal to or even higher than the number who
died, and the same trend is observed in Toledo, Valladolid and
Burgos.[38] On the other hand, in the absence of medical care the
mortality rate could reach 80.2 per cent, as in Pamplona,[39] a figure
similar to that recorded in later epidemics in the seventeenth century
(73.9 per cent in Malaga in 1678 and 83.3 per cent in Cadiz in
1649).[40]

3. DEMOGRAPHIC CONSEQUENCES OF THE CRISIS

It would be rash to speak of the effects of the epidemic in the 'empty
cohorts' of subsequent years, save in order to make some conjectures
which are reasonably probable but which could only be verified if a
census of the population broken down into age groups were available for the seventeenth century. One would no doubt see the
progress during the first half of the century of the hollow generations savaged in the last years of the previous century. The infant
mortality rate resulting from the crisis and the subsequent fall in the
number of births undoubtedly had negative effects on the demographic structure in the medium or long term in the areas that fell
victim to the plague. In many cases, and in almost all those that have

38 Bennassar, *Recherches sur les grandes épidémies*, p. 78.
39 A total of 276 deaths is recorded in 344 cases of the plague, *ibid.*, p. 79.
40 Villalba, *Epidemiología española*, II, p. 81 (the plague of 1678), and AHN, Consejos, leg. 51,378 (Cádiz, Jan.–Apr. 1649). Other data on hospital mortality rates in
times of the plague concord with the data indicated above: mortality among
sufferers in the Capuchinos Hospital in Zaragoza, up to 17 September 1652,
amounted to 56.5 per cent (AHN, *ibid.*); and in Valencia during the plague of
1647–8 mortality rates of 41.8 per cent and of slightly more than 50 per cent,
respectively, were recorded among the patients in the General Hospital and in
Arguedes Hospital, Mariano Peset et al., 'La demografía de la peste de Valencia de
1647–1648', *Asclepio* 26–27 (1974–5), 206, 222. Naturally, there may also be
doubts regarding the nature of the diseases suffered by all the 'sufferers from the
plague' treated in hospitals during epidemics.

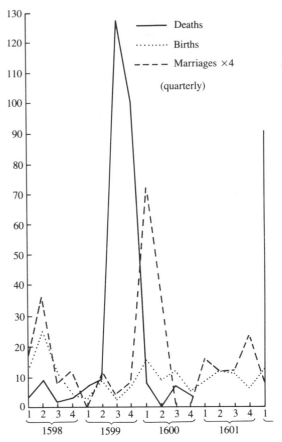

Figure 2.3 Short-term demographic effects of 1599 plague in Chiloeches
Source: As for figure 2.1

the fullest and most detailed records, the high mortality in the year
of the crisis was accompanied by a simultaneous decrease in the
number of marriages and in the number of children conceived,
reflected a few months later, generally in the overall figures for the
year following the crisis, in a clear fall in births compared with the
normal mean number of baptisms. In certain cases it is the 'abnormal' trends in these other variables, that is, in the numbers of
marriages and births, characteristic of times of crisis, that reveal to
us the existence of the crisis where we lack reliable mortality figures.

In some cases we only have evidence of the fall in the number of births following the plague year, and in others a decrease in the number of marriages (for example, in Hervás), followed immediately by a sharp increase that fully compensated for the many deferred marriages with the new opportunities for many second marriages, as was the case in Burgo de Osma, Navalcarnero or Talavera de la Reina.

In other locations included in our sample the joint evolution of the different demographic variables can be observed, the trends in marriages and births moving in opposite directions after the crisis, in Otero de Herreros in 1601, in Villacastín in 1600 and in Sobradillo in 1602. The complete pattern of internal demographic change during and immediately following the crisis is reflected in other locations, such as Retortillo or Lumbrales, and with archetypal features in Chiloeches (Guadalajara), a case which merits detailed examination, as may be seen in Figure 2.3.

Clearly the evolution of the different demographic variables in the majority of the locations studied conforms to what we already know about the 'mixed' nature of the crisis. The shortage of food, the presence of epidemic mortality and, in all certainty, the existence of a general psychological climate of anguish and uncertainty, all played a part in the evolution of all the demographic mechanisms. The very nature of the disease, the paralysis of will in the face of its terrible symptoms and, furthermore, the absence of viable alternatives available in normal times, would undoubtedly lead to a reduction in the usual number of marriages recorded in years of demographic stability. The presence of the epidemic would discourage weddings, and would make them impossible to celebrate if the future spouses were from different locations, however close, once the strict system of blockades, quarantines and controls on people's movements was introduced. Of all the demographic factors registered in the entries in the church records, marriage is clearly the least instinctual, or the most rational, the factor that may be the most coldly calculated and for the longest time. It is also clearly the factor on which both general and personal economic circumstances have the most influence. A time of plague was certainly not the best time to consummate an event that had been arranged and planned in a time of normality; nor could all the usual alternatives be kept going in a time of such abrupt changes in both economic and demographic conditions. A sharp reduction in available income (due to the depletion of family resources, discontinuation of normal work, and diversion of resources to unforeseen and immediate needs) would be added to the many other demographic effects upon the marriage market; some marriages would have to be postponed for these reasons, or because one of the betrothed had fled the centre of the epidemic; others would have to be cancelled altogether on account of the death of one or both of the future spouses. Only when the death rate, and with it the rhythm of daily life, returned to normal could some of the marriages that had been postponed during the crisis take place, together with others arranged after the crisis, as young orphans who had inherited the family wealth appeared on the marriage market. All these couples could rethink their earlier expectations in better circumstances, for 'those wishing to own land could do so with little money, since by virtue of the disappearance of so many, the land was worth less and there was a need for growth'.[41] Naturally, the total number of marriages was also increased by virtue of the considerable number of widows and widowers who remarried, and the cases of Sobradillo and Otero de Herreros provide excellent examples of this trend over time.[42] All this indicates that irregular trends in marriage numbers are not necessarily peculiar to a certain type of crisis, since there is a varied combination of circumstances that may set this mechanism in motion, combining both economic and material factors, as well as others which are strictly demographic, psychological or social.

As to the decrease in the number of infants conceived during times of crisis, reflected in the fall nine months later in the number of baptisms, we already know that in theory this may occur involuntarily, by virtue of amenorrhoea due to famine in a situation of food shortages, and as a result of the emotional disorders caused by a state of depression, or of great anguish or fear. For this reason both the economic crisis and a strictly epidemic crisis that resulted in abnormally high mortality and that was accompanied by a whole

---

[41] Francisco Franco, *Libro de enfermedades contagiosas y de la preservación dellas* (Seville, 1569), p. 65; see A. Carreras, *La peste y los médicos en la España del Renacimiento* (Salamanca, 1976), p. 138.

[42] In Sobradillo a high number of widowed men and women are recorded among the marriages registered, which also increased in number, in 1732, 1807 and 1810–11, following the mortality crises of 1730–1, 1805 and 1809, respectively; and in Otero de Herreros in 1806, following the high mortality rates of the previous years.

series of dramatic circumstances, as in the case of the plague, could explain the decrease in the number of births. However, there are also other factors, though less unanimously accepted, that on the evidence could be relevant in certain cases. Widespread, regular birth control at that time must be considered improbable and, had it existed, it is unlikely there would be any references to it. Nevertheless, mention must be made of certain forms of voluntary birth control. The cases of infanticide among a number of rural families in the countryside around Ciudad Rodrigo, denounced by the bishop in 1603, and in Medina del Campo in 1599, must be closely connected to the crisis that we have been studying, and must be considered an extreme form of 'ex-post' birth control.[43] Furthermore, the spread of the practice of *coitus interruptus* among the population, which was regarded as a matter of fact and denounced on moral grounds in 1607 in the important work of the Jesuit, Tomás Sánchez, together with other practices connected with abortion, must be directly linked to the circumstances of the final years of the sixteenth century and the first years of the seventeenth.[44] Voluntary abstinence from sexual relations was explicitly recommended during the years of the plague by various specialists in the disease, such as Dr Guevara of San Sebastián, Luis Mercado,[45] Pedro Ciruelo, who in 1519, quoting St Paul, had recommended that all married men should act in those circumstances as if unmarried,[46] or Andrés Laguna in 1556.[47] The demographic trends themselves could also explain in part this decrease in the number of births immediately following the crisis since it is clear that the higher rate of adult mortality during the epidemic must have affected a much higher

---

[43] W. Petersen, *La población. Un análisis actual* (Madrid, 1968), p. 324.

[44] Tomás Sánchez, *Disputationum de sancto matrimonii sacramento* (Antwerp, 1607). See also on this point, André Venard, 'Deux contributions à l'histoire des pratiques contraceptives (I. Saint François de Sales et Thomas Sanchez)', *Population* 4 (1954), 683–92, and, in general, the suggestions of P. Vilar, 'Quelques problèmes de démographie historique en Catalogne et en Espagne', *Annales de Démographie Historique*, 1965, p. 16. Also in 1606, in *Diez privilegios para mugeres preñadas*, Juan Alonso de los Ruizes includes a large number of references to abortion and the substances used to bring about abortions, Luis S. Granjel, *La medicina española del siglo XVII* (Salamanca, 1978), p. 204.

[45] Luis Mercado, *El libro de la peste* (1921 edn), p. 251.

[46] P. Ciruelo, 'Hexameron theologal sobre el regimiento medicinal contra la pestilencia', Alcalá de Henares, 1519, in Carreras, *La peste y los médicos en la España del Renacimiento*, p. 118.

[47] 'Discurso breve sobre la cura y preservación de la pestilencia', *ibid.*, p. 150.

than usual proportion of pregnant women,[48] meaning that a certain number of future births would be lost. Furthermore, the reduction in the number of marriages during the crisis must also have played its part in the immediate decrease in the number of births, since in former times the proportion of young or recently married couples to the total was much higher than at present and, in consequence, of all children born within a specific period the proportion of first-born would also be higher.

It is difficult to discover the 'wave effects' of the generations depleted by high rates of child mortality or low numbers of births due to the crisis, on the basis of the only quantitative data available, namely, for the first half of the seventeenth century, the records of baptisms and marriages. In the case of baptisms, negative effects could be expected when the generations born at the end of the sixteenth century reached marriageable age and bore their first children. For this purpose regional or local data on the mean age at which couples entered into their first marriage would clearly be necessary, since these data may vary considerably according to the time and place.[49] Nevertheless, a decrease in the mean number of baptisms performed in the decade may be perceived in the 1620s. An extensive survey conducted in eighteen locations included in our sample effectively shows that the mean annual number of baptisms performed between 1621 and 1630 was, in the majority of these locations, lower than in the first two decades of the century. However, although these figures reflect the demographic decline in the interior of Castile during the first half of the seventeenth century, they are not sufficient evidence of the effect of the epidemic of 1596–1602 since, with the exception of one location which records the lowest mean number of baptisms in the aforesaid decade, in almost all the areas analysed that suffered a crisis in the final years of the sixteenth century the lowest levels of births were recorded in the decade after, the 1630s. In addition, there are four

[48] Villalba, *Epidemiología española*, II, p. 79, relating to the epidemic of 1678 in Malaga.
[49] This age is very difficult to specify for these dates. In the eighteenth and part of the nineteenth centuries in certain areas of Segovia it ranged from 23 to 26 years of age in men and from 20 to 23 years of age in women, as is shown in a detailed statistical study conducted on the basis of the records of Mozoncillo and Otero de Herreros, Vicente Pérez Moreda, 'Matrimonio y Familia. Algunas considera-ciones sobre el modelo matrimonial español en la Edad Moderna', *Boletín de la Asociación de Demografía Histórica* 4 (1986), 3–51.

Table 2.4. *Mean annual number of baptisms*

Location	1601–10	1611–20	1621–30	1631–40	1641–50
Ciudad Rodrigo	83	98	97	100	153
Fuente de S. Esteban	110	101	102	100	?
Lumbrales	114	142	119	100	128
Villavieja	157	117	128	100	?
Sobradillo	159	208	158	100	110
Martiago	81	82	90	100	72
Motilla del Palancar	105	109	110	100	80
Fuenterrebollo	?	173	142	100	134
Otero de Herreros	133	?	106	100	103
Villacastín	257	213	178	100	104
Navares de Enmedio	191	121	83	100	105
Vallelado	107	136	105	100	146
Hervás	119	109	107	100	117
Cereceda	109	119	104	100	87
Mantiel	209	158	164	100	105
Chiloeches	102	92	106	100	87
Burgo de Osma	85	125	118	100	102
S. Esteban de Gormaz					
(N. Sra. del Rivero)	262	271	176	100	182

(Base: 1631–1640 = 100)

other locations in which the lowest number of recorded births is in the years 1641–50, see Table 2.4.[50]

This decline in the number of baptisms, which would appear to be centred on the 1630s,[51] is undoubtedly influenced by other circumstances, some much more immediate, such as the agrarian and mortality crisis of 1630–1, which had significant and widespread effects throughout the interior, in addition to the high mortality rates that largely affected infants during the first years of the century. Emigration throughout the early decades of the seventeenth century is another important point to be borne in mind, and a probable massive decline in fertility, which should be the subject of serious study, may also have played an important part. Finally, we should not dismiss the influence of the later generations depleted

---

[50] One of these four locations, Martiago, situated close to the Salamanca border with Portugal, reflects the depopulation caused by the war fought with Portugal during these years.

[51] This has also been shown in the studies conducted by Angel García Sanz on an extensive sample of locations in Segovia, *Desarrollo y crisis del Antiguo Régimen en Castilla la Vieja* (Madrid, 1977), pp. 51–3.

Table 2.5. *Mean annual number of marriages*

Location	1601–10	1611–20	1621–30	1631–40
Sobradillo	263	233	100	119
Villacastín	189	165	100	177
Hervás	133	127	100	121
Chiloeches	121	130	100	75
Talavera de la Reina	100	85	100	96
Otero de Herreros	65	62	100	88
Barajas de Melo	90	62	100	93

(Base: 1621–30 = 100)

in the aftermath of the epidemic of 1596–1602, generations which, by the 1640s, had become couples married for some years but still well within the fertile age group.

The impact on nuptiality is also open to different interpretations, as well as being based on a much smaller number of cases. It was only to be expected that the reduced numbers of births in and around 1599, together with the high infant mortality rates during that period, would lead to a reduction in the mean annual numbers of marriages around the 1620s. In four of a total of seven locations in which both the mortality rates and the other demographic variables correspond to the typical crisis pattern, the mean number of marriages between 1621 and 1630 is lower than in previous decades and lower than in the following decade, with the sole exception in respect of this last point in the case of Chiloeches. In the other three locations this trend is either not observed, or is inverted, see Table 2.5.[52]

It is very possible, in light of these results, that the fall in the number of marriages years after the crisis may be due not only to the possible consequences of important migratory movements that are difficult to specify in real terms, but also to the effects of a crisis mortality centred in particular on infants or children. For example, a disproportionately high mortality rate in the 0–1 or 0–4 age groups would lead to a reduction in the number of marriages in the 1620s.

[52] Talavera records high immigration, as from 1620, particularly from Galicia and Old Castile, González Muñoz, *La población de Talavera de la Reina*, p. 259, and from that date Otero de Herreros records the most expansive phase of its pastoral activities as a location typically dedicated to Mesta transhumance.

On the contrary, predominant mortality rates among the 5–9 or 10–14 age groups could have been the cause of the decrease in the number of marriages between 1611 and 1620, if it is assumed that couples entered their first marriages at an average age of 25 and that the crisis occurred precisely in 1599. This pattern may be seen in the last three cases analysed in Table 2.5 and could be explained, if we leave aside for the moment the question of migratory movements or possible changes in marriage patterns, by the different intensity of the epidemic at the local level on different age groups of infants and children. Only by examination of a wider sample of cases may sounder conclusions be reached in this respect.

Bennassar also suspected that the sharp but fleeting increase in the number of marriages in the years immediately after the epidemic was followed by a subsequent decrease, but he attributed this phenomenon, which the above data clearly corroborate, to a possible high ratio of males in the youngest adult age groups, as a consequence of the high female mortality that he assumes existed during the crisis.[53] This would lead to an extension of male celibacy and to the consequent reduction in the total number of marriages, a phenomenon which was certainly criticised in the literature of the *arbitristas* during the first decades of the century.[54] Nevertheless, we have seen that Bennassar's evidence regarding this allegedly high female mortality rate was not very convincing, since it was based on very few data which, in addition, related only to the adult population. The sources used do not specify in all cases the sex of the infants and adolescents whose deaths are recorded during this period, which would be the most essential information for this purpose, and yet Bennassar not only accepts high rates of both infant and female mortality as a result of the epidemic, but he would also appear to combine the two phenomena, assuming in addition a high rate of female mortality among infants and juveniles. Even if this were the case, it would not appear to be the most important mechanism responsible for the decrease in the numbers of marriages and births in the decades following the plague. Infant mortality, by itself, even if it was not relatively higher than adult mortality during the crisis, and with no clear difference between the sexes, must necessarily determine an important reduction in the number of

[53] Bennassar, *Recherches sur les grandes épidémies*, p. 70.
[54] See Domínguez Ortiz, *La sociedad española en el siglo XVII*, pp. 86ff.

marriages when the survivors of the generations depleted by the effects of the plague reached marriageable age. Clearly it cannot be denied that, together with other social manifestations typical of the period, the figure of the bachelor became more common. However, the most reasonable view would be to consider that both the criticism contained in the contemporary literature and the concerns of the short-lived Junta de Población[55] were intended to denounce the general decrease in demographic activity, rather than the specific consequences of a particular social attitude. Female celibacy due to the low ratio of males as a result of migration, and more specifically of male emigration to the Americas, was undoubtedly a significant factor of decline in many areas.[56] That is, precisely the opposite of Bennassar's theory. Had the *arbitristas* had the means to corroborate 'a possible numerical disequilibrium between men and women'[57] as the cause of the demographic decline, they may perhaps have done so in the opposite sense to Bennassar; that is, the criticisms of the emigration to the Americas and other parts of the empire as a factor of depopulation could have been made bearing in mind all the points indicated above.[58]

It is clear that the negative effects of the great epidemic in Castile of 1596–1602 played a part in the demographic decline seen in Castile, particularly in Old Castile and in the central area of the interior, during the first half of the seventeenth century, but it is impossible to trace the path of the epidemic clearly by following the curves of marriages or births. Even if these figures do fall to their

---

[55] Some notes on the 'demographic policy' adopted after 1609 and on the activities of the Junta de Población during the 1620s in J. Reglá, 'La época de los dos últimos Austrias', in *Historia social y económica de España y América*, ed. J. Vicens Vives (Barcelona, 3rd edn, 1972), III, p. 209, and Domínguez Ortiz, *La sociedad española en el siglo XVII*, pp. 96–8.

[56] Domínguez Ortiz, *La sociedad española en el siglo XVII*, pp. 95ff. A reflection of this may be the high number of 'widows' recorded in the 'census' of 1646.

[57] Bennassar, *Recherches sur les grandes épidémies*, p. 70.

[58] This was the view of Pedro Fernández de Navarrete in 1626 when he indicated that one of the principal causes of the depopulation of Castile was 'the large number of colonies' and 'that each year more than forty thousand people leave Spain', with very few 'marrying and reproducing', *Conservación de monarquías*, Discurso VIII. The criticisms expressed by Lope de Deza of emigration and the overextension of the Spanish empire may also be understood in this sense: 'so many states and kingdoms beyond her own continent and circuit, such as the Americas, Flanders, Italy, and others ... mean that many native sons are required, to go out to the foreign kingdoms and provinces', *Gobierno político de agricultura* (Madrid, 1618), ff. 21v.–22.

lowest levels in the 1620s and 1630s, we cannot conclude that this was exclusively due to a wave effect deriving from the great crisis of the end of the sixteenth century, and that for several reasons. Firstly, because other less serious crises were to be repeated in the following years and their consequences must be even closer to the central years of demographic decline. And secondly, because the other components that regulate population trends may also vary in a period of economic instability and not only as a 'response' to a mortality crisis; the decrease in nuptiality and fertility could thus contribute to check the growth of population. However, apart from these factors, which are difficult to measure and in respect of which we have no more specific data than the diatribes of the critical literature of the period, there is the question of emigration which is, in many places and in entire areas, an essential point for comprehending the demographic decline. During the first half of the seventeenth century the evident relative depopulation of north and central Castile was not only attributed to high mortality, but also, and in some locations it was the principal cause, to the constant loss of population through emigration.[59] Madrid, as the seat of the Court, Andalusia and also New Castile, at least as an area of transit, in addition to the American continent, absorbed some of the population losses of places that were not especially severely punished by the catastrophic mortality crises of the seventeenth century, or that were at least no more severely punished than other peripheral areas. This migratory current, which already existed in the sixteenth century and which was undoubtedly accelerated as a result of the temporary movements away from the centre of the epidemic that were typical of periods of crisis, must have been consolidated as a result of the plague of 1599. The still unpublished study of Professor Domínguez Ortiz into the annual regional purchase of Crusade Bulls during the seventeenth century summarises, by means of a

[59] As was the case in Villacastín, Angel García Sanz and Vicente Pérez Moreda, 'Análisis histórico de una crisis demográfica: Villacastín de 1466 a 1800', *Estudios Segovianos* 24: 70 (1972), 119–42. Similar to this case, in which the incidence of the 1599 plague was relatively slight, is that of Medina del Campo, where 'it would appear to be improbable ... that the population decline was due to an extension of contagion, although the plague certainly helped to accentuate this process, but rather to the fact that a large number of the inhabitants left the town', Alberto Marcos Martín, *Auge y declive de un núcleo mercantil y financiero de Castilla la Vieja. Evolución demográfica de Medina del Campo durante los siglos XVI y XVII* (Valladolid, 1978), p. 71.

58   VICENTE PÉREZ MOREDA

series of graphs of great interest, a number of conclusions that are in agreement with this hypothesis concerning the internal movements of population to which we refer. Moreover, the small sample of locations in New Castile that we have been able to analyse reflect, in respect of baptisms in the years around 1600, completely opposite trends to those recorded in the majority of the locations analysed in more northerly areas of Castile. In Los Yébenes, Orgaz, Madridejos, Belmonte, etc., there is a sharp and continuous increase in the number of baptisms from 1598 and 1599 throughout the first years of the seventeenth century. These figures give the impression that there was emigration southwards during the years of crisis in which high mortality rates were recorded in the north. Catastrophic mortality is, therefore, by no means the only cause of the depopulation of the interior of the kingdom.

It must also be borne in mind that the mortality rate alone could not have played such an important role. It is true that, at a local level, many rural areas felt the effects of the epidemic more than the majority of the towns and cities of Castile, despite the fact that the decline of the cities and of the semi-urban areas was accelerated as a consequence of the great crisis, once other economic factors came into play. However, there were also many villages in which the mortality rate did not reach genuinely catastrophic levels, sufficient in themselves to determine the progressive depopulation of the area. Authoritative critics have indicated that in order to bring about a clear reduction in numbers of births in the medium and long-term, in any one year catastrophic mortality must carry away at least 20 per cent of the population.[60] Only in the most serious cases did the crisis of 1599 reach figures of 30 or 40 per cent, in very specific, isolated and generally small areas, whereas for the whole of the kingdom it would not represent, at most, a reduction of more than 7.5 or 8 per cent of the total population. If the crisis is understood, therefore, to be the sole cause of the internal development of the demographic mechanisms, it would not have had decisive consequences had it not been for the combined effect, whether simultaneous or immediately subsequent, of the other variables that guide population trends. If we compare the towns and cities of Castile

[60] See the contributions by D. E. C. Eversley and Gustaf Utterström in D. V. Glass and D. E. C. Eversley (eds.), *Population in History. Essays in Historical Demography* (London, 1965), pp. 52, 541.

with those of the Levante, Catalonia (specifically in 1589–92 and 1629–30) and all the Mediterranean periphery in the seventeenth century, the results speak for themselves: in the interior the catastrophic mortality crisis would not have had lasting or decisive effects on subsequent population trends had it not been for the presence of other concomitant factors, the majority of which are located on or originate in the strictly economic plane and do not, therefore, depend on the simple endogenous operation of demographic mechanisms.

3. The agrarian 'depression' in Castile in the seventeenth century

GONZALO ANES

Although the sources necessary to reconstruct the tithe series needed to study changes in the agrarian economy in the sixteenth century do exist in parish, cathedral, diocesan and private archives, the tithe figures now available are still too few and too fragmentary to permit valid general conclusions to be drawn from the limited number of cases where the fluctuations and trends of output can at present be known. Price series for agricultural produce, together with other supplementary information, however, make it possible to sketch out the trend of agricultural production in some places and some regions of Castile and Andalusia.[1]

The increase of the urban population in the sixteenth century guaranteed the peasantry a firm market for their products and in some specific cases, as the demand from towns and cities grew, it elicited a response from the agrarian sector in the form of an extension of the area under cultivation and a diversification of crops. It also allowed, where possible, specialisation in the products in greatest and most regular demand by the urban population. To the increase in urban demand must be added the increase and diversification of overseas demand, which has in the past been given

---

[1] The price series and indices constructed by E. J. Hamilton, *American Treasure and the Price Revolution in Spain, 1501–1650* (Cambridge, MA, 1934) remain indispensable. When Jean Paul Le Flem publishes his *La mercurial de Segovia, 1560–1715*, we shall have a source of great importance, analysed with statistical rigour, which will permit appropriate comparisons and revivify the study of price history. The so-called *Relaciones Topográficas* ordered by Philip II (more properly and less anachronistically, *Relaciones para la descripción e historia de los pueblos de España*), are also of great interest for the study of agriculture in New Castile, providing quantitative data on more than 600 towns in the years 1575–80; see Noël Salomon, *La Campagne de Nouvelle Castille à la fin du XVIe siècle d'après les "Relaciones*

greater importance than it deserves. The figures we have for trade with the Indies, despite the uncertainty concerning the quantities of agricultural produce exported, are indication enough that exports could not have set off the growth of the agrarian sector. Nevertheless, overseas demand for Castilian and Andalusian agricultural produce did contribute to agricultural growth in areas from which it was profitable to export, since it promoted production for the market and the specialisation that followed from it. That demand helped stimulate a process of expansion which had its origins in behavioural changes within the rural population resulting from the readjustments that took place during the fifteenth century to changes in average yields, in labour productivity, in wages and consequently in the rents and dues demanded by the lords, and in the relative price of agricultural and manufactured goods.

The population of the Crown of Castile grew during the sixteenth century. Figures for twenty Castilian cities in 1530 and 1594 show an increase of 84 per cent.[2] Though the growth of urban population was not solely the result of immigration, the most active commercial and manufacturing cities tended to absorb a considerable influx of population from the countryside. The figures for baptisms in rural parishes confirm the growth of population in the sixteenth century established on the basis of the censuses. Those figures show an upward trend until 1570–80. From then on checks on growth were beginning to operate, and the baptismal records show a clear downward trend in every rural parish that has been studied.[3]

topográficas" (Paris, 1964) and José Gentil da Silva, *Développement économique, subsistance, déclin* (Paris, 1965).

[2] Ramón Carande, *Carlos V y sus banqueros*, (Madrid, 1943), I, p. 60. The general trend is not invalidated by there being cities whose population fell between those dates. Those falls were slight, and the total population of the thirty-one cities for which we have information and which we can regard as a representative sample of the whole urban population, was 361,445 in 1530, 593,845 in 1594, an increase of 64 per cent. The fall in the eleven cities of those thirty-one which lost population was only 20 per cent.

[3] That the downward trend in the number of baptisms was a symptom that the number of people was beginning to exceed the food supply is corroborated by the evidence of the aforementioned *Relaciones*. Salomon pointed out that the *Relaciones* as a whole give the impression that the population had increased from the end of the fifteenth century to the middle of the sixteenth, but by the time the *Relaciones* were being compiled the beginnings of a downward movement were visible in a large number of places, Salomon, *La Campagne de Nouvelle Castille*, pp. 45–9. The tables published by Gentil da Silva show that in places in the provinces of Madrid, Cuenca and Toledo, where population had been rising during

The profitability of growing more food enabled an expanding population to be sustained and that in turn allowed more land to be cultivated. The ploughing up and cultivation of poor land was the one response the farmers had to the ever increasing need for agricultural produce as the population of the towns and villages grew. Intensification of production was not possible given the almost total absence of technical change in the sixteenth century. For that reason, although it is true that good harvests could be got in newly broken land in the early years, the soil in poor, low-quality land, cultivated with archaic techniques, was soon exhausted. Average yields per acre and the productivity of labour, therefore, tended to fall, and the costs of production in hours of labour tended to rise.[4]

The ploughing up, sowing and cultivation of woodland, scrub and pasture reduced the area of permanent grazing, and necessarily also reduced the number of cattle and sheep maintained in each village in line with the loss of feed.[5] This parallel increase in land under cultivation and decrease in permanent grazing was probably at the root of the shortage of plough-teams. With more land to plough, more plough-teams were needed, but with less grazing there were inevitably fewer cows and oxen, assuming that prior to the need to increase cultivation there had been a balance in each district

the sixteenth century, the locals were complaining in 1575–80 of a lack of land for cultivation, a shortage of pasture, and the poor quality of the soil.

[4] The evidence for the extension of cultivation related to the increase of population is abundant. In Valdaracete (Madrid), the increase of population was explained in 1580 'by the ploughing up of the land in the town's district, which has therefore been able to feed and support more people', Carmelo Viñas Mey and Ramón Paz (eds.), *Relaciones de los pueblos de España ordenadas por Felipe II. Provincia de Madrid* (Madrid, 1949), p. 627. The increase of population in Valdelaguna (Madrid) was also explained by 'the people having turned to arable farming and ploughed more land than they used to', *Relaciones. Madrid*, p. 635. The fall in average yields with the cultivation of marginal land and the corresponding decline in labour productivity was soon to lead to a fall in population. That was implicitly recognised by the inhabitants of Chamartín (Madrid) in 1579 when they said that the village had decayed because of the cultivation of 'very poor and thin soils', *Relaciones. Madrid*, p. 214. The inhabitants of Cerralbo (Toledo) declared in 1576 that they grew 'wheat, barley, oil, vetches, and a few chick peas', as well as wine, 'but none of it in any abundance' because the soil was 'very much exhausted' and 'very difficult', *Relaciones. Toledo*, I, p. 299.

[5] There is a lack of quantitative data for the decline of cattle, sheep and goats; but see the evidence of Almoguera (Guadalajara), where in 1575 it was said that 'there used to be many sheep and goats', but now 'there are very few, because the ground has been ploughed up and largely cleared', Salomon, *La Campagne de Nouvelle Castille*, p. 94.

between arable, pasture and woodland. The shortage of ox-teams was gradually overcome by the use of mules as draught animals. Mules did not need permanent grazing; they could be fed on straw and barley, and the supply of straw and barley tended to increase as more land was put under the plough. Mules are, of course, faster than oxen and can on average plough the same area of land in a third the time a team of oxen would need. The slowness of oxen also made it less worthwhile to use them on plots a long way from their stables, and that also encouraged their replacement by the mule. So too did the increasing amount of land given over to vines, since the mule was better suited to draw the light ploughs used in the vineyards, which, moreover, did not provide grazing.[6] The rising price of mules during the sixteenth century was the consequence of the increased demand arising from the need to put more land under the plough and of the higher costs of fodder for their maintenance. Contemporary writers who dilated on the disadvantages of using mules as draught animals emphasised that their high cost prevented poor farmers from owning them, which was why they had to continue to use the cheaper and less demanding oxen.[7] On the Cantabrian fringe, where there was plenty of pasture and the fields were not far from home, the peasants always used oxen for the plough. The advantage of the much stronger ox was that it ploughed more deeply and that both its flesh and its hide could be used once its useful working life was over.

The expansion of agriculture in the sixteenth century, therefore, involved putting more land under cultivation. That made it necessary to overcome the contradiction between an ever increasing area of cultivated land and the parallel reduction of permanent pastu-

---

[6] Miguel Caxa de Leruela was convinced that the planting of vines had made it necessary to use mules at the plough 'and hindered working with oxen', *Restauración de la antigua abundancia de España* (Naples, 1631), in a new edition by Jean Paul Le Flem (Madrid, 1975), p. 105. The advantages and disadvantages of using mules instead of oxen were the subject of a real debate which acquired particular interest at the end of the eighteenth century. On this see the works referred to by Braulio Antón Ramírez in his *Diccionario de bibliografía agronómica y de toda clase de escritos relacionados con la agricultura* (Madrid, 1865), p. 991. Such ideas were spread by men of letters with no practical knowledge of agriculture, and were ignored by the farmers who did what suited them.

[7] The shortage of cattle was already apparent by 1552. A pragmatic of 23 April decreed that everyone with 1,500 head of sheep grazing on municipal fields was to keep 6 breeding cows for every 1,000 sheep, *Nueva Recopilación*, ley XV, título VII, libro VII.

rage, or to move from a five, four or three-year rotation to more frequent cropping. Where the soil was fertile enough to permit a harvest every other year, that tended to become the norm and consequently, lacking permanent plots of fallow and sufficient grazing, there was a tendency to do without cattle and sheep, with the results we have just noted.

The area dedicated to the vine tended to increase in suitable regions under the stimulus of rising prices. The tithe series for the must confirm the growth of output throughout the whole of the sixteenth century. In places the grape was the principal item of the harvest and, when pressed into must and wine, the most important source of income for agriculturalists who were true specialists, selling a product on the market to raise the money to buy everything else they needed for their sustenance. The 'Topographical Relations' corroborate the evidence of the tithes concerning crop specialisation.[8] The marketing of wine away from its place of production led to competition and to an improvement in quality.[9]

The planting of olives in New and Old Castile, La Mancha and Extremadura in the sixteenth century seems to have been due more to internal than to external demand,[10] but the expansion of olive-

[8] In addition to the places where the importance of wine production can be shown in absolute terms, it is of interest to point out that, in some places, it was also important in relative terms. In Algés (Toledo), the residents chosen to reply to the questionnaire in 1576 explained that the village's crop was 'wine belonging to residents and landowners from Toledo'; the remaining crop was 'very little'. Although it is true that here crop specialisation was due to the fact that the soil was not good for grain, being 'rocky and stony over most of the district', in Burguillos it was said in 1576 that there was no 'other farming of importance' than 'the growing of vines'. Their wine was sold in Toledo, and 'the grain and animals' they needed they bought in La Mancha and Toledo, *Relaciones. Toledo*, I, pp. 87, 156–7. The two residents of Ciruelos deputed to answer the questionnaire in 1576 declared that the whole district was under cultivation and that the greater part of it was 'planted with vines and olives', while not much was ploughed and sown; they also said the village's 'greatest lack' was grain, which they procured from La Mancha, *ibid.*, I, 308; and similar evidence from Cuervas, Chueca, Esquivias, etc., *ibid.*, I, pp. 333, 400.

[9] The residents of Extremera declared in 1580 that their wine was 'of such quality and renown' that it was sought by buyers from Madrid, Toledo, Seville and elsewhere; 'oil of good quality and value' and 'much saffron, of a higher value than in other places', were also highly regarded for their quality by merchants, *Relaciones. Madrid*, pp. 248–9. In Mondéjar (Guadalajara), they said they produced 'a lot of wine, of excellent quality' and made 'very select whites'; in Tendilla and Sayatón similarly.

[10] The olive groves in Castile were concentrated in the valley of the Tagus, especially in Guadalajara province, and also in Toledo, see Salomon, *La Campagne de*

groves and vineyards in Andalusia was a response to the movement of prices and to the greater ability to adapt to the market permitted by its situation, soil and climate.[11]

The extension of the cultivation of cereals, vines and olives was compatible with the continuance of horticulture and fruit-growing and with the availability of other complementary products for the supplementation of family needs.[12] In some cases the growth of population did not require that foodstuffs had to be produced by unbalanced methods which in the long run put the brake on growth and in adverse climatic conditions led to a disequilibrium which inevitably meant a loss of population. In regions with the greatest population growth, the first shortages were of grazing and of timber because the pastures and the woodlands had been ploughed up. In the villages of the uplands of Toledo, Cuenca and other parts of Castile and Andalusia, the rise in the birth rate does not seem to have generated in the long run the classic conflict between population and subsistence because of a tendency of their populations to migrate to the more fertile lowlands. We know about this migration although we are still a long way from being able to put a figure on its significance.[13]

An increased population made possible and required that more land be devoted to cereals and other agricultural produce. Urban demand encouraged farmers to shift between crops as relative prices, price fluctuations and the trend of prices against foreseeable costs of production in each particular case dictated.

The expansion of land under cultivation continued in Old Castile at least until 1570–80, although it is always possible to find exceptions to this general trend.[14] The estimates of population and agri-

Nouvelle Castille, p. 86. There were also olive groves to the north of the central cordillera, but essentially for internal demand, Jesús García Fernández, *Aspectos del paisaje agrario de Castilla la Vieja* (Valladolid, 1963), pp. 2–6.

[11] Carande, *Carlos V y sus banqueros*, I, pp. 135–6.

[12] Hontarejo, Illescas, *Relaciones. Toledo*, I, pp. 459, 493–4.

[13] See the comments of Ignacio Olagüe on this point, *La decadencia española*, (Madrid, 1950), I, pp. 267–8.

[14] See the 'Relación de lo que han informado los corregidores de Castilla la Vieja y Nueva, la Mancha, Extremadura y Andalucía acerca del remedio que tendrá para la conservación de la labranza y crianza', Biblioteca Nacional, Madrid, Ms. 9372. The *corregidor* of Burgos informed that in some areas the land was no longer being worked 'because of the lack of people and the great increase in wage rates', and the *alcalde mayor* of the *Adelantamiento* of Burgos also claimed land was not being worked 'because the area was mountainous and infertile', eroded by rains. In the

cultural production, as indicated by the tithes, confirm the upward trend of both these variables. The direction of the trend, despite some contrary evidence and the particular circumstances and needs of individual places, cannot be in doubt. As there were no improvements in agricultural methods of any consideration, the need to grow more meant the need to plough up pasture and woodland;[15] the subsequent shortage of grazing meant that soon the number of cattle and sheep had to be reduced and the ox had to be replaced by the mule in order to establish a new balance in agriculture. The shortage of timber, which also resulted from the breaking up of the woodland, also meant that the town councils had to step in to save the woods and promote reforestation.[16] The repeated complaints about the lack of grazing because of the spread of the arable and the denunciations by the Council of the Mesta forced the Crown to order the protection and preservation of woodland. Nevertheless, the need to repeat royal pragmatics and decrees over and over again indicates that they were of very little effect.[17]

The common practice of burning woods in order to extend pastures was frequently denounced. In reply to petitions of the Cortes in 1555 and 1560 against the burning of woods in Andalusia, Extremadura, the kingdom of Toledo and elsewhere, to provide young shoots for better grazing for goats, Philip II ordered that animals should not be allowed into newly burned wooded areas for

Adelantamiento of León, Medina del Campo, Logroño, Zamora and Avila, the officials said there was good land uncultivated for lack of labour and the poverty of the peasants, 'resulting from the great burden of taxes, *alcabalas* and *millones*', and similarly in Jerez, Ecija and Puerto Real, Carmona and Antequera, for a variety of reasons, including bad harvests, emigration, the oppression of judges and *poderosos*, high taxes and high wages for labour.

15 Again see the 'Relación de lo que han informado los corregidores ... acerca del remedio que tendrá para la conservación de la labranza y crianza', in particular the reports of the officials of Zamora, the Siete Merindades of Old Castile, Ciudad Rodrigo, Gata, Cordoba, Jaén, Gibraltar, Lorca, Alhama, Mérida, Almadén, Brozas, Trujillo, Badajoz, Montánchez.

16 The 'Topographical Relations' show how many places had to cultivate inferior land (12 per cent of those in Cuenca, 15 per cent in Madrid, 29 per cent in Toledo), were short of wood and woodland (48 per cent in Cuenca, 64 per cent in Madrid, 43 per cent in Toledo), or did not have enough pasture for their animals (19 per cent in Cuenca, 34 per cent in Madrid, 27 per cent in Toledo). The calculations are based on the tables in Gentil da Silva, *Développement économique, subsistance, déclin*, pp. 56–61. Salamanca's municipal ordinances of 1568 required that for every *fanega* of woodland put under the plough, thirty trees had to be left.

17 See the laws in *Nueva Recopilación*, título VII, libro VII.

five or six years in order to preserve the holm-oak and other trees. Despite the heavy penalties, it was not a success.[18]

The shortage of wood and pasture and the consequent decline in the number of cattle and sheep in the villages of Castile, Extremadura and Andalusia, seem clearly to have been the result of the disruption of the balance between arable, pasture and woodland resulting from the over-extension of cultivation. The outcome was harvest failures when climatic conditions were adverse, violent fluctuations in supply, and a rise in the death rate. The extension of cultivation and crop specialisation made possible an increased population and its continued growth. The expansion of the vine and the olive during the sixteenth century led only exceptionally to the abandonment of self-sufficiency by the peasantry. Crop diversity was maintained in the villages, even into our own days, in order to ensure a food supply that the market, ill-supplied and distorted by the bulk stocks of agricultural produce derived from rents and tithes, could not guarantee. The peasantry did not have the purchasing power needed for there to be an organised market in agricultural produce. The little money that came their way had to go to pay the lesser tithes, which usually had to be paid in coin, rents and taxes. They did not have enough coin for regular purchases in the market.

Keeping abreast of the increasing demand for food during the sixteenth century, the breaking of infertile ground, its cultivation and the transition to a system of cropping in alternate years, together with the larger supply of labour and the use of mules for ploughing, made possible as we have seen the continued growth of the population. By the end of the century the shortage of land seemed to some to be the fundamental limitation on the continued growth of population in the villages. There were complaints of the 'tightness' to which they were being reduced by the lack of cultivable land and of houses. The increase in the marriage rate was not only caused by an increased birth rate, but also by a slow change in the age of marriage. As they said in the village of Carabaña in response to the investigations of 1576, 'people are now marrying younger'.[19]

The increased demand for cereals led to a progressive increase in grain prices during the sixteenth century. Because of the declining

---

[18] *Nueva Recopilación*, ley XXI, título VII, libro VII.
[19] See the quotations assembled by Gentil da Silva, *Développement économique, subsistance, déclin*, pp. 19–22.

yields of the harvests, supply did not keep up with demand and grain had to be imported. The gap between production and consumption was always filled in coastal areas by imports.

Cereal prices tended to rise from the beginning of the sixteenth century, as much in Andalusia and Valencia as in New and Old Castile. In New Castile grain prices tended to rise not only throughout the century, wheat especially in the first half, but also throughout the first half of the seventeenth century. As we have seen, the high price of wine had stimulated the planting of vines from the beginning of the sixteenth century, even on land previously dedicated to cereals.

Cereal prices increased less in Old Castile and León and fluctuated less violently. The price of wine rose by 360 per cent between 1501–1600, and that very large increase must have stimulated farmers to plant vines, even in the first half of the seventeenth century, as prices continued to hold up, putting on another 13 per cent between 1590–1600 and 1640–50. Such a modest increase in prices, however, suggests that production and supply had increased sufficiently to satisfy the market. The decree of Philip IV in 1633, claiming that 'the planting of vines was excessive and damaging to arable and animal husbandry', must have been a reflection of that saturation.[20] Between 1540–50 and 1590–1600 the price of wheat had risen by 114 per cent, but it tended to stabilise during the next half century. That stabilisation also tends to confirm the realignment of supply and demand in those years. During the first half of the seventeenth century the price of meat tended to rise faster than that of grain and wine in Old Castile and León, and that must have encouraged farmers to keep more animals and so to look for more pasture.

The rise in the price of wheat was greater in New Castile during the second half of the sixteenth century than during the first. It continued to rise, though less sharply, during the first half of the seventeenth. The price of barley, on the other hand, tended to rise faster, perhaps because of the great demand for fodder for the mules. The rise in the price of meat in the first half of the seventeenth century must have stimulated animal husbandry, as in Old Castile and León, but the increase in wine and oil prices tended to die out after the mid-sixteenth century.

---

[20] Thereafter, a licence was needed to plant vines, *Nueva Recopilación*, ley XXVII, título VII, libro VII.

The rise in the price of wine was much more intense in Andalusia in the first half of the sixteenth century than in the two Castiles, increasing by 179 per cent between 1501–10 and 1540–50. Urban and overseas demand had something to do with this increase and stimulated the planting of vines. There was also a large increase in oil prices, 139 per cent during the same period. The rise of wine and oil prices continued during the second half of the sixteenth century and the first half of the seventeenth, though at a slower rate.[21] The expansion of the vine and the olive under the stimulus of the movement of wine and oil prices was, of course, a sign that conditions were being created there for the involvement of their growers in the market, since the quantity of wine and oil produced by the farmer in areas where the vine and the olive predominated was generally greater than he needed for his own consumption.

The great fluctuations in the price of cereals during the second half of the sixteenth century and the first half of the seventeenth were the result of violent swings in output caused by adverse weather conditions which led to deficient harvests, sharp reductions in supply and price increases. Not only did output fall in these years, but demand rose, since there were farmers who scarcely grew enough for their own use even in normal years. In bad years they had to buy on the market, or get on credit the grain they needed for their bread during the 'long months'. The municipal granaries and charities helped to regulate the supply of grain by storing it after the harvest so that it could be distributed on credit to the needy in the 'long months', most especially in bad harvest years. The vendors of agricultural produce, who always harvested more than they needed for their own families, and those who received produce in payment of rents and tithes would hold on to grain in years of abundance and sell it, either in their own granaries or in the local market, when there was a scarcity. Taking advantage of the high prices of years of dearth, they could maximise their money incomes. This practice was so usual that some constitutions of the diocesan synods made it obligatory.[22] In this way the hoarders, in addition to maximising

---

[21] Price data from Hamilton, *American Treasure and the Price Revolution in Spain.*

[22] The synodal constitutions of the diocese of Astorga, drawn up, published and decreed by the bishop of Astorga, Fray Don Pedro de Roxas, in Salamanca, 1553, required that 'the church stewards sell grain stocks, and the season's rye, barley and wheat at the time of the year when prices are highest, with a view always to selling for the highest possible price' (*Constitución* XXI, *capítulo* V), p. 255 of the

their prices, unintentionally also helped, in the same way as ecclesiastical charity, to regularise supply and mitigate the catastrophic effects of bad harvests.

As we have seen, the population of the cities and towns tended to rise at least until the 1570s. How more people could have been fed in urban centres at the same time that average agricultural productivity per labourer was tending to fall would seem to be a paradox. In fact, it is not, since, as we have said, by cultivating more land more was produced, and this increased the tithes. Land rents also tended to rise during the sixteenth century. Whenever landowners could set higher rents, whether in money or in kind, they tried to do so. The need generally to cultivate more land allowed lessors to take advantage of the situation, particularly in areas where they were not inhibited by a separation between usufruct and eminent domain. They therefore tried to reduce the length of the rental agreements.[23] There was thus a tendency for the quantity of agricultural produce extracted from the countryside in the form of tithes and rents in kind to increase. As the beneficiaries of this surplus product consumed only a part themselves, and that part did not change from one end of the century to the other, the rest of what they received, which did tend to increase, was sold at the highest price it would fetch, even if on occasion the legal maxima (*tasa*) had to be observed. What was sold to the peasants who had not produced sufficient for their own needs allowed them to survive in the short term, but in the long run it was impossible for them to sustain those levels of debt. The increasing quantities sold in the towns and cities permitted a larger urban population to survive. The interdependence of country and city during the sixteenth century can begin to be understood if these relationships are kept in mind. What they also meant was the need for a shift to crop specialisation where

---

printed edition of the *Constituciones* (Salamanca, 1799). There was also an edition in 1595.

[23] On land rents in New Castile at the end of the sixteenth century, see Salomon, *La Campagne de Nouvelle Castille*, pp. 238–45. It is not possible to give more information about the tendency to shorten rental contracts because no work has yet been done on the rich notarial sources of the *archivos de protocolos*. The tendency is apparent, however, in the instructions issued to clerics and administrators in, for example, the synodal constitutions of Astorga, cited above: 'they are not to sell, nor mortgage for life or in perpetuity, nor make any disposition of anything without our permission or that of our vicar general, nor lease for more than three

possible and the involvement of peasant families in craft manufacturing and trade.[24]

At the end of the sixteenth century the total burden of dues, taxes and rents absorbed half the peasant's harvest. It is understandable then how impossible it was to maintain oneself for long from the cultivation of poor quality land, which carried burdens in the same proportion as more fertile land. Settlements in areas where the land was poor therefore tended to lose population, or even to disappear. Complaints about the depopulation of the kingdom and references to uninhabited villages were commonplaces in the writings of the *arbitristas* who propounded measures and remedies to prevent the ruin and depopulation of Spain. It is these writings which have been the most easily usable sources to prove the existence of an economic depression in Castile in the seventeenth century.

The first question to consider in a study of 'decline' is the extent of the fall in the number of inhabitants. That fall would have been brought about by large increases in death rates, resulting from subsistence crises, combined with famines and mortalities of a *catastrophic* nature and with rural emigration to the towns and cities in the expectation of succour from ecclesiastical charity. It is not comprehensible that a large number of people could have existed in the cities if the tendency to the depopulation of the countryside had been so general and so marked.

Nobody doubts that at different times during the century there were areas where population tended to fall. There are numerous examples of whole villages, generally very small ones, being depopulated, even in the sixteenth century. But the fact that some places were depopulated is not conclusive proof of a general trend of depopulation in the seventeenth century, even in districts in which there were villages which had become uninhabited.[25] Contemporaries were misled by the depopulation of villages. Their accounts are couched in the dark tones so much in vogue in the art of the period, and manifested in the painting and the literature of the

years the lands and properties of the said churches' (*Constitución XXI, capítulo* V), p. 254 of the 1799 edition.

24 Salomon, *La Campagne de Nouvelle Castille*, pp. 97–132.

25 The 'Topographical Relations' make it possible to draw up a catalogue of deserted villages in New Castile and to list the not particularly numerous reasons for their depopulation adduced at the time, the most frequent being health issues, *Rela-*

Baroque in which ruins, as a theme, have such an important part. There is a clear parallel between Lope de Vega's portrayal of the 'Neglected Garden',[26] Rodrigo Cano's ruins of Italica,[27] some passages of Góngora's *Soledades*,[28] Carrillo de Sotomayor,[29] or Salazar y Torres versifying over the ruins of a castle,[30] and the words Guillén Barbón y Castañeda uses about the houses of rich farmers in the 'poorest villages of this kingdom': 'their rich construction, buildings sumptuous with ornamentation and well-furnished homes' of which nothing more is now to be seen but 'green ivy and croaking jackdaws';[31] or those of Mateo de Lisón y Biedma when he talks about the 'many villages that have become depopulated and abandoned', 'churches in ruins, houses fallen down, estates in decay'.[32] These images have influenced every historian involved in the study of the *decline*.

The concern of political writers for agriculture in the last years of the sixteenth and the first half of the seventeenth century was associated with what José Antonio Maravall calls the 'desire to change reality, refusing to accept it as it is'. The plaints about the decadence of agriculture were directed not at public opinion, but at the rulers. The belief that the yield from agriculture could be improved if the soil were cultivated better, and that its fluctuations

---

ciones. Toledo, I, pp. 74, 230–1, 237, 357; *Relaciones. Madrid*, pp. 227, 303–4, 602, 699–700, 702–3.

[26] 'Otra Numancia de árboles y vides,
un Sagunto de flores y retamas
las piedras hojas y los muros ramas.'

[27] Where, in the 'despedezado anfiteatro', with its 'mármoles y arcos destrozados', grow 'zarzales y amarillos jaramagos'.

[28] '... y sus desnudas piedras
visten piadosas yedras;
que a ruinas y a estragos
sobre el tiempo hacen verdes halagos.'

[29] In which, 'la hiedra, huésped que se abraza en ella
o ella, se esconde en ella, de afrentada.'

[30] Describing some ruins with rooms 'que antes pulieron láminas y espejos,/ camarín de vencejos/ y alcoba aún no capaz para los grajos'.

[31] *Provechosos arbitrios al consumo del vellón, conservación de plata, población de España y relación de avisos importantes a las cosas que en ellas necesitan de remedio* (Madrid, 1628), p. 9.

[32] *Discursos y apuntamientos de don Mateo de Lisón y Biezma, señor del lugar de Algarinejo, veinticuatro de la ciudad de Granada y su procurador de Cortes, en las que se celebraron el año pasado de 1621, dados a Su Majestad en su Real Mano* (Madrid, 1622), p. 3.

depended not on the weather (which could not be controlled, whether good or ill) but on the way man applied his energies, brought some writers to concentrate on the study of agronomy. The adoption of measures to bring about the ends they desired was the business of the state. That was why there was so much written about the failings of agriculture from the middle of the sixteenth century, designed for the public authorities, 'by imposing some measure or other', to 'stop its dismal progress'.[33] The conviction of the need for the crown to intervene to improve agriculture was what made Pedro de Valencia want the king to be not only the supreme judge and captain general, but also 'head farmer and supervisor of his peasantry'.[34] In spite of this approach, which implies a belief in a sort of physiocracy *avant la lettre* on the part of Castilian 'agrarianists' of the end of the sixteenth century and the first decades of the seventeenth, the disruption of the balance between population and subsistence, resulting from a long process of adaptation and readaptation to changing social and material conditions, led inevitably to a series of adjustments which happened spontaneously and automatically without the public authorities being able to do very much to direct or advance them, because they had neither the theoretical understanding nor the means to take the necessary political action.[35] It is understandable, therefore, that their *ad hoc* responses should have been different in each case and should have had conflicting results.

[33] José Antonio Maravall, *Estado moderno y mentalidad social (Siglos XV a XVII)* (Madrid, 1972), II, pp. 325–6.

[34] José Antonio Maravall, 'Reformismo social-agrario en la crisis del siglo XVII: tierra, trabajo y salario en Pedro de Valencia', *Bulletin Hispanique* 72 (1970), 1–2; and *Estado moderno y mentalidad social*, II, p. 339.

[35] The physiocracy of the Golden Age, precursor of that influential eighteenth-century movement, was, according to Salomon, an expression of the interests of the 'great landlords' or the large and middling sheep-owners of the Mesta, disinclined to accept 'the new forms of a manufacturing and monetarised economy' which were rising with the growth of the cities. For Salomon, most of the writers saw things from the viewpoint of the 'clase nobiliaria' whose income derived essentially from the land, even though they had abandoned their country residences to live at Court or in the cities, Noël Salomon, *Recherches sur le thème paysan dans la 'comedia' au temps de Lope de Vega* (Bordeaux, 1967), p. 206. The concerns of the agrarianists were much wider than simple expressions of landlord or sheep-owning interests. It is worth pointing out that they believed the government could intervene successfully in the economy through appropriate legislation. For Martínez de Mata, the remedy for the ills of the kingdom was to be found, not in any new scheme, but in carrying out the laws passed when Spain was prosperous, Gonzalo Anes (ed.), *Memoriales y discursos de Francisco Martínez de Mata* (Madrid, 1971), Discurso VIII, para. 75, 231.

In a situation of concealed unemployment, the fall in population and in the working population, did not necessarily mean that agricultural production also fell. Cereal production could have been maintained, or even increased, in those places where the fall in population permitted a better relationship between the share of the land devoted to arable, permanent pasture and woods. Where the working population tended to decline and with it the area of land under cultivation, the increased amount of untilled land could have enabled the peasants to keep a larger number of animals, resulting in an increase in the size of the sedentary flocks. Klein claims that at the end of the seventeenth century sedentary sheep raising had increased throughout Castile at the expense of arable agriculture.[36] That increase was due to the fact that the sheep had more pasture in the villages, and each village therefore could keep more sheep without the locals having to take their animals to other areas in search of feed. But they needed to protect their own pastures from the incursion of the transhumants, and so the increased amount of land available for pasture, when taken advantage of by the sedentary flocks, may not have benefited the flocks of the Mesta.

Thus, in the districts in which population was falling from the end of the sixteenth century, the amount of land under cultivation also tended to fall. The poorest land was given over to pasture, with the result that, as the available labour was employed on the best land in each district, which was also better fertilised by the penning of a larger number of sheep on it and their grazing the stubble, average yields per cultivated acre and labour productivity tended to rise. The decline in population implied a fall in the working population in the countryside. With less labour applied to the cultivation of the land and that only to the cultivation of the best land, average yields per acre should have risen even though less land was being worked and total output was falling. There were no technical changes in agriculture in the seventeenth century other than the greater rate of substitution of mules for oxen as draught animals.[37] An increase in

[36] Julius Klein, *The Mesta, 1273–1836* (Cambridge, MA, 1920), pp. 341–2.
[37] Maize cultivation, which had an important role in the agricultural growth of the coastal regions of Galicia, Asturias, the Montaña and the Basque country in the seventeenth century, needed too much moisture to gain a foothold in Castile. The cultivation of maize began in Guipúzcoa in 1576 (*mijo de Indias*), although it spread very slowly before 1630. Thereafter, it spread widely; see José de Vargas y

yields and productivity was, therefore, the effect of a cutting back of cultivation by the abandonment of the poorest soil. To what extent that increase was influenced by the natural readjustment between pasture and arable brought about by the abandonment of marginal land is something that can only be posed as a question that needs investigation. So far, the figures we have for grain seed-ratios in parts of New Castile show a tendency to rise throughout the century. That trend is confirmed by yield series drawn up by Pierre Ponsot for wheat and barley in five farms in the Cordoban champaign.[38]

Average yields per acre tended to rise as the cultivation of the poorest lands was abandoned and as the arable was cultivated less frequently. Labour productivity and gross agricultural income per family also had to rise, especially in areas where population fell. It is that which explains the growth of population in some cities in the seventeenth century, notably in Madrid and in some cities of Andalusia. Specialisation in vine growing, very marked in some regions, and a surge in sedentary sheep numbers in others, enabled peasants to supply the urban markets.

The tithe series show divergent tendencies, depending on the region and on the crop. In Segovia, whilst some wheat and barley tithe series show a stagnant trend, the tithe series for rye show a rise, especially in the second half of the century.[39] Such differences demonstrate that when talking about the agrarian sector it is not possible to continue to adhere to the notion of a general depression of the seventeenth century, since, although it is true that there were

Ponce, 'Estados de vitalidad y mortalidad de Guipúzcoa en el siglo XVIII' (1805), Real Academia de la Historia, 9–27–3–E71, núm. 2, Vargas Ponce.

[38] The richness of the documents used by Ponsot has enabled him to study yield ratios and production in the farms owned by the cathedral chapter of Cordoba in the Cordoban Campiña. See his two studies, 'Rendement des cereales et rente foncière dans la Campiña de Cordove au début du XVIIe et au début du XIXe', *Cuadernos de Historia. Anexos de la Revista Hispania* 7 (Madrid, 1977), pp. 475–89, and 'Malthus n'était-il pas prophète en Andalousie? Les rendements des cereales en Basse Andalousie du XVIIe au XIXe siècle', Paper given to the Colloque préparatoire au 7e Congrès International d'Histoire Économique d'Edimbourg on the theme 'Préstations paysannes, dîmes, rente foncière et mouvement de la production agricole à l'époque pré-industrielle', held in Paris, 30 June–2 July 1977, which contains the series referred to here.

[39] Gonzalo Anes and Jean Paul Le Flem, 'La Crisis del siglo XVII: producción agrícola, precios, e ingresos en tierras de Segovia', *Moneda y Crédito* 93 (1965), 3–53.

places, and even whole regions, where for certain periods of the century wheat production was falling, in some of them the production of other cereals was increasing. Everything leads one to believe that the production of must, oil, wool and meat, and the ratio between harvests and sown land were also rising.

The seventeenth-century *depression* in the agrarian sector in the two Castiles, Extremadura and Andalusia was rather a matter of slow and self-regulating readjustments and readaptations. Its outcome was a new balance between the food supply and population. Of crucial importance in this harmonisation were the decisions of peasant families on whom the production of foodstuffs depended. Seignorial and ecclesiastical authority and government legislation impinged on the freedom with which those decisions were taken. Adaptation to the new circumstances tended to strengthen those authorities as they took advantage of peasant migration, absorbing private and communal plots into their old or newly established estates. The emigration of peasants from overpopulated areas, the most notable case being the forced emigration of the *moriscos*, implied a reorganisation of cultivation, with the result that the land that was least fertile and furthest from the villages where its cultivators lived was left barren. In some cases the lords encouraged that process of reorganisation, but that is a subject that needs further study.

4. Castilian agriculture in the seventeenth century: depression or 'readjustment and adaptation'?

ENRIQUE LLOPIS AGELÁN

In the following pages I shall tackle two closely related matters. I shall begin by raising again the question of the existence or non-existence of a genuine agrarian recession in Castile during the seventeenth century. I shall then reflect on the extent of the changes which took place in the rural economy of Castile in the final decades of the sixteenth century and the first half of the seventeenth century.

I. SPANISH AGRICULTURE FROM THE FINAL DECADES OF THE SIXTEENTH CENTURY UNTIL THE FIRST YEARS OF THE SEVENTEENTH CENTURY: DEEP DEPRESSION AND SLOW RECOVERY

Until recent years, regardless of the basis from which they approached the argument and of their differences over timing, geography and extent, virtually all experts, historians and economists recognised the existence of a prolonged and widespread economic crisis in the Spain of the later Habsburgs. In two articles published in 1978, Gonzalo Anes challenged this near unanimous assessment of productive activity in our seventeenth century.[1] Whether we agree or not with Anes's revolutionary pages, there is no doubt that they have encouraged new thinking about and research into the behaviour of the Spanish economy in the seventeenth century.

Anes maintains that the so-called agrarian 'depression' in Castile

---

[1] Gonzalo Anes, 'La "Depresión" agraria durante el siglo XVII en Castilla', *Homenaje a Julio Caro Baroja* (Madrid, 1978) [chapter 3 of the present volume]; 'Tendencias de la producción agrícola en tierras de la Corona de Castilla (siglos XVI a XIX)', *Hacienda Pública Española* 55 (1978).

during the seventeenth century actually consisted of a 'series of readjustments and adaptations which took place automatically, bringing food production into line with the population'.[2] He bases his views on the following data and arguments.

First, there is no evidence of a 'general trend toward depopulation' in the seventeenth century. Second, the tithe figures available do not permit us to determine the trends in agricultural production in Castile during the seventeenth century, amongst other reasons because of the lack of data on grape and olive harvests and on sheep-shearing. Moreover, the results of the analysis of the published data rather point to a change in the composition of agricultural production than to a slump. Third, if we take into account the fact that there generally existed a high level of 'hidden' unemployment, and that the reduction in the area of land under cultivation increased the average productivity of that land and facilitated the expansion of sedentary sheep flocks, then agricultural production did not necessarily fall in those areas where the numbers of the actively employed dropped. In other words, following on the fall in productivity and yield-ratios resulting from the extensive exploitation of new land in the sixteenth century, the population decline could actually have meant increased productivity.

I shall now examine some of Gonzalo Anes's arguments and try to establish a balance-sheet of the performance of Castilian agriculture in the seventeenth century. I have concentrated on the behaviour of six basic factors: population, grain harvests, per capita cereal production, wool exports, relative agricultural prices, and land rents.

We know that between 1600 and 1700 the population in Castile grew very little or actually remained static; at best it is improbable that it reached growth rates of over 0.15 per cent.[3] Vicente Pérez Moreda has shown that mortality changes were not the cause.[4] As a result, the stagnation or very low increase in the population of Castile is hard to explain without a drop in the birth rate and/or migration to other areas of the Peninsula and to the Indies. Now, migration and the falling fertility must have been caused by a

[2] Anes, 'Depresión agraria', p. 100.
[3] Francisco Bustelo, 'Algunas reflexiones sobre la población española de principios del siglo XVIII', *Anales de Economía* 15 (1972), p. 106.
[4] Vicente Pérez Moreda, *Las crisis de mortalidad en la España interior, siglos XVI–XIX* (Madrid, 1980), pp. 294–326.

deterioration in the economic condition of a considerable percentage of Castilians. Not only that, almost all the baptismal records available show a downward trend in the first forty years of the seventeenth century, at least. In short, the demographic evidence corroborates, in my opinion, the hypothesis of the existence of a persistent contraction of Castilian agriculture during the seventeenth century.

In recent years little work has appeared on the performance of agricultural production in Castile during the seventeenth century, but our knowledge of the problem has advanced considerably with the publication of tithe series for the vast Archbishopric of Toledo.[5] This has enabled me to draw up a production series for bread-corn ('pan') in twenty different archdeaconries.[6] [See Statistical Appendix, Table 4.1 and Figure 4.1]

From a brief examination of the data three observations can be made:

1 Shortly before the end of the third quarter of the sixteenth century, the upward trend of grain harvest returns was reversed in the lands of the Archbishopric of Toledo. In an extensive area of New Castile, the pause in the upward movement of cereal production occurred some years earlier than in the Bureba region further north,[7] and in the countryside around Segovia.[8]

2 Grain harvests in New Castile declined sharply from the early 1570s until the end of the 1630s. By the latter date average yearly cereal production barely exceeded half of what it had been around 1570.

3 Even after the nadir of the slump at the end of the 1630s, no genuine revival took place until shortly before the 1670s, and before 1680 the halting revival did not succeed in recovering much

[5] Jerónimo López-Salazar and Manuel Martín Galán, 'La producción cerealista en el Arzobispado de Toledo', *Cuadernos de historia moderna y contemporánea* 2 (1981), 56–101.
[6] Alcalá de Henares, Alcaraz, Alcolea de Torote, Brihuega, Buitrago, Calatrava, Canales, Escalona, Guadalajara, Hita, Illescas, Madrid, Montalbán, Ocaña, Rodillas, Santa Olalla y Maqueda, Talamanca, Talavera de la Reina, Vicaría de la Puebla, and Zorita de los Canes y Almoguera. The only two archdeaconries that could not be included are Toledo and La Guardia.
[7] Francis Brumont, *Campo y campesinos de Castilla la Vieja en tiempos de Felipe II* (Madrid, 1984), pp. 145–50.
[8] Angel García Sanz, *Desarrollo y crisis del Antiguo Régimen en Castilla la Vieja. Economía y sociedad en tierras de Segovia 1500–1814* (Madrid, 1977), pp. 105–6.

more than an eighth of what had been lost since the maximum reached in the early 1570s.

It is worth examining this depression in greater detail. Five phases can be distinguished. (a) In the first phase, from the mid-1570s to the mid-1580s, cereal production fell on average by roughly 13 per cent. (b) In the second, which ends in the early years of the seventeenth century, the main feature is a fleeting recovery, thanks to good harvests in 1585, 1586 and 1587, which gave way to a stagnation at a level similar to that of the later stages of the first phase. (c) In the third, which covers the central years of the first decade of the seventeenth century, there is another and more severe drop in harvests to an average level roughly 18 per cent lower than that of the previous phase. (d) Between the late 1600s and the late 1630s, the outstanding feature is stagnation. (e) The 1630s, as in other areas, were dramatic years. In New Castile, from a very low level, grain harvests fell yet again by more than 20 per cent. In sum, in the Archbishopric of Toledo the key periods in the movement of contraction were, in order of intensity, the 1630s, the middle years of the first decade of the seventeenth century, and the ten years from the mid-seventies to the mid-eighties of the sixteenth century.

In Table 4.2, I have brought together the limited and fragmentary data which I have been able to piece together on the movement of grain production in Trujillo and its surrounding area.[9] Although these figures leave a lot to be desired, certain things are worth noting. (a) In 1550 and 1560 more than twice as much grain was harvested as the average between 1711 and 1734. (b) It is even more significant that in no year from 1711 to 1734 did cereal harvests reach 80 per cent of that of 1550. (c) The relative importance of barley and particularly of rye as a proportion of total cereal production increased substantially between the middle years of the sixteenth century and the first third of the eighteenth. The partial substitution of mules for oxen, even though this process did not apparently reach its peak in the province of Cáceres until after 1850,[10] must have

---

[9] The *tierra* of Trujillo comprised the following towns and villages: Cañamero, Zurita, Aldeanueva, Bercozana, Logrosán, Cetenera, Acedera, Orellana, Orellanita, Navalvillar, Campo, La Zarza, Alcollarín, Erguijuela y Portera, Santa Cruz, Abertura, Escorial, Puerto, Valhondo, Villa Mesía, Madrigalejo, Robledillo, Santa Ana, Ruanes and Plasenzuela.

[10] In the province of Cáceres in 1891 yokes of bovines still made up 62.5 per cent of the total. I owe this information to Santiago Zapata.

contributed to the increased importance of barley. The growing of rye was related to the need to cultivate poor quality land due to the enclosure of municipal land and to the extension of pastureland for the benefit of the Mesta.

In short, the average level of cereal production must have been a good deal higher in the 1550s than during the first thirty years of the eighteenth century. Furthermore, during the second half of the sixteenth century and in the seventeenth century, there was a significant change in the relative importance of the different cereals which seems to point to an impoverishment of the diet, at least in that portion made up of cereals. It is also more than likely that there was a severe agricultural depression in the Trujillo area during the seventeenth century, even if we cannot detail its form and characteristics.

Cereal production in a number of areas of the province of León also shows a downward pattern from the later 1580s to the early 1690s. Wheat, barley and rye tithes, in spite of the fact that some of the enclosed pastureland was put under the plough in the seventeenth century, fell by 42.8 per cent between 1583–91 and 1685–91.[11]

Cereal production in Amusco, Monzón, Piña and San Cebrián de Campos also fell considerably. Average annual grain tithes in these municipalities in the province of Palencia fell by approximately 50 per cent between the 1580s and the 1660s.[12] A similar drop in grain production, 45.8 per cent between 1580–9 and 1630–9, occurred in twenty-two townships in the province of Segovia.[13] Wheat and barley harvests in fifteen townships in the eastern part of Tierra de Campos fell by 51.3 per cent and 43 per cent respectively between 1580–9 and 1660–9.[14]

[11] Villaverde de Sandoval, Villarroena, Navatexera, Valdesaz de Oteros, Matanza and Fuentes de Carvajal and the *cotos redondos* (enclosed pastures) of Valdellán, Corrales and Valsemana, Membrillán; Libros de Panera, AHN Clero, libros 5,185 and 5,190–91. José Antonio Sebastián Amarillas kindly supplied me with a number of tithe figures for villages in León.
[12] Alberto Marcos Martín, *Economía, sociedad y pobreza en Castilla: Palencia 1550–1814*, 2 vols. (Palencia, 1985), I, pp. 234.
[13] García Sanz, *Desarrollo y crisis*, p. 105.
[14] Bartolomé Yun Casalilla, 'Producción agrícola en Tierra de Campos y Segovia: contrastes, similitudes y problemas en torno a la agricultura castellana en los siglos XVI a XVIII', Paper presented at III Congreso de Historia Económica, Segovia 1985, p. 30; and in a similar vein by the same author, 'Poder y economía. Algunas propuestas para el estudio de la historia agraria de Castilla la Vieja y

In short, it is hard to doubt the collapse of cereal production in the first half of the seventeenth century. It is highly likely that the drop in both Castiles and in Extremadura was over 30 per cent. The process of recovery was slow in almost all areas. The level of grain harvests in the 1580s was not surpassed in the Segovia area before 1750–9; in Tierra de Campos not before 1770–9; in New Castile as a whole not until after 1700; and in the Trujillo area in all probability not until after 1814.[15]

If the total area of land under cultivation decreased on account of declining demand for staple products resulting from a fall in population in the first half of the seventeenth century, one would expect a recovery in per capita cereal production as cultivation became more restricted. However, the figures do not confirm that expectation. In Tierra de Campos during the first thirty years of the seventeenth century cereal production fell more rapidly than did population. Not only that, during the seventeenth century per capita cereal production never surpassed that of the late sixteenth century. In the Segovia area there was a rise in per capita cereal production, but this only took on significant proportions after 1640, that is, after the recession had reached its lowest point.[16] In the territories of the Archbishopric of Toledo the population would have had to have fallen by half for per capita cereal production to have increased in the first half of the seventeenth century. From the data available it seems unlikely that the fall in population reached such dramatic proportions in New Castile in the seventeenth century. In short, there does not seem to have been a per capita increase in cereal production to accompany the contraction of the harvests.

Nevertheless, if the fall in the total amount of cereals coincided with a substantial rise in livestock figures and in grape and olive harvests, then there might not have been much of a reduction in agricultural production as a whole. Although the data available at present do not permit us to ascertain the trends of wine, oil and livestock production during the seventeenth century, I shall neverthe less attempt to determine, from figures for the export of fine wool

León durante la edad moderna' in Reyna Pastor (ed.), *Relaciones de poder, de producción y parentesco en la edad media y moderna* (Madrid, 1990), pp. 375–409.
[15] García Sanz, *Desarrollo y crisis*, pp. 94–110; Yun Casalilla, 'Producción agrícola en Tierra de Campos y Segovia', p. 30; López-Salazar and Martín Galán, 'La producción cerealista en el Arzobispado de Toledo', pp. 56–101.
[16] Yun Casalilla, 'Producción agrícola en Tierra de Campos y Segovia', pp. 13–15.

and from the relative prices of agricultural produce (cf. Statistical Appendix, Tables 4.3–4.7), whether during the first half of the seventeenth century there were strong enough incentives to bring about the conversion of grain land to alternative uses.

According to L. M. Bilbao's estimates based on fiscal sources, Castilian wool exports tended to fall during the seventeenth century, by 41 per cent between 1612–20 and 1662–70.[17] Considering the limited domestic demand for high-quality fleeces and the slump in the cloth industries of the Castilian towns, it seems almost impossible that the recession in cereal production could have coincided with a boom in wool production.

If we were to accept Hamilton's tables of New Castilian wine prices as reliable and representative (which we ought not to do until more up-to-date research allows us to make the requisite comparisons), we should have to admit that the movement of prices in this region not only did not justify the planting of vines on arable land during the first half of the seventeenth century, but in fact did the very opposite. The other wine price series that I have used is much more reliable, since it lists the market prices fetched by a fairly standard product, the wine produced by the monastery of La Estrella in La Rioja. In this region (cf. Table 4.4), it would not appear that, except for 1618–26, the terms of trade were such as to encourage the planting of vines on arable land. Thus in the first half of the seventeenth century, the relative movement of prices could not have been the cause of any significant change in the composition of agricultural production in the direction of an increase of viticulture at the expense of cereals.

Neither does the relative movement of prices appear to have stimulated the planting of olive trees on the arable during the first half of the seventeenth century. Wheat tended to become more expensive relative to oil between 1560 and 1650, by somewhat more than 60 per cent between 1563–80 and 1635–53 (see Table 4.5).

Having rejected wine and oil as options, is it possible that livestock production could have compensated for the recession in cereals? During the first decades of the seventeenth century, the number of head of transhumant sheep, according to Jean Paul Le

---

[17] Luis María Bilbao Bilbao, 'Exportación y comercialización de lanas de Castilla durante el siglo XVII, 1610–1720', in *El pasado histórico de Castilla y León* (Burgos, 1983), II, p. 227.

Flem's estimates,[18] did not tend to increase. Frequently it did not reach 60 per cent of the peaks of either the first half of the sixteenth century or the second half of the seventeenth century. L. M. Bilbao's estimates of wool exports and the conclusions he reaches from a study of the accounts of the monastery of Guadalupe's transhumant flocks seem to point in the same direction.[19] In the last years of the sixteenth century and the first four decades of the seventeenth, the fortunes of the Mesta must have gone through a period of severe crisis as a result of the greatly increased cost of winter pasturage and the relative weakness of overseas wool demand, aggravated at certain times, as Jonathan Israel has shown,[20] by the problems the wars created for international trade. The data presented in Table 4.6 confirm that the terms of trade in the first forty years of the seventeenth century did not favour the transhumant sheep-herders. Thus only the possibility that a significant increase in sedentary flocks could have prevented the slump in cereal production from causing a sharp drop in agricultural production in general in Castile during the first half of the seventeenth century stands in the way of the rejection of the hypothesis.

It is true, as Gonzalo Anes has shown[21] and as Table 4.7 of our Statistical Appendix confirms, that in Old Castile the price of meat tended to increase more steeply than that of wheat during the first half of the seventeenth century. However, if we take as a starting-point the 1560s and 1570s, the pattern is not so favourable to the meat producers. Besides, the relative movement of prices is not enough to explain the expansion of sedentary flocks, since a sharp rise in production costs could have meant a drop in profits for the sheep-owners. There is proof that communal pasture land shrank considerably in the second half of the sixteenth century in face of the plough, enclosure, or privatization, and the planting of vines. This

---

[18] Jean Paul Le Flem, 'Las cuentas de la Mesta (1510–1709)', *Moneda y Crédito* 121 (1972), pp. 99, 68–70.

[19] Enrique Llopis, 'Crisis y recuperación de las explotaciones trashumantes: la cabaña del Monasterio de Guadalupe (1597–1679)', *Investigaciones Económicas* 13 (1980), 125–68.

[20] J. I. Israel, 'Spanish Wool Exports and the European Economy, 1610–1640', *Economic History Review*, 2nd series, 33 (1980), 193–211.

[21] Anes, 'Depresión agraria', p. 93; and by the same author, 'Comercio de productos y distribución de rentas' in G. Anes, A. Bernal, J. García Fernández, et al., *La economía agraria en la historia de España. Propiedad, explotación, comercialización, rentas* (Madrid, 1979), p. 287.

process very probably continued into the first three decades of the next century. This meant, as contemporary writers claimed,[22] and as the accounts of the monastery of Guadalupe and the numerous contracts for the renting of pasture in the Cáceres district show, that prices for pasturage moved strongly upwards between approximately the 1550s and the 1630s.[23] Bearing in mind that this represented a high percentage of livestock breeders' production costs, it seems fairly likely that the numbers in the sedentary flocks did not in fact increase during the first half of the seventeenth century, but actually tended to fall.

Considering that the demand for meat must have fallen sharply in Old Castile in the first half of the seventeenth century owing to population decline, to the serious urban crisis and to the general economic difficulties, in my opinion the increased cost of meat is proof enough of the decline in sedentary stock-raising. In the 1620s, Caxa de Leruela wrote that, 'Of the flocks we call "estantes" (sedentary), which used to be four times more numerous than those we call "trashumantes" (transhumant), three-quarters have gone'.[24] Even if Caxa le Leruela, who had been *alcalde mayor entregador* (chief judge for the affairs of the Mesta), was exaggerating, it is hard to deny the existence of a severe crisis in the sedentary sheep population if we consider the seriousness of the problem of pasturage and the movement of meat prices in a period when demand must have shrunk considerably.

In Extremadura, the terms of trade between wheat and the various types of livestock (Table 4.8) would appear to follow a different pattern from those in Old Castile. In Extremadura cereal prices, except relative to the price of sheep, moved ahead, at least during the 1630s and 1640s when the decline in cereal production probably reached its nadir. The rise in wheat prices in terms of cattle and horses as cereal production moved to its lowest point of the century could have been due to a severe shortage of bread-grains,

[22] Miguel Caxa de Leruela, *Restauración de la antigua abundancia de España* (Naples, 1631), pp. 105–6.
[23] Between 1515–24 and 1628–37 the price of wheat in New Castile, according to Hamilton's figures, multiplied by 5.54 and that of the pastures of the monastery of Guadalupe by 8.33 (Llopis, 'Crisis y recuperación', p. 144). The value of grazing rights on the *dehesas* of Cáceres increased by 2.72 between 1540–9 and 1590–9, A. Rodríguez Sánchez, et al., 'El sistema de ventas y arrendamientos en tierras de Cáceres en el siglo XVI', *Norba* I (1980), 351.
[24] Caxa de Leruela, *Restauración*, p. 49.

and/or to a precipitous drop in the demand for livestock combined
with a rather less severe fall in supply in comparison with other
parts of the Peninsula. Therefore, whatever the reason, there does
not appear to have been sufficient motive in Extremadura, in the
first half of the seventeenth century, to replace arable farming with
animal husbandry, especially if we bear in mind the fact that the cost
of pasturage rose strongly in the final decades of the sixteenth
century and the first decades of the seventeenth.

In conclusion, the relative movement of prices, whether because
of the direction, the brevity, or the shallowness of the movement,
was not capable it would seem of preventing the slump in cereal
production from turning into a marked decline in Castilian agricultural production as a whole in the first forty years of the seventeenth century. Moreover, it is probable that the reduction of
communal pastureland contributed to the fact that the falling trend
in cereal harvests was accompanied by a sharp decline in sedentary
flocks. It is true that sheep-farming was to recover, but as Pérez
Moreda has noted for the Segovia region,[25] that recovery must have
begun only *after* the agricultural depression had touched bottom.

There is possibly an even more pertinent argument against the
hypothesis that the expansion of livestock and other crops could
have compensated for the fall in cereal production. When the sale
and utilisation of a good deal of the soil was severely restricted,
when only a small part of the total agricultural production reached
the market, when a high percentage of working farmers lacked the
means of improving their farming methods, and when the main
preoccupation of the majority of peasant-farmers was the production of bread-grains in order to safeguard their own alimentary
needs, fluctuations in relative prices could have had only a limited
effect on the reallocation of resources. In the context of the
economy of *ancien-régime* Castile, changes in the terms of trade
were unlikely to generate changes of any substance in the structure
of agricultural production. Indeed, Gonzalo Anes himself, after
studying the 'Relaciones Topográficas' compiled for Philip II,
admits that

> those places where the cultivation of wheat, vines, or olives
> predominated were very few in the sixteenth century. Crop diver-

[25] Vicente Pérez Moreda, 'La Transhumance estivale des merinos de Segovie: le
"pleito de la montaña"', *Mélanges de la Casa de Velázquez* 14 (1978), 296–7.

sification has been the norm in Spain in every locality, to the present day, as a means of guaranteeing food supplies, which, because the purchasing power of the peasant was low, the market could not do. They were thus forced to produce almost all their own needs.[26]

The rent of arable land fell significantly during the first fifty years at least of the seventeenth century. Rents of seven properties belonging to the monastery of El Escorial (Modua, Peromingo, Marugán, Muñomer, Bernuy, Chavente and Jimenagorda) fell by 64.9 per cent between 1575 and 1660;[27] the rents of arable land belonging to the monastery of Sandoval in León fell by 63.9 per cent from 1590 to 1689;[28] the rent of the grain-lands of the Chapter of Segovia fell by 30 per cent only, between the final years of the sixteenth century and the 1650s.[29] All these figures refer to payments in kind. The fall in arable rents could not have been due solely to falling demand, but also, in some regions at least, to the increased supply of land resulting from the private use of municipal lands. In any case, such a significant drop in arable land rents is hard to explain unless we accept a sharp reduction in agricultural activity in Castile during the first half of the seventeenth century.

2. SOME COMMENTS ON CHANGES IN AGRARIAN ORGANISATION

In the Castile of the seventeenth century, the movement of population, grain production and land rents would be hard to account for in an agrarian system in which no changes had taken place. If this had been the case, then the fall in population in making possible larger holdings, an improvement in the average quality of arable land, an increase in permanent pasturage and a drop in land rents, should have brought about an early end to the recession and a rise in per capita agricultural production, even when fiscal pressure on the rural areas was on the increase. However, the figures seem to refute such a prediction. The downward trend continued for at least four decades and per capita cereal production did not begin a real

[26] Anes, 'Tendencias de la producción agrícola', p. 101.
[27] Gregorio Sánchez Meco, *El Escorial y la Orden Jerónima. Análisis económico-social de una comunidad religiosa* (Madrid, 1985), p. 61.
[28] Libros de panera, AHN Clero, libros 5, 185 & 5, 190–1.
[29] García Sanz, *Desarrollo y crisis*, p. 300.

recovery until after the trend had troughed. As a result, the Malthusian corrective mechanisms could not prevent the depression in Castilian agriculture from becoming extremely severe in many areas. That suggests that the relative ineffectiveness of such mechanisms has to be explained not by the intrinsic incoherence of the Malthusian model, but by other changes that were taking place in the agrarian system of inland Spain at exactly the same time.

On the other hand, if we accept that in Spain between the beginning of the sixteenth and the end of the nineteenth centuries, without any significant changes in farming methods, both population and the area under cultivation more than doubled, then we cannot continue to consider the Malthusian model as the only, or even the main, explanation of change in the long-term trend of agricultural output in the early modern period. Bearing in mind that many areas had a low density of population, especially New Castile and Extremadura, and that their repopulation continued throughout the sixteenth to the nineteenth centuries, it is not surprising that Malthusian type models should prove especially inadequate for any analysis of the evolution of Spanish agriculture.

In short, the depression can only be understood in the context of the changes which took place in the Castilian agrarian system, changes which were not predetermined, but were in great part the result of specific historical circumstances in the different areas.

What changes took place in the Castilian agrarian system in the final decades of the sixteenth century and the first half of the seventeenth century? I do not think that in the present state of research it is possible to give a satisfactory answer to that question. However, I do think that among the most important were the changes in the use and/or distribution of the soil, effected or determined by the sale of wastes (*baldíos*), the increased exploitation of municipal land for revenue purposes, the unlawful appropriation of the commons, the grave crisis in sedentary sheep flocks and the partial replacement of oxen by mules in some areas. Perhaps the privatisation of the ownership and use of public land, resulting from the measures granted to the municipal authorities to enable them to raise their tax quotas for the *millones*, was the most important of these changes since it led to a substantial reduction in the area for cultivation and pasture available free of charge, or at very little charge, to many peasant families. Although David E. Vassberg's claim that, in the mid-sixteenth century, the communitarian system was the keystone of the social and economic structure of rural life and the support of agriculture and animal husbandry is something of an exaggeration,[30] there is no doubt that the reduction in rights to the commons must have led to important changes in their role in production and in costs for the small-scale peasant, the basic productive unit in Castilian agriculture. Not only were the peasants deprived of the use of certain resources, but also on occasion they had to carry increased costs because they now needed to rent arable or pasture land which they had formerly worked free of charge. Moreover, this was happening at a time when peasant economies had to face the aggravation of other problems.

During the second half of the sixteenth century, most small farmers were faced with a steep increase in fiscal demands and in land rents, which, according to Bartolomé Yun, rose to as much as 40 per cent of the gross output of certain farms in Tierra de Campos.[31] Many of them were also affected by the growing shortage and increased cost of pastureland, by soil exhaustion (resulting from the need to increase the number of harvests), by the working of poor-quality soil, by the widely fluctuating prices of cereals, and by the restriction of rural credit as a result of the greater credit demands of the monarchy, the town councils and the nobility. The high cost of breaking new ground, as Gonzalo Anes has rightly emphasized,[32] prevented many peasant-farmers from resorting to this way of solving their increasing problems of subsistence. They were forced to intensify their efforts on land already in use, even when those efforts were not normally accompanied by improvements in farming methods or greater concentrations of fertilizer.

The steep growth of public spending was the main cause of the privatisation of many wastes and public lands. In the final decades of the sixteenth century, at a time when economic expansion in Castile had come to a standstill and many small farmers found themselves in a critical situation, the exchequer had to resort to the sale of certain public lands and to the concession to the town councils of expedients to enable them to pay the new taxes, their

---

[30] David E. Vassberg, *La venta de tierras baldías. El comunitarismo agrario y la Corona de Castilla durante el siglo XVI* (Madrid, 1983), p. 53.

[31] Yun Casalilla, 'Producción agrícola en Tierra de Campos y Segovia', p. 8.

[32] Gonzalo Anes, 'El sector agrario en la España Moderna', *Papeles de Economía* 20 (1984), 4.

own municipal debts and the expenses of reacquiring their commons.[33]

The common lands sold represented, at least in some areas, a considerable part of the municipalities' hinterlands. Bartolomé Yun estimates that the lands sold might well have accounted for 30 to 40 per cent of the total area of the Tierra de Campos,[34] and in the district of Coca the figure was 18 per cent.[35] It is true that much of the land sold was bought by the peasants who had previously been farming it or by the municipalities themselves,[36] but the financing of those purchases created serious problems. Many councils and farmers had to take out heavy mortgages, a real worry given the narrow margin of their economic viability, especially for the latter, and given the fact that the sales, many of them in the 1580s, coincided with the end of a period of expansion and the start of a recession. Besides, not infrequently the councils in the event had to rent out part of their land and/or increase the payments from their citizens in order to meet their obligations. In short, one way or another, the sale of commons, apart from reducing the area of land in the public domain, led to changes in the way the municipal properties were exploited which tended to diminish the area of arable and pasture available for use by the townsfolk for free or for a small fee.

With the introduction and successive renewals of the *millones*, there came a proliferation of royal authorisations for the councils to break up, sell, mortgage, enclose, or rent out their municipal properties. From then on the process of privatisation of public land was intensified. The authorisations seem to have consisted of a more or less explicit compact, under the watchful and acquiescent eye of the clergy and the nobility, between the municipal authorities and the Crown. The former agreed to make available increased contributions to the exchequer in return for greater freedom to modify the use and management of their extensive municipal properties. The

---

[33] Angel García Sanz, 'Bienes y derechos comunales y el proceso de su privatización en Castilla durante los siglos XVI y XVII: el caso de tierras de Segovia', *Hispania* 144 (1980), 113.

[34] Bartolomé Yun Casalilla, 'La crisis del siglo XVII en Castilla: indicadores, cronología y factores en la Tierra de Campos (1580–1640)', in *El pasado histórico de Castilla y León* (Burgos, 1983), vol. II, p. 267.

[35] García Sanz, 'Bienes y derechos comunales', pp. 117–18.

[36] Vassberg, *La venta de tierras baldías*, pp. 234–6.

power of the councils was, of course, subject to restrictions. The raising of taxes could not come from measures which would have borne chiefly on the privileged groups in society. Thus the *millones* ended up being paid by the consumers of certain staples.[37] On the back of the pressing needs of the royal fisc, the local bosses (*poderosos*) managed to gain control of vast agricultural resources. This put them in a position of advantage from which they could look after their own interests as disposers of agricultural surplus product, as employers of labour, as pastoralists and as lessors. Inevitably, they acted as far as they could to reallocate agricultural resources to suit the requirements of their own agri-businesses. The very reduction in the output of communitarian agriculture benefited them as suppliers of produce, as employers of labour, and as landlords. Of course, the nobility and the clergy were also well placed to make the most of the situation. The acceleration of differentiation within the peasantry and the rise of local 'bosses' seem to me to have been two of the most singular features of the social and economic development of seventeenth-century Castile.

Apart from the sale, mortgaging and renting out of public lands which took place within the law (even if the councils or royal commissioners at times exceeded the bounds of their legal authority), straight usurpations by the nobility and the *poderosos* also helped accelerate the process of privatisation of common land and rights. The depopulation of a number of villages and the sale of jurisdictions and of judicial exemptions contributed to the general 'assault' on public properties.[38] The confirmation of dubious titles to land by means of financial settlements with the Crown also reveals the extent of the illicit encroachment into public land that had taken place, as Domínguez Ortiz has suggested.[39]

In sum, the notable decline in the communitarian use of the land in Castile during the final decades of the sixteenth century and the first half of the seventeenth cannot be doubted. This must have affected the arable farming and in particular the pastoral activities

[37] Felipe Ruiz Martín, 'Procedimientos crediticios para la recaudación de los tributos fiscales en las ciudades castellanas durante los siglos XVI y XVII: el caso de Valladolid', in A. Otazu (ed.), *Dinero y crédito (siglos XVI al XIX)* (Madrid, 1978), pp. 43–5 [chapter 8 of the present volume].

[38] García Sanz, 'Bienes y derechos comunales', pp. 120–2.

[39] Antonio Domínguez Ortiz, *Política fiscal y cambio social en la España del siglo XVII* (Madrid, 1984), p. 230.

of the peasantry. The privatisation of the ownership and the usufruct of common land necessarily reduced the 'property' of its
previous cultivators and forced them to try to rent more land.
That in turn partially or wholly cancelled out the benefits they had
derived from the fall in arable rents from the end of the sixteenth or
the beginning of the seventeenth century. Thus one of the factors
which should have helped restore the balance in agriculture, the fall
in land rents, was offset, at least in part, by the reduction in the
availability of communitarian farmland.

The intensive ploughing up of new lands and the growth of
sedentary flocks caused the cost of pasturage to rise sharply from
the 1540s on.[40] This trend continued, though more moderately,
during the first decades of the seventeenth century and provided an
incentive to private owners and town councils to enclose pastureland.[41] This phenomenon, noted by contemporary writers,[42] has
been corroborated by Fermín Marín after an exhaustive study of the
papers of the Mesta.[43] From 1630, at the latest, condemnations for
enclosing pastureland became by far the most common of the fines
imposed by the judges of the Mesta. As a result, in spite of the fact
that the declining population created conditions favourable to the
expansion of pastoralism, the enclosure and privatisation of communal and municipal land prevented many peasant-farmers from
making use of the increased land available as grazing for their
draught animals. Bearing in mind that the pastoral activities of the
small farmers depended largely on their access to the common
pastures, it is understandable that the expansion of their flocks did
not take place until the slump in arable farming had left enough land
unused for permanent pasturage to compensate for the common
rights they had lost with the enclosure and privatisation of public
lands. This apparently did not occur in much of Castile before 1640.
Consequently, the effectiveness of another of the most important
corrective mechanisms in this type of economy (increased pasture-

---

[40] José Pereira Iglesias, *Cáceres y su Tierra en el siglo XVI. Economía y Sociedad*
(Cáceres, 1991), pp. 182–7.
[41] Llopis, 'Crisis y recuperación', p. 149.
[42] Caxa de Leruela, *Restauración*, pp. 122–9.
[43] Fermín Marín Barriguete, 'La Mesta en los siglos XVI y XVII: cañadas, rotura-
ciones de pastos, arrendamientos e impedimentos de paso y pasto', doctoral thesis
of the Department of Modern History, Universidad Complutense, Madrid, 1985,
pp. 1345–52.

land as a result of population decline) was diluted by the changes which were taking place in the system of land use.

In the first half of the seventeenth century the livestock option was necessarily restricted to those landowners who did not have to pay out large sums for the upkeep of their animals, either because they owned the pasturage themselves or because they were in a position to graze large numbers of animals on communal land. Furthermore, the fall in wool exports, the decline of many of the Castilian cities and the introduction of excises on meat tended to undermine the profitability of livestock farming. In short, it seems likely that the trends in both cereal and livestock production in Castile during the first half of the seventeenth century were of the same order, negative.

We cannot accept, in the way David E. Vassberg claims, that the ox was ousted during the sixteenth century from its position as the principal draught-animal in the Castilian countryside,[44] although there is no doubt that its partial replacement by the mule began in that century. This was encouraged by the rising demand for animal-power (due to the tilling of new ground, and sometimes to deeper ploughing), by the increased trade in agricultural produce, by the greater average distance of the land being cultivated from the towns, and by the spread of vineyards.[45] But in all probability the lack of common pasture-land was the most important factor in this change. It forced some peasant farmers to recrop, increasing the area given over to barley at the expense of that intended for bread-grains. Consequently, the need to substitute mules for oxen lowered the standard of living of many farmers. Besides, not all peasant farmers were in a position to buy and keep a pair of mules, since that required a minimum area of arable land on which to combine the production of cereals for fodder with that of grain for human consumption. Thus the loss of benefits from the commons was to result in the decapitalisation of many small farmers.

On the other hand, the increased number of mules necessitated

[44] David E. Vassberg, *Land and Society in Golden Age Castile* (Cambridge, 1984), pp. 158–63.
[45] Much of the planting of new vineyards at the end of the sixteenth and the first decades of the seventeenth century was connected to the increasing need of the peasantry for coin to meet heavier tax burdens. The expansion of supply together with a simultaneous fall in demand accounts for the collapse of wine prices in the second quarter of the seventeenth century.

more extensive farming which, together with the exhaustion of the soil due to lack of fertilizers, meant, at least in some cases, the need to maintain or even increase the area under cultivation even in places where the population was falling. So the partial replacement of oxen by mules helps to explain the continued breaking of new ground even in the midst of a recession, a phenomenon pointed out by Felipe Sánchez Salazar,[46] and that in turn made it more difficult to restore the balance between arable, pasture and woodland.

In conclusion, the privatisation of a significant part of the municipal lands, spurred on by the considerable increases in the cost of pasturage and in municipal spending, and authorised by a state which had to resort to any means of augmenting its revenues, contributed to the decline of the basic unit of agrarian production in Castile, the small peasant farmer. There cannot be the least doubt that the reduction in the availability of the common lands brought about a serious deterioration in the conditions of access to arable and pasture land for the direct cultivator. This change was not only irreversible, it became more and more pronounced during the course of the *ancien régime*.

The image which prevailed until recently of a Castile whose agrarian structures remained practically unchanged throughout the *ancien régime* is slowly but surely disappearing. While it is true that there were apparently no great changes in technology, in techniques, in forms of cultivation, or in yield-ratios, this does not preclude significant changes in the basic structures of agrarian organisation, such as the forms of access to the exploitation of the land. There is thus a need, even an urgency, for further investigation into the tensions to which the use of communal and municipal properties gave rise, as well as into the social and economic consequences of their deployment. Much of the social conflict of the time was related to it, but the generally unspectacular nature of those conflicts has contributed to the scant attention Spanish historians have so far paid to these questions.

We need to remember that these changes in agrarian organisation took place during a period of depression or of very slow recovery. Considering that the production levels of the 1580s were not

---

[46] Felipe Sánchez Salazar, 'La extensión de cultivos en el siglo XVIII', doctoral thesis of the Department of Modern History, Universidad Complutense, Madrid, 1984, pp. 90–100.

reachcd again until well into the eighteenth century, we can state that in Castile economic growth ceased for approximately one and a half centuries. This brings us to a topic of immense interest which requires thorough research and thought in the next few years. I refer to the frustration of the growth which had taken place in the sixteenth-century Castilian economy, as manifested by the definitive collapse as manufacturing and commercial centres of many of the cities of the central mesetas of Old and New Castile.

I am well aware of the shortcomings and failings of this short essay. On the one hand, I have concentrated almost exclusively on the period of depression and all but ignored a subject of undoubted interest which needs to be tacklcd if one is to achieve an overall picture of the seventeenth century, the slow recovery which followed it. On the other hand, while concentrating on the impact of changes in the exploitation of community lands on the peasant economy, I have omitted other subjects of fundamental importance, such as the interrelation between rural and urban depression, changes in the seignorial regime, monetary instability, the special difficulties of the smallest villages,[47] peasant indebtedness and the growing importance of usury and money-lending. In no way have I pretended to offer an all-embracing explanatory model; it would be enough if these lines were thought to have brought something new into the discussion, or if they were to incite colleagues to look again at the issues I have raised.

---

[47] This issue was raised by Antonio Domínguez Ortiz in a magnificent pioneering article, 'La ruina de la aldea castellana', *Revista Internacional de Sociología* 24 (1948), 99–125.

Statistical Appendix

Table 4.1. *Grain production in the archdiocese of Toledo (Index numbers)*

Years	Annual averages	Years	Annual averages
1565–1573	100.00	1628–1636	63.91
1574–1582	91.54	1637–1645	56.78
1583–1591	93.71	1651–1659	61.16
1592–1600	84.82	1658–1666	56.08
1601–1609	75.87	1668–1676	63.79
1610–1618	76.09	1672–1680	61.86
1619–1627	72.22		

Note: Base 100 for period 1565–1573
Source: From the series published by J. López Salazar and Manuel Martín Galán 'La producción cerealista en el Arzobispado de Toledo', *Cuadernos de historia moderna y contemporánea 2 (1981), pp. 56–101.*

Table 4.2. *'Tercias reales' of city and region of Trujillo (in 'fanegas')*

Years	Wheat	Barley	Rye	All cereals
1550	2,943.58	688.62	403.16	4,035.36
1556	1,214.04	299.31	109.31	1,622.66
1559	1,562.33	278.58	77.72	1,918.63
1560	3,148.68	522.37	185.45	3,886.50
Annual averages				
1711–1734	904.82	360.16	598.31	1,863.29

Sources: Hojas de Gracias and *Hojas de pan*, Archives of the Monastery of Guadalupe, legajos 143, 149.

Table 4.3. *Price ratios: wheat and barley*

Years	León	Years	New Castile
1583–1592	1.85	1560–1569	1.92
1593–1602	1.96	1591–1600	2.72
1603–1612	1.73	1609–1618	1.97
1613–1622	1.70	1627–1633	2.53
1623–1632	1.67	1640–1649	1.64
1633–1642	1.72	1654–1663	2.03
1643–1652	1.64	1664–1678	1.79
1653–1662	1.64	1680–1685	1.76
1663–1672	1.79	1687–1699	1.91
1673–1682	1.63		
1683–1692	1.59		
1693–1702	1.56		
1583–1600	1.97		
1601–1625	1.65		
1626–1650	1.70		
1651–1675	1.66		
1676–1700	1.63		
1701–1725	1.63		
1726–1760	1.60		

Sources: For León, prices of wheat and barley sold by the Monastery of Sandoval (supplied by José Antonio Sebastián Amarillas, from Libros de Caxa, AHN, Clero, libros 5169, 5174–76); for New Castile figures are from E. J. Hamilton.

Table 4.4. *Price ratios: wheat and wine*

Period	La Rioja	Period	New Castile
1572–1580	100.00	1563–1560	100.00
1581–1589	145.27	1582–1602	132.88
1590–1598	154.72	1606–1625	136.00
1600–1608	114.56	1627–1633	164.68
1609–1617	96.06	1635–1653	150.66
1618–1626	76.77		
1631–1640	121.25		
1641–1660	117.71		
1661–1660	119.29		

Note: Index numbers of annual averages. On base 1572–1580 for La Rioja, 1563–1580 for New Castile.
Sources: Figures for La Rioja from prices for wheat and wine sold by the Monastery of La Estrella (AHN, Clero, libros 5.966, 5.978, 6.000); for New Castile from E. J. Hamilton for wheat and wine.

Table 4.5. *Price ratios: wheat and oil*

Years	New Castile
1563–1580	100.00
1582–1602	131.50
1606–1625	154.79
1627–1633	147.94
1635–1653	160.27
1655–1686	112.32
1687–1699	97.26

Note: Index numbers of annual averages. On base 100 for 1563–1580.
Sources: E. J. Hamilton, *American Treasure and the Price Revolution in Spain 1501–1650* (Cambridge, MA, 1934), pp. 340–7, 370–5; and *War and Prices in Spain, 1651–1800* (Cambridge, MA, Harvard University Press, 1947), pp. 238–41.

Table 4.6. *Price ratios: wheat and wool*

Years	Wheat
	Fine wool
1603–1638	100.00
1639–1676	67.58
1677–1708	76.45
1713–1750	56.26

Note: Index numbers on base 1603–1638.
Sources: Annual prices for wheat sold by the Monastery of Sandoval de León and fine wool of the Cabildo of Segovia were kindly supplied by A. García Sanz (from the Libros de Menudos of the Archivo Capitular of Segovia).

Table 4.7. *Price ratios: wheat and meat*

Years	Wheat / Beef	Years	Wheat / Mutton
1577–1585	100.00	1572–1577	100.00
1586–1594	117.21	1579–1585	117.64
1595–1603	101.98	1586–1592	130.88
1604–1612	94.70	1593–1599	147.05
1613–1621	86.75	1601–1607	108.82
1622–1630	67.54	1608–1614	89.70
1631–1639	98.67	1616–1621	89.70
1640–1644	98.01	1622–1627	73.52
1646–1650	79.47	1629 1634	122.05
		1635–1640	101.47
		1642–1660	98.52

Note: Index of annual averages on base 1577–1585 for beef, 1572–1577 for lamb.
Sources: Series derived from prices of wheat sold by the Monastery of La Estrella and
E. J. Hamilton's beef and lamb prices in Old Castile.

Table 4.8. *Price ratios: livestock and wheat*

Years	3 yr-old steers / Wheat	Sedentary sheep / Wheat	Years	Mares / Wheat
1598–1612	100.00	100.00	1597–1612	100.00
1628–1652	72.36	100.00	1628–1652	69.05
1653–1677	132.70	150.87	1659–1677	94.96

Note: Index of annual averages on base 1598–1612.
Source: Hojas de ganados, accounts of the Monastery of Guadalupe, legajo 127.

Figure 4.1 Grain production in the archdiocese of Toledo (index of annual averages on base, 1565–1573)
Source: E. Llopis Agelán, 'El agro castellano en el siglo XVII', *Revista de Historia Económica* 4:1 (1986)

5. Wool exports, transhumance and land use in Castile in the sixteenth, seventeenth and eighteenth centuries

L. M. BILBAO and E. FERNÁNDEZ DE PINEDO

Throughout the course of the sixteenth, seventeenth and eighteenth centuries the economy of Castile was heavily influenced by interests associated, directly or indirectly, with the production and exportation of wool. Much of the wool exported was produced by the transhumant merino sheep supervised by the Honrado Concejo de la Mesta, the Honourable Council of the Mesta, recipient of numerous royal privileges.[1] The economic interests sustaining this transhumance – small landowners in the mountains of the north, nobility and clergy owning livestock and pasturelands, the Crown, which levied taxes on sacks sent abroad, exporters and foreign cloth manufacturers – were strong enough to subordinate the agricultural sector and the craft industry of Castile to wool production. Wool production in turn depended above all on foreign demand. In this way the economy of Castile, basically agricultural, was directed by foreign interests.

Data on the movement of wool exports from Castile, preserved in the Archivo General de Simancas for the period 1560–1800, are unfortunately scarce. The figures are not usually for wool, but for revenue from taxes on wool. To make the series as nearly homogeneous as possible, the original data have been converted into *arrobas* of wool (1 *arroba* = 11.5 kg) and then into tonnes (Table 5.1). The figures for this 200-year period, though incomplete, show that the maximum came in the 1570s (4,025 tonnes), the minimum in 1664–70 (1,840 tonnes). The seventeenth century, then, was weak, with a collapse at the beginning of the last quarter of the century.

[1] J. Klein, *The Mesta. A Study in the Economic History of Spain 1273–1836* (Cambridge, MA, 1920); F. Braudel, *The Mediterranean and the Mediterranean World in the Age of Philip II*, 2 vols. (London, 1972), I, pp. 91–4.

Table 5.1. *Wool exports, 1561–1796 (annual average in tonnes)*

period	annual average (tonnes)
1561–1569	3,165
1571–1579	4,025
1589–1594	2,587
1610–1615	3,105
1620–1626	2,760
1654–1657	2,875
1664–1670	1,840
1723–1730	3,474
1750–1759	4,453
1760–1769	5,108
1770–1779	5,138
1787–1796	4,237

From then on there seems to have been a recovery, and strong growth in the eighteenth century leads to the highest figures of the entire series, the 5,138 tonnes of 1770–9.[2]

Since on average a transhumant merino flock of 100 animals (ewes, rams and lambs) produced 17 *arrobas* of wool,[3] half that weight after washing (8.5 *arrobas*), our figures show that the transhumant flocks could not on their own have been responsible for all the wool exported. The figures for transhumant sheep come from Julius Klein (actual figures for 1510–63) and J. P. Le Flem (actual figures for 1510–62, and estimates for 1616–34).

Table 5.2, based on the figures of J. P. Le Flem, summarizes his data after first eliminating two extreme years (1622 and 1634).[4] Klein, while not giving concrete figures, states that in the second half of the seventeenth century there were seldom more than 2 million transhumant sheep and more often there were fewer.[5] It is, however, completely in keeping with the agricultural situation in the sixteenth century that the peak for transhumant sheep should have come at the start of the century when the effects of the depression of

---

[2] AGS Dirección General de Rentas, 1ª remesa, legs. 2506–2565, 2579–2596; AGS Tribunal Mayor de Cuentas, legs. 726–749, 834; AGS Expedientes de Hacienda, legs. 540–542; AGS Contadurías Generales, legs. 2700–2702, 2302, 2126–2138.

[3] These are average figures derived from the transhumant flock of the Monastery of Santa María del Paular between 1680 and 1729, AHN Clero, libro 19,782.

[4] Klein, *The Mesta*, p. 27; J. P. Le Flem, 'Las cuentas de la Mesta (1510–1709)', *Moneda y Crédito* 121 (1972), 68–9.

[5] Klein, *The Mesta*, p. 342.

Table 5.2. *Transhumant sheep (annual average)*

years	annual average numbers of sheep
1511–1519	2,854,865
1520–1529	2,692,835
1530–1539	2,566,653
1540–1549	2,628,315
1550–1559	2,363,729
1560–1562	1,945,753
1616–1619	1,891,561
1620–1629	1,764,643
1630–1633	1,642,869
1708	2,100,000
1746	3,294,136
1765	3,500,000

the fifteenth century were still being felt. In the second half of the century more land was cultivated, leaving less available for pasture and causing progressive decreases in the numbers in the flocks.

The almost 2 million transhumant sheep of the 1560s produced, we calculate, 1,902 tonnes of washed wool, and the 1,764,643 average for the 1620s, 1,725 tonnes. These figures are well below the average quantities exported in the same two periods (3,165.5 t. and 2,760 t.). The wool exported came, therefore, from both transhumant and sedentary merinos. It is impossible to understand the problems of the Mesta without taking the latter into account.

The demand for merino wool came from the quality cloth industry, both foreign and domestic, but with the decline of the Castilian textile industry from the end of the sixteenth century, a decline which continued throughout the seventeenth century and even into the eighteenth, the demand for merino wool came almost entirely from abroad. In this way the development of the foreign cloth industry, through its demand for raw materials, was to determine the number of transhumant Mesta sheep in the seventeenth century and for much of the eighteenth. The general development of the textile industry as a whole is clearly a separate issue.

In the fifteenth century Castilian wool overtook English wool in quality. The advance of enclosures in England contributed to better feeding of the sheep, and this in turn to an increase in length of wool and loss of fineness. By the end of the century Castilian wool had come to be better than English wool, and in the second half of the sixteenth century 'not even English writers could deny that Spanish wool was the finest in the world'. This high-quality wool was naturally used to make the finest cloth. The demand, then, for Castilian wool throughout the sixteenth, seventeenth and eighteenth centuries was dependent above all on the market for luxury cloths. We know that in England, while the trade in woollen cloth was booming during the early Tudor period, the production of worsteds was on the decline. On the other hand, throughout the seventeenth century, the fine broadcloth industry languished in an almost continual state of chronic depression and decay. At the same time the production of coarse woollens had increased. Moreover, the lower quality of English wool favoured the production of cheaper material and the development in England of the 'new draperies', but forced producers of fine cloth to import Castilian wool. In the 1620s certain English manufacturers began to use Spanish raw material, and some time afterwards abandoned the production of broadcloth to produce a new high-quality product made wholly or in part from fine Spanish wool. By the 1630s the new industry had become firmly established, and it continued to expand throughout the remainder of the seventeenth century. The deterioration in the quality of English wool had made Castilian wool indispensable to the manufacture of luxury cloth in England.[6]

The economic circumstances of the seventeenth century were not, however, ideal for the consumption of quality cloth. Broadcloth exports from England declined. The high-quality cloth industry in Venice fell away throughout the seventeenth century. The cloth industry in Florence, which used the best Castilian wool, suffered a similar fate.[7] The manufacturers in the towns of Flanders and Brabant who had reorganized their textile industry, reorientating it towards quality cloth, from the mid-seventeenth century onwards

---

[6] P. J. Bowden, *The Wool Trade in Tudor and Stuart England* (London, 1971), pp. 34, 43–4, 47.

[7] M. Carmona, 'La Toscana face à la crise de l'industrie lainière: techniques et mentalités économiques aux xvie et xviie siècles', in M. Spallanzani (ed.), *La lana come materia prima. I fenomeni della sua produzione e circulazione nei secoli XIII–XVIII* (Florence, 1974), pp. 151–2; C. M. Cipolla, 'The economic decline of Italy', in C. M. Cipolla (ed.), *The Economic Decline of Empires* (London, 1970), pp. 196–201; R. Romano, 'A Florence au XVIIe siècle. Industries textiles et conjoncture', *Annales ESC* 7 (1952), 511; D. Sella, 'Les Mouvements longs de l'industrie lainière à Venise aux XVIe et XVIIe siècles', *Annales ESC* 12 (1957), 30–1;

could not withstand the converging tariff offensives of France, Holland and England.[8] The 'new draperies' used cheap carded wool, mostly of local or regional origin, to make fabrics which were virtually unfulled, with lighter, brighter colours, and which were a great success in the Mediterranean and colonial markets. Fortunes were made in Hondschoote, then Leiden, then England. The development of the 'new draperies' affected the demand for raw material because these new fabrics did not require such expensive wool. Consequently from 1620 onwards the Dutch ports received substantial cargoes of wool from the Baltic ports.[9] Although there was some development in the Leiden cloth industry towards more expensive products – in the form of the famous *lakens*, which required top-quality raw material – Leiden was not dependent on Spanish wool until after 1648,[10] and this was for a specific type of fabric.

The collapse from 1620 onwards of Italian quality woollens, the difficulties of the quality cloth industry in general, and the triumph of the 'new draperies' using cheap, finer wool, explain the lack of dynamism in foreign demand for Castilian wool for much of the seventeenth century. The ruin of the Castilian cloth industry made it impossible to redirect the sacks of wool for absorption into the internal market.

The difficulties got worse from the 1650s onwards. The fall in Segovian fine wool prices on the Amsterdam market (see Figure 5.1, constructed from the data of Posthumus) coincides with falling Castilian wool exports: from 2,875 tonnes in 1654–7, to 1,840 tonnes in 1664–70.[11]

If the export of fine wool from Castile was a reflection of the demand for raw material by the quality European industry, then the seventeenth century was for this branch of manufacturing a time of clear decline. This can be explained by falling production in Italy, as

F. Ruiz Martín, *Lettres marchandes échangées entre Florence et Medina del Campo* (Paris, 1965), p. xxxv.

[8] P. Deyon, 'La Concurrence internationale des laines aux XVIe et XVIIe siècles', *Annales ESC* 27 (1972), 28.

[9] N. W. Posthumus, *De Geschiedenis van de Leidsche Lakenindustrie* (The Hague, 1939), III, p. 765, table 80.

[10] J. I. Israel, 'A Conflict of Empires: Spain and the Netherlands, 1618–1648', *Past and Present* 76 (1977), 61–2.

[11] N. W. Posthumus, *Inquiry into the History of Prices in Holland* (Leiden, 1946), I, pp. 268–70.

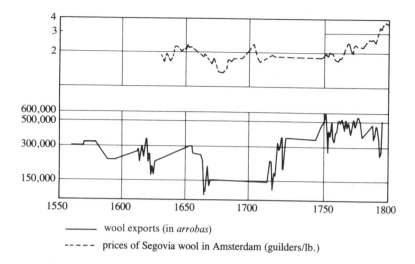

———— wool exports (in *arrobas*)

- - - - - prices of Segovia wool in Amsterdam (guilders/lb.)

Figure 5.1 Exports of Castilian wool, 1561–1796
Source: P. García Martín and J. María Sánchez Benito, *Contribución a la historia de la trashumancia en España* (Madrid, 1986)

Castilian wool exports via the south-eastern ports of the Iberian Peninsula were the ones which collapsed. It should be pointed out, however, that the gap left by the decline of the Italian quality cloth industry was not filled by cloth of similar quality from the Northern European countries importing Castilian wool. Total sacks of wool exported via the Cantabrian ports and Seville between 1571–9 and 1620–6 tended to fall, if only slightly. During the same period exports via south-eastern ports were halved, and in 1664–70 exports for the whole of Spain were little higher than those via the Cantabrian ports and Seville in 1561–9 and 1571–9.

Depopulation in Castile in the seventeenth century had caused many farms to be abandoned, leaving abundant pastureland and opening up opportunities (in theory at least) for the production of cheap, high-quality wool. However, this abundance of pastureland was clearly not enough to stimulate the production of quality wool for export. Despite the drop in population, the falling demand for quality wool brought down the numbers of transhumant sheep (see Table 5.2). Depopulation combined with reductions in transhumant flocks would have left plenty of land for the development of seden-

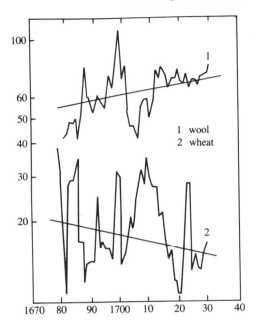

Figure 5.2 Prices of wool and wheat of the Monastery of Paular
Source: As for figure 5.1

tary livestock, which according to various authors increased throughout the seventeenth century.[12]

From 1670 the Crown farmed out its export taxes on wool instead of administering them itself, and until the 1720s exact overall figures are not available. It was precisely during this half-century (1670–1720) that factors at home and abroad combined to start creating the conditions for the recovery of transhumant livestock.

The decline in wool exports in the seventeenth century came about almost entirely because of a fall in international demand, but both external and internal factors played an important part in the recovery. The French situation suggests some recovery in high-quality cloth made with Spanish wool at the end of the seventeenth

---

[12] See Klein, *The Mesta*, pp. 342–3; Le Flem 'Las cuentas'; F. Ruiz Martín, 'Pastos y ganaderos en Castilla: la Mesta (1450–1600)', in Spallanzani, *La lana*; A. García Sanz, *Desarrollo y crisis del Antiguo Régimen en Castilla la Vieja. Economía y sociedad en tierras de Segovia, 1500–1814* (Madrid, 1977), pp. 123–4.

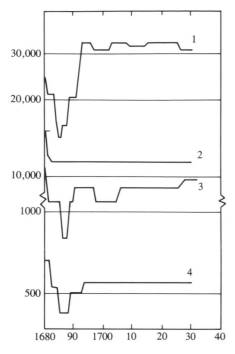

1. Millares de Cogolludo
2. Dehesa de Sancti Spiritus
3. Puerto de Carracedo
4. Puerto de Barbelta

Figure 5.3 Value of pasturage leases, 1680–1740
Source: As for figure 5.1

century and especially at the start of the eighteenth century.
Colbert's economic policies, protectionism plus Crown investment
in factories, seem to have eventually brought positive results. The
factory set up by the Dutchman, Van Robais, at Abbeville in 1665,
took off quite remarkably, despite some difficult periods, and used
the best Spanish wool, which came to it via Bilbao. We are told that
the first factory in Sedan was founded in 1644 and the second in
1688, and in Amiens most of the varied and interesting products
were created around 1675–85. At the time of the 1692 survey, in
Sedan 'the cloths were made of Spanish wool' (from Segovia,
Albazin, Albarracín, Soria), in quantities in excess of 3,500 pieces.

Abandoning products of mediocre quality, the manufacturers of Sedan worked almost exclusively with fine materials. Instead of domestic wool from the Ardennes, they eventually used top-quality wool imported from Spain for almost all their goods. Cloth production in Sedan rose regularly from 1700 to 1730; but Spanish wool was not only used in the most important centres of Champagne, the fine double-twilled cloths of Châlons were also made with wool from Brie and Spain. The short-pile materials were made with Segovian wool. In Beauvais, Spanish wool was used in top-quality cloth (ratine, Spanish serge, flannelette); at Pau, in the south, they made fine cloth with wool from Segovia; in Toulouse, the fabrics known as londrins for export to the Levant were made with fine Spanish wool (from Soria and Segovia); in Carcassonne, part of production used wool from Soria.[13] It has been estimated that in France, around 1692, the manufacture of woollen cloth needed 14,150 tonnes of wool, of which 4,750 came from abroad.[14]

This recovery in foreign demand came at a time when wool and wheat prices within Castile were going in opposite directions; as cereal prices fell, wool prices rose. Both Amsterdam prices and those at Paular in Castile rose sharply from 1680 to 1700 and remained at those levels through the 1710s and 1720s (see Figure 5.2).[15] The buying power of sellers of wool in terms of wheat increased significantly, which acted as an incentive to produce more wool. At the same time, as can be seen in Figure 5.3, pasture prices both in summer and winter remained quite stable once the 1680 law fixing prices at 1633 levels took effect. The transhumant sheep of the Castilian monastery of Santa María del Paular, for which we have figures, grew by a clear 42 per cent between 1680–9 and 1720–9. The transhumant livestock of the Mesta as a whole rose to 2,100,000 sheep in 1708. In our opinion it was the combination of falling agricultural prices and rising international wool prices which encouraged sheep farming until the 1750s. From then on, despite the recovery in agricultural prices, international demand – which was quite dynamic to judge from figures for English imports of Castilian

[13] T. J. Markovitch, 'L'Industrie française au XVIIIe siècle. L'industrie lainière, sous la Régence et au début du règne de Louis XV', *Economies et Sociétés. Cahiers de l'ISEA* 2 (1968), 1529–45.
[14] L. Fontvieille, 'Les Premières enquêtes industrielles de la France, 1692–1703', *Economies et Sociétés. Cahiers de l'ISEA* 6 (1969), 1101.
[15] AHN Clero, libro 19,782.

wool – would seem to have prevented the reversal of the tendency, though at the expense of agriculture. As can be seen in Table 5.1, wool exports increased into the 1770s. The same applies to trans-humant herds: the 2,100,000 sheep in 1708 increased to 3,294,136 in 1746, and then to 3,500,000 in 1765. In the 1770s the figure probably remained at between 3,200,000 and 3,500,000 head. In the eighteenth, as in the sixteenth and seventeenth centuries, however, the sedentary merinos were also involved in wool production for export. Some estimates of numbers of sedentary merinos are avail-able to us; in 1765 the number was put at 2,100,000. The 3,500,000 transhumant, plus the 2,100,000 sedentary sheep, all merinos, could produce 5,474 tonnes of washed wool, close to the figure for the annual average exported in the 1760s, 5,108 tonnes. The difference would be due to consumption by the Spanish industry, and of course inaccuracies in data.

The growing flocks needed substantial pastureland, particularly in winter. The upturn in livestock at the end of the seventeenth and the start of the eighteenth centuries had come at a time when the Spanish population reached its lowest level – 8,800,000 inhabitants; but by around 1750 population had risen to 9,855,000. Fallow land abandoned during the depression of the seventeenth century was returned to cultivation. Very often these lands had become pastures. It became inevitable that there would be a conflict between feeding more mouths and interests linked with wool production and exporting.

Winter pastures in the south (Extremadura, La Mancha, Andalu-sia) were of two types: those which belonged to the villages and those which were private property. Both types could be cultivated for some years and classified either as *dehesas de pasto y labor* (pasture and cultivation meadows), or given over exclusively to pasture and called *dehesas de solo pasto* (pasture only meadows). The seventeenth-century drop in population had turned many *dehesas de pasto y labor* into *dehesas de solo pasto*. Once such a change had taken place, the 'right of possession' enjoyed by the Mesta prohibited a return to the land's former use. The owner of a piece of land who had leased it out to flocks administered by the Mesta could only have them removed if he was going to occupy the land with his own sheep. In 1763 several cities of Extremadura, in a joint petition, complained that the transhumant flocks were taking over the whole region, occupying more and more land every year and never surrendering anything, and that they were on the way to driving out any resident husbandmen who had some livestock. The *corregidor* (royal governor) of Trujillo produced documents to demonstrate the enormous drop in harvests since the beginning of the seventeenth century: in 1614–18 the average wheat tithe came to 9,829 *fanegas* a year; by 1749–53 it was only 2,829. The city of Badajoz also complained of falling harvests. In 1721–5, 390,460 *fanegas* of wheat and 271,660 of barley had been harvested in its territory; in 1759–63, only 234,500 and 166,560 respectively. The land in the possession of the transhumants had quadrupled since the beginning of the century. After the Spanish Succession War (1701–14), 'like a rushing torrent held back for a long time, they flooded the provinces and occupied them all'. The farmers were reduced to cultivating a narrow strip of land along the Portuguese frontier.[16] The advance of transhumance had also reduced sedentary livestock. The number of cattle fell from 6,490 in 1721–5 to 3,770 in 1759–63. In Mérida the reduction seems to have been even more drastic, from 3,170 cattle in 1728–32, to 1,333 in 1758–62.[17] Without manure or draught animals, agriculture declined.

The sole purpose of those complaints was to demonstrate the negative effect that the development of transhumance had had on sedentary stock raising and on agriculture. For that reason, the figures might be thought suspect. However, the responses to the Ensenada *Catastro* of the mid-eighteenth century show the enormous extent of pasturage in Extremadura (see Table 5.3).

The area used for pasture was, then, very great indeed. In almost all the towns and villages every year half the cultivated land lay fallow, and in some villages two-thirds of it. These data are confirmed by the tithes. In Trujillo in the mid-eighteenth century, quinquennial averages of grain and lesser tithes came to 135,263 *reales*, whereas tithes on transhumants sold in the city amounted to 192,400.

These immense areas of pastureland were for the most part private property. Communal pastures occupied very limited areas. Half of the land of Mérida was used for pasture, and this was divided into 37 *dehesas*: 7 belonged to the king; 8 to the town (as

[16] E. Larruga, *Memorias políticas y económicas sobre los frutos, fábricas, comercio y minas de España* (Madrid, 1785–1800), XXXVII, p. 299.

[17] *Ibid.*, p. 316.

Table 5.3. *Land use (percentages of total surface area)*

	Trujillo	D. Benito	Mérida	Cáceres	Alcántara
Major towns					
pastureland	80.38	61.48	50.00	50.00	64.51
arable land	16.33	7.92	25.00	36.66	31.40
uncultivated	3.28	30.59	25.00	13.33	04.09

Small villages	(1)	(2)	(3)	(4)	(5)	(6)	(7)	(8)
pasture	50.00	89.29	33.34	71.28	33.34	06.35	50.00	33.33
arable	25.00	10.71	66.65	28.71	50.00	24.64	50.00	33.33
uncultivated	25.00	–	–	–	16.66	69.00	–	33.33

Note: (1) Cordovillo   (4) Esparragalejo   (7) Trujillanos
        (2) Carrascalejo   (5) La Nava   (8) Carmonite
        (3) Aljuzen   (6) Navasfrias

Table 5.4. *Income from pasture (in reales)*

recipients	summer	winter	total	%
nobility	10,700.00	49,375.00	60,075.00	35.88
church	422.11	22,264.80	22,686.19	13.55
commoners	600.00	51,808.26	52,408.26	31.30
communities	17,321.27	10,300.00	27,621.27	16.50
unknown		4,620.00	4,620.00	02.76
	29,044.40	138,368.00	167,412.40	99.99

bienes de propios) but, of these 8, 5 were in mortgage and were going to have to be allocated out to creditors; of the remainder, 8 belonged to the great nobility, 3 to the clergy, 9 to commoners, 1 to the community of the town and the last to an *encomienda*.[18] From another source we can confirm the unimportance of communal pastures at the end of the seventeenth century, particularly in the south, in Extremadura. We have worked out the sums paid by the monastery of Santa María del Paular in 1688 for the lease of summer and winter pastureland for their flocks. Table 5.4 sets out how much was received by each group of owners of the pastures.

The northern pastures were cheaper, even considering that flocks

[18] AGS Dirección General de Rentas, 1ª remesa, libro 144.

used them for only three months (June, July, August), whereas the winter pastures in Extremadura were occupied for six months (October to March inclusive); 60 per cent of these payments went to municipalities. Nonetheless, the nobility received a very substantial 37 per cent. The southern pastures cost almost five times as much as those of the mountains of the north. In this area, there was little communal property, and it was predominantly the nobility, the clergy and individual commoners who were the owners.

The distribution of the profits from the flock gives us an idea of the interests behind the expansion of sheepfarming. According to the 1688 data for the monastery of Santa María del Paular, the monastery paid 131,834.5 *reales* in wages (in money and in kind) and for the sheep trails (*cañadas*); 167,412.4 for summer and winter pastures; 111,127.29 for washing the wool, transporting it to Bilbao and for customs duties; leaving a profit of 228,575.30 *reales*. In this way we can more clearly appreciate the interests of all those involved in transhumance: the great owners of pastureland, the sheep owners, shepherds, traders, and the king. Considerable sums of money were being distributed among a very small group of people. The 1764 Cáceres survey pointed out that 1,000 head of livestock needed 1,000 *fanegas* of land and provided work for only four to six men; the same 1,000 *fanegas* under cultivation could provide a living for 154 people.[19]

The structure which dominated the Castilian economy, especially in the seventeenth and eighteenth centuries, gained strength from the consolidation of a socioeconomic bloc dependent on the export of wool. Numerically they were a minority, but some of them had strong links with the political power base of the *ancien régime* – nobility, clergy, the treasury – and enjoyed high incomes precisely because of wool exporting. The frail attempts of the domestic cloth industry in Castile, around 1520 (the Comunero Revolt) and at the beginning of the seventeenth century (the *arbitristas*), to take the English road, limit wool exports and develop native manufacturing, failed. The only possibilities of economic growth in the sixteenth, and again in the eighteenth century, were limited to agriculture and

[19] *Memorial ajustado hecho en virtud de Decreto de Consejo del Expediente consultivo ... entre D. Vicente Paino y Hurtado de Extremadura y el Honrado Concejo de la Mesta* (Madrid, nd [1771]), fol. 124v°.

livestock raising. However, when pastureland resources were abundant, foreign demand for wool slumped, and when demand recovered in the eighteenth century it held back the growth of agriculture. By themselves, the farmers were incapable of breaking the stranglehold maintained by the pasture and merino interests.

6. *Andalusia and the crisis of the Indies trade, 1610–1720*

A. GARCÍA-BAQUERO GONZÁLEZ

After a long spell of almost continuous growth during practically the whole of the sixteenth century, the sole exception being the recession of 1550–62, the upward trend of Spanish trade with the Americas was interrupted between 1593 and 1622. There then followed a sharp decline which lasted for the rest of the century. Not until well into the eighteenth century was there a recovery. In effect, after the period 1593–1622, when there were both obvious signs of prosperity (not for nothing did Chaunu call 1608 'the year to beat all records') and also unmistakable signs of uncertainty, clear symptoms of an impending reversal of the previous trend, the American trade entered upon a pronounced, irreversible and sustained depression (as our shipping and tonnage tables prove) which was still strongly in evidence between 1700 and 1715. In sum, despite some signs of decline, the level of activity held up between 1593 and 1610; but from 1611 to 1622 the trend reversed, with repeated and uninterrupted falls which were not halted until the first third of the eighteenth century.

Needless to say, this deep and prolonged crisis was rooted in a whole series of flaws and weaknesses, some inherent in the nature of the monopoly and Spain's fragile commercial system, others in the peculiarities of the colonial economies themselves. Amongst the former we might single out the Crown's own commercial policy, cramping trade by restrictive and ineffective legislation; the disastrous administration, particularly in fiscal matters; the slow and costly convoy system; the rudimentary trading system, permanently short of liquidity; and the short-sightedness of Spanish traders who kept supply scarce with a view to increasing prices and profits. Amongst the latter, the trend towards self-sufficiency which was emerging in the colonies, together with the increase in local capital invested in the regional economies, was the most significant. Finally, we must not forget the challenge of other European powers, which was felt increasingly as Spain's military and political power declined.

Not surprisingly, a crisis of such serious dimensions and such diverse origins made an impact on the national economy, regionally, insofar as it was involved, and most of all on the Seville–Cadiz axis, manifested in a sad, confused and self-interested dispute over preference, privileges and profits.

I. THE MODIFICATION OF THE ATLANTIC CONJUNCTURE

Until recently, the profile of the fluctuations in the Indies trade during the seventeenth century could be expressed graphically in the figures of the number of ships and the annual volume of tonnages compiled by H. and P. Chaunu up to 1650, and by me from 1680 onwards.[1] These figures reveal clearly enough, despite the gap in the series between 1650 and 1680, a sustained downward trend after 1620, which persisted in the period 1682–1716 and which suggests that it was almost impossible that there could have been any significant recovery, or any recovery at all, in the missing years. In any event, the intervening thirty years, and the whole second half of the seventeenth century in general, were in need of fuller investigation. It is precisely this gap that the work recently published by L. García Fuentes has filled,[2] enabling us now to construct (with some reservations) a homogeneous series on the basis of the tonnages of merchant ships alone. The series, presented in graphical form (see Figure 6.1), reveals clearly enough a trend which would not be significantly altered by the data from the warships with the fleets and from the ships involved in the slave trade, which it has not been possible to use. As a final caveat, it needs to be remembered that tonnages of ships are not the same as tonnages of capacity. The

[1] H. and P. Chaunu, *Séville et l'Atlantique*, 12 vols. (Paris, 1955–60), and A. García-Baquero González, *Cádiz y el Atlántico (1717–78)*, 2 vols. (Seville, 1976). It should be understood that at no time have I thought that these two factors could be considered the only, or even exceptionally good measures of trade trends. They are simply a substitute for the information we really should be using, the real volume of merchandise shipped and its monetary value. The absence of this information gives the number of vessels and the tonnages a role in the analysis of the trade that they cannot easily fill, and that leads to the uncertainties inevitable with such data.

[2] L. García Fuentes, *El comercio español con América (1650–1700)* (Seville, 1980).

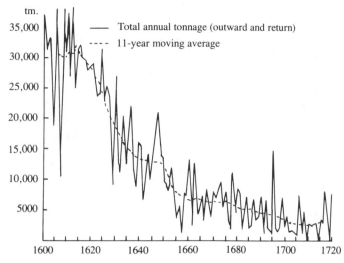

Figure 6.1 Total tonnage of merchant shipping, 1600–1720
Source: A. García-Baquero, 'Andalucía y los problemas de la Carrera de Indias', *Actas II Coloquios Hª Andalucía* (Cordoba, 1983), Vol. I, 537–9.

relationship between the two is complex and does not always permit conversion from one to the other. Nevertheless, the movement of shipping tonnages can be taken with some confidence to represent the overall movement of trade.

The first thing that is apparent from the curve of Spanish American trade in the seventeenth century, derived from the usable data from these three studies, is that the view we presented at the beginning of this chapter is fully confirmed. The moving average of the overall movement of tonnages (outwards and inwards) shows with absolute clarity that between 1615–20 and 1710–15 the trend is irreversibly and continuously downwards. The fall is precipitous in the earlier decades, levelling out in 1639–45, only to fall again fairly steeply to 1660. After a stable period until 1675, there is another fall until 1689, followed by renewed stability until 1695, when the last, decisive fall begins, troughing in 1709. This unremitting decline must be assessed not only in terms of the constancy of the trend, but also in terms of the magnitude of the fall. If we look at the gross figures of the moving average, we find, in 1615, an average of 31,092, falling to 13,498 in 1639, and to 6,693 in 1661; the averages then stabilise around that figure until 1675, when they again begin to fall, to 4,307 in 1689, and to 2,640 in 1709. If, to be absolutely sure, we take gross tonnages in 10-year averages, we have for 1611–20 an average of 30,026 tons; for 1631–40 15,275 tons; for 1651–60 8,800 tons; for 1681–90 5,062 tons; and for 1701–10 2,783 tons. As these figures show, the downward trend is continuous, as is the rhythm of decline. In effect, that rhythm marks out two important phases, to judge by the severity of the falls. The first is from 1611–15 to 1656–60, when 76 per cent of the initial tonnage was lost; the second, from 1656–60 to 1706–10, with a loss of a further 53 per cent. Even if we split these two phases into shorter periods, we still find a persistent loss of tonnage. Between 1611–20 and 1631–40, tonnage is 49 per cent down; between 1631–40 and 1651–60, 47.5 per cent down; between 1651–60 and 1681–90, 36 per cent down; and between 1681–90 and 1701–10, 45 per cent down. By 1701–10, 91 per cent of the 1611 tonnage had been lost. So it would appear that there is little need of further proof of a sustained trade crisis in the seventeenth century. Furthermore, if instead of total tonnages we take figures for the number of ships, up to 1665 the results are virtually identical, after which date there is a slight increase in shipping until 1675. This did not last, however, since in 1690 the moving average (Figure 6.2) is at the same level as it had been in 1664. If we start with the average number of ships in 1615, a century later we find a reduction of exactly 90 per cent.

It is obvious that the value we place on these figures in defining the crisis depends very much on whether we accept tonnage and shipping figures as representative of the trend. For most experts they are, but there are exceptions, the most famous being Professor M. Morineau, who has very serious and profound doubts about the correlation between these figures and the prosperity or decadence of the Indies trade. He argues that there is no clear correlation and no parallelism between the reduction in tonnage and the catastrophic drop in returns of precious metals during the first half of the seventeenth century (on E. J. Hamilton's evidence). This is confirmed by a similar comparison for the phase of expansion in the sixteenth century, when there was, in his opinion, a disparity between the increase in tonnage and that of silver shipments. Morineau affirms that whilst between 1506–10 and 1591–5 tonnage increased eightfold, silver imports increased forty-three fold; and in

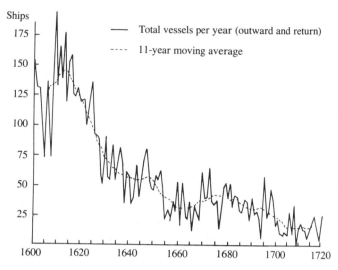

Figure 6.2 Total shipping movements, 1600–1720
Source: As for figure 6.1

the recession phase from 1591–5 to 1646–50, whereas tonnage fell by
about a third (32 per cent to be precise), bullion imports fell to a
third (by 66.5 per cent). All of which goes to show, firstly, the
impossibility of 'establishing an automatic parallelism'; and,
secondly, that 'the related argument using tonnage as evidence for
the evolution of returns of precious metals has little consistency'.[3]
While it is in no way my intention to become involved in a dispute
with Morineau over the figures (especially because the point was of
marginal importance to him and does not basically affect the nub of
his conclusions about the problem of precious metals, as we shall
see), I should simply like to argue that his total exclusion of tonnage
as a valid measure of the movement of trade is not well founded. At
best, it would perhaps be more reasonable if he were to take the
same view about other factors, such as imports of precious metals,
for example. What is really surprising is that Morineau has actually
considered the possibility of a 'perfect correlation' or an 'automatic

[3] M. Morineau, *Histoire Economique et Sociale du Monde*, II, *Les Hésitations de la
croissance (1580–1730)* (Paris, 1978), p. 81.

parallelism' between tonnage volumes and precious metals. For this to be the case, he would have to assume that bullion imports were almost the exact counterpart of the goods exported to America, and Morineau himself is the first to admit that this was not so. On the one hand, the bullion shipments included the monies both of the royal exchequer and of private individuals, which in turn included sums belonging to settlers, emigrants and government officials – dead or alive – sending their fortunes back home, as well as to merchants exporting goods to the Americas. On the other, even they did not always trade their products for specie, but often invested part of their profits in spices and other local produce. Secondly, price relativities would also logically distort that relationship and contradict any 'automatic parallelism'. Not only were bullion imports *not* the exact counterpart of exports to the Indies, but each of these factors was constantly subject to changes in value because of price fluctuations, which means that the equilibrium between them could hardly attain the degree of automatism claimed by Morineau. All this, however, does not mean that we simply accept the 'lack of parallelism' or 'indeterminacy of correlation' between total tonnage and bullion shipments. To refute this, we need only calculate their correlation coefficients, retaining Morineau's periodisation. The results entirely confirm our opinion of his extremism in rejecting tonnage as a valid measure of trade: for the period 1506–10 to 1591–5 the coefficient of correlation is 0.88; for 1591–5/1646–50, it is 0.81. The figures speak for themselves. There is, then, clearly a correlation, even though, as is to be expected, it is not a perfect one, and so there is no reason at all why tonnage should be rejected as a measure of trade trends.

Morineau's mistrust of tonnage figures for the definition of trade is in reality little more than the preliminary skirmish in the battle over the bullion totals. In fact, the author himself points out that the correlation between bullion and tonnage has its weaknesses, and that the fundamental problem continued to be just how much silver actually reached Europe in the seventeenth century. According to official figures, at least until 1660, bullion imports follow the general pattern of crisis. It is precisely to contradict those figures that Morineau unveils other sources (his now famous *gazettes hollandaises*) to prove that the volume of precious metals was very much greater than had come to be accepted. The statistical series of bullion imports of the various

Table 6.1. *Bullion imports, 1601–1700*
(in millions of pesos of 272 maravedís)

Years	Hamilton	Domínguez Ortiz	García Fuentes	Morineau
1601–5	40.3			40.3
1606–10	51.9			51.9
1611–15	40.5			43.1
1616–20	49.8			49.8
1621–5	44.6	56.4		46.1
1626–30	41.2	38.3		52.5
1631–5	28.3	33.4		46.2
1636–40	26.9	41.6		46.0
1641–5	22.7	23.8		46.9
1646–50	19.4	20.1		22.7
1651–5	12.0	16.6	11.7	21.4
1656–60	5.5	9.2	5.5	50.1
1661–5		7.5	6.8	86.9
1666–70			4.3	70.0
1671–5			4.2	56.3
1676–80			3.9	84.5
1681–5			1.9	67.0
1686–90			2.2	75.5
1691–5			0.7	69.8
1696–1700			1.9	66.0

Sources: E. J. Hamilton: *American Treasure and the Price Revolution in Spain, 1501–1650* (Cambridge, MA, 1934), p. 34; A. Domínguez Ortiz: 'Las remesas de caudales preciosos de Indias en 1621–1665'. *Anuario de Historia Económica y Social* 2 (1969), 561–85; García Fuentes: *El comercio español con América (1650–1700)* (Seville, 1980), pp. 388–9; Morineau: 'Gazettes hollandaises et trésors américains', *Anuario de Historia Económica y Social* 2 (1969), 289–347; 3 (1970), 139–209; P. Leon (ed.), *Histoire economique et sociale du monde* (Paris, 1978), II, p. 83.

authors involved in the dispute are shown in Table 6.1 (in millions of *pesos* of 272 *maravedís*).

It is clear that, though the dispute is centred on the second half of the seventeenth century, the basic disagreement is over the five years from 1626 to 1630, thirty years before the law exempting merchants from the requirement to register their imports of precious metals could serve as an explanation for such an enormous difference in the figures.[4] Morineau's confidence in his own figures leads him to seek the explanation of this difference in a qualitative change in the

---

[4] After 1660 the compulsory registration of treasure imported from America was abolished.

goods exported. I quote: 'Tonnage is a rather crude measure of trade. It is only a true representation when we are dealing almost exclusively with bulky cargoes. Was this the case in the American trade? No, or to be more exact, it was no longer the case in the first half of the seventeenth century. Pierre Chaunu admits this: "At the beginning of the seventeenth century, an increasingly more varied and less bulky range of products began to be shipped." '[5]

What can we deduce from the recent figures of García Fuentes on Spanish colonial trade in the second half of the seventeenth century? In the first place, we must stress that so long as we are ignorant of the exact nature of the merchandise shipped, our hypothesis remains nothing more than a conjecture, and it will remain so until a source is discovered other than the 'official registers', since they simply list the majority of manufactured goods laden as bundles, bales, packs, boxes, etc., without specifying their contents. Secondly, we can, nevertheless, revise the key point of Morineau's argument, which is that heavy and bulky agricultural produce gave way to manufactured goods of less bulk and increasingly greater value.

Let us examine the changes in the proportion of agricultural products during the second half of the seventeenth century, and compare them, if not with all manufactured goods (since, as García Fuentes presents them, it is impossible to reduce them to common terms), at least with the so-called *efectos de palmeo*, which can almost certainly be equated broadly with textile goods. One last observation: up to 1679, the volume of agricultural produce refers strictly to that shipped from Cadiz and Seville, while after that date the figures include produce shipped in the Canary Isles. Notwithstanding this difference, which would logically swell the total of agricultural produce shipped from 1679 on, the results are as shown in Table 6.2.

In the light of these figures, the impression is one of almost absolute stability in the percentage of agricultural produce in the total tonnage, whereas the percentage of textiles almost triples. But are these figures sufficient to confirm a structural change in the nature of the trade? While it cannot be denied that the evidence would seem to suggest it, we cannot be certain that the stability of agricultural products and the increase in *efectos de palmeo* were a sufficient cause of the increase in bullion returns detected by

[5] Morineau, *Hésitations*, p. 81.

Table 6.2. *Exports to the Indies, 1650–1699*

Years	Total	Agric. prod.	% Total	*Efectos de Palmeo*[a]	% Total
1650–1659	40,922	6,414	15.7	549	1.3
1660–1669	50,488	11,076	21.9	1,927	3.8
1670–1679	45,158	11,030	24.4	3,734	8.3
1680–1689	40,439	9,128	22.6	2,742	6.8
1690–1699	40,773	8,683	21.3	3,654	9.0

Note: [a] Largely textiles.

Morineau. If the changed nature of the trade was not enough to account for the fall in tonnage and the increase in bullion, then these shifts can have been the result only of increased levels of contraband. Morineau is inclined to accept this, as is Kamen, who in his recent survey of Charles II's reign writes:

> The available figures suggest an absolute decline in shipping from Cadiz, but it does not follow that the volume of wealth from America also declined absolutely. Smuggling was so extensive that the amount of goods registered from the Indies was invariably only a proportion of the real amounts; as little as a half, according to a source of 1691. The problem of contraband has regularly confused the study of bullion imports. As the commodity most likely to be smuggled, bullion would rarely have been registered in the correct quantity.[6]

All the same, Kamen himself suggests figures of his own for bullion imports which do not coincide with Morineau's and still less with those which García Fuentes himself believes to be too low, considering that there was no compulsory registration after 1660.

At this point we return to the original question concerning the existence or not of a crisis in Spanish colonial trade in the second half of the seventeenth century, statistically demonstrable from shipping and tonnage figures. There can be no definite answer at present since this very much depends on the reliability of a single type of source. On the other hand, whatever the answer may be with regard to bullion import figures, there are certain things that could lead to the recognition of a crisis, at least of Spanish commerce.

[6] H. Kamen, *Spain in the Later Seventeenth Century, 1665–1700* (London, 1980), pp. 134–5.

Even if we do not accept, or want to modify, the bullion import figures, the force of the other variables obliges us to admit the existence of a crisis. But if we do accept those figures, albeit with modifications, we also have to accept as essentially correct the claim for a change in the nature of the trade, and this in turn forces us to recognise the increased dependence of Spanish trade on European manufactures.

Not as an example, but simply as an indication of the kind of crisis I am talking about, we might recall the remark cited by Morineau that a ton of lace was worth a thousand tons of wine. It goes without saying that lace was not a Spanish product, whereas wine was. Even accepting that there was a revival in trade between America and Europe in the second half of the seventeenth century, we would argue that it was a revival precisely at the expense of Spanish goods, and that the very fact of a revival, therefore, actually implied a crisis for Spanish trade.

It is true that such a situation was nothing new in the Indies trade. What was new was the aggravation of a long-standing situation of dependence, already in itself burdensome enough, with all the economic repercussions that one might expect. While the increase in exports which García Fuentes stresses would appear to contradict what we have said, in my opinion it actually confirms it, since the goods exported most successfully were (apart from brandy) not Spanish manufactures. It is precisely in the context of this deterioration in Spanish and Andalusian commercial interests that the regional aspects of the crisis need to be considered.

2. THE COLONIAL TRADE CRISIS AND ITS IMPACT ON THE REGIONAL ECONOMY

Let us now look at the real purpose of this analysis of overseas trade, which is the recognition of its direct effect on the economic structure of Andalusia in general, and western, or Lower Andalusia in particular. There has been so little research into this subject that it is difficult to piece together even the most tentative conclusions. What is needed is data, data of almost every kind. The problem is not one of interpretation, but of information. Given the lack of research, I shall do no more than single out a few ideas for consideration and reflect on possible lines of investigation.

In view of the conclusions we arrived at concerning the correlation between the movement of trade and tonnage and shipping variables, we might with some confidence suppose it impossible for the economy of Lower Andalusia to have been able to make any significant recovery, or any recovery at all, in the second half of the seventeenth century. Such an evaluation holds good so long as we start from the assumption that there was an effective link between the Andalusian economy and the American trade. If this was so, obviously the profile of the crisis would be extended to those aspects of production which could have been affected by the monopoly, and that must have included both agricultural produce and manufactured goods. If on the contrary this link did not exist, at least in any direct and immediate form, we might find some sign of recovery independent of the general curve of the Atlantic trade.

It is hard to believe, on the basis of the so-called *tercio de frutos* (oil, wine and brandy), whose area of supply was limited to western Andalusia, that there was no effective connection between agricultural production (at least of those products included in the *tercio de frutos*) and trade. In the case of manufactured goods the connection might, perhaps, have been much weaker. Our enquiry into the question of whether the symptoms we have are of an economy (rural and/or urban) in recession, or independent of the movement of the Indies trade, is thus limited to three lines of investigation: the analysis of population behaviour during the period in question, especially in the key cities; the analysis of urban production; and a survey of the agrarian sector, based on the evolution and extension of crops, fluctuations in production, particularly that intended for the American market, and the movement of agricultural prices and rents.

(A) As to the movement of population during the century, in particular in that part of Andalusia affected by the Indies trade monopoly, the first thing we should point to is the marked increase in the information available to us, both quantitative and qualitative. In fact, we have parish records for all the main towns in the region. For Seville, thanks to the efforts of a research team headed by Professor Alvarez Santaló, continuous data have been reconstructed for six of the most representative parishes.[7] For Cordoba,

---

[7] L. C. Alvarez Santaló, 'La población de Sevilla en las series parroquiales: siglos xvi–xix', in *Actas II Coloquios Historia de Andalucía. Andalucía Moderna* (Cordoba, 1983), I, 1–19.

Fortea Pérez has made an exhaustive study of all fourteen parishes.[8] For Huelva, we have Pulido Bueno's recent study, unpublished as yet, of one of the two parishes which existed in the seventeenth century.[9] Lastly, for Cadiz, we have some preliminary figures of the parish records published by Ponce Cordones,[10] as well as Porquicho Moya's unpublished study of the first half of the seventeenth century.[11] In addition to these studies of urban demography, there is the occasional study of rural demography, as well as other works on the remainder of the Andalusian capitals.

In the case of Seville, capital of the monopoly system, the graphs of the parish records show a population, after the initial check to its expansion in the final decades of the sixteenth century, beginning to decline gradually from 1620, and much more perceptibly after 1638. The crisis of 1649 then aggravated an already weakened situation, and from then on Seville's population sank to a level from which it was not to recover for the rest of the century. The relatively weak attempts at growth visible around 1670 appear to be rather the normal reaction to the catastrophic losses of 1649 than the start of a sustained and coherent recovery. The figures that follow give an idea of the gravity of the situation created by the crisis of 1649: in the parish of El Sagrario, after 1649 baptisms fell by almost 60 per cent; the figure was the same in the parish of La Magdalena, and in San Nicolás, Santa María la Blanca and San Martín even reached 70 per cent. The collapse was less brutal in the parish of Santa Ana, but no less irremediable. The hecatomb suffered by the population of Seville was not stanched after 1649, irrefutable proof being the fact that from 1690 to 1708 baptisms were the same as in 1650.[12]

In contrast to the behaviour of Seville (which follows reasonably faithfully the pattern of trade), we have the anomaly of Cadiz whose

[8] J. I. Fortea Pérez, 'La evolución demográfica de Córdoba en los siglos xvi y xvii', in *Actas I Congreso Historia de Andalucía. Andalucía Moderna* (Cordoba, 1978), I, 371–96, and the same author's *Córdoba en el siglo xvi: las bases demográficas y económicas de una expansión urbana* (Cordoba, 1981).

[9] I. Pulido, 'Perfil socioeconómico de Huelva en el siglo xvii', unpublished *tesis de licenciatura*, Universidad de Sevilla.

[10] F. Ponce Cordones, 'Dos siglos claves en la demografía gaditana. (Breve estudio sobre la evolución de la población de Cádiz en las centurias xvii y xviii)', *Gades* 11 (Cadiz, 1983), 417–51.

[11] I. Porquicho Moya, 'Cádiz. Población y Sociedad: 1597–1650', unpublished *tesis de licenciatura*.

[12] Alvarez Santaló, 'Población de Sevilla', p. 4.

population (on the data available) tripled during the first half of the seventeenth century, and doubled again between 1650 and 1700,[13] a growth which is difficult to account for by natural causes, and still less in a period such as the one we are examining. Alongside these two extremes – Seville typifying the crisis pattern, with no recovery throughout the seventeenth century, and Cadiz characterised by a spectacular and uninterrupted growth, particularly after the mid-century – Cordoba follows the pattern of Seville, albeit in a less drastic form, while Huelva takes an intermediate position, clearly lagging behind Cadiz's growth, but showing some degree of recovery during the second half of the seventeenth century. In short, as Alvarez Santaló points out, rather than a distinct pattern for each town, what we have is a general climate of stagnation, varying in degree, affecting Seville, Cordoba and Huelva, with Cadiz the exception. Nevertheless, it is worth noting that the great centres of population do not have the monopoly of regional demography, and although we do not know much about rural populations, we know enough to detect differences.

Are we then justified in establishing a tight correlation between the crisis of the American trade and the regional demographic crisis? If we take the case of Seville, the temptation to do so is very strong since even chronologically the two crises fit perfectly. Cadiz (with all due reservations as to the limitations of the data) could also fit, not so much with the movement of trade, as with the impetus to growth deriving from its becoming the base for the Indies trade. On the other hand, for Cordoba and Huelva the link is not so clear; nor is it with the growth trend established by Vincent, Rabasco, Sanz Sampelayo and others, for eastern Andalusia, undoubtedly less affected by the American trade. In sum, in view of the wide variety of circumstances and the uncertainties of our knowledge, it would be advisable to wait for more relevant data before coming to any conclusions.

(B) As to productive activity in the towns, we shall try to establish, from the fragmentary data presently available, whether or not there was a crisis and then link it to the crisis of the American trade.

All the information we currently have points to the period as one of recession. We have quantitative data for the two great urban

---

[13] Ponce Cordones, 'Demografía gaditana', pp. 427–8.

centres traditionally regarded as the emporia of manufacturing in Lower Andalusia, Seville and Cordoba. The figures for Seville show that the totality of guild activities suffered a severe recession during the course of the century, and much more marked in the guilds of the tertiary sector than in the strictly manufacturing guilds. That in turn means that the latter were essentially tied in to the local or regional market, whereas the main reason for the collapse of the commercial guilds was clearly an external factor.[14]

These conclusions are supported by the following facts. Firstly, the fall in sales-tax payments by the guilds of Seville between 1601 and 1714. If we compare the sums paid by a number of guilds in 1714 with those paid by the same guilds in 1601, there is a drop of 78 per cent, a figure which speaks volumes for the significance of the seventeenth century for the guild system in Seville.

Secondly, the very different impact of the crisis on the secondary and the tertiary sectors is revealed by the same document of 1714, which shows that since 1601 the contributions of the commercial guilds had fallen by 83.5 per cent, whereas those of the manufacturing guilds fell by only 47 per cent. In another document, allocating contributions amongst the guilds of Seville in 1667, the share of the manufacturing guilds amounts to 66.5 per cent of the total, whereas that of the commercial guilds was 32 per cent, a complete reversal of the proportions which prevailed throughout the whole of the sixteenth century. Further confirmation is provided by a similar document (a donative demanded of the guilds of Seville by the Junta de Guerra in 1713), which indicates that the manufacturing guilds contributed 56 per cent, and the commercial guilds only 35 per cent of the total.

In sum, these figures reveal, firstly, the existence of a crisis, and secondly, the uneven repercussion of the crisis on the two groups of guilds. We should point out, however, that the greater proportional importance which the manufacturing guilds acquired during the seventeenth century was merely the result of the collapse of the commercial guilds, that is to say due not to an increase in manufacturing, but to the decline in commercial activities.

In Cordoba, the other great manufacturing centre, the effects of the crisis seem to have been similar, although there are no figures for

<hr />

[14] A. M. Bernal, A. Collantes de Terán and A. García-Baquero, 'Sevilla: de los gremios a la industrialización', *Estudios de Historia Social* 5–6 (1978), 234–41.

one of the principal areas of activity, the cloth industry, so that we have to rely on the other mainstay of local industry, silk. The existence of a crisis in this industry is undeniable. According to Fortea Pérez's figures, the 832 looms which existed in the period 1594–7 were, in a survey of 1690, reduced to 337, and by 1714 to a mere 98.[15] The collapse is too spectacular to require further comment.

We know very little about the other towns in Lower Andalusia. We are beginning to learn something of the economic activity of Huelva, albeit indirectly, from the work of Pulido. That indicates a very clear depression in mid-century, with an apparent, but modest revival in the final decades of the century, although it should be stressed that the figures are not for production but for investment. In any event, although not representative of manufacturing, the wills, rental agreements and contracts of sales drawn up in Huelva during the century reveal the total lack of economic resources among the artisans. Only the Church and the liberal professions seem to have had the capacity to play a leading role in the economic life of the city.

For Cadiz, we also have very little.[16] It has been emphasised by all those who have worked on the subject that the artisanate of Cadiz was of no importance and that productive activity in the city must have been dominated by activities associated with the fitting-out of ships (careening, caulking, rope and gunpowder making, etc.), about which we have no concrete information. The only sector manifesting significant activity was construction, obviously contingent upon the demographic growth reflected in the parish records cited above and upon the increasing need to fortify the port. If we link this demographic growth to the progressive transfer to Cadiz of the headquarters of the Indies trade, we must conclude that the increase of population was not the result of a general expansion of trade. In short, we lack information, but what we have argues against any correlation between manufacturing output and the American trade.

This, then, is the general overview of what we know. The picture

---

[15] J. I. Fortea Pérez, 'La industria textil en el contexto general de la economía cordobesa entre fines del siglo xvii y principios del xviii: una reactivación fallida', in *Actas II Coloquios Historia de Andalucía. Andalucía Moderna* (Cordoba, 1983), I, 443–65. [Chapter 7 of the present volume.].

[16] On this see, A. Domínguez Ortiz, 'La burguesía gaditana y el comercio de Indias desde mediados del siglo xvii hasta el traslado de la Casa de la Contratación', in *La burguesía mercantil gaditana (1650–1868)* (Cadiz, 1976), pp. 3–11.

that emerges very clearly is a crisis in the commercial sector, together with a somewhat less severe recession in the urban manufacturing sector. The immediate question is whether this crisis was determined directly, or at all, by the Indies trade. Unfortunately, the answer cannot at present be conclusive. According to the figures for manufacturing in Seville during the seventeenth century, there appears to be no connection at all. The figures for seventeenth-century Cordoba, in the opinion of contemporaries, showed a direct correlation between the silk industry and exports to America. According to those involved, speaking at the end of the century, 'shipment of the said goods (silk) to the Indies has ceased, bringing total ruin to those manufactures, and as long as foreign trade with the Indies is not stopped, Spanish industry will not prosper'.[17] In Cadiz, the absence of any connection is palpable, and there never seems to have been more manufacturing there than the minimum necessary to cover the most basic urban requirements. Finally, the figures for Huelva, by their very nature, do not clarify matters at all. So it would seem that as things stand we are unable to give any definite answer and must continue to tolerate a certain ambiguity. Nevertheless, what should be stressed is the apparent absence of any correlation between manufacturing output in the Lower Andalusian region and the Indies trade, since in the only case where this link is affirmed, Cordoba, it clearly was not due to a slump in exports, but to an increased penetration of foreign goods, against which Cordoba was unable to compete.

(C) Finally, it remains to consider the sector which is always believed to have had the closest links with the Indies trade (if only because of the *tercio de frutos*), namely agriculture. Here, as with population and manufacture, we shall attempt to establish the existence of a crisis and then determine its connection, if any, with the American trade.

We ought to make it clear first, as A. M. Bernal has recently done, that any attempt to establish the possible existence of an agrarian crisis in seventeenth-century Andalusia is seriously limited by two basic factors: 'On the one hand, the deep-rooted image of the seventeenth century in Andalusia as a period of severe crisis has

---

[17] Fortea Pérez, 'Industria textil', p. 460, n. 4.

come to be an unquestioned assumption. On the other, the seventeenth century is a great void in the historiography of Andalusia'.[18]

If we began this section by referring to the general dearth of studies on Andalusia's economic history in the seventeenth century, when we come to agrarian history this dearth is even more serious. A demonstration of the neglect of our rural history in the seventeenth century is the fact that of fifteen papers on rural history in the recently published *Actas de los II Coloquios Historia de Andalucía: Andalucía Moderna*, not one deals with the seventeenth century.[19] Nevertheless, as Bernal says, the image persists of Andalusia as the perfect exemplar of the seventeenth-century agrarian crisis. In the most frequently consulted texts, but without concrete evidence to support the claim, our region is always pictured as the area where the salient characteristics of the crisis are to be seen in their purest form, and where the signs of the economic recession are soonest and most easily detectable.[20] Amongst the many arguments deployed in support of the existence of an agricultural crisis in Andalusia during the seventeenth century, and more particularly in the second half of the century, the most solidly based are the references to food shortages and adverse weather conditions. These references, the majority of which have been collected by Domínguez Ortiz himself, tell of frequent and repeated crises of subsistence in the middle of the century and in its last third, aggravated by disastrous weather conditions, with drought and flood alternating in a panorama of desolation.[21] Though varying in intensity from one district to another, the crisis apparently affected the whole region, as is suggested by the simultaneous appearance of popular disturbances. Of the eighteen localities which experienced hunger riots between 1647 and 1652, twelve were situated in western and the rest in eastern Andalusia.[22] Nonetheless, however suggestive this might be, it is clearly not by itself sufficient evidence of the movement of the agrarian economy and still less of its possible relationship with the Indies trade.

[18] A. M. Bernal, 'Andalucía Occidental: Economía rural, 1590–1765', in *Historia de Andalucía*, VI (Madrid, 1981), p. 187.
[19] *Actas II Coloquios Historia de Andalucía. Andalucía Moderna*, 2 vols. (Cordoba, 1982).
[20] Bernal, 'Andalucía Occidental', p. 187.
[21] A. Domínguez Ortiz, 'La crisis de Castilla en 1677–87', in *Crisis y decadencia de la España de los Austrias* (Madrid, 1969).
[22] A. Domínguez Ortiz, *Las alteraciones andaluzas* (Madrid, 1973).

So if this route does not get us very far, is there any quantitative data that might help solve the problem? Looking at the material published so far, the answer could not be less hopeful. What we have is not only so little, but worse it is so fragmented that it is confusing, not to say contradictory. Thus, for cereal production, the data is limited to: (a) the curve of wheat tithes in the archbishopric of Seville, published by G. Anes,[23] which shows a tendency to growth from 1652 to 1682, followed by a stronger and more sustained period of growth until 1706; (b) the curve of tithes in four towns in the province of Huelva (Calañas, Puebla de Guzmán, Bollullos del Condado and Lucena del Puerto) and two in the province of Cordoba (Castro del Río and Espejo), published by P. Ponsot.[24] These contradict the trends revealed in the curve for Seville. The curves for Huelva show an overall stagnation in wheat production for the whole of the century, and even the period 1660–1720 shows contradictory trends. The curve for Castro and Espejo shows a steady decline of output, broken only by a period of stagnation at a very low level from 1652 to 1675; (c) lastly, the tithe curves drawn up by R. Benítez Sánchez-Blanco, for the county of Casares, Antequera, Setenil and the whole of the bishopric of Malaga.[25] These are different again. They show a period of pronounced recession between 1630 and 1655, a recovery to 1670, production at a complete standstill from 1670 to 1680, followed by another recovery to the end of the century.

So few examples and such very different patterns of development make the possibility of saying anything about the existence or non-existence of a crisis extremely problematic. However, this truly depressing picture will change radically with the publication in the near future of Pierre Ponsot's *Album-Atlas Histórico de Andalucía* [published 1986], since in it he includes a fair number of curves of grain tithes for our period, together with wine and oil tithes, products, as we know, more closely linked to the Indies trade.[26]

[23] G. Anes, *Las crisis agrarias en la España moderna* (Madrid, 1970), pp. 466–7.
[24] P. Ponsot, 'En Andalousie occidentale: les fluctuations de la production du blé sous l'Ancien Régime', *Etudes Rurales* 34 (1969), and 'La Dîme, source d'histoire rurale et urbaine; réflexions méthodologiques et analyse d'un cas cordouan', in *Actas II Coloquios Historia de Andalucía. Andalucía Moderna*, I, 353–62.
[25] R. Benítez Sánchez-Blanco, *Moriscos y Cristianos en el Condado de Casares* (Cordoba, 1982), pp. 217–21.
[26] Relevant in this respect is the existence of the so-called *tercio de frutos de la tierra* in the cargoes of the *flotas* of New Spain, composed essentially of wine, oil and

How far will these new figures go towards confirming or refuting the existence of a crisis? Ponsot presents a total of thirty-three curves of grain tithes for a like number of townships in the provinces of Seville, Huelva, Cadiz and Cordoba. In none of these places did cereal production increase in the seventeenth century. In twenty-three it stagnated, in five it fell, and in the remaining five alternated between sharp rises and equally severe losses. So the preponderant trend of cereal production in the seventeenth century would appear to be stagnation, thus confirming the curves for Huelva. As for oil, Ponsot gives us a total of eighteen curves of tithes. In three places production increased throughout the century; in five others it increased only in the second half of the century; in three cases it stagnated throughout the century, and in another during the first half of the century only; production fell throughout the century in five places, and in the last only in the second half. Summing up, the dominant tendency is once again stagnation. Wine production increased throughout the century in only two localities out of twenty-two, and in another two in the first half of the century only; in five places it remained static, but fell over the long-term in thirteen, and in the second half of the century in the remaining two.[27] The main trend of wine production, therefore, was downwards.

In the light of these new figures, as Ponsot himself says: "The seventeenth century in Andalusia confirms the notorious reputation it has in most of Europe as the "Iron Century", although the century is not all of a piece.'[28] The seventeenth century was not, of course, an homogeneous block, and that ought not to surprise us. However, whether or not our sample represents more or less faithfully the evolution of regional production, and that would confirm the theory of zonal differences, it does bring out a significant number of major contradictions in productive activity. The analysis should proceed from two starting points. The first is the analysis of the crisis in relation to expansion, the second the analysis of the crisis in relation to recession. In the first case, the stagnant nature of

brandy. Of the total tonnage of any vessel, one-third was reserved for the merchants of Cadiz who participated in the monopoly; the rest was divided into three parts, two-thirds for manufactures and re-exports, one-third for domestic agricultural products, i.e. *el tercio de frutos de la tierra.*

[27] P. Ponsot, *Album-Atlas Histórico de Andalucía* (Granada, 1986), pp. 9–10.

[28] *Ibid.*, p. 9.

the trend is clear, indicating a situation which was worse than before but not catastrophic; in the case of oil, growth is represented in 40 per cent of the sample. In the second, the overall view is less grave since stability was the predominant trend, with recession showing in only 30 per cent of the grain and oil series, but, more seriously, in some 60 per cent of the wine series. In short, if the concept of crisis necessarily implies recession, then its application to the present case is somewhat excessive. If it implies merely stagnation, then it certainly does seem that there was a crisis. Moreover, the lack of homogeneity has to be understood within similar chronological limits, as an entire century cannot be labelled under the single heading of either stagnation or recession.

Let us see what the analysis of other variables might suggest, before giving a final verdict, beginning with prices. Economic historians have placed great weight on price series for the analysis of the economy, and thanks to Hamilton's classic study,[29] together with the new series compiled by Ponsot,[30] we are well-informed for our region. On the whole, the movement of the prices of the various agricultural products is as follows: (a) grain prices fall into three quite distinct phases – stagnation until 1640, a rise from 1640 to 1680, and a very sharp fall thereafter; (b) oil prices describe two contrasting tendencies – a rise throughout the first two-thirds of the century, and a fall after 1665–70, continuing until the beginning of the eighteenth century; (c) wine prices divide into two half centuries of stability, separated by a fierce increase between 1648 and 1652, making the first half century a period of stagnation on a low price plateau, and the second a period of stagnation on a higher plateau. In sum, prices reveal a marked downward tendency after mid-century, confirming the impression that this was also the most critical period for production. This would hint at the possibility that the agricultural crisis in Andalusia was basically limited to the second half of the century.

Thanks yet again to Professor Ponsot, we also have a third series of data which may help to confirm this impression, namely land-rents.[31] Here stagnation is once more the keynote. Where rents were

[29] E. J. Hamilton, *American Treasure and the Price Revolution in Spain, 1501–1650* (Cambridge, MA, 1934), and *War and Prices in Spain, 1651–1800* (Cambridge, MA, 1947).

[30] Ponsot, *Album-Atlas*, pp. 13–14.   [31] *Ibid.*, pp. 16–17.

paid in specie, long-run stagnation is represented in twenty-five holdings, decline in one, and rise in none. Where rents were paid in kind, the pattern was identical: stasis in five cases, increase in one, and a fall in another. Rents are perhaps the variable that gives the clearest diagnosis of stagnation and, therefore, some guarantee of the acceptability of the general view of an immobile agricultural sector in the seventeenth century. To complicate the picture further, Ponsot points out that rents collapsed totally after 1680, not to revive until the early eighteenth century.

In view of all this, dare we risk a new diagnosis of the relationship between the Indies trade and Lower Andalusian agriculture? It is undeniable that there was a progressive reduction in the volume of agricultural produce shipped to the Indies as well as in the percentage of agricultural exports in the total American trade. The determining factor in the process of recession was wine (a purely regional product), while the increased exports of brandy (basically a foreign product) were not enough to compensate. But that does not necessarily mean that there was a causal relationship with the Andalusian agrarian crisis. If we explained the agricultural expansion which took place in the sixteenth century less in terms of the Indies trade than in terms of internal and European causes, there is no reason to reverse the causation now. A more than probable decline in the population of the region and a general continental crisis would be quite sufficient to explain the phenomenon without the need to seek the ultimate cause in the Indies trade and to make that the scapegoat.

7. The textile industry in the economy of Cordoba at the end of the seventeenth and the start of the eighteenth centuries: a frustrated recovery

JOSÉ IGNACIO FORTEA PÉREZ

This chapter is an attempt to analyse the problems of the Cordoban economy at the end of the seventeenth century and the efforts made by the city to try to overcome them. The basic documentation consulted consists of the various inquiries carried out from 1686 by the *corregidor* of Cordoba, Don Francisco Ronquillo Briceño, in response to an order from the Royal Board of Commerce (Real Junta de Comercio) asking for information about 'all the businesses that there have been in this city and its kingdom, their present condition, the reasons for their diminution, and the measures that could be taken to expand them and introduce new ones'. Although the scope of the survey was wide, it ended up being restricted to the city limits and, within those limits, to the textile industry. There is no doubt that this was the sector most in need of large-scale reorganisation; it was also the one in which contemporaries had placed their greatest hopes. New orders, town council reports and memoranda from the city's mercantile and craft circles throw light on the situation of the textile sector in subsequent years. These form a second corpus of documentation which enables us to understand the nature of the problems that the textile industry was experiencing at the end of the seventeenth and the start of the eighteenth centuries, and to evaluate the results obtained.[1]

The present chapter, however, does not try to answer all the

[1] All the documentation consulted comes from the Cordoba Municipal Archive (hereafter AM Cor.), Sección VI, serie 7, leg. 17, docs, 1 to 5 and leg. 18, docs, 33, 39, 41, 44, 46, 48, 53 to 55, 62 and 64. I have also consulted the *Actas capitulares* (hereafter AC) of the years 1686–8. The reports for 1686 include the replies of Cordoba and the towns of Baena, Montilla, Castro del Río, Rute, Cañete, Espejo, Puente Genil, Montoro, La Rambla, Bujalance, Priego and Montemayor. Unfor-

questions involved in a consideration of this subject. Rather, it raises some of the problems and suggests hypotheses that may help to solve them.

The overall predominance of agrarian activity in the economic structure of Cordoba, the persistence of certain centres of industrial production and the utter prostration of the economic activities of the area in general are immediately obvious in the reports of 1686. In fact, agriculture, as the representatives of the Cordoba farmers (*labradores*) pointed out, 'is the only sustenance of this city and its district'. It was an agriculture based on the cultivation of cereals, although in some places, Baena for instance, vineyards had become increasingly important, in Montilla they were preponderant, and olive plantations had spread considerably in the districts of Puente Genil and Bujalance.

However, within a context in which the agrarian economy predominated, the presence of some textile activity could be detected in certain places. Cloth-making is mentioned in Rute, Cañete, Espejo, Montoro, La Rambla and Bujalance. Silk was produced also in Espejo and, above all, in Castro del Río, Puente Genil and Priego. Part of the output was exported unfinished, but the rest was used in the manufacture of certain cloths, such as the flannels of Castro, or the taffetas, veils and handkerchiefs of Priego. The economic activity of Cordoba also included the making of woollens and silks.[2] However, with some exceptions and leaving aside the villages of Los Pedroches, textile manufacturing does not seem to have been an independent activity in these places in the seventeenth century. It was, rather, a subsidiary activity carried out by the peasants for their own consumption. Nevertheless, the town councils of Rute, Montoro and Cañete stated that some of the cloth they made was sold in places nearby. Bujalance was the most explicit in defining its commercial space, which included locations in the Alpujarras, Guadix, Baza, the Condado de Niebla and other unspecified parts of Andalusia.[3] However, it was undoubtedly the silk industry that

tunately, I have not found any trace of those of the villages of Los Pedroches, if indeed they did respond to the city's questionnaire.

[2] According to the city councillor, Don Martín Antonio González de Quiral, 'The main trades of this city are silks, cloths and agriculture', AC 16 Feb. 1687.

[3] AM Cor. Sección VI, serie 7, leg. 18, doc. 33, 'Auttos y diligenzias hechos en virtud de zedula real despachada por los señores de la Junta de Comerzio para la introduzion de nuebas fabricas de lanas y sedas', 1686.

supplied the most extensive commercial channels. Cordoban silk fabrics had been in much demand not only in Andalusia, Portugal and Extremadura, but also in the Indies. The Indies market, however, was already declining and was to be all but lost during this period, thereby seriously threatening the future of the sector.[4]

In any event, both agricultural and artisanal activities suffered an acute crisis in the 1680s. 'Farming and the dependence of everything on it is in the direst of straits', complained Cordoba's husbandmen. Nor were other reports any more encouraging. The land under cultivation in the district of Baena had been reduced to a third of what had once been usual. Many vine-growers from Montilla and Baena had been forced to give up their vineyards because wine prices were too low. The floods of 1684 had destroyed Puente Genil's market-gardens, depriving the town of the profits that it had obtained from the sale of its fruit and vegetables throughout the region. The oil yield had also been very meagre throughout the period 1682–5. The town of Bujalance complained of similar problems. In short, extreme poverty was stalking the Cordoba country-side. This was in part the result of bad weather, the alternation of droughts and excessive rain that had ruined the crops and decimated the cattle. All the reports we have seen insist on this point, although for some it was not the fundamental reason for the crisis, as we shall see.

The problems of agriculture undoubtedly had an effect on the craft sector, which the documents show to have been in an even worse depression. Indeed, in the 1680s the production of woollens and silks had stopped completely in places like Espejo and Rute. In Castro the making of ordinary cloths had been abandoned, while silk-thread production had been interrupted by the loss of the mulberry trees in the floods. Puente Genil had to face the same problems. Other places still kept up their industrial activity, though to a much lesser extent than previously. Cañete de las Torres went on making only heavy cloth. In Priego the number of spinning

---

[4] The loss of the Indies market was attributed to the Cordoba merchants' scanty assets and to foreign competition, see AC session 4 Mar. 1687, and Sección VI, serie 7, leg. 17, doc. 4. The latter document includes a memorandum of the silk merchants, dated 1715, in which it says, among other things, that because of the penetration of foreigners into the trade with the Indies 'the shipment of these silks to the Indies has stopped, which is the absolute ruin of these manufactories. As

wheels and looms had diminished considerably, and of those still working only a few were kept running all year. La Rambla described its cloth output as being 'very low'. But perhaps it is the memorandum submitted to the *corregidor* of Cordoba in 1686 by the *jurado* Antonio de Mesa that reveals most dramatically the sector's decline. According to this document, the silk industry in Cordoba had boasted nearly 2,000 looms 50 years earlier. There had also been a notable production of black and coloured ribbons that had provided work for about a hundred spinners. The making of the cloths known as *anafayas* was also important, both because they had an assured sale in many markets, and because it kept a large number of people busy at a low cost, as well as enabling the apprentices to practise the skills of the trade. For all these reasons, the *jurado* Antonio de Mesa had no hesitation in describing the silk industry as 'the largest of Cordoba's manufactures and the most necessary for the common good'. But there was also a considerable woollen industry. The 100 looms then operating in Cordoba wove some 4,000 brown cloths, while each year 8,000 pieces from Los Pedroches were fulled and dyed in the city. However, of this happy (if, in my opinion, exaggerated) state there was barely even a memory by the date of the memorandum. All that remained were 50 silk looms and 30 spinners, of which only 6 were working. The production of *anafayas* had also ceased. Nor was the position of the woollen industry very different. The number of looms had dwindled to 5, the number of cloths manufactured in the city to about 100, and only 200 pieces a year were now brought in from Los Pedroches.

Such is the dispiriting picture that the documents reveal. Only a couple of small centres of production, Montoro and Bujalance, were unaffected.[5] It is true that we lack precise information on the development of the textile industry in the Valle de los Pedroches. The output of the villages in the area could have remained at a higher level than the drastic decline in the quantity of exports sent to the city suggests. In either case, the document is revealing a fact of

long as the trade of the foreigners with the Indies is not denied them, Spanish manufactures will be unable to flourish.'

[5] In Montoro the situation was really one of stagnation. 'This trade is exactly the same today – the town's response states – except that there are never any better years than others.' In Bujalance the manufacture of woollens was the activity that had declined the least, despite the general contraction of the economy, 'because the

fundamental importance, the virtual disconnection of Cordoba, its merchants and its capital from any involvement with the rural textile industry. This is the complete opposite of what had happened in the sixteenth century. Then the importance of Cordoba's cloth industry had rested precisely on the matching of the merchants' interests to the opportunities presented by the existence of a rural area traditionally devoted to the production and weaving of woollens. Although the disconnection between the two had started much earlier, it seems to have reached its peak at the end of the seventeenth century when the rural industry was abandoned to its own devices.[6]

There are many reasons why that happened. Contemporaries stressed one above all, the invasion of foreign merchandise, which had catastrophic consequences. Not only did it accentuate the shortage of capital in the area, but it also ruined the local industry by depriving it of its domestic and foreign markets. Foreign penetration was also felt to be based on a fraud. The foreign textiles, according to the documents, *looked* very good, but were really deceptions and very short-wearing. The home-made textiles, on the other hand, were of intrinsic worth because they were manufactured according to legal regulations, with proper specifications and proof of authenticity. The terms in which this comparison was made reveal the vast distance that separated the Cordoban cloth industry, and Spanish industry generally, from the more dynamic industries of north-western Europe. The gulf between the two had opened up much earlier, but the crisis and the outcome of the crisis with which the seventeenth century began gave the latter such great competitive advantages that they were able to secure the domination of the European and overseas markets.[7]

There is no need to say much about the nature of the 'new draperies'. Their main technical characteristic was the use of combed long-fibred wool, scoured before spinning, which needed much less fulling and sizing after weaving and so reduced pro-

---

poverty from the loss of jobs and income means that most people who live in this city have to work in cloth making'. Sección VI, serie, 7, leg. 18, doc. 33.

[6] For the situation of Cordoba's cloth manufacturers in the sixteenth century see my book, *Córdoba en el siglo XVI: las bases demográficas y económicas de una expansión urbana* (Cordoba, 1981), pp. 268ff. 335ff.

[7] On this subject see J. de Vries, *The European Economy in an Age of Crisis, (1600–1750)* (Cambridge, 1976), pp. 98ff.

duction costs. The finished product was a light, thin cloth, with its texture and the pattern of its weave evident at a glance. During the course of the seventeenth century the north European manufacturers introduced further innovations, mixing other fibres (silk, linen, etc.) with the wool, for example, which enabled them to vary the range of their products indefinitely. At the same time, the improvements introduced into the dyeing processes gave the cloths a vivid colour which made them extremely attractive. It was, however, the perfection of the final stages of the sizing process that guaranteed a demand for the new draperies.[8] Basically this was the use of special presses which gave silk or woollen fabrics a sheen and a brilliance impossible to achieve in the local workshops, as the Cordoban manufacturers eventually realised.[9] A document of 1715 sums up the disastrous effects the new fabrics had on the local production of silks and cloth. It reads:

The foreigners have introduced different wool and worsted fabrics so extremely fine that their lightness is like that of silk, and although they are fine and of little substance, their dyes and colours are so clear that, together with their low price compared with silk, these fabrics are bought and not the silks ... As a result, not only the silk guild has lost out, but the cloth guild as well.[10]

Such were the characteristics of the serge, worsted and druggets of France and England that completely dominated the Cordoba market. Not all the imported fabrics, however, were of this fineness and lightness. The so-called 'Alconcheste' (Colchester), or hundred-thread flannels, were coarser and more hard-wearing, and were in great demand in Spain for monastic habits. This was also true of the burlaps, an attempt being made to start the production of these in Cordoba at this time. Nonetheless, the coarse brown cloths of the Campiña, or the heavy *veinticuatrenos* of Los Pedroches could offer only token resistance to the products of the 'new draperies'.

It is worth saying more about the criticisms made in Cordoba at

[8] On the technical aspects of the new drapery, see P. Deyon, *Amiens, capitale provinciale. Etude sur la société urbaine au XVIIe siècle* (Paris, 1967), pp. 181ff. According to Deyon, the Amiens dyers managed to come up with processes to fix colours which up till then had been considered false, p. 189.

[9] The documentation provides contradictory evidence on this point. The makers of the new fabrics recognised their technical inferiority. The artisans and some of the merchants, however, did not, and for them the imported fabrics were false and fraudulent.

[10] AM Cor. Sección VI, serie 7, leg. 17, doc. 4.

the time of the foreign fabrics. They were accused of being all show, without substance, fake and short-wearing, so much so that, according to the *jurado* Antonio de Mesa, it would be enough to ban the entry of fabrics with 'sheen, smoothness, and finish' for the higher specifications and harder-wearing quality of the Cordoban products to be evident. Such quality was not to be found in the foreign fabrics, which explained their low price and provided sufficient reason for condemning them as fake. What this meant was that the local cloths were more expensive than the imported ones and that, in the view of the Cordobans, it was impossible to reduce the costs of production because of the strict regulations that controlled their manufacture and that were their guarantee of real quality. The Cordoban manufacturers tended to associate this with the life of the fabric, which in turn depended on a number of factors, particularly important being not only the quality of the fibres and the fastness of the dyes, but also the density and weight of the fabric, that is, the number of threads of wool or silk used in its weaving. The open weft of the foreign fabric and its lightness and thinness betrayed its fraudulence and explained its low price. If this line of reasoning is accepted, it is very possible that the best traditional cloths were, in fact, superior in price and quality to their competitors. That does not mean that all foreign cloths were of a uniformly low quality, it was simply that different conceptions of production and consumption were being applied.

This is why the attacks on the foreign fabrics revealed an absolute incomprehension of the inherent possibilities of the new draperies. They also concealed the obvious technical inferiority of the Cordoba workshops. To attribute the low price of foreign fabrics to fraudulent manufacturing practice implies lack of understanding and ignorance of the immense effort made in the countries of northern Europe to reduce production costs, which was achieved thanks to more economical production techniques and the decided boost given to rural, cottage industry. Indeed, this technical inferiority was admitted by the Cordoba manufacturers themselves, when they decided to imitate their competitors. One of them, Don Bernardo de Pineda, embarked on this course around 1683–6, but he pointed out that it was first necessary 'to bring over master-craftsmen, since those in Spain lack the experience and the disposition needed to imitate the sheen and perfection of the foreign product'.[11]

[11] AM Cor. Sección VI, serie 7, leg. 18, doc. 33.

But what tied the noose of foreign domination and made any possibility of recovery for the Cordoba textile industry very difficult was the export orientation of the raw materials market. There was no wool for the craftsmen of Los Pedroches, nor for any other centre of production in the Cordoba district. Foreign merchants, or their agents, signed up most of the wool at shearing time for export. Nor were there sufficient quantities of silk for the Cordoba looms from the traditional areas of supply, Valencia and Murcia. Some of the best of the Murcian and Valencian silk was now being exported, but more importantly, the silk was also being increasingly used by the strong silk industry in the areas that produced it, that is, in Valencia.[12] The exporting of raw materials is in fact one of the reasons most forcefully alleged to explain the decline of the Cordoban textile industry, both in the memorandum of 1686 and in later documents. This problem was certainly not new. Even during their best moments, the local cloth workshops had been threatened by the disequilibrium in wool supplies caused by the export market. The manufacturers and merchants could, however, have resorted to their option to buy at the going rate, as the laws of the kingdom allowed, but it seems that by the end of the seventeenth century this right had fallen into disuse. Moreover, the Cordoba merchants were not supplying the same quantity of raw materials to the looms of the area as they had done previously.[13]

The consequences of these difficulties in the supply of fibres were not exactly the same for the cloth as for the silk industry. In the cloth industry, at the end of the seventeenth century, the craftsmen

[12] 'Representación y manifiesto que hazen las artes de la labor de la seda ... a Su Señoría, la Muy Noble y Muy Leal ziudad de Córdoba sobre el atraso en que se hallan todas sus fábricas, por razón de la concurrencia y entrada de todas ropas de otras partes, las quales sin excepción alguna se labran en esta ziudad, para que por medio de su autoridad y patrocinio se embarace dicha entrada' ['Representation and manifesto made by the arts and crafts of silk work ... to the Most Noble and Most Loyal City of Cordoba on the recession in all manufacturing, because of the concurrence and entry of every kind of clothing from elsewhere, which are all made in this city as well, so that by means of your authority and protection this importation be stopped'], reproduced, along with many other documents, by J. de la Torre and J. M. Rey Díaz in their *El Arte de la Seda en Córdoba* (Cordoba, 1928), typed copy, Biblioteca Municipal, Cordoba, fols. 613–53.

[13] In his memorandum, the *jurado* Antonio de Mesa claimed the right of *tanteo* (the option to buy at the same price) for the weavers of Los Pedroches, referring to a consignment of 4,000 *arrobas* of wool (one *arroba* equals 25 lbs./11.5 kilos) dumped in Hinojosa del Duque on the death of the buyer, a foreigner whose nationality is not given: AM Cor. Sección VI, serie 7, leg. 18, doc. 33.

were procuring their own supplies of wool almost entirely, helped by the existence of important sources of wool in certain areas. This is indicated in the references to Los Pedroches in Antonio de Mesa's memorandum, but the same thing also happened elsewhere. The people of Bujalance devoted themselves, according to their town council, 'to the making of cloths, everyone according to his financial capability'. Montoro claimed, at the same time, that 'the cloth trade depends on the ability of the people to farm'.[14] Naturally this fact put a considerable restriction on the productive possibilities of the textile industry. The city merchants seem to have left the craftsmen to their own devices. But the point here is that the fact that the craftsmen were supplying themselves, at a time when the tendency was for wool to be exported, was clearly reflected in the high cost of local manufactures. The weavers lacked the means to accumulate raw materials. Once shearing time arrived, in April and May, they obtained what they could with their scant resources at the same time as merchants, resident in Cordoba or elsewhere, were making massive purchases on behalf of foreigners. As a result, once they had sold their cloths they had no wool with which to start working again. Unless they were able to buy some from retailers, they were faced with unemployment. This would seem to be the only way of explaining the marked fluctuations recorded by Antonio de Mesa in the price of manufactures from Los Pedroches during the course of the year. At the time of the 'wool harvest', they were sold at 10 ducats the piece; at the end of the year, the price went up to 22 ducats.

With silk the situation was somewhat different. The local output of silk was not appreciable, and its poor quality meant that it had to be kept for cheap fabrics. That apart, the craftsmen depended on supplies from the city that had come from Murcia or Valencia. Traditionally the Cordoba merchants had controlled this traffic, but by the end of the seventeenth century they had to a large extent abandoned it. This helps explain why the memoranda and reports from the craftsmen are harshly critical of the Cordoba merchants and blame them directly for the prostration of the industry. The silk industry, said a document of 1710, has suffered 'a total collapse because of a lack of capital among its exponents ... the main cause of this ruin being the changed nature of the trade this city once had

14 AM Cor. Sección VI, serie 7, leg. 18, doc. 33.

with the kingdoms of Valencia and Murcia, from where a large part of the silk used to come'.[15] In former times, continued the memorandum, there were three kinds of silk merchants in the city. First, there were the so-called *desk* merchants (mercaderes de *escritorio*), over thirty in number. They contracted large quantities of the raw silk, and had it spun. A second group of merchants bought this spun silk and redistributed it among the weavers. Finally the silk fabrics then went to retail merchants (mercaderes *de vara*), who sold it. However, according to the craftsmen, all this had stopped some time ago. Now only the retail merchants existed, and they 'have procured that the raw silk is now brought here ready prepared, that is spun and for the most part woven, so that the only silks that come in for manufacture are the skeins for silk sewing-thread'. In this way the disengagement of the merchants deprived the craftsmen of work, which is why they were accused of being idle, 'timid men', more interested in their own self-interest than in the common good.[16]

The absence of mercantile involvement was not, however, total. As a document of 1713 has it: 'It is common knowledge that because they are ruined and lack capital the manufacturers do not make any material with their own silk, but only with that of the merchants.'[17] What this means is that the Cordoba silk industry, however low its level of production, revolved round the activity of the merchants; in other words, it still functioned at the end of the seventeenth and the start of the eighteenth century along the lines of the classic *Verlagssystem*. There is no need to expand on this and the advantages it offered the merchant to adapt to economic fluctuations.[18] It is enough to remember that in this mode of production, credit was the crucial, decisive element. The merchants gave credits to the

[15] 'Representación y manifiesto'. The argument is also reproduced in another document dated 1715. It is a memorandum submitted to the city council by the Silk Guild. AM Cor. Sección VI, serie 7, leg. 17, doc. 4.

[16] AM Cor. Sección VI, serie 7, leg. 17, doc. 4. Resentment against the merchants can be seen in the view expressed in the 'Representación y manifiesto' of the Silk Guild referred to above, 'What Your Majesty needs are manufacturers rather than merchants, useful people, whoever they are.'

[17] AM Cor. Sección VI, serie 7, leg. 7, doc. 4.

[18] For industrial organisation in this period, see B. Supple, 'The Nature of Enterprise' in *The Cambridge Economic History of Europe*, V *The Economic Organization of Early Modern Europe* (Cambridge, 1977), pp. 392–461. In the same volume, H. Kellenbenz, 'The Organization of Industrial Production', pp. 462–548. A brief summary of the English case can be found in D. C. Coleman, *Industry in Tudor and Stuart England* (London, 1975).

producers in the form of advances, either of money or of raw materials, which the craftsmen had to repay with their labour. But neither should it be forgotten that the commercial systems of the time also made very intensive use of credit, from the moment when merchants accepted payment for the products they sold in the form of 'obligations', which were nothing more than acknowledgements of debt and promises to repay at a certain date and on certain conditions.[19] It was precisely this combination of credit to the consumer and credit to the producer that had made possible the significant growth of Cordoba's textile industry in the sixteenth century. It seems not to have been possible to keep this going in the conditions of the seventeenth century. Moreover, it is the crisis of the credit system that, in my opinion, goes a long way to explain the disengagement of the merchants and with it the decline of the industrial sector.

In fact the Cordoba area experienced numerous crises of agricultural production in the second half of the seventeenth century. An accumulation of bad harvests impoverished the population and restricted their capacity as consumers. In this sense it is symptomatic that the town council of Priego, in 1686, explained the decline of its taffeta 'manufactories' by claiming that 'the consumption of silk fabrics has fallen because the purchasers, driven by want, make do only with what they absolutely need, and even the most spendthrift avoid extras'. Nor is this the only document that makes the same point. At the same time, Castro del Río referred to 'low population and widespread poverty' to explain the difficulties of its textile industry. Undoubtedly, in this context of general impoverishment and the many problems that made business profits so chancy, credit had lost much of its attraction. Merchants thus had ready pretexts to justify their withdrawal from industrial activity or the reduction of their involvement with industry, as it suited them. The marketing of new-style fabrics from abroad, which were also cheaper than those they themselves could have made, presented them with unbeatable opportunities of making a profit without committing their capital to the production cycle. However, the under-capitalization of the textile sector resulting from this attitude created extremely unfavourable conditions for the backers of the new manufactories,

---

[19] For the role of bonds in the commercial systems of the sixteenth century, see R. Gascon, *Grand commerce et vie urbaine au XVIe siècle. Lyon et ses marchands*

in whose opinion only a rapid turnover or the granting of credits would permit the reactivation of the textile industry. The town council of Priego was quite explicit in this respect when it pointed out in 1686 that the new manufactories of plushes, serges and brocades could only successfully establish themselves and expand, 'if these fabrics are sold as quickly as possible and with credits to ease the cost'.[20]

But these problems were even more complex if it is borne in mind that the seventeenth century introduced further disruptive elements into economic life: monetary chaos, the massive minting of copper coinage, and the crazy dance of devaluations and revaluations which took place until 1686. The effects of all this are well-enough known: credit was weakened, trade faced a mountain of obstacles, the investment of capital fell away, and the circulation of good money became scarce. This situation was seen in Cordoba from different angles. For one gentleman of the city council the shortage of coin in the city was not so much the consequence of the monetary manipulations, as of the increased export of silver abroad to pay for the import of wheat and textiles. True or not, it was said in the city council that 'in the past the exchange of *reales de a ocho*, the commonest silver coin, for copper was a profitable business and great fortunes were made, but now a *real de a ocho* is something special ... from which it is clear that silver only lasts the year it enters, and that very little of what comes from the Indies remains'.[21]

The city's merchants saw the problem from a different angle. A document they were responsible for at the start of the eighteenth century was highly critical of the House of Austria's monetary policy for having severely damaged the textile industry. What is curious is that they should have referred to the devaluation decreed in 1680, the stabilising effects of which on the country's economy were felt very quickly. In the opinion of the merchants, however, the measure had not only caused a general impoverishment, but it had also meant 'the beginning of the decline of the factories, *the financing of them being impossible*, bringing to one and all the

(Paris, 1971), pp. 273ff. For the situation in Cordoba at the same time, Fortea Pérez, *Córdoba en el siglo XVI*, pp. 407–11.

[20] All the documentary references in the text are in AM Cor. Sección VI, serie 7, leg. 18, doc. 33.

[21] AM Cor. AC, session of 4 Mar. 1687.

poverty in which they may now be found'.[22] This text dates from 1715. It does not seem, therefore, that the monetary stability that began to be perceptible from 1680–6 had any appreciable effect on the future of the industry. By now too much ground had been lost to its competitors for an improvement on one front alone to be enough to revive it.

Such were the problems that faced the economy of Cordoba at the turn of the seventeenth century. Contemporaries sought to overcome these problems by applying a varied programme of reforms, which will now be examined.

As far as agriculture was concerned there was little that was new. It is surprising that, given the very serious situation of agriculture in Cordoba at the time, the only remedy thought of was a ban on importing foreign wheat and the repeal of all those laws that restricted the free circulation of foodstuffs: the grain price maxima and the banning of exports. As is well known, the provisioning policy of the municipalities had been based for a long time on the alternating or simultaneous application of each one of these. It was thought this would prevent the social tensions that could arise from the high cost of grain and market shortages in times of bad harvests. In Andalusia the dangers were exacerbated by the strong latifundist structure of landownership and the concentration of population in substantial urban centres or medium and large-sized villages. The memory of the hunger riots so widespread in Andalusia in the middle of the seventeenth century maintained these measures in full force. Bad harvests in the 1680s led authorities to have recourse to them again, particularly where cereal imports were involved. But from the perspective of the Cordoban peasantry this was at the very root of the agricultural crisis. Besides, it was, in their view, an absurd policy. The fear of hunger was an over-reaction in a countryside as fertile as that of Andalusia, where a good year could make up for four bad harvests. Imported wheat was of bad quality, less dense than their own, and so much more expensive that the payment for the massive purchases made in previous years would have emptied Andalusia of cash. There was also the fact that the grain had to be transported from distant countries and often arrived in bad

---

[22] AM Cor. Sección VI, serie 7, leg. 17, doc. 4.

condition, causing sickness.[23] But also, and this is the essential point, the importation of cereals ruined the peasant because his earnings were related to the variability of the harvests. The high prices of the bad years made up for losses in periods of plentiful harvests. Strictly speaking, the report complained, 'the peasant, whether the harvest is poor or good, always loses if his income is calculated at harvest prices; however, if he can hold the grain until a better time, he can not only recover any loss, but, if it is not too great, even make something on it'.[24] The profits to be made out of grain speculation, which the document exposes as common practice, were thus openly recognised. There can be no doubt that importing wheat in these conditions conflicted with the interests of the farmers because it evened out the prices. This is how the petition justified asking for the import of cereals to cease and for the price maxima and the ban on exports to be abolished. 'The wheat trade must be free', the document concluded, 'Necessity will bring wheat from Tierra de Campos to Seville, and take our products there. The inns and carters and other trades will be preserved, silver will stay in Spain, and simply by the movement from one place to another, without fixing prices, prices for wheat and bread will fall, not because of a law, but because everyone will want to sell.'

There is no need to stress the fact that the petitions in the memorandum quoted above represent the interests of the big land-owners, accumulators of rents in kind. Nor is it surprising that these points of view should have been listened to by the *veinticuatros* and *jurados* who comprised the city council. But their role as city fathers, charged with the maintenance of public order, made them moderate the radical nature of the proposal, in view of existing conditions, and revitalise the bodies which had once been responsible for palliating the effects of crisis. In this way, in 1687, much was made of a project, apparently on the cards for some time, to establish a public granary (*pósito*) in the city. The measure could be extended to all the towns of the district. This is interesting because, along with other things, it gives an idea of how big a drop there had been in the conditions of life in the city during the seventeenth century, since in

[23] Imported wheat was even blamed for spreading the plague, see AC session of 18 Feb. 1687, intervention of Don Antonio de los Ríos y Argote, vizconde de Miranda.
[24] AM Cor. Sección VI, serie 7, leg. 18, doc. 33.

the sixteenth century the whole of municipal provisioning policy had centred on the operations of the public granary.[25]

Neither the memorandum of the farmers nor the discussions on the subject held in the meetings of the city council in 1686 and 1687 contain any other measure to indicate a desire on the part of the landowners or the public authorities to improve the conditions of agricultural production or to lighten the burdens that weighed upon the peasantry. The documents we have reveal an immobile agrarian structure. If it was obvious to everybody in Cordoba that a prosperous agriculture was an indispensable condition for any subsequent take-off of the economy in general and of the textile industry in particular, nothing was done to channel or direct the process. In short, the welfare of the countryside was still dependent on the fluctuations of the harvests, or on the action of outside influences.[26]

The attitude of the authorities and of minority sectors of Cordoban society towards the programme of industrial revitalisation was much more mixed and infinitely more selfish.[27] Certainly many hopes were vested in it. It was known that an important textile industry had existed in Cordoba in the past, and there was no fundamental reason why it should not be able to recover its former glory, given the belief that the conditions that had made that possible still existed. Thus the abundance of wool and dye-stuffs in the area was extolled, as was the capacity of its inhabitants to work

[25] By about 1680, neither the customs house for silk nor the wool washing places, which had seen so much activity in the sixteenth century, were functioning. I do not know when the city's public granary stopped functioning. In 1592 the council had decided to create a new granary free of charges, due to the heavy debts of the one that had been operating previously. The then bishop of Malaga, who was a Cordoban, gave it alms of 1,000 ducats, AC session of 10 Jan. 1594.

[26] Nor did Andalusian agriculture experience important transformations in landownership in the eighteenth century. The *latifundio* system was consolidated, see R. Herr, *The Eighteenth Century Revolution in Spain* (Princeton, NJ, 1958), ch. 4.

[27] The attempts at reactivation would, it was hoped, be extended to other Cordoban crafts. In 1686 the count of Gavia also asked for tax exemptions for 'trades now completely extinct, like embossers, counterpane makers, handkerchief weavers who have totally stopped'. AC 27 Nov. 1686. All these industries had been very active in the sixteenth century, especially that of the embossers. Their reputation was such that the Cortes of Castile had to prohibit leather embossed elsewhere being sold as if it had been embossed in Cordoba, *Actas de las Cortes de Castilla*, IV, 479 (1573). For all this see Fortea Pérez, *Córdoba en el siglo XVI*, pp. 223–52. The Strapmakers' Guild, also important in the sixteenth century, took steps in the eighteenth century to obtain privileges to help it out of its prostration, AM Cor. Sección VI, serie 7, leg. 17, doc. 4. It was also thought that the relaunching of the textile industry would benefit other craftsmen like carpenters and blacksmiths.

with wool and silk. It was said, with a certain exaggeration, belied by other contemporary documents, that if Cordoban manufactures were different from the foreign ones, that was not due to ignorance, but to a strict observance of the regulations. But what was valued above all was the employment potential of the textile industry which, so the Cordoba silk masters insisted, was greater even than that of agriculture. The relaunching of the textile industry would, therefore, enable many of the problems that affected Cordoban society to be eradicated, the most pressing of which arose from mendicancy and unemployment. But it would also be possible to revive trade and increase the value of royal taxes. It was even taken for granted that an indirect consequence would be the moderation of agricultural wages, since the day labourers' wives would be able to supplement the family income by spinning, and that would stabilise the agricultural workers' wages.[28] It was believed, in short, that determined action would permit the achievement of the desired objectives by following a course of action suggested by earlier reflections on the causes of the decline.

It fell to the *corregidor* of Cordoba, Don Francisco Ronquillo Briceño, to take the initiative in the programme of reforms, a programme for which he was able to obtain the collaboration of certain sectors of the Cordoban merchant classes. A French master craftsman, resident in the city, one Esteban Cortado, also played a very active part in this process. The main obstacle to be removed was the invasion of foreign cloths and the lack of raw materials. It was soon realised that the only effective way of counteracting the importation of foreign cloth was to imitate it. However, bearing in mind that deep down the technical inferiority of the Cordoba drapery was recognised, it was first necessary to attract foreign craftsmen who would disseminate the secrets of the 'new drapery' throughout the city. But it was also necessary to provide the Cordoba workshops with adequate technology, including the presses that gave the imported cloths their attractive appearance. In addition, it was essential to ensure the supply of raw materials and avoid the manufacture of cloths and silks being faced with the problems of financing that had so impaired it. The programme of reforms was, indeed, extensive, and it is true to say that an attempt was made to operate on all fronts.

[28] See the 'Representación y manifiesto' of the Silk Guild of 1715.

Indeed, a document of 1696 confirms that during the previous ten years no fewer than twenty-two foreign masters, from France, Flanders and England, had arrived in Cordoba and taught their trades in the city and its surroundings. Esteban Cortado calculated that over 2,000 people in Cordoba and Andújar had learned how to spin wool at his expense. Two city merchants undertook to maintain stocks of wool and silk, for which they made a small charge, to guarantee work for the workshops. A third merchant opened a place for washing wool on the outskirts of Cordoba where, according to his own statement, up to 400 people came to work.[29] The city promoted such initiatives in very different fields with some vigour. They gave money from public funds to the foreign masters who engaged to teach the new techniques to apprentices. Timber was distributed among the manufacturers for building looms. The weavers were helped financially with the making of heddles, cards and the other tools of their trade. Funds were provided for the construction in Cordoba of the presses necessary for the finishing of the fabrics. The city also undertook to place apprentices with masters who were given public money to help with the cost of the manufacture of the new cloths. Lastly, the city provided premises where women skilled in lace-making and needlepoint could teach the poor girls of the city, defraying in part the costs of the school.[30] At the same time they drew up a multitude of protectionist measures and privileges for the manufacturers which were sent up to the Junta de Comercio for its approval. They asked for exemption from the sales tax on first sales, or exemption from municipal and general taxes for a certain period. They pressed insistently for a ban on the export of silks to Valencia and Murcia, or at least preference for purchases by native merchants, and the recognition of their option to buy first at the going rate, as the laws of the kingdom allowed. They wanted the Indies market reserved for native manufacturers, to block foreign penetration.

[29] AM Cor. Sección VI, serie 7, leg. 78, doc. 1. This is a report sent to the city council by Esteban Cortado in 1696 about the state of his workshops. Cortado was one of the manufacturers who brought foreign silkmasters to Cordoba. Despite their varied origins, the majority must have been French or Flemish, as certain witnesses state in this document of 1696. Four other merchants also attracted foreign silkmasters to the city, Eulogio de Valenzuela, Juan de Padilla, Bernardo de Pineda and Pedro Marín, AM Cor. Sección VI, serie 7, leg. 18, doc. 3.

[30] AM Cor. Sección VI, serie 7, leg. 18, doc. 33, various inquiries before the *corregidor* between 1686 and 1688.

But at the start of the eighteenth century the city's craft elements pressed for more radical protection. No kind of silk, either spun or woven, from anywhere else should be allowed into Cordoba, even if it was not being made there. The export of raw silk should also be banned, and all that was produced in Cordoba and its province should be used internally in the weaving of cloths. These petitions appealed to similar privileges which the Crown had previously granted to other cities, such as Valencia, Granada and Toledo, although there was much discussion among the artisans and merchants of Cordoba about whether these privileges were or were not actually applied by their beneficiaries. What is more, they also asked that

nobody could be a silk merchant who did not have the looms corresponding to his resources and to the size of his shop, and that nobody could sell any kind of silk fabrics who was not also a manufacturer or who did not put out silk for manufacture, because manufacturers are discouraged seeing that the only outlets are for fabrics from outside.[31]

What they wanted, under the aegis of the programmes of reactivation, was a strengthening of the Guild, and that would undoubtedly have provoked the suspicions of the city's mercantile circles.

What were the results of all this effort? For some time it looked as if the longed-for recovery was possible. Indeed, in 1687 everything was got ready for the opening of five girls' schools where they could learn lace-making and needle-point. The same year 14 city merchants undertook to keep 68 looms running for the manufacture of the new cloths and silks, which they would increase in the future to a total of over 100, once the initial operation was established.[32] A year later note was taken of the existence in the city of 159 silk looms for the new fabrics. Finally, a register dated 1690, but which we know about from a later document, listed up to 330 looms for all types of silk, both old and new, as well as 50 spinners, and 8 dye shops. In all,

---

[31] See the 'Representación y manifiesto' of the Silk Guild.

[32] Four city merchants undertook to install at once up to forty looms for silver cloth, Mallorca samite, mohair, Geneva satin, thick taffetas, plush Rome serges, Italian braids, tussores, silk flannel and silk and worsted flannel, and grounds, all involving the Silk Guild. In the woollen sector, a further ten merchants installed twenty-eight looms for English flannel, French estamins, druggets, Rome serges, Bruges serges, scarlets and burlap, AM Cor. Sección VI, serie 7, leg. 18, doc. 33.

they provided work for 954 people with their families, and over 28,000 women (obviously an exaggeration) were involved in the weaving of coloured ribbons. Comparing these statistics with those provided by Antonio de Mesa in 1686, one would have to conclude that remarkable progress had been made. It was not, however, lasting.[33]

The greatest failures occurred in the woollen sector. In fact the makers of woollens faced serious problems from the start. Despite the fact that the experts' analyses of the new Cordoba fabrics were almost invariably favourable and that the fabrics were said to have been well accepted by the consumers, the truth is that technically their quality hardly matched those they were imitating. The colours were not as vivid as the foreign cloths. The press used in the city was of poor quality and the fabrics came out defective. There were not enough foreign masters and even they, out of either ignorance or malice, sometimes ruined the fabrics on which they were working. The women who prepared the worsted yarns were unreliable, because during the important moments of the agricultural calendar they abandoned the work they had contracted. But, above all, the collaboration of the bulk of the Cordoba merchants was lacking. They refused to buy the cloths their colleagues were making, alleging their poverty, amongst other pretexts. What was worse was that they discredited the new manufactures and discouraged those who had embarked on their production by making it seem a very risky venture.[34]

It is not surprising that in these conditions a majority of the manufacturers should have asked the *corregidor* in 1688 to absolve them from their commitments. The good harvest that year saved the situation at the last moment, but only for a short time. In effect, in 1692 only Don Rodrigo Muñoz de Velasco and the Frenchman Esteban Cortado were still persevering with the enterprise, having some twelve worsted looms still in operation. Esteban Cortado was still fighting for his workshops between 1705 and 1715, but he ended up ruined. Around 1727 another manufacturer, Don Francisco de

---

[33] The 1690 Register is included in the 'Representación y manifiesto' of the Silk Guild. On 23 Dec. 1692 there was a count made of the looms for new fabrics that had been in operation during that year and the previous one. In 1691 the total was 44, and in 1692, 38. As can be seen, there had been a considerable drop from the 159 new looms in the 1688 Register, Sección VI, serie 7, leg. 18, docs. 33 and 39.

[34] AM Cor. Sección VI, serie 7, leg. 18, doc. 33.

Reina, took over the baton. We find him at this time seeking privileges and exemptions to protect his flannel and camlet manufactures, all apparently to no avail. A register of 1776 listed only eight masters of the wool guild existent in Cordoba, and they basically produced thick *paños catorcenos* and *dieciochenos*, serges, worsteds, flannels, baize and swanskin, almost all of them coarse cloths in traditional style.[35]

The situation of the silk industry was more uneven, but no less negative overall. The evidence of the various registers of looms drawn up from the end of the seventeenth century shows that the industry experienced considerable fluctuations within a generally declining trend. The 330 looms in 1690 had been reduced to 86 in 1707, and in 1714 there were about 100. But after 1714 there seems to have been a considerable upsurge in the activity of the Cordoba weavers, given that in 1730 mention is made of 307 looms, 20 or 24 spinners and 10 or so dye shops. By 1743, however, there were only 144 looms functioning, 6 spinners and 4 or 5 dye shops. The register of 1756 puts the number of looms up to 168, but twenty years later there were only 95.[36]

Even more than the number of looms themselves, what is interesting is their distribution. Is it possible to detect any change in the structure of the Cordoba silk industry? There were certainly very few novelties with regard to its most expensive products, what was then regarded as the finest work of the silk-makers art (*Arte Mayor*

---

[35] AM Cor. Sección VI, serie 7, leg. 18, doc. 39 (1692) and leg. 17, docs 1, 2 and 4 (1707, 1715, 1727). The 1776 Register in the same section and series, leg. 19, doc. 64. Most of the foreign silkmasters who arrived in Cordoba had left the city by 1696. In that year only three remained, according to one of them. In justification it was said that many Cordoba people had learnt their trade from them, but it can also be taken as an indication that the new cloth works had not managed to consolidate themselves in the city, Sección VI, serie 7, leg. 17, doc. 1.

[36] AM Cor. Sección VI, serie 7, leg. 17, doc. 2 (1707 Register), leg. 18, doc. 44 (1714 Register), doc. 55 (1730 and 1743 Registers), leg. 19, doc. 62 (1756 Register) and doc. 64 (1776 Register). For the 1690 Register, see note 33. The 307 looms noted in 1730 are doubtful. Statistics are included in the 1743 Register. On the other hand a document of 1728 talks of the 'tan deteriorado' state of the silk industry. As proof it is adduced that 'there are more workers than the merchants have cloths, so that the merchant picks the ones with the best reputation, and the others get work as bricklayers and other jobs since they are not able to work at their own trade'. It is possible, therefore, that some of the 307 looms of 1730 were not in operation at the time. According to the document of 1743 the prostration of the silk industry was evident thirteen years earlier and it had continued until then, see the document of 1728 in Sección VI, serie 7, leg. 18.

de la Seda). Indeed, throughout the period under consideration, the predominance of the production of taffetas, shawls and plushes is absolute and, in percentage terms, increasing. At the end of the seventeenth century, 70 per cent of all the looms were producing such fabrics, and the proportion grew to 90 per cent in the second half of the eighteenth century. It was, however, a production in frank decline. In fact, the most important changes in the Cordoba silk industry at this time originated not in the manufacture of fine silks, but on the margins of the industry. Already in 1690 Cordoba and the other towns of its kingdom had secured a royal privilege to breed the so-called 'heavy silk' *(seda de peso)* within their boundaries. This was a low-quality silk whose use had been prohibited, for that very reason, in the making of the new fabrics by the ordinances of 1684. This was the only silk that had always been produced locally and it had been kept for low-cost manufactures. We also know that around 1710 the Cordoba weavers were complaining that almost the only silk that reached Cordoba from Valencia and Murcia was *capillejos* for sewing-thread, which was also low grade. It was thus the nature of the raw materials available in Cordoba at this time that forced the local industry to move away from the opulent velvets, satins and damasks, and even from the more modest taffetas and shawls, towards the production of sewing silk, ribbons and a very varied range of different coloured braids. In fact the 1776 register, to which reference has already been made, reveals the existence in the city of 42 masters of *capillejos*, and 621 small looms for ribbons, 13 for braids, and 166 looms for passementerie, on which trimmed braids, shaded plush silk, etc, were worked. This was the only branch of the silk industry that was able to keep going, and even expand during the eighteenth century. Indeed, its predominance was already assured in the early years of the century, at least, according to a memorandum of the silk merchants of 1715, which claimed that 'a distinction should be made between the manufactures of the city, which are not composed solely of fabrics. *They are the lesser part.* It is the output of the *capillejeros*, who make fine, ordinary and heavy silk thread for sewing, that provides the main activity and employment for the workshops of this city.'[37]

Thus the long process of the decay of the Cordoban silk industry

---

[37] AM Cor. Sección VI, serie 7, leg. 17, doc. 4. A copy of the privilege of 1690 in De la Torre and Rey Díaz, *Arte de la Seda.*

from the end of the sixteenth century reached its lowest point. It is symptomatic that throughout the sixteenth century the term *Arte Mayor de la Seda* had been restricted to the masters of velvets, satins and damasks. It was they who effectively controlled the Guild, keeping the taffeta makers out of positions of power, because they considered them specialists in a minor branch of the art. However, between the end of the sixteenth and the middle of the seventeenth century, important changes took place in the orientation of the Cordoban silk industry. The production of taffeta now became predominant, and so the taffeta masters succeeded in getting offices as inspectors (*veedores*), at first quietly, but later only after a fierce struggle within the corporation, which came to a head in 1643 and 1644. A hundred years later what *Arte Mayor de la Seda* meant essentially was taffetas, plushes and shawls, with hardly a trace of velvets, satins and damasks.[38] The retreat of the manufactures that in the past had been the original nucleus of the Cordoba silk industry had therefore been profound, although Cordoba still produced a certain amount of these kinds of fabrics as late as 1690. New products, which it was hoped would compete with foreign goods, were also beginning to be made, silk *teletones*, Rome serges and silk serges, which are mentioned in the register for that year. Finally, efforts were made to introduce sheer silks and camlets, Geneva satins and Italian ribbons and braids. Some of the products which had been recently introduced were still being made in the city around 1714, if credit can be given to the register for that year (see Appendix). However, none of this was to survive in the eighteenth century. Of the fabrics then being made in Cordoba, the only really new ones were the plushes, and these had begun to be made even before the city decided on the renewal of the silk industry. The reality is that, just as in the woollen industry, the reform programme

[38] The 1776 Register, which only includes one loom for velvet, two for satin and none for damask, was compiled under the auspices of the Silk Guild. On the evolution of the Guild in the sixteenth and the first half of the seventeenth century, see my *Córdoba en el siglo XVI*, and De la Torre and Rey Díaz, *Arte de la Seda*. The latter provides statistics of the amounts of silk imported into Cordoba in the years 1700–29 and 1766–82. In 1700–29 the average amount imported was 19,687 lbs a year, and in 1766–82 27,333 lbs a year. Bearing in mind the decadence of the silk industry in Cordoba at this time, the increase could reflect the rise in the production of ribbons and braids. At the end of the sixteenth century 35,000 lbs of silk were distributed every year, according to the sales tax investigations of

for the silk industry, begun with such enthusiasm and energy at the end of the seventeenth century, ended up an almost total failure.

Cordoba's industry revealed an absolute incapacity to adapt itself to the demands of the market in the transition from the seventeenth to the eighteenth century. This failure is even more lamentable if it is remembered that conditions in the country were beginning a marked change for the better. Spain's demographic growth and economic progress in so many areas in the eighteenth century could well have acted as a stimulus for the renovation of technique and production that was the only guarantee of the future of the industry.[39] What is even more distressing is to find that documents of 1727 or 1743 still point to the persistence of the same factors that years before contemporaries had seen as explaining the decadence of the Cordoban textile industry in the second half of the seventeenth century: foreign competition, fiscal pressure, loss of markets, lack of raw materials and the lack of merchant involvement.[40]

1590–5, although it must be admitted that such a figure is perhaps rather low, Archivo General de Simancas, *Expedientes de Hacienda*, leg. 85.

[39] For the origins of the revival in Castile at the end of the seventeenth century, see A. Domínguez Ortiz, 'La crisis de Castilla en 1677–87', in his *Crisis y decadencia en la España de los Austrias* (Madrid, 1973), pp. 197–217; V. Vázquez de Prada, *Historia económica y social de España*, III, *Los siglos XVI y XVII* (Madrid, 1978), pp. 332ff; E. J. Hamilton, *War and Prices in Spain, 1651–1800* (Cambridge, MA, 1947). The most recent and innovative study of this subject is H. Kamen, *Spain in the Later Seventeenth Century, 1665–1700* (London, 1980), pp. 67ff.

[40] AM Cor. Sección VI, serie 7, leg. 18 (1728) and doc. 54 (1743). I have only scant information about the fiscal pressure on the textile industry in this period. The cloths of residents and outsiders paid 40,880 *reales* in sales tax and *cientos* (the *cientos* were four 1 per cent additions to the sales tax); and the clothiers, doublet makers, ragmen and weavers contributed 1,700 *reales* in the same period. The payments for cloths fell to 24,000 *reales* in 1683, and were fixed at 30,500 in 1685, whilst the payments of the others fluctuated between 1,700 and 1,650 *reales* in these two years. Finally, the cloths of residents and outsiders together paid 18,000 and 19,000 *reales* in 1692 and 1694, while the contribution of the clothiers et al. had risen to 2,200 *reales* in 1692. The document reveals nothing about the method of collection or the rate of the tax; nor does it distinguish between what residents and outsiders paid separately; nor does it throw light on whether these fluctuations reflected some kind of preferential fiscal treatment for the cloth dealers. As regards the Silk Guild, their contribution stayed at 40,475 *reales* from 1730 to 1733; it went up to 42,337 *reales* in 1734–42, and settled at 51,420 *reales* in 1743. The Guild felt that this fiscal pressure was excessive, bearing in mind the sector's decline, Sección VI, serie 7, leg. 18, doc. 41 (*paños*/drapery) and doc. 55 (*sedas*/silks). I have not found any evidence in the documents of what was paid for the cloth tax in the eighteenth century.

If then the analysis made around 1686 was correct and if the measures adopted were going in the right direction, what exactly went wrong? The answer is undoubtedly a complex one, requiring much more evidence than is available at the moment. Nonetheless, the sources we have do point to certain hypotheses and research possibilities, along the following lines.

The first problem worth examining is the financial profitability of the enterprises on which the reform programme was to be based. The woollen industry is the one that offers the most interest in this respect, as can be seen from an examination of the efforts of Esteban Cortado and, above all, Francisco de Reina. The former, at his peak, was running eight looms for the newly introduced fabrics, and he was thinking of increasing them to twelve, all of them in his Cordoba workshops. The case of the latter is more spectacular. In Francisco de Reina's 'factory', twenty-four looms were working, together with spinners, 'redinas', warping-frames, pinners, boilers for dyeing, presses and all the other impedimenta necessary for the treatment of the wool and the weaving and finishing of the fabrics until the moment of their sale. Despite its small scale it was a real factory. No Cordoba merchant in the sixteenth century had run so complete and wide-ranging a workshop. Yet it has to be asked whether any consideration was given to the exploitation of the rural workforce, which because of its low cost was being used so success-fully in the countries of northern Europe and to which the Cordoba merchants of the sixteenth century had also resorted? It is true that Esteban Cortado had worsted spun at Andújar and that Francisco de Reina had wool sent to be spun at Pozoblanco and Los Alcarace-jos, where he also had some cloths woven for him. However, the bulk of the production of both men in all its phases was done in their urban premises. They were, in any case, exceptional. A document of Torrecampo, dated 1721, praising the quality of their manufactures, claimed that 'when these cloths were sold to the merchants of the city of Cordoba, they used to pay a better price for them than they paid for those of the other towns of this district of Los Pedroches'.[41] At that time the residents of Torrecampo had contracted to supply *paños veinticuatrenos* to the 'royal troops of His Majesty'. The production was calculated as 144 pieces of cloth per year that, significantly, was not being sent to Cordoba, but to the town of

---

[41] AM Cor. Sección VI, serie 7, leg. 17, doc. 5.

Pedro Abad for its final fulling. It is uncertain how far this document is applicable to the rest of the region. In any event, the documents do not give a clear indication as to whether any thought was given to the restoration of the close links which had previously existed between the looms of Los Pedroches and the fulling mills, carders and dye-shops of Cordoba. All the programmes of industrial recovery for which we have information were based essentially on the city, and this is a fact which in my view was to have important consequences for the future of Cordoba's cloth industry.

In effect, of all the different ways of organising the production process, what was chosen was the most expensive and the least profitable. It is very possible that in some cases this choice was made inevitable by special circumstances, as we shall see. What is certain, however, is that Francisco de Reina's 'factory' tied up the not inconsiderable amount of over 170,000 *reales de vellón* in wool, cloths, equipment and plant, such as the fulling mill with two troughs built beside the river. A business of this kind needed a sound financial structure to ensure its future, either in the form of adequate reserves of cash, or a flexible credit backing, or government subsidies. Protectionism, by means of privileges and tax exemptions, was another possibility. It was this last option that was followed, but it was not to be enough. Esteban Cortado ended up ruined. The merchants with whom he had formed the company left him in the lurch at the first sign of trouble. Nor was Francisco de Reina granted the advantages he had asked for.[42] Consequently, although there were notable national and international precedents for the setting-up of large-scale textile concerns (many of which also had the same problems), the decline of the Cordoba woollen industry was almost certainly due to the under-use of the rural workforce.

[42] The only ones granted were those then enjoyed by the burlap makers of Cuenca, which in any case are not specified. They requested exemption from royal and municipal taxes on their wool purchases for twenty years, that they be given the right of *tanteo*, and that they should have preference over foreign merchants when buying, exemption from tolls, bridge tolls and customs for twenty years, exemption from taxes for the same period for the introduction into Cordoba of 30 *arrobas* of oil, 10 of soap and 10 of vinegar for each loom maintained in their workshops, freedom from sales taxes on their first sales, monopoly of the production of the drapery at present in their factories. Apart from the burlaps, no privilege was obtained for any other fabrics that they might make, AM Cor. Sección VI, serie 7, leg. 18, doc. 53.

Production in the city was to end up reduced to the making of coarse cloth and flannel.[43] The question is, how was it possible to fail at something that had been done successfully in the sixteenth century? The root of the problem probably lies in the fact that whereas throughout the sixteenth century a type of textile production that had been widespread in the area for a long time, particularly in the Valle de los Pedroches, was expanded and perfected, there was now an attempt made to replace it with something completely new, the technical aspects of which were unknown. What is more, such attempts were made in very disadvantageous circumstances for the Cordoba manufacturers, not only because of the more advanced level of development reached by the new drapery in countries like England, Holland and certain parts of France, but also for other, technical reasons. This is especially true in the case of fabrics like the *bayetas de Alconcheste* (Colchester baize), which had so much success in the Cordoba market and which some of the Cordoba manufacturers tried to imitate. These baizes were made with long-fibred English wool of not very good quality. The wool available in the Cordoba area, especially in Los Pedroches, was a fine wool, used traditionally in the choicest fabrics. Using it to imitate these kinds of flannel was not only unsatisfactory, it could also hardly be profitable. On the other hand, the problems of training and product control inherent in employing a rural workforce to make a kind of cloth whose production techniques were unknown, probably made it necessary to concentrate the production process in the city in enterprises close to the factory model, and that in turn compromised their profitability even more.

However, there were also other foreign fabrics of better quality, made, moreover, with Spanish wool, coming into the Cordoba market. It might be imagined, therefore, that their imitation in Cordoba would have been more feasible. Such was the case with the 'stammels' or 'scarlets', which had begun to be made very successfully in Wiltshire and Gloucestershire at the beginning of the

---

[43] AM Cor. Sección VI, serie 7, leg. 17 (no doc. number) and leg. 19, doc. 64. The most recent study of the achievements and problems of the textile industry in Spain in the eighteenth century is A. González Enciso, *Estado e industria en el siglo XVIII: La Fábrica de Guadalajara* (Madrid, 1980); see also his 'Inversión pública e industria textil en el siglo XVIII. La real fábrica de Guadalajara. Notas para su estudio', *Moneda y Crédito* 133 (1975), 41–64.

seventeenth century. These fabrics, being made entirely of wool, were closer to the traditional manufactures, but they were not for that reason less of a novelty. Probably the *estameñas de Inglaterra* (English serges) and the *escarlatines* (scarlets), which they tried to produce in the city at the end of the seventeenth century, were thought to be Cordoban replicas of English models. But here again there was not a glimmer of success. The fundamental reason for the failure was the persistent problem of financing and, above all, the inability to copy the techniques of production skilfully enough. Something said in Cordoba in 1688, about some imitations of French and English serges made in the city looking more like the cloths of Cobos, Toledo and Alcudia, is in this context very revealing.[44]

A second question of interest is the nature of the barriers placed by the existing guild structures in the way of the reform programme. This problem can be examined with respect to the silk crafts. During the course of the second half of the seventeenth century the sector's ordinances had been falling into oblivion in parallel with the worsening crisis of the industry. According to 'The Petition and Manifesto of the Silk Guild' in 1710, every artisan chose his own rules. What is more, believing that foreign competition was exclusively a problem of cost, many masters felt that the only effective way to counteract it was to adulterate their fabrics, making them up short of what the regulations prescribed, 'so as to match the lower

---

[44] With regard to the Colchester baize, it was said in Cordoba around 1688 that their manufacturers, amongst whom were mentioned Bernardo de Pineda and Rodrigo Muñoz de Velasco, had had to enquire 'in the ports and elsewhere about the conditions that such flannels need' and that all they ended up with were losses. It was necessary to bring in master craftsmen, but this was not a success either (see note 35). On these points see the declarations of Juan de Figueroa, 28 Feb. 1688, AM Cor. Sección VI, serie 7, leg. 18, doc. 33. With regard to the characteristics of these flannels, the stammels and the scarlets and of the textile industry in general in England in this period, an excellent synthesis is C. Wilson, *England's Apprenticeship, 1603–1763* (London, 1965), pp. 66ff. On the decisive changes which the English wool and textile market experienced in the first half of the seventeenth century, see also B. E. Supple, *Commercial Crisis and Change in England, 1600–1642* (London, 1959), and D. C. Coleman, 'An innovation and its diffusion: the New Draperies', *Economic History Review*, 2nd series, 22 (1969), 417–29. The repercussions that this reorganisation of the European textile industry in the seventeenth century had on the Castilian wool trade have been studied by L. M. Bilbao Bilbao and E. Fernández de Pinedo, in the essay printed in the present volume. The similarities of Cordoba's imitation foreign serges to those of Cobos,

prices of the foreigners'.[45] It was only logical that the prestige of the Cordoban fabrics should have suffered badly in consequence. On the one hand, they showed themselves incapable of imitating the foreign fabrics, and on the other they did not comply with their own ordinances. Hence when the reactivation programme was begun, craftsmen and authorities were at one on the need to adhere to the regulations.[46] Specifically, it was the general ordinances of 1684 which they wanted strictly observed. But the craftsmen also recognised the opportunity they were presented with of securing for themselves a privileged position in the control of the process of production. This is why in 1710 they drew up petitions for the prohibition of the importing of any kind of silk fabric and the exporting of raw silk, in order that all the silk produced locally would have to be used in manufacturing, and for the reunion of the production and marketing functions, which until then had been separate. But the Silk Guild wanted something more – the creation of a local Trade Council consisting of five representatives of the city council and five of the manufacturers, without a mention of the merchants.[47] The other aim was to get the merchants to go back to the old way of marketing silks, so that the artisans would be guaranteed employment. This was an implicit recognition that the role of the merchant was indispensable; his collaboration might be required, but his activities had to be controlled. Conflict between the two was thus inevitable. Already in 1715 the merchants, in defence of their freedom of action, opposed the ban on imported silk fabrics, or, if the craftsmen's petition were to be heeded, demanded the narrowest interpretation of it, forbidding only those fabrics which were also produced in the city. In view of market movements, they also wanted the modification of some obsolete regulations governing the making of fabrics for which there was no longer any demand.[48] However, they

---

Toledo and Alcudia were pointed out by Rafael de Padilla and Esteban Cortado, 15 Apr. 1688, in the document cited earlier in this note.

45 AM Cor. Sección VI, serie 7, leg. 17, doc. 3.

46 In 1688 and 1714 inspections were carried out on the weavers to check if the fabrics were being worked in accordance with the ordinance, and in some cases infractions were uncovered and penalised. The artisans wanted these inspections to be regular, AM Cor. Sección VI, serie 7, leg. 17, doc. 7 and leg. 18, doc. 44.

47 See the 'Representación y manifiesto' of the Silk Guild of 1710.

48 AM Cor. Sección VI, serie 7, leg. 17, doc. 4. Earlier, in 1713, the merchants had offered 'the agreement in accordance with the ordinance for newly invented fabrics'. At that time the following were being woven in accordance with the

came up against the rigid attitude of the Guild to the application of the regulations. In the Guild's view anything not in conformity with the ordinances was fraudulent, an assessment which embraced a wide range of products, including the taffetas and ribbons of Ecija, Jaén and Priego which, nonetheless, were much in demand in the area. The fact that these were not being made in accordance with the regulations was enough reason for the craftsmen to want them not to be made in Cordoba. They concluded their argument by insisting that their opposition was not designed to conceal their ignorance of the techniques required to make this type of fabric; on the contrary, Cordoba's products were superior to those of the towns mentioned and its operatives well able to make any article, however select. Lastly, if the Cordoba merchants wanted outside manufacturers allowed into the city, it was only because they sought to cheat the consumer and make big profits by selling as a quality product something that was intrinsically inferior. In 1721 there were renewed conflicts over the double taffetas of Ecija, single flannels, crimson and red plushes, mixed cotton and silk handkerchiefs, and silk ribbons. These were all variants of fabrics made in Cordoba but included some changes in the weight of the fabric, in the dyes used, or in the mix of the different fibres, things not foreseen in the existing regulations. Despite this, their manufacture had been introduced in various places with obvious success. The double taffetas of Ecija, for example, were much in demand in Portugal and other kingdoms according to the merchants. The inspectors of the *Arte de la Seda* had nonetheless condemned them as false and prohibited their production and sale in the city, despite the merchants' insistence that they were dealing with 'variants and new types not covered by the general regulations'. Besides, prohibiting their manufacture in Cordoba harmed everybody, because the city would be deprived

---

regulations of 1684: velvets embroidered with satin background, damasks, brocades, grograins and camelhair, silk serges, medium-thick taffetas called *catalufas*, Seville cloaks, handkerchiefs and ribbons. The following had either never been worked, or the production of them had stopped: terry velvets, plushes, satins embroidered with silk twist, striped satins, thick taffetas and mourning cloaks. Finally, the merchants asked for modification of the regulations dealing with plain plushes (so that they could be worked with less warp than was laid down) and plain satins (the same). Authorisation was also requested to make in Cordoba the thick taffetas of Ecija, the plain taffetas of Priego and the plain flannels, which were very much in demand. All these products were banned by the inspectors of the Cordoba Silk Guild.

of a market that would simply move to places which exhibited a more flexible approach to the regulations.[49]

The inflexibility of the Cordoban crafts, therefore, created many more obstacles for the merchants than they were inclined to overcome. But neither were the craftsmen, locked into their old obsessions with the intrinsic value of the fabrics and quality understood merely as hard-wearingness, able to impose their own point of view. And so the penetration of cloths from outside went on and the silk craft continued on its downward path without any change in the craftsmen's subordinate position. The register of looms, master weavers and cloth owners drawn up in 1756 is explicit on this point. It named eighty-four masters who possessed 168 looms of different kinds. However, only eighteen of them wove cloths on them for themselves. The others worked for twenty-five other people whose profession is not specified, but who were, presumably, in most cases, merchants. In fact, only three of the names included in the list of masters are repeated in the list of cloth owners. Moreover, the average number of looms per master was two, but almost half of them had only one loom. Those who ordered the fabrics were normally involved with three or four masters at the same time, maintaining an average of five looms at a time. In short, the 1756 loom-register reveals that most of the craftsmen had very little productive capacity. That said, the cases of Francisco de la Cruz, Ignacio Romero and Francisca López must be mentioned; together, directly as owners, or indirectly by ordering cloths, they controlled the output of fifty-nine looms, more than a third of the total.[50]

A third aspect worthy of interest is the figure of the Cordoba merchant. Our sources do not show him to have been a man of wealth, rather the opposite. Already in 1686 the loss of ground in the Indies market was blamed on the inability of the city's

---

[49] AM Cor. Sección VI, serie 7, leg. 18, doc. 46. As can be seen, there are no signs in Cordoba, or only exceptionally, of the ability that some Barcelona textile workers showed of reviving the city's textile industry despite the obstacles of the guilds, see P. Molas Ribalta, *Los gremios barceloneses del siglo XVIII* (Madrid, 1970), pp. 198ff.

[50] Francisco de la Cruz had four looms of his own and he had put out cloths for weaving to six other masters, who owned sixteen looms. Ignacio Romero, with four looms of his own, also worked with three other masters, each of whom had a loom. Finally, Francisca López controlled twenty-two looms, eight of her own and fourteen belonging to ten masters to whom she put out cloths for weaving, AM Cor. Sección VI, serie 7, leg. 19, doc. 62.

merchants, because of their lack of means, to participate in a trade which was by then so totally disorganised that profits were not only uncertain, but also long delayed.[51] Again, around 1728, it was the poverty of the merchants that was held to explain the high level of unemployment among the city's craftsmen. However, although this is a factor to be taken into account, more so in the silk than in the woollen sector, its significance should not be exaggerated in explaining the ultimate failure of the Cordoba textile industry. Before the Industrial Revolution, rather than plenty of disposable capital, what an entrepreneur needed was the ability to adapt himself to shifts in the market and the dynamism and flexibility to reduce the costs of production. These were not qualities that, taken as a whole, the Cordoban merchant class of the time had. The rigid social, economic and institutional context in which they had to operate, together with their own mistakes in the planning of the enterprises they promoted, in the occasional cases when this happened, ended by aborting their initiatives.[52] Proof of the scant business capacity of the Cordoba merchants is the fact that they did not manage to regenerate the woollen industry, despite having almost complete freedom of action in that sector. This was not the case with the silk industry, where the guild system had kept itself

[51] The deputy *alguacil mayor* of Cordoba pointed out in 1687 that the reconstruction of the city's textile industry would be possible (among other reasons) only
if the voyages of the (Indies) fleet and galleons were uninterrupted and the foreign nations could not find other routes to export their cloths to the Indies. In that way cloths from Spain would find a better market, and if there were a voyage every year profits would be regular. But with delays of two or three years, they look for new business and abandon the Indies trade, since they have limited resources and one voyage cannot repay them the costs of such a long wait'. AC session of 4 Mar. 1687

[52] On the failure to take advantage of the opportunities opened up in Andalusia by the colonial trade during the eighteenth century in anticipation of a possible industrialisation of the region on the model of other countries, see the observations of A. García Baquero González, *Cádiz y el Atlántico (1717–1778)* (Seville, 1976), I, pp. 566–7. In his opinion, which I share, the failure is explained by the rigidity of the social context and economic conservatism. To get round the social prejudice towards the 'mechanic trades', the town council of Priego requested in 1686 that 'the lords of vassals, each one in their localities, in accordance with the kind of cloth that can be made there, introduce workshops at their own expense, which will make them useful and be an example for the nobles, acting as intermediaries, to begin in trade, which is a very suitable way for them to maintain and advance themselves', Sección VI, Serie 7, leg. 18, doc. 33. In 1682, as is well known, a pragmatic had been issued that made the status of nobility compatible with dedication to commerce and industry.

alive, despite the very low level of its activity in the second half of the seventeenth century.

At the same time, the failure of Cordoba's textile industry must be seen in the context of the changes that were taking place at the end of the seventeenth and the start of the eighteenth centuries in the industrial map of Spain as a whole. In the silk industry, the decline of Cordoba coincides with the remarkable expansion that was beginning in Valencia. Contemporaries sensed the consequences for Cordoba of this divergent evolution.[53]

However, all the factors of decadence that have been examined can be explained as operating in a climate pervaded by the rigidity of the social structure and by economic conservatism at every level. In contrast to what was happening at the same time in other parts of the country, the reform programme in Cordoba lacked the necessary social basis. Given these conditions, any protectionism or any measure to reactivate the economy from outside the social body would eventually be shown to be unviable. Thus, the Cordoba area, despite enjoying some of the conditions for the development of rural industry in the case of woollens, as well as a long manufacturing tradition in the case of silks, missed its last chance to share in a process that, from the second half of the eighteenth century, would radically transform the social and economic structure of Europe.[54]

---

[53] This is what is implied in the 'Representación y manifiesto' of the Silk Guild.

[54] On the role that the development of rural industry played in other countries in the encouragement of production for the market, the transformation of the economy and the countryside, and the modification of demographic structures, see De Vries, *Age of Crisis*. The same problem, on the eve of the Industrial Revolution, is examined in a special number of the *Revue du Nord, Aux origines de la Révolution Industrielle. Industrie rurale et fabriques*, 61: 240 (1979). There is an interesting review of the current state of the question and methodological suggestions in P. Deyon's introductory chapter to the above volume, 'L'Enjeu des discussions autour du concept de proto-industrialisation', pp. 9–15. The most systematic treatment of the subject is by P. Kriedtke, H. Medick and J. Schlumbohn, *Industrialisation before industrialisation* (Cambridge, 1981).

Appendix 7.1. Types of silk looms in use in Cordoba between 1690 and 1776

Type of loom	1690	1714	1756	1776
velvets	30			1
gold satins	10	1		
embroidered satins	23			
tram satins		1		
satins		13	5	2
damasks	6	1	10	
terry velvet	4			
gold and silver cloth		12		
tussores	7	1		
flannels	12	4		
Roman serges	6			
silk estamenes	4			
thick taffetas	74	5	55	17
medium-thick taffetas			1	
plain taffetas	16	2	1	2
cloaks	109	29	49	13
lamés		4		
mittens		2		
brocades		7		
handkerchiefs			1	
grisettes			7	3
mantillas				2
plushes	20	14	39	55
grounds	9			
unspecified		2		
Total	330	98	168	95

Note: The Register for 1730 gives the following distribution of looms: 54 plushes, 96 damasks and others, and 157 satin cloths. The Register for 1743 has 25 plushes, 16 'work clothes', and 103 satin cloths (flannels, taffetas, cloaks and handkerchiefs). There were 285 looms at a standstill.

8. Credit procedures for the collection of taxes in the cities of Castile during the sixteenth and seventeenth centuries: the case of Valladolid

FELIPE RUIZ MARTÍN

My purpose in this chapter is very simple; it is to try to clarify the procedures employed for the collection of taxes during the sixteenth and seventeenth centuries in the forty districts into which the eighteen provinces of the kingdom of Castile were divided, with emphasis on the cities. However, my aim may be considered over-ambitious, since I want to provide an explanation of something of vital importance in the history of Spain. In the interior of Spain, on the *meseta*, from the fifteenth century at least, there had been a marked predominance of large centres of population of all kinds and regardless of their economic and socio-professional structure. However, by the beginning of the seventeenth century, these centres of population were gradually diminishing in number and beginning almost to fall into decay. When in the eighteenth century a general revival took place, they proved unable to recover their old importance or to regain even a remotely similar share of the total population of the country to that which they had had in the previous two or three centuries. This assertion can easily be proven by comparing the population figures that were carefully compiled in 1591 with the number of inhabitants contained in the reliable census conducted by Floridablanca in 1787. In 1591 the centres of population with more than 2,500 families (*vecinos*), the equivalent of those with 10,000 inhabitants in 1787, were incomparably greater in number. Save for Madrid which, for reasons to do with politics and the Court, was a case apart, the economic role and the social structure of the towns and cities of the Duero and Tagus basins also declined. Economically, they ceased to be the driving force of productive activity in both urban and rural areas, although it was a service for which they had certainly charged a high price. Socially, a polari-sation between a small number of wealthy, both laity and clergy,

169

and a large number of poor replaced the diversity of intermediate social groups characteristic of the fifteenth and sixteenth centuries. This checked what was arguably a large-scale development of a middle class, and thus also had important attitudinal implications, as José Antonio Maravall has maintained and incontrovertibly documented. The bureaucratic negligence of the seventeenth century, contrasting with the bureaucratic diligence of the century before, does not allow a quick or complete analysis of this most important question, but the evidence we have is both clear and unequivocal. When the Bourbons were installed on the Spanish throne and sought to heal the wounds that troubled Old and New Castile, they came up against a lethargy in the towns and cities of those regions which left them unable to respond, even with the encouragement of government aid. They were held back, as we shall see, by restraints inherited from the past, and specifically from the seventeenth century. Some groups of people, though small in number, were able to take advantage of this situation, and in the eighteenth century, when the winds of change began to blow more favourably, they become proponents of an incipient bourgeoisie which made the most of the land sales resulting from the disentailments decreed in 1836 and 1855. In this way Old and New Castile entered the nineteenth century without having been able to overcome a structural defect which, it seems to me, was consolidated in the seventeenth century.

This course of development, which may be subject to some modification, is described clearly and in very similar terms, though with varying degrees of accuracy and competence, by the *corregidores*[1] in the reports they produced between 1784 and 1785 at the request of the ministers of Charles III. The most discerning and careful of those reports condemned the source of the corrosive evil that had led to such serious deterioration, namely the municipal debts of their own administrative capitals. Following the researches of Ramón Carande on the reign of Charles V, which have been continued along the lines set out by him into the eighteenth century, the extent of state indebtedness is well known. The consolidation of the debt in the form of *juros*[2] is also well known, as is the history of

---

[1] The *corregidores* were appointed by the Crown and held both judicial and governmental functions.

[2] The *juros* represented loans made to the Crown on which interest was paid.

those bonds until their long overdue abolition in the nineteenth century. However, little account has been taken to date of municipal indebtedness, the extent and incidence of which will, when analysed, come I suspect as a surprise. During the sixteenth century it was not necessary for the municipal authorities of the district capitals (*cabezas de partido*) to have recourse to credit in order to pay their taxes to the Treasury, since taxes were paid on a corporate basis by associations of the people who were liable for them, associations which were set up and institutionalised precisely for that purpose (the revival of the guilds was thus promoted in a way rather different from what is imagined). As a result, throughout the sixteenth century there was very little development of municipal indebtedness. In exceptional circumstances, in a year in which the harvest was poor and when, therefore, there was a shortage of cereals, the municipal council could take a loan on its assets in order to get resources to supply the bakeries or the *pósito*, the municipal granary.[3] The same would be done if shortages of wool or oil created problems for the crafts which worked with these materials, for example, or if the community as a whole bought assets of any kind, buildings, sites, land, offices, royal licences or grants of extra powers, and so on. In the sixteenth century, however, these loans were all quickly repaid; municipal indebtedness was low and the towns did not get enmeshed in its throes. This curse was to appear in the seventeenth century and was to strangle the towns and cities, so that in the eighteenth they were unable to breathe freely. It is worth taking the time, therefore, to get to the bottom of this change, the secret of which surely lies in the devices employed for the collection of taxes, particularly the heaviest of them, the *alcabalas* (or sales taxes) in the sixteenth century, and the *alcabalas* and *millones* after 1590.

In theory, the *alcabalas* comprised 10 per cent of all purchases and sales. In practice, however, only half, or one-third, or even one-fifth of this 10 per cent was collected, depending on the goods or property involved and the place and time of the transactions. This substantial reduction was the result of the system of *encabeza-mientos*, composition agreements between the Treasury and the

---

[3] The term *pósito* referred to both the municipal institution responsible for storage of grain for times of shortage, and the actual premises in which this grain was stored.

taxpayers for the payment of a fixed sum. These agreements, which were made via the Cortes[4] and were first successfully introduced sporadically at a local level, were extended between 1534 and 1536 to the eighteen provinces of Castile and to the forty sub-districts of those provinces (*partidos*). The disadvantage of these agreements for the fisc was that the basic assessment of trade in merchandise, animals, personal property and real estate was always on the low side. This meant that potential revenue was reduced from the start, and this problem would clearly be magnified when trade was growing, as it was then doing. Nevertheless, the advantage offered by these agreements, namely prior knowledge of the exact amount of revenue that would be received, was something both essential and for which there was no alternative. Tax revenue, which included one-fifth of all the treasures extracted from the mines of the American continent, was regarded by the rulers of the House of Austria as a means of meeting their 'ordinary' expenses; the small amount that was left did not come near to meeting their 'extra-ordinary' expenses, caused overwhelmingly by war. In order to meet these extraordinary expenses, recourse was had to advances from the bankers, effected by means of the famous *asientos* (loan con-tracts), for the repayment of which assignments were made against tax revenues, primarily, naturally enough, against those revenues whose amount could be known in advance. It is for this reason that the government never renounced the *encabezamiento* system for the *alcabalas*. Philip II's councillors of finance, with knowledge no doubt of the investigations carried out in 1553–4 (now in the library of the Escorial), were well aware that the fixed sum established between 1534 and 1536 in respect of the *alcabalas* and the *tercias*[5] (which were also always included in the *encabezamientos*) had become very much eroded. Although the *encabezamiento* of just over 333 million *maravedís*[6] was increased by 37 per cent in 1562/3, and was increased again in 1576 (but by too much it would seem, since in 1577 it had to be cut back again by 1 million ducats), it was never assumed that these sums approached even remotely the

---

[4] The Cortes were representative assemblies of the kingdoms, called by the Crown, for consultation on matters of government and, in particular, for the authorisation of taxes.

[5] A tax consisting of two-ninths of the ecclesiastical tithes payable on produce or income.

[6] The *maravedí* and the ducat were once Spanish coins.

nominal 10 per cent, either then, in the 1570s, or later in the 1580s and 1590s. It was in order to verify this assumption, which gave the lie to the complaints and laments of the proctors of the Cortes, that the remarkable fiscal inquests known as the *expedientes de hacienda* were compiled.[7] In 1561, in 1584, and again in 1596 it was demonstrated that if the full 10 per cent of the *alcabalas* was exacted, plus the *tercias*, a much larger sum would enter the coffers of the Treasury than the *encabezamiento* produced. Nonetheless, nothing was changed, in spite of Philip II's own inclinations, and that was because the consortia of Genoese businessmen, whose opinions counted, were unanimously against any such change. Although these groups still competed for *asientos*, they were as one in preferring fixed and predictable sums which could not be concealed or falsified, and which would eliminate risk, to the uncertainties of purely hypothetical returns.

The *encabezamientos*, therefore, continued. We need to look briefly at how they operated. The overall sum that had been decided upon was divided among the forty districts of the eighteen provinces of the kingdom of Castile, and each was allocated a quota. The district capital, in cooperation with the towns and villages within its jurisdiction, was responsible for reapportioning this quota amongst them, deducting, first of all, the amount they estimated would be obtained from the *tercias*. There was, therefore, no abuse of the system, and a reasonable give and take resulted in balance and moderation. The municipal authority (*ayuntamiento*) of the district capital then called a meeting of the elected representatives of the different, specialised, trading sectors – 'miembros' – which paid tax (though in different degrees) on their transactions, in order that they should see to the equitable distribution of the part for which they were responsible. There would be arguments and disputes, but in the end an agreement would be reached among the 'miembros'. Each group would then work out what percentage of the value of the transactions that they calculated would be effected by their sector as a whole during the period in question would be sufficient to meet the sum required for their share of the tax. There would be more

---

[7] This enormous mass of paper, classified in alphabetical order of towns and districts, is now held in the Archive of Simancas in the section entitled appropriately, 'Expedientes de Hacienda'. It is currently the subject of study by a number of young students who have recently presented or are currently preparing splendid doctoral theses in the University of Valladolid.

arguments and more disputes, this time among colleagues, louder and bitterer disputes since at this point the conflict was between the bold and the cautious. The former would argue for low rates, convinced that transactions would increase; the latter, more pessimistically, would defend high rates. However, as is always the case, the bold generally prevailed over their more cautious colleagues and a low percentage rate would be established for future transactions. At this point the cautious traders would break away, though undertaking, nevertheless, to observe religiously the rate that against their will had been established (to the others' advantage, as they believed) and to submit their businesses to the audit of their bolder colleagues. To use the vocabulary of the time, the cautious traders stuck with the market (*al viento*),[8] whereas their more optimistic colleagues would be *matriculados*,[9] gambling on a prior commitment which made them responsible, each according to his position, for making up any shortfall in the amount obtained from the traders *al viento*, to complete the sum established in the *encabezamiento* for the 'miembro' as a whole. In addition to this distinction between the 'matriculados' and the traders 'al viento', a distinction was also made between the traders 'al viento' resident in the city and outsiders.[10] The outsiders 'al viento' were generally worse treated, and somewhat higher demands were made of them than were applied to the resident traders 'al viento'.

I do not intend to describe how the 'matriculados' or bold traders controlled and collected the sales tax from the resident traders and outsiders 'al viento'; it is sufficient to note that this function was either 'administered' by agents, or, more frequently, 'farmed' for a specific sum. Nor do I want to say anything about the ways the rules and regulations were stretched by the taxpayers, and even more so by the tax collectors, under the guise of concessions and by devices designed to encourage trade and attract it to their sector in order to produce a more favourable balance than would have resulted from strict application of the rules. I will insist, however, although it is an obvious point, that this system was viable as long as economic activity continued to expand. Cessation of growth led to a chain of

---

[8] Literally translated, *al viento* means 'in the wind'.
[9] Literally translated, *matriculados* means 'registered'.
[10] Outsiders *al viento* were those who sold goods in the town or city and who were required to pay the corresponding tax on the goods sold.

bankruptcies, and recession was to have even worse consequences. A chronology both of the bankruptcies and of the more serious consequences can be established in the cities of the Duero and Tagus valleys, with the exception, as always, of Madrid. In other words, these data enable us to determine the beginnings of stagnation and of the fluctuations of the depression in the urban centres of both Old and New Castile. This stagnation, just as the depression, came sooner or later depending on the character of each urban agglomeration, for, as can be seen from the range of their 'miembros' and the relative level of each 'member's' contribution to the sales tax, the situation in all these centres was not the same. From the last two decades of the sixteenth century, we begin to get requests from individual districts (*partidos*) asking to withdraw from the *encabezamientos* and submitting, without any remission, to the full 10 per cent of the sales tax. If these withdrawals from the *encabezamientos* are arranged by place and date, the geography and the chronology of the onset of the process of decline and its gradual development in time and space can be clearly mapped. These withdrawals were accepted by the Council of Finance, although they complicated its accounting, because the king had granted this option to the Cortes. However, as we shall see, when withdrawals from the *encabezamientos* became widespread, restrictions had to be imposed.

The symptoms of stagnation and, subsequently, of decline in the trading of goods, animals, personal property and real estate that were reflected in the decline in revenue from the *alcabala* became evident in both Old and New Castile in or around 1578, and this decline is even greater if account is taken of inflation. Taxation, however, was not checked, nor could it have been, given the demands of royal credit which, although administered independently, was inextricably linked to the public revenue. And as the revenues could not grow from the roots by indirect taxation, which meant in effect the sales tax, recourse had to be had from 1589 to direct taxation, in what would be its most characteristic form, namely the *millones*. Breaking with a tradition whereby the privileged classes, the nobility and the clergy, were exempt from direct taxation, the burden of which was borne overwhelmingly by the lower classes, the 'pecheros', the *millones* exempted neither the nobility nor the clergy, who were required to contribute, in accordance with their wealth, in the same way as everyone else. This was a revolutionary change which first required an estimate of the number of nobles and clergy, calculated as a percentage of the 'pecheros' in each of the forty districts of the eighteen provinces of Castile, as established by the inquiries of 1528–36 and their rectification in 1540. The protests of the nobles and the clergy against this affront to their standing and, what hurt them most, to their purses, were not inconsiderable. In his historical novel entitled *La gloria de Don Ramiro*, Enrique Larreta has given us a faithful description (based on reading and research in impeccable sources) of the protests that took place in Avila, and this city was not unique. Philip II silenced these protests with much bloodshed, and crushed the protesters. In 1591, in order to ensure that there were no objective grounds for complaint, since both the nobles and the clergy claimed there were fewer of them than the figures derived by the application of a set coefficient to the number of commoners, he ordered a careful census to be taken of all the houses of commoners, nobles and clergy throughout the kingdom of Castile. So meticulous was the census that it even detailed the monks and nuns in the convents and monasteries.

The introduction of the *millones* should not be understood as a replacement for the sales tax, but rather as a supplement designed to offset the losses resulting from the leakage inherent in the mechanism of its collection that has been described above, and which threatened the breakdown that was soon to occur. For this reason, it was not desirable to adopt for the *millones* a system similar to the *encabezamientos* used for the sales tax, which placed its success in the hands of interested parties. Instead, a complex machinery was set up, the management and responsibility for which was laid upon public officials, the *regidores* (or municipal councillors) of the community as a body. The *millones* were invariably set as specific amounts to be paid in their entirety, as was preferred by those providing advances to the Crown, whose need for *asientos* did not diminish, given the failure of the persistent attempts to replace them with public loan banks between 1576 and 1620 and, though more sporadically, thereafter. The *millones*, a direct tax on wealth, were voted by the Cortes, with a greater or lesser degree of enthusiasm, each time for an increasing sum and for a fixed number of years. Just as with the *encabezamientos de alcabalas*, the *millones* were divided among the forty districts of the eighteen provinces of Castile. It should be repeated, however, that, contrary to what was the case with the *encabezamientos*, in each of these areas it was not private individuals involved in trade who were in charge of the collection of the *millones*, but the public officials, the *regidores* of the town as a body, who were required to settle accounts with the Treasury. These officials took good care of themselves. Moreover, as it was not in their interests to damage other wealthy people like themselves, they contrived in due course, or learned, means of evasion which both avoided angry disputes with their friends and relatives, or even with their patrons among the nobles and the clergy, and also enabled them to carry out to their own advantage the task of collecting the *millones* imposed on them by the Treasury. This evasion involved the employment of indirect measures: the alienation of municipal assets; the granting of licences to plough up previously unworked land; the diversion of money from the municipal grain store (*pósito*); and the imposition of *sisas* (excise duties)[11] on all kinds of items. The *regidores* did not hesitate to employ devices such as these which had the effect of transforming the *millones*, originally conceived as a direct tax on wealth, into an indirect tax. It was a fraud on society, but who dared complain when, after 1608, despite the tragic effects of the plague of 1598–1602, the supply of labour so exceeded demand that wages were falling again below the index of prices! At the same time, the government was tightening the reins. The modern state in Castile was changing from authoritarian to absolutist, and, in turn, the municipal authorities were becoming dictatorial. There was no room for grumbling. It was thought that with the accession of Philip III and his favourite, the duke of Lerma, there might be a clash between the municipal authorities and the modern state; but it was not long before an understanding was reached between the two, for the municipal authorities gave the Court what it most urgently needed, money.

Of all the measures that were employed for the payment of the *millones* indicated above, the *sisas* on foodstuffs proved to be the most versatile. A supplement would be added to the normal price of meat, bread, fish, milk, and so on, and the appropriate quantity would be deducted from the weight of the goods sold. No research has been conducted into the eating and drinking habits of the inhabitants of Castile, nor into the quantities they consumed,

---

[11] The *sisas* were taxes charged on foodstuffs, and levied by means of reduced measures rather than monetary charges.

although it would be perfectly feasible from the tax records for the reign of Philip II in Simancas mentioned earlier. Unfortunately there are no comparable sources for the seventeenth century. Nonetheless, I believe that the deeply ingrained image of a starving population, derived from the picaresque novels, must be reexamined and most probably corrected, at least for the period before 1640. This pejorative view does not accord with the returns obtained from the *sisas*, which not only paid for the *millones* but also, at a later date, for the *encabezamiento* of the *alcabalas*, when their payment ceased to be the responsibility of the 'members' of the various branches of the local economy, or of tax-farmers or administrators, and came to depend instead on the ruling magistracy of the local corporations that governed the main towns and villages of the provinces of the kingdom of Castile. The *sisas* were a panacea for the councillors. With the money they extracted by these tortuous means, by cutting daily rations of food and drink and, if necessary, firewood, timber, lime and bricks also, they settled the bill for the *millones* and *encabezamiento* and were able to embark on the most outrageous expenditures. The *sisas* were a magical resource drained to excess by the municipal authorities in the seventeenth century; they were the most copious fountain of their coffers.

Before long, in imitation of the close linkage between royal credit and the finances of the state, and using identical forms and a similar vocabulary, a municipal credit linked with the *sisas* came into being. This *sisa*-linked municipal credit also had its *asentistas*, not foreigners in this case but local people, consortia from the most prominent guilds, whose associates were generally shopkeepers with their own premises and clientele. When the *regidores* asked the guilds for an advance, in order to pay the *millones* or *alcabalas*, or whatever, the guilds, adding on interest and other benefits, after studying future prospects and weighing up the possibilities, would demand the introduction of a *sisa* on some foodstuff, the collection of which they would control in mortgage for their loan. The guilds involved in the loan contract would then share out among their members the rights accorded to them in that contract, in the form, if we may use the term, of shares. These shares would be placed by their owners with families or institutions (hospitals, churches, monasteries, convents) that had funds to invest. Had the municipal authorities acted in strict compliance with the public commitments they made in order to silence public opinion whenever a *sisa* was introduced, declaring that the sacrifice being demanded of the community had a precise purpose and was, therefore, only temporary, the disease would not have become endemic. But it was not the case. If the municipal authorities imposed a *sisa* to repay in full a loan they had sought, only rarely did they repay the principal of the advance with the amount received from the *sisa*; more often they merely paid the interest due to the guilds for non-repayment, as contracted. In this way, a substantial burden of municipal debt was built up, more substantial in some cities than in others, but everywhere high. As a result, the cost of living in the cities, and first of all the cost of food and drink, was raised artificially above the level of market prices, again more in some places than in others. Moreover, as this additional burden affected certain social groups more than others, the gap between rich and poor widened.

The situation described above was experienced in all the towns and cities of both Old and New Castile, though analysis of the process, when it is done, will reveal important variations. However, there is one city, Valladolid, for which data is available, as a result of the intelligence and the indignation of a man who was *diputado del común*[12] in the city in the eighteenth century. This post gave him access to the account books of the city council, which he studied minutely and on the basis of which he wrote a voluminous book, full of figures and names, which is of inestimable value. The name of this inquisitive and critical official was José Ruiz de Zelada and the title of his book, *Estado de la bolsa de Valladolid: examen de sus tributos, cargas y medios de su extinción; de su gobierno y reforma* (State of the treasury of Valladolid: study of its taxes, debts, and of the means of their elimination; its management and reform). He was not allowed to publish the work, or perhaps he did not wish to do so until he was on firm ground; but in 1777, when he was recorder to the Council of Castile and corresponding academician of the Royal Academy of History of Madrid, he gave the book to the printing firm of Don Tomás de Santander with the permission of the Royal Chancellory of Valladolid. The book was published in a quarto volume of almost 400 pages of fascinating reading, in which one after the other he details the mortgages given to the guilds of Valladolid by the municipal authority, how much each was for, how it was secured

---

[12] The post of *diputado del común* was an elected municipal office created in 1766.

(usually against *sisas*), how the rights or shares that were issued were marketed, and who got them. Ruiz de Zelada's *Estado de la bolsa de Valladolid* is an inexhaustible mine of information. The gradual growth of Valladolid's civic debt until it reached gigantic proportions is recorded in minute detail. It was a phenomenon of the seventeenth century that was to be projected, unimpaired, into the eighteenth.*

The reason for this is that the Bourbons, who by decree dared to cut the state debt despotically, if not to a minimum, at least very substantially, did not dare to touch municipal indebtedness. I must confess that this was not something I had taken into account until I discovered the magnificent work of José Ruiz de Zelada. Bedazzled by the *juros*, I had taken no account of the rights or shares in the municipal debt (sometimes called *censos*) that had turned the *sisas* into an impenetrable thicket which choked the growth of creative activities in the cities of Castile. An impenetrable thicket because their beneficiaries, who were, it would appear, more powerful than the *juro*-holders, opposed their eradication. Neither Philip V nor Ferdinand VI hesitated to take drastic measures with the *juro*-holders, but they did not touch the holders of municipal *censos*. For that reason, when in 1785 the *corregidor* José Colón de Larreátegui informed Charles III of the economic prostration in which he found Valladolid (his report, in 172 folios, is in the Biblioteca Universitaria de Santa Cruz), his basic argument was that the city was still dragging the weight of the *sisas* which had been loaded onto it in the seventeenth century. There was simply no means of removing them, and the high price of food caused by their exaction forced wages up and made the cost of any kind of manufacturing activity uncompetitive. Colón de Larreátegui gives a series of examples in his report, but I will cite just one which speaks volumes. A textile factory, enjoying royal privilege and tax exemptions (their value is specified) was established in Valladolid. These advantages proved, however, to be far from sufficient to offset the difference in prices and, in consequence, in wages that had to be paid in Valladolid over and above those paid in other places where there were no *sisas* on foodstuffs, or where the *sisas* were lower.

The debts of the municipalities, just as the remnants of the state debt, passed into the nineteenth century. We know that in the

---

* There is a modern edition of Ruiz de Zelada by B. Yun (Valladolid, 1990), see below p. 310, n. 40.

disentailment decrees of Mendizábal and Madoz, in 1836 and 1855, those bidding for auctioned properties were given the option of paying part of the price in bonds. I am not sure whether there had been a prior conversion of municipal debts into the state debt, but it does seem to me that, in the same way as the state debt at that date, if municipal indebtedness did not melt like a snowball in the sun, it did at least decrease considerably. In the 1840s and 1850s, stimulated by the introduction of the railway, Valladolid endeavoured to escape from the morbidity into which it had sunk some 250 years earlier. The fact that those attempts at industrialisation failed, although not totally, does not contradict the evidence that the obstacles which Colón de Larreátegui had insisted upon in his report, namely the high costs resulting from the *sisas*, had by now evaporated.

9. *Urbanisation and deurbanisation in Castile, 1500–1800*

JUAN E. GELABERT

In line with the general evolution of urban population in Europe between 1500 and 1800 recently proposed by Jan de Vries,[1] Spain experienced a long-term movement composed of three distinct phases of successive urbanisation and deurbanisation. The first of these phases culminated in the late sixteenth century and was marked, for the most part, by a notable increase in the population of the cities, such as was not again to be repeated. Then, at the turn of the sixteenth century, the bulk of the Castilian urban network underwent an acute demographic crisis, whether measured in absolute or in relative terms. Finally, in the eighteenth century, there was some recuperation of the losses of the previous century, without, however, a return to pre-1600 levels.

The criterion arbitrarily chosen by Jan de Vries for the definition of a *city* is that it should have housed 10,000 inhabitants at some point between 1500 and 1800. Other scholars prefer other limits, but I prefer to follow de Vries for the simple reason that his figures are the most wide-ranging in both space and time and offer the best overall view for the purposes of comparative analysis throughout the three centuries in question, both within a single country and for Europe as a whole.

According to de Vries's figures, there were twenty cities in Spain in 1500, thirty-seven in 1600, twenty-two in 1700, and thirty-four in 1800. City dwellers comprised 6.1 per cent of the total population in 1500, 11.4 per cent in 1600, 9 per cent in 1700, and 11.1 per cent in 1800. On either count the three phases of the movement are clear.[2]

---

[1] Jan de Vries, *European Urbanization, 1500–1800* (London, 1984), ch. 8.

[2] *Ibid.*, Tables 3.1, 3.7. There is also a brief compendium of data on urban demography for the period 1600–1850 in Pilar Correas, 'Poblaciones españolas de más de

In comparative terms, the 11.4 per cent of urban population in 1600 is a respectable figure. The European average was about 7.6 per cent, and Spain was headed only by the Low Countries (24.3 per cent in Holland, 18.8 per cent in Flanders), the Italian peninsula (between 12.5 and 16.6 per cent according to the region), and Portugal (14.1 per cent).

However, the expression *Spain* covers a variety of differences, not only of a political and social nature, but also of economic and demographic experience. It is precisely during the two phases of urban concentration and demographic dispersion in the sixteenth and seventeenth centuries that these differences are of most significance.[3]

The first difference of note is that between the Crown of Castile and the Crown of Aragon. Although, despite their very different geographic, demographic and economic resources, there was not much divergence in their gross levels of urbanisation at the end of the sixteenth century, Castile, with three-quarters of the territory of the Peninsula (excluding Portugal) and four-fifths of the population, was a genuinely urbanised country with a widespread distribution of cities. In the territories of Aragon and Catalonia, on the other hand, and to a lesser extent in Valencia, city population was highly concentrated (Zaragoza in Aragon, Barcelona in Catalonia, Valencia city, Alicante and Orihuela in Valencia). Of the forty-one cities which existed in peninsular Spain in the period from 1500 to 1699 (the forty-second was Palma in the Balearics, and the forty-third, after 1700, Bilbao), thirty-six were in Castile and only five in the Crown of Aragon.

Barcelona, in demographic terms the only city in Catalonia, housed 10.4 per cent of the total population of the Principality at the end of the fifteenth century (1497); in 1718 (in the aftermath of the damaging War of the Spanish Succession) that figure had fallen to 8.5 per cent; but by 1787 it had risen again to 13.8 per cent.[4] Zaragoza, the capital of the kingdom of Aragon, housed 7.7 and

5.000 habitantes entre los siglos XVII y XIX', *Boletín de la Asociación de Demografía Histórica* 6 (1988), 5–23.

[3] For the differences between Castile and Catalonia, for example, see Pierre Vilar, *La Catalogne dans l'Espagne Moderne*, 3 vols. (Paris, 1962), I, pp. 522ff.

[4] Jordi Nadal Oller, 'La Vraie richesse: les hommes', in Joaquim Nadal Farreras and Philippe Wolff (eds.), *Histoire de la Catalogne* (Toulouse, 1982), pp. 61–90; see also Pierre Vilar, 'Les Élans du XVIIIe siècle', in *ibid.*, pp. 377–409.

7.85 per cent of the population in the censuses of 1495 and 1560 respectively;[5] and in the kingdom of Valencia, immediately prior to the expulsion of the *moriscos* in 1609, the capital, together with Alicante and Orihuela, had no less than 18.4 per cent of the population of the region.[6] In sum, though similar in terms of their overall demographic proportions, Castile and Aragon differed so much in the shape of their urban networks and in the dynamics of their evolution that they cannot properly be treated together. It is on Castile, therefore, that I shall concentrate.

The rhythm of demographic growth in the cities in Castile in the sixteenth century was very different from that in their rural hinterlands. Whereas population overall increased by 48.4 per cent between 1526–8 and 1591, the population of the cities increased by at least 62 per cent.[7] In Segovia, for example, between 1531 and 1591 the average annual rate of growth of the city was double that of the surrounding countryside (0.67 and 0.31 per cent respectively).[8] Between 1528 and 1591 the population of Zamora grew by 73.47 per cent, whilst its hinterland increased by between 12.1 and 38.6 per cent. The expansion of Burgos (192 per cent between 1530 and 1561) greatly exceeded that of its countryside (19.2 per cent between 1528 and 1591), as did that of Palencia (43.1 and 21.3 per cent respectively), and Guadalajara (109.4 and 51.5 per cent). Such examples, taken from Molinié-Bertrand's very full analysis of Castilian population in the sixteenth century, could be multiplied.[9]

In the last quarter of the sixteenth century, however, the population of Castile as a whole was beginning to show signs of exhaustion. In the northern Meseta, along the line Salamanca-Valladolid-

[5] G. Colás Latorre and J.A. Salas Ausens, *Aragón bajo los Austrias* (Zaragoza, 1977), p. 34.
[6] Data derived from James Casey, *The Kingdom of Valencia in the Seventeenth Century* (Cambridge, 1979), Table 1; Bernard Vincent, 'Récents travaux de démographie historique en Espagne (XIVe–XVIIIe siècles)', *Annales de Démographie Historique* (1978), 453–81; Armando Alberola Roma, *Jurisdicción y Propiedad de la tierra en Alicante (ss. XVII y XVIII)* (Alicante, 1984), ch. 1, 1.2.
[7] J. Gelabert, 'Economía y sociedad', in *Historia de España. El siglo de oro* (Barcelona, 1988), pp. 207ff; J. Nadal, *La población española (siglos XVI–XIX)* (3rd edn, Barcelona, 1986); V. Pérez Moreda, 'La población española', in M. Artola (ed.), *Enciclopedia de Historia de España* (Madrid, 1988), pp. 345–431, at pp. 370–1.
[8] A. García Sanz, *Crisis y desarrollo del Antiguo Régimen en Castilla la Vieja. Economía y sociedad en tierras de Segovia de 1500 a 1814* (Madrid, 1977), pp. 46–7.
[9] A. Molinié-Bertrand, *Au siècle d'or: L'Espagne et ses hommes. La population du royaume de Castille au XVIe siècle* (Paris, 1985).

Burgos, the rural population of the ancient provinces of Burgos,
Valladolid and Palencia seems to have reached a peak around the
time of the census of 1586, since five years later it had fallen by 6 or 7
per cent.[10] The 1586 figure was also a maximum in the Bureba
district,[11] and it is in that same quinquennium that baptisms in the
nearby district of Tierra de Campos reach a peak.[12] On the limits of
Old Castile, further to the south, a population of 47,574 individuals
in 1561 rose to 51,762 in 1584, and then fell to 41,179 in 1591.[13] In
the ancient kingdom of León, as well, 1587 has been seen as the peak
of the rural population increase.[14] What we have in effect is a
chronology which places the reversal of the general trend in the last
five years of the 1580s.[15]

As is well known, the urban centres did not follow the chronology
of rural population change at all closely. Medina del Campo, for
example, had more tax-payer households in 1528–36 (3,872) than its
entire population in 1561 (3,297). The movement of births after 1560
confirms the early reversal of its demographic growth.[16] Burgos,
Salamanca and Zamora also recorded their highest levels of population in 1561, the 1579–84 surveys revealing lower figures and
placing the reversal of the trend somewhere in between.[17] Population peaks were also reached in Avila and León around 1571,
although in Valladolid, Segovia, Palencia, Medina de Rioseco and
Villalón population held up until 1585–90.[18]

[10] F. Brumont, 'L'Evolution de la population rurale durant le règne de Philippe II.
L'exemple du Nord-Ouest de la Vieille-Castille', *Mélanges de la Casa de Velázquez*
14 (1978), 249–68.

[11] F. Brumont, *Campo y campesinos de Castilla la Vieja en tiempos de Felipe II*
(Madrid, 1984), p. 83.

[12] B. Yun Casalilla, *Sobre la transición al capitalismo en Castilla. Economía y
sociedad en Tierra de Campos (1500–1830)* (Salamanca, 1987), pp. 156–7.

[13] *Ibid.*, p. 172.

[14] L.M. Rubio Pérez, *La Bañeza y su tierra, 1650–1850* (León, 1987), p. 74.

[15] See also, B. Bennassar, *Valladolid au siècle d'or. Une ville de Castille et sa
campagne au XVIe siècle* (Paris, 1967), p. 170; García Sanz, *Crisis y desarrollo*,
p. 55.

[16] A. Marcos Martín, *Auge y declive de un núcleo mercantil y financiero de Castilla la
Vieja. Evolución demográfica de Medina del Campo durante los siglos XVI y XVII*
(Valladolid, 1978), pp. 62, 92.

[17] Molinié-Bertrand, *Au siècle d'or*, p. 135; F.J. Vela Santamaría, 'Salamanca en la
epoca de Felipe II', in *El pasado histórico de Castilla y León* (Burgos, 1983), II,
pp. 281–322; J.C. Rueda Fernández, 'La ciudad de Zamora en los siglos XVI y
XVII: estudio demográfico', *Studia Zamorensia* 2 (1981), 116–34.

[18] Serafín de Tapia, 'Las fuentes demográficas y el potencial humano de Avila en el
siglo XVI', *Cuadernos Abulenses* 2 (1984), 31–88; V. Fernández Vargas, *La
población de León en el Siglo XVI* (Madrid, 1968), p. 37; Bennassar, *Valladolid au
siècle d'or*, p. 183; Yun Casalilla, *Sobre la transición*, pp. 156–7.

Movements in New Castile and Andalusia were not dissimilar. The most general information we have about the overall movement of population, the investigations ordered by Philip II between 1575 and 1580 in the ancient provinces of Madrid, Toledo, Guadalajara, Cuenca and Ciudad Real, better known as the 'Topographical Relations', reveal that population was rising in 234 villages, stationary in 37, and falling in only 99.[19] A sample of 25 villages in the Montes de Toledo shows population rising between 1576 and 1590, and recent researches on the neighbouring region of La Mancha also defer the commencement of the downward trend to the 1590s.[20]

The information we have on the evolution of population in the cities in New Castile and Andalusia, however, reinforces the impression of a much earlier peaking. Ciudad Real rises from 1,810 to 2,049 households between 1561 and 1591, with the high point for births around 1575, as in Talavera de la Reina (1570–4). Cuenca reached its maximum in 1561, with 3,534 households, after which population fell in every decade to 2,691 at the end of the century. In Extremadura, the population of the city of Trujillo never exceeded the peak of 1561, the figures for 1579, 1584 and 1591 all being lower, whereas the population of the villages of its jurisdiction rose from 8,654 in 1579–84 to 8,693 in 1591.[21] Although the situation of Toledo was more complicated, the overall picture was in line with the general pattern. Its population was never greater than around 1571 (12,412 households), and by 1591, with 10,933 households, a falling away was already noticeable. Thanks to a continuous series of parish registers, the more detailed movement of baptisms reveals that the first crisis of growth took place during the 1560s, resulting in part from the movement of the capital to Madrid in 1561. In fact, after 1571, the settlement of a concentrated group of *moriscos*

---

[19] N. Salomon, *La Campagne de Nouvelle Castille à la fin du XVIe siècle d'après les "Relaciones Topográficas"* (Paris, 1964), p. 44.

[20] M.R. Weisser, *The Peasants of the Montes. The Roots of Rural Rebellion in Spain* (Chicago, 1976), p. 60; J. López Salazar Pérez, *Estructuras agrarias y sociedad rural en la Mancha (siglos XVI–XVII)* (Ciudad Real, 1986), p. 74.

[21] C. Rahn Phillips, *Ciudad Real, 1500–1750. Growth, Crisis and Readjustment in the Spanish Economy* (Cambridge, MA, 1979), pp. 22–7; M. González Muñoz, *La población de Talavera de la Reina (siglos XVI–XX). Estudio socio-demográfico* (Toledo, 1975); A. Diaz Medina, 'Cuenca en 1587: estructura socio-profesional', *Studia Histórica* 1 (1983), 29–64; A. Molinié-Bertrand, 'Contribution à l'étude de

expelled from the kingdom of Granada delayed the demographic decline of the city, a decline apparent in Christian parishes by the end of the 1570s.[22] Finally, Cordoba's population perhaps reached a peak in 1575–6, 1571–5 seeing by far the highest number of baptisms.[23] Some other large towns of Andalusia, like Baeza, Andújar, Ubeda, Jerez de la Frontera, Ecija, Carmona, experienced a marked reduction in their rates of growth between 1561–79 (from 100 to 115.6) and 1579–91 (from 100 to 104.8).[24]

It is arguable, therefore, that the process of demographic growth in the sixteenth century favoured the concentration of population in the larger centres, and that the cities grew at a markedly faster rate than their hinterlands. It is also true that the same thing was happening at a lower level, with the larger towns growing more than the smaller. In La Mancha, in 1530 there were only two centres of around 4,000 inhabitants; in 1591 there were seventeen; those of between 1,000 and 4,000 increased from twenty-seven to fifty-nine, and those of under 1,000 from sixty-two to seventy.[25] In the Tierra de Campos, between 1530 and 1591 the population of villages of under 75 *vecinos* increased by only 4.2 per cent, whereas larger villages of up to 500 *vecinos* recorded increases of between 19 and 33.7 per cent.[26]

On the other hand, once the reversal of the general trend of demographic growth was underway, it was the larger centres which were the first to decline, the great cities leading the way. In Cordoba, for example, whilst the large towns of over 1,000 *vecinos* were showing signs of exhaustion by the second half of the century (index 100 1557, 105 1579, 102 1590), the smaller ones were holding up much better (117 1579, 118.5 1590).[27]

The cases of Madrid, Seville (its population peaking in 1597 in sequence with the curve of Spanish–American trade), and Murcia

---

la société rurale dans la province de Trujillo au XVIe siècle', *Mélanges offerts à Ch.V. Aubrun* (Paris, 1975), II, pp. 125–38.

[22] M.R. Weisser, 'The Decline of Castile Revisited: The Case of Toledo', *Journal of European Economic History* 2 (1973), 614–39; L. Martz and J. Porres, *Toledo y los toledanos en 1561* (Toledo, 1974), p. 7; L. Martz, *Poverty and Welfare in Habsburg Spain. The Example of Toledo* (Cambridge, 1983), p. 95.

[23] J.I. Fortea Pérez, *Córdoba en el siglo XVI: las bases demográficas y económicas de una expansión urbana* (Cordoba, 1981), p. 140.

[24] Molinié-Bertrand, *Au siècle d'or*, pp. 261ff.

[25] López Salazar, *Estructuras agrarias*, p. 59.

[26] Yun Casalilla, *Sobre la transición*, p. 163.   [27] Fortea Pérez, *Córdoba*, p. 114.

are the exceptions to the rule of the earlier cessation of growth in the cities.[28] This provokes two considerations, at least. The first is that we ought to look again at the overall percentage of the population attributed to the cities of Spain, and therefore in Castile, in 1591. Taking the figures worked out by Jan de Vries on the basis of the 1591 census, it looks as if some Castilian cities were no longer at their peak, and that a decade earlier the figures would have been rather different, and in all probability a good deal larger.

It is likely that at the root of the marked increase of urban population until the 1570s or so was a continuous migratory movement from the countryside to the cities. This is the only way that such a clear increase in the proportion of the urban population to the whole can be explained. If the populations of the cities tended naturally to decline or at best to reproduce themselves, being in general subject to fewer growth factors (higher death rates, higher incidence of celibacy, lower birth rates, etc.), then it was the arrivals from outside who influenced the timing and the rate of the growth and decline of the cities. In short, when there were fewer immigrants, the cities had to rely on their own natural demographic balance and as a result they stagnated, and then underwent a slow decline, which in the Castilian case lasted through the seventeenth and eighteenth centuries. Although the seventeenth century is poorly served with sources for demographic history, the limited information available gives an idea of the scale of the decline. Toledo, for example, went from 12,412 *vecinos* in 1571 to 4,889 in 1639. Avila had 2,475 *vecinos* in 1571, 1,190 in 1632, and 1,146 in 1692.[29]

It is arguable, therefore, that from the later sixteenth century the population of Castile was undergoing a process of dispersal, or rather ruralisation, meaning that the chances of resistance or growth were better in the smaller centres of population. In turn, when demographic recovery came, it was to take on an overwhelmingly rural character which largely passed the urban world by.

---

[28] D.R. Ringrose, *Madrid and the Spanish Economy (1560–1850)* (Berkeley–Los Angeles–London, 1983); J. Sentaurens, 'Séville dans la seconde moitié du XVIe siècle: population et structures sociales. Le recensement de 1561', *Bulletin Hispanique* 77 (1975), 321–90; F. Chacón Jiménez, *Murcia en la centuria del Quinientos* (Murcia, 1979), p. 117.

[29] J. Montemayor, 'Toledo en 1639', *Mélanges de la Casa de Velázquez* 18 (1982), 135–63; Tapia, 'Fuentes demográficas', p. 88.

At some point between the second half of the seventeenth and the start of the eighteenth century population began to recover. Recent estimates put the total population of Castile around 1700 at only 5 per cent less than it had been in 1591.[30] What is striking, however, is that by 1789 there were fewer centres with a population of 2,500 *vecinos*, or 10,000 inhabitants, than there had been in 1591. In other words, the great majority of the large towns do not seem to have participated in the demographic growth of the later seventeenth and eighteenth centuries. To take the case of Segovia and its hinterland once more; the rural areas grew from 122 per cent of their 1591 population in 1752, to 157 per cent in 1789; the population of the city, on the other hand, only 80 per cent of its 1591 size in 1752, actually fell slightly by 1789.[31] Castile (excluding Madrid) lost much of its urban population during the crisis of the seventeenth century, as can be seen in Table 9.1 below.

Furthermore, the intensity of deurbanisation is directly proportional to the size of the original urban population. Between the end of the sixteenth century and the mid-eighteenth century, the Castilian urban network all but vanished, leaving only the administrative capitals of the provinces, and sometimes not even them, able to escape the process. By 1800, according to Jan de Vries, some cities, like Avila, Cuenca, Medina del Campo, Medina de Rioseco, and Segovia, were virtually indistinguishable from the urban landscape of Castile. The collapse of the urban network was most marked in the northern sub-meseta where none of the 'cities' of the late sixteenth century was anything like the same size in the nineteenth. In the south of the central urban network the same process was visible in Toledo and Cuenca, though Madrid, of course, was different. Within the two-thirds of Castile contained within an imaginary line drawn from the Guadalquivir to the Cantabrian coast, and excluding Madrid and Santiago de Compostela, there were sixteen cities with a smaller population in 1800 than in 1600.[32] It was only in the region between the Guadalquivir and the Straits of Gibraltar that there was any real resistance to this urban malaise. Of

---

[30] Unpublished data from a current research project on the principal Spanish censuses from 1591 to the end of the eighteenth century. I am very much indebted to Professor Eiras Roel for advice on this and many other questions relating to demographic matters.

[31] García Sanz, *Crisis y desarrollo*, pp. 46–7.

[32] De Vries, *European Urbanization*, appendix 1.

Table 9.1. *The deurbanisation process in 11 provinces of Castile,*
1591–1750

Provinces	A^a		B^a		C^a	
	1591	1750	1591	1750	1591	1750
Burgos	13,43	8.30	4.06	3.75	2.78	2.07
Soria	13.55	10.97	6.50	5.29		
Segovia	25.37	12.56	15.85	10.25	13.34	7.17
Avila	17.07	13.80	7.48	5.22	7.48	
Salamanca	18.88	15.27	10.82	11.86	10.82	12.37
Madrid	40.06	79.00	28.08	66.89	28.08	66.89
Extremadura	41.46	46.67	24.13	27.20	4.97	
Toledo	40.52	50.19	28.61	25.68	16.77	8.82
La Mancha	73.99	71.28	33.79	38.74		4.61
Cuenca	29.05	25.10	10.93	5.34	4.72	
Guadalajara	31.96	15.50	4.91	5.13		
Total	31.39	31.69	15.92	18.66	8.08	9.26
Total (not including Madrid province)	30.52	26.96	14.70	13.84	6.08	3.50

Note: ^{a}Percentage of urban population in towns above 500, 1,000 and 2,000 households (respectively columns A, B, and C).
Sources: Data of 1591 in González, *Censo . . .*, Madrid (1824); for 1750, see notes 55,
56 and 57.

the three areas distinguishable in Molinié-Bertrand's atlas of Castilian population: the first situated in Old Castile (Valladolid, Salamanca, Avila, Segovia, Burgos), the second in New Castile (Toledo,
Cuenca, the big towns of La Mancha, like Ocaña), and the third in
southern Andalusia and the kingdom of Murcia; in the first the
urban network disappeared completely; in the second only Madrid
survived; and in the third, twelve of the nineteen centres came
through. The eighteenth-century recovery affected a few cities
between Gibraltar and the Guadalquivir (Cadiz, Jerez de la Frontera, Seville and seven others), some cities on the Mediterranean
coast (Murcia, Cartagena), and Madrid and Santiago. In the Peninsula outside Castile, Bilbao became a city and the cities of Aragon,
Catalonia and Valencia, as a whole, also grew. In other words,
whereas in the seventeenth century the larger centres were the
preferred victims of deurbanisation, the obstacles to the restoration
of the urban network that existed in Castile in the eighteenth
century were not operative in the other territories of the Peninsula.

It needs to be asked, therefore, what it was that made the atmosphere of the cities of Castile so unbreatheable in the seventeenth century and stunted their demographic and economic development even in the more buoyant eighteenth century. It is not my intention to examine every possible cause or condition for this profound change in the demographic geography of early modern Castile. Besides such classic explanations as that implicit in the work of D. R. Ringrose, who portrays Madrid as a hydra sucking into itself the urban life of Castile, one could point to other general factors, and clearly it would not be difficult to find specific reasons for each individual case of urban decline. It would seem to be true, for example, that the decline of Burgos in the 1570s was the result of the effects of the crisis of the wool trade to Flanders. In the same way, a causal relationship could be established between the reversal of the trend in the Spanish–American trade and the decadence of Seville. Nor would it be rash to relate the early agonies of Medina del Campo to the effects of the first bankruptcy of Philip II, the disruption of the system of exchange fairs, and the banking crisis, all of which took place from 1557 onwards.

I want to propose a more general explanation of the decline of the Castilian urban system. It seems to me that various fiscal measures adopted in Castile at the end of the sixteenth and in the early seventeenth century contributed both directly and indirectly to throttling the great vitality the urban system had manifested until then. Those measures seem to have had a not negligible impact on economic activity in the towns and on their functions as territorial centres, jurisdictional capitals and spaces for the exercise of political power and fiscal administration. Without these central-place functions, intimately connected with a specific hinterland of its own, the existence of a city was inconceivable.[33]

It is important to stress how closely the fiscal system of the Castilian monarchy was dependent on the institutional role of the cities within the structure of government. Such a link was not, of course, a peculiarity of the Crown of Castile. Referring to a similar

[33] B. Clavero Salvador, 'El mito histórico de la ciudad burguesa', *Ciudad y Territorio* 57–8 (1983), 37–43; A.M. Guilarte, 'Estudio preliminar', to A. Sacristán y Martínez, *Municipalidades de Castilla y León. Estudio histórico-crítico* ([1877], Madrid, 1981), pp. 24–5; M. Berengo, *Nobili e mercanti nella Lucca del Cinquecento* (Turin, 1974), p. 293; A.M. Hespanha, *As vesperas do Leviathan. Istituciones e poder politico. Portugal sec.XVII* (Lisbon, 1986), I, p. 475.

situation in France, B. Chevalier speaks of 'an unwritten compact'.[34] In Castile the compact was much nearer to being a written one, particularly in regard to the taxes which in the sixteenth and seventeenth centuries comprised by far the most important sources of royal income, the *alcabalas*, the *servicios* and the *millones*.

The *alcabalas*, originally a municipal tax which the crown succeeded in extending to the whole kingdom as a regalian right, was transformed around 1494–5 from a variable indirect tax bearing on all individuals and all commercial activity, into a fixed levy unrelated to levels of trade, which the cities obliged themselves to remit every year to the royal treasury, taking responsibility at the same time for the allocation of the burden among the populations of their regions.[35] The attractions of this system, known as the *encabezamiento*, for the cities of Castile were obvious. Together with an increased political and administrative role for the municipal oligarchies, the new system allowed them to consolidate and increase their fiscal control over the city's hinterland. Moreover, for the merchants resident in the cities it meant in effect the freezing of the burden of the tax that most immediately affected them and, in the course of time, a declining incidence of taxation on production, profits and economic activity in general. It was in this climate that for a period in the sixteenth century economic activity in Castile experienced a considerable expansion.[36]

It can be said, therefore, that the *encabezamiento* system (finally established for the kingdom as a whole in 1536) deprived the royal Treasury every year of an increasingly large flow of funds, whilst at the same time the wealth of the kingdom was growing considerably

---

[34] B. Chevalier, *Les Bonnes villes de France du XIVe au XVIe siècle* (Paris, 1982), pp. 97–103.

[35] On the role of the cities in the politics of the monarchy, see Pablo Fernández Albaladejo, 'Monarquía y Reino en Castilla, 1538–1623', in his *Fragmentos de Monarquía. Trabajos de historia política* (Madrid, 1992), pp. 241–83. For more on the *encabezamiento*, R. Carande, *Carlos V y sus banqueros* (Madrid, 1949), II, pp. 230–5, and Charles David Hendricks, *Charles V and the 'Cortes' of Castile. Politics in Renaissance Spain* (Ann Arbor, Mich., 1976), ch. 8.

[36] M.A. Ladero Quesada, 'Para una imagen de Castilla (1429–1504)', in his *El siglo XV en Castilla. Fuentes de renta y política fiscal* (Barcelona, 1982), pp. 88–113. Low fiscal pressure and economic growth have been associated by Bartolomé Bennassar: 'Il est évident que cet affaiblissement de la fiscalité constitue une circonstance particulièrement heureuse pour le développement économique de Valladolid', *Valladolid au siècle d'or*, pp. 302–3.

thanks to the favourable economic climate. Low fiscal pressure, together with the generally prosperous economic situation, was responsible for the harmonious political climate between king and kingdom.

Charles V's imperialism was made possible by bullion from the Indies and recourse to external and internal credit. It was, however, a financial system too difficult to maintain for long, as the balance between credit and tax revenue began to weigh too dangerously against the latter. The sum of all these circumstances led to the disastrous financial straits in which Charles left his son Philip, and to the latter's first bankruptcy in 1557.

Philip II had no option but to fix his attention on the dwindling *alcabalas*. In 1562 a new general *encabezamiento* agreement 37 per cent greater than the previous one came into effect.[37] Despite the substantial increment, both the cities and the royal Treasury were aware that the amount was far from constituting any real burden, and as Philip II's financial problems did not get any better with the passage of time, the king was forced again to look to the *alcabalas* as the revenue source most susceptible to an increase. In 1575 the *encabezamiento*, which should have run to 1577, was unilaterally abrogated by the king, and a new figure set at no less than three times that of the old *encabezamiento*. That sum proved impossible to collect and from 1578 a somewhat reduced figure was agreed upon, though still more than double the pre-1575 *encabezamiento*.[38]

The effects of this increase were felt immediately by the cities. The suddenness of the tax rise and the fact that it coincided with the recession of the end of the century must have dealt the cities a severe blow. Medina del Campo and its district paid 8.5 million *maravedís* prior to 1562, 12.5 million until 1575, and then was assessed at 40 million. The town council offered half, but the rural district accepted the quota of 3,168,000 assigned to it. Even so, in the five years 1576–80, the town was only able to raise 20, 17.2, 18.9, 19.7 and 21.6 millions respectively. A new agreement was reached for 1582–8 at 17.5 million, but, as the town could not raise it, an administrator was sent. He, however, was unable to collect more than 11.5 million. Finally, in 1599 the Crown had to accept a

---

[37] Modesto Ulloa, *La Hacienda real de Castilla en el reinado de Felipe II* (2nd edn, Madrid, 1977), p. 175.
[38] *Ibid.*, pp. 177–80.

ten-year agreement at a figure of 6.4 million.[39] In Cordoba, the city's *encabezamiento* increased from 16,635,000 to 56,250,000 *maravedís* in 1575. The first year it was collected; but losses began in 1576. A new figure of 47 million was set for 1577–8, and cut again to 34 million in the *encabezamiento* of 1578. Cuenca, and even the wealthy Seville, underwent similar experiences.[40]

It was the coincidence with generally worsening economic conditions that made the increased fiscal pressure particularly damaging. The fiscal pressure inaugurated in 1575 hit urban manufacturing activity hard. The lesser resistance to the new quotas in rural districts suggests that they expected to be able to withstand the increase, or perhaps that in the countryside the burden was less. In the countryside the *alcabala* had lost its character as a sales or transactions tax because of an insufficient degree of commercialisation, and had become a tax on the person. Textile manufacturing, on the other hand, paid something at every stage of the productive process. A piece of cloth made in Cordoba paid 102 *maravedís* in taxes in 1557, 282 in 1579, 258 in 1580, and 375 in 1590. Contemporaries are witness to the damaging fiscal burden of 1575 on 'industrial' cities like Segovia, Cuenca and Toledo.[41] The case of Cordoba shows how the damage done by the tax increase was at the root of a diversion of industrial and commercial capital into alternative investments in the public and private debt (*juros* and *censos*) or into offices, etc.[42] Rather than deurbanisation *per se*, what was often happening in Castile was a process of decay resulting from the deindustrialisation of the urban network.

But an even greater financial effort was to be demanded of an already overburdened Castile. From 1590, as a result of the disaster of the Armada against England, the cities of the Cortes granted Philip II a 'service' of 8 million ducats to be paid over six years. These *millones*, originally conceived as an extraordinary, once-for-all aid, were to be both regranted and increased, and in the course of time came to be the main source of Crown revenues. In the kingdom

[39] Marcos Martín, *Auge y declive*, p. 69.
[40] J.I. Fortea Pérez, *Monarquía y Cortes en la Corona de Castilla. Las ciudades ante la política fiscal de Felipe II* (Valladolid, 1990), pp. 207–56.
[41] Fortea Pérez, *Córdoba*, p. 440; Diaz Medina, 'Cuenca en 1587', pp. 29–64; Marcos Martín, *Auge y declive*, p. 69.
[42] Fortea Pérez, *Córdoba*, p. 460.

of Seville, for example, the effect of the *millones* was to increase the gross tax-burden sevenfold between 1590 and 1650.[43]

Although initially the cities and the district capitals remained individually responsible for the choice and the administration of the measures used to raise them, after 1601 the *millones* were levied throughout Castile by excises (*sisas*) on wine, vinegar, oil and meat, in the belief that this would be more equitable and of more universal impact. There was no certainty, however, that the greater consumption of the rich would be translated into greater fiscal contributions. Leaving aside the fact that the rich were more easily able to defraud the Treasury than the poor, they were also able to avoid paying on their own domestic production, or on their consumption of luxuries. Yet again, whilst the urban oligarchies looked for a form of fiscal extraction which least affected them, supporting excises on items of general consumption, it was an option which caused grave damage to the bulk of the population and contributed to depressing the living standards of the wage-earners. It was also clear that the raising of taxes from consumables sold in the markets bore less heavily on a self-sufficient countryside where, as had been noted in 1589, 'the villages were so small that they had neither taverns nor butchers' and it was extremely difficult to raise taxes at all.

During the last quarter of the sixteenth century not only was fiscal pressure increasing relatively more in the urban centres, but the cities were also losing jurisdictional control over their rural districts and with it the possibility of exploiting their authority to shift at least part of their share of the fiscal burden onto the countryside. At least two factors contributed to a marked reduction of the power of the city over its countryside during the last quarter of the sixteenth and the first decades of the seventeenth century. In the first place, the Crown, impelled by its financial needs, began to detach some of the rural areas belonging to the cities and to grant them almost complete judicial independence. The Crown also accepted large sums from villages and private individuals to buy out their *alcabalas* and to administer them themselves. The result was that the tax quotas came to be borne by a decreasing number of people. In 1574 it was calculated that 63 million *maravedís* should be deducted from the *encabezamiento general* to allow for the contributions of districts

[43] Ildefonso Pulido Bueno, *Consumo y fiscalidad en el Reino de Sevilla: el servicio de millones en el siglo XVII* (Seville, 1984), p. 81.

withdrawn from the jurisdictions of the cities since 1537.[44] Given that the sale of *alcabalas* continued uninterruptedly and that no corresponding reductions were made to the overall figure of the *encabezamiento*, the burden of the tax continued to grow year by year.

The creation of new territorial units by separation from the ancient domains subject to the jurisdiction of the great cities is to be seen as a response to the tyranny exercised by the cities over their territories for which there is evidence from the end of the fifteenth century. In effect, using the 'abuses and oppression' of the cities in the way they reallocated the fiscal burden on their villages as a pretext, the Crown began after 1537 to review the 'unjust privileges' granted in the late middle ages. From then on the Crown was prepared to sell privileges of exemption and also to allow the cities the possibility of paying an equivalent sum in order to retain their territories intact. Seville, Cordoba and Toledo offered 13.87, 6.75 and 4.5 million *maravedís* respectively to prevent the alienation of any village from their jurisdictions, and Soria paid 4,000 ducats to prevent the sale of exemption to Nobiercas.[45]

The ransoms paid by the cities prevented further alienations from their territories, though the Crown did not always honour its bargains. The soundness of municipal finances at that time saved the majority of the great cities from the dangers of this first round of alienations, and most of the exemptions concerned middle-sized cities like Mérida, Trujillo, Huete, and Almagro. However, the process moved up a gear in the second half of the century. By 1565 Alcalá de Henares had lost control of fifteen of its twenty-four dependent villages. When it heard that two others, Corpa and Pozuelo de Torre, wanted to follow the same route, 'in order to escape the abuses suffered by the inhabitants of the villages at the hands of the justices of the towns and cities to which they are subject', it offered 3 million *maravedís* to stop their secession, well aware of the value of its jurisdictional control over its territory, 'without which, in the event of food shortages, it would be without provisions and sustenance, being unable to compel the said villages to supply them; the same would be true of timber and firewood and

[44] Ulloa, *Hacienda real*, p. 231.
[45] Hendricks, *Charles V and the 'Cortes' of Castile*, pp. 241–2; Carande, *Carlos V y sus banqueros*, III, p. 208; Ulloa, *Hacienda real*, pp. 670–1.

other necessities, for they would cut down the woods from which the city was supplied, and there would be other damage and harm suffered'.[46]

Under Charles I and Philip II, however, alienations were minor compared with those granted by Philip IV.[47] In two provinces, Valladolid and Cordoba, where it is possible to reconstruct the process from the end of the sixteenth to the end of the seventeenth century, twenty-six grants (about half the total of fifty-five) were made by Philip IV, twenty by Charles I and Philip II, eight by Philip III, and one by Charles II. There were as many alienations during the 44 years of Philip IV (1621–65) as in the previous 119 years.[48]

The process of judicial emancipation and the creation of new towns followed a similar course. Their effects were also similar. The sale of the right to collect taxes not only increased the burden on the larger centres of population, given that most alienations involved medium and small places, it also resulted in constant changes in the fiscal burden within a particular territory. The separation and creation of new towns contributed to a redistribution of population, not so much because new settlements were being created as because their new autonomous jurisdictional status undoubtedly brought with it a diminution of the quotas reallocated by the city from which they had been liberated.

It is not easy to say how many people subject to their jurisdiction the Castilian cities lost by the end of the seventeenth century when the process of alienations came to an end. In the middle of the eighteenth century, around 1754, the exempt towns comprised a not negligible proportion of the population in some provinces. There seem not to have been any exempt towns in Burgos, but in Soria they comprised 19 per cent of the population, in Segovia 30.1 per cent, in Avila 16.7 per cent, 13.6 per cent in Toledo, and 12.4 per cent in Salamanca.[49]

[46] AGS M y P, leg. 252.
[47] S. de Moxó, 'La venta de alcabalas en los reinados de Carlos V y Felipe II', *Anuario de Historia del Derecho Español* 41 (1971), 487–554; A. Domínguez Ortiz, 'Ventas y exenciones de lugares durante el reinado de Felipe IV', *Anuario de Historia del Derecho Español* 24 (1964), 163–207.
[48] AGS DGT, Inventario 24, leg. 320, 'Relazion de las alcaualas y tercias vendidas . . . hasta el año de 1632' (though the information actually goes into the eighteenth century).
[49] M. Artola (ed.), *La España del Antiguo Régimen*, fasc. III *Castilla la Vieja* (Salamanca, 1967), Appendix 1; fasc. IV *Castilla la Nueva y Extremadura* (Salamanca, 1971), Appendix 1; fasc. 0 *Salamanca* (Salamanca, 1966), pp. 35–6.

As far as the sale of *alcabalas* is concerned, it was obvious that the lordship of the cities over their territories, together with the administrative authority over the excises which the district capitals had for a long time exercised, meant that there was gross inequality in the distribution of their tax quotas as between the capitals and their territories. The same can be said of the allocation of the *millones* over which the formal grants to the king had given the cities vast judicial powers. It was only to be expected then that all the cities would abuse their administrative and judicial powers and their authority in fiscal matters, whilst their districts would do everything they could to liberate themselves from it. The purchase of *alcabalas* was a guarantee of autonomy in the administration of the tax in the expectation that it would result in lower contributions.[50]

The bidders for the *alcabalas* were usually the municipalities themselves, members of the aristocracy, and sometimes high officials of the Council of Finance. Of the bids accepted in the provinces of Cordoba and Valladolid in the sixteenth and seventeenth centuries only seven out of fifty-five went to the municipalities. That meant that the aristocracy could get control of the *alcabalas* more easily than any of the other potential purchasers. As from the late middle ages the exaction of a substantial part of the *alcabala* was in the hands of the aristocracy, and not much had been reincorporated by the Crown, it is not too much to suppose that with the concessions made in the sixteenth and the seventeenth centuries the aristocracy held the lion's share.

This leads to another issue relevant to the urban crisis in Castile in the first two centuries of the modern age, the existence of a current of migration of men and of resources from the cities and territories of the royal domain to seignorial jurisdictions. It was a phenomenon frequently denounced at the time, and some comments on it are in order.

The difference in the way the *alcabala* was collected in seignorial and royal jurisdictions goes back to 1451 when, because of the obstacles the lords put in the way of the collection of royal taxes in their domains, the Crown agreed to accept fixed sums in return for

---

[50] P. Fernández Albaladejo, 'Monarquía, Cortes y "cuestión constitucional" en Castilla durante la Edad Moderna', *Revista de las Cortes Generales* 1 (1984), 13–34, at note 39; Fortea Pérez, *Monarquía y Cortes*, pp. 218, 248; Serafín de Tapia, 'La documentación fiscal concejil en el siglo XVI. Un instrumento imprescindible para la historia social', in *Los archivos y la investigación* (Avila, 1988), pp. 49–70.

the nobility's accepting a common responsibility for the monies that were owed. The sums originally set in 1455–8 (*tasas*) were reasonably high, but by 1465 they had fallen substantially. The freezing of the sums they owed for sales taxes enabled the seignorial territories to benefit from low rates of tax forty years earlier than the royal jurisdictions. It is from that time that we get complaints against the migration of population into seignorial territories to take advantage of the more favourable fiscal regime.[51] The situation got worse in the sixteenth century as the increase in the *alcabalas* in the royal domain accentuated the difference. Seignorial vassals and in general all those who remained outside the *encabezamiento* could be thought to be advantaged.[52] Every time the king alienated *alcabalas* the agents of the cities concerned claimed quite rightly that an appropriate deduction should be made from their overall obligation, for otherwise the existing burden would have to be supported by a declining number of taxpayers.[53]

Not only was the fiscal regime different, but during the sixteenth and seventeenth centuries, the situation was, if possible, getting worse as the increase in the number of exempt villages made the difference in the fiscal pressure on the royal domain more visible, and from 1575 it was becoming critical. As soon as the increased *encabezamiento* was registered business houses moved in waves into seignorial jurisdictions: 'the information is that from Cordoba, Soria, Salamanca, Murcia and Cuenca merchants are moving to Yecla, Cartagena, Almansa, Orihuela, and other exempt towns'.[54]

After 1575, when the level of taxation on the royal domain was becoming insufferable, the preferential treatment of seignorial jurisdictions was clear for all to see, and under Philip IV the discrimination between the various fiscal regimes was extreme. Though ministers of the Crown denied it, seignorial territories were seen as taxhavens for the oppressed. The proctor of Salamanca in the Cortes in 1625, Don Antonio Carvajal, claimed that:

> the towns of these kingdoms which belong to lords are clearly less burdened than those in the royal domain, so it seems to people that they would be better off as seignorial vassals. From this it can

---

[51] M.A. Ladero Quesada, *La hacienda real de Castilla en el siglo XV* (La Laguna, Tenerife, 1973), p. 78; S. Haliczer, *The Comuneros of Castile. The Forging of a Revolution, 1475–1521* (Madison, Wisc., 1981), p. 67.

[52] AGS M y P, leg. 251.   [53] AGS M y P, leg. 255; AGS CJH, leg. 580.

[54] Fortea Pérez, *Monarquía y Cortes*, pp. 84, 86, 229, 325, 335, 344.

be seen how detrimental is the sale of jurisdictions because of the extra tax quotas which fall on royal cities, and that is not because they are naturally more prosperous, but because there is nobody to defend royal towns from the taxes that rain upon them and to try to alleviate their burdens.[55]

It did not matter whether the lord held only criminal and civil jurisdiction or had the right to the *alcabalas*, or whether the municipalities administered the taxes themselves in the king's name or had judicial exemption. The reality was that the chance to buy privileges existed and that privilege was a barrier against the attempts of the royal fisc to exact taxation. In effect, throughout the two centuries, the sources reveal a fear, a diffidence on the part of royal tax collectors to enter seignorial jurisdictions. In 1648, the *corregidor* of Arévalo wrote to the Council asking whether he should collect the donative in the three seignorial villages within his district, or not.[56] In the same year, the *corregidor* of Cordoba complained that 'the greatest difficulties are in seignorial territories where most of the tax arrears are concentrated, because my predecessors have not been able to do more than they have done'.[57] In 1627, the President of the Council of Finance told Philip IV that 'many grandees, nobles and gentlemen of the kingdom have not complied with the donative offered, nor have they made their vassals contribute. This is a bad example for the vassals in Your Majesty's jurisdiction and grounds for discontent that seignorial vassals are exempt from paying.'[58]

It is not easy, however, to relate this piecemeal evidence to demography. It is even questioned whether different fiscal treatment could in the long term generate different demographic patterns. It has been written, for example, though with some caution: 'It cannot be said that the seignorial regime benefited its vassals . . . but neither can the opposite be claimed.'[59] Other writers have observed of the sixteenth and seventeenth centuries that 'the populations subject to the lords grew at a faster rate and probably for longer than those in royal jurisdictions'.[60] A recent study of seignorial territories in the province of Cordoba offers some confirmation

---

[55] Quoted in A. Domínguez Ortiz, 'La ruina de la aldea castellana', *Revista International de Sociología* 24 (1948), 99–124.
[56] AGS CJH, leg. 923.   [57] AGS CJH, leg. 924.   [58] AGS CJH, leg. 632.
[59] López Salazar, *Estructuras agrarias*, pp. 101–2.
[60] Fortea Pérez, *Córdoba*, p. 117.

of the existence of a twin-track system.[61] Doña Mencia, for
example, increased in population from 289 *vecinos* in 1591 to 471 in
1701; Lucena in the 1690s had nearly 4,000 households, as many as
in the best moments of the sixteenth century; Montilla in 1680 had
more inhabitants than it ever had in the sixteenth century; Rute,
during the seventeenth century, experienced a constant increase in
its population.[62] Even in the second half of the seventeenth century,
a degree of demographic vitality is visible in seignorial populations
in the province of Salamanca. Commenting on the phenomenon,
not without a certain surprise, the author of the study writes, 'The
double demographic current caused by the growth of population in
seignorial jurisdictions and in the smaller villages contrasts with
prevalent views of Spanish demography in the ancien régime.'[63] In
the provinces of Burgos, Soria, Segovia and Avila, thirty-seven
cases where population grew by more than 50 per cent were in royal
jurisdictions, and seventy-three in seignorial (including two ecclesiastical). Conversely, in Avila the enormous majority of cases of
depopulation (eighty-one of eighty-eight) were in the royal
domain.[64]

But it was not only population which fled to 'fiscal paradises'. The
evidence available indicates that the progress of manufacturing
activity in Castile ran parallel to the movement of population. We
have already seen how the excises on foodstuffs substantially
reduced real wages and thus the living standards of Castilian
workers after 1611.[65] In Valladolid towards the middle of the
seventeenth century taxes increased the price of wine and oil by
50 per cent, and that was not exceptional but the rule in most of
the cities of Castile well into the next century.[66] In due course local
taxes came to surpass royal taxes.[67] Inevitably, the maintenance of a

[61] J. Calvo Poyato, *Del siglo XVI al XVIII en los señorios del sur de Córdoba* (Cordoba, 1986), p. 150.
[62] B. García Jiménez, *Demografía andaluza. Rute en el Antiguo Régimen* (Cordoba, 1986), p. 52.
[63] Mª. Dolores Mateos, *La España del Antiguo Régimen*, fasc. 0 *Salamanca*, p. 37.
[64] Mª. Pilar Calonge Matellanes, et al., *La España del Antiguo Régimen*, fasc. III *Castilla la Vieja*, pp. 41–2.
[65] Fortea Pérez, *Monarquía y Cortes*, p. 340.
[66] A. Gutiérrez Alonso, 'Un aspecto poco conocido de la crisis del siglo XVII: el endeudamiento municipal. El ejemplo de la ciudad de Valladolid', *Investigaciones Históricas* 6 (1987), 8–37.
[67] For Madrid, see J. Fayard, 'Crédit publique en Espagne au XVIIe siècle: les emprunts sur la ville de Madrid', *La documentación notarial en la historia*

living wage by the urban labour force was passed on into higher costs of production and higher prices of manufactured goods. Some time ago, comparing nominal wages in Madrid and Barcelona, Pierre Vilar noted how much higher they were in the capital and in the rest of Castile, adding that, 'Social structures, attitudes, the role of the capital as an administrative centre and as a centre of conspicuous consumption, the effects of the economic malaise of the seventeenth century had all left the region less responsive to the improved economic conditions of the eighteenth century and therefore less able to take advantage of them.'[68] Along the same lines, an informed resident of eighteenth-century Valladolid observed: 'As the costs of production increase in line with the increase in taxes, it is necessary to raise the price and as a result, since in neighbouring districts which are not so taxed they work with greater ease, everybody rushes there for supplies and in a short time the city which has such high taxes is left depopulated, and its commerce, arts and industry lost.'[69] What is certain is that in comparison with the seventeenth century not only did the output of manufacturers of such cities as Segovia, Ciudad Real, Toledo and Guadalajara fall considerably, but also the bulk of production took place in the countryside.[70] Thus, the heavy fiscal burdens on the urban centres, both municipal excises and royal taxes – which after 1575 had been responsible for a restriction of commercial and manufacturing activity, and the generalisation of taxes on foodstuffs from the early years of the seventeenth century affected salaries and prices in the

(Santiago, 1984), II, pp. 253–65. To see how the vestiges of municipal taxation of comestibles persisted into the nineteenth century, H. Peñasco de la Puente, *Las sisas de Madrid. Apuntes para escribir su historia* (Madrid, 1890), is still worth consulting.

[68] Pierre Vilar, 'Slancio urbano e movimento dei salari: il caso di Barcellona nel Settecento' in *I prezzi in Europa dal XIII secolo ad oggi. Saggi di storia dei prezzi raccolti e presentati da R. Romano* (Turin, 1967), pp. 375–417, at p. 406; see also his 'Historia de los precios, historia general. Un nuevo libro de E.J. Hamilton', in *Crecimiento y desarrollo. Economía e historia. Reflexiones sobre el caso español* (Barcelona, 1974), pp. 163–85.

[69] Quoted in González Alonso, 'Un aspecto poco conocido', p. 33.

[70] A. González Enciso, 'La industria lanera en la provincia de Soria en el siglo XVIII', *Cuadernos de Investigación Histórica* 7 (1983), 147–70, presents data of 1745, 1760 and 1785–95 for textile production both in old industrial towns (Palencia, Segovia, Guadalajara and Toledo), and in rural centres. At all those dates, rural production stands well above that of urban origin: 30,291 pieces of cloth against 14,788 in 1745; 10,437 against 7,688 in 1760; and 33,358 against 20,696 in 1785–95.

urban economies and combined to cause serious damage to productive activity in the towns.[71] As has already been noted, the depopulation of some Castilian cities was immediately preceded by a downturn in craft activity and commerce which sought alternative places to work and outlets for investment.

Yet, if emphasising the negative aspects one can speak of urban depopulation, one can also, stressing the positive response, speak of ruralisation. It is clear not only that the rate of urbanisation of the Castilian population declined markedly between 1500 and 1800, but that, once the general crisis phase of the last years of the sixteenth and the first half of the seventeenth century was past, the new impetus to the growth of population did not benefit the greater part of the existing urban network. The countryside resisted the impact of the crisis better, something not apparently unique to Castile.[72] Among several possible explanations, the wide variety of forms of fiscal exaction which came into effect after 1575 and which in all probability bore less heavily on the countryside, has already been suggested. The increased fiscal exactions encouraged the establishment of new settlements in which fiscal pressure was more bearable, especially when compared with that which the cities and district capitals loaded onto their subject territories. In 1634 the *corregidor* of Soria made this comment on the situation: 'In this province there are other subject villages, although different in size, and now they do not want to join with each other but would rather break apart.'[73]

Contemporary sources also make frequent reference to emigration towards the Basque Provinces and the territories of the Crown of Aragon, which all enjoyed privileged fiscal systems compared with that of Castile.[74] The town of Haro, for example, with 234

---

[71] Antonio Domínguez Ortiz, *Política fiscal y cambio social en la España del siglo XVII* (Madrid, 1984), p. 74. The cry against high taxation as a serious obstacle to industrial development is a commonplace in contemporary literature; see, among others, the authorities quoted by James C. La Force, Jr, *The Development of the Spanish Textile Industry, 1750–1800* (Berkeley and Los Angeles, 1965), ch. 7; and Agustín González Enciso, *Estado e industria en el siglo XVIII: la fábrica de Guadalajara* (Madrid, 1980), pp. 215–17.

[72] L. Faccini, *La Lombardia fra '600 e '700. Riconversione economica e mutamenti sociali* (Milan, 1988), p. 26.

[73] AGS CJH, leg. 725.

[74] C. Viñas Mey, *El problema de la tierra en la España de los siglos XVI–XVII* (Madrid, 1941), ch. 4.

families in 1667, a third less than it had twenty years before, attributed its decline to emigrants going 'to live in the provinces of Alava, Guipúzcoa and Vizcaya, which are exempt from the taxes here'.[75] Even earlier in the century, Mateo de Lisón y Viedma described how farmers 'move from place to place to seek alleviation, or go to other kingdoms and provinces where they do not have to pay Your Majesty the *millones*, *alcabalas* and other *servicios*, the burden of which and the humiliations meted out by the tax-collectors are the cause of this depopulation'.

In conclusion, one could say that the most salient characteristic of the crisis of the seventeenth century in Castile was a widespread geographical redistribution of the population. What was happening at the turn of the sixteenth century was a general relocation of population from the cities to the countryside. The population of Castile was reorganising itself into a pattern of medium and small-scale concentration characteristic of the demography of the eighteenth century. This was followed by the acquisition by these small communities of the judicial, administrative and institutional mechanisms which allowed them to escape the burdens weighing so heavily on their former fellows in the cities. Migration to seignorial areas was another way of attaining the same goal. Castile was undergoing a process of institutional atomisation and autonomisation. The sale of *alcabalas*, the exemptions of towns, the restoration of primary jurisdiction to the towns of the Military Orders, the creation of new seignorial jurisdictions, etc., all had important consequences for the geographical distribution of population in the Crown of Castile in the seventeenth century. This redistribution severely damaged the urban network because those centres once marked by a prospering manufacturing and commercial sector (Medina del Campo, Cuenca, Segovia, Toledo, Villalón, Medina de Rioseco, Burgos, etc.) were in the eighteenth century all underpopulated and impoverished cities. It might be suggested, therefore, that the redistribution of the population of Castile between the end of the sixteenth and the eighteenth century had its roots in the greater resistance of the rural areas than the towns to the crisis, thus reversing the previous tendency which had run from the end of the late middle ages and for most of the sixteenth century. As the effects

---

[75] Henry Kamen, *Spain in the Later Seventeenth Century, 1665–1700* (London, 1980), p. 99.

of catastrophic mortality had only a secondary role in determining Spain's demographic evolution during the course of the sixteenth and seventeenth centuries, normal mortality did not improve significantly, and fertility variations had negligible effects overall, the most active element in the 'marked change in the demographic trend' has to be ascribed to migration.[76] Reasons for that change can be found in the practical alternatives available to make the obvious difficulties of urban life more supportable, and those difficulties would certainly include among other things the pressure of the fisc and the gradual establishment of a fiscal system which weighed much more heavily on the towns than on the countryside.

[76] Vicente Pérez Moreda, *Las crisis de mortalidad en la España interior, siglos XVI–XIX* (Madrid, 1980), ch. 17.

10. *Fiscal pressure and the city of Cordoba's communal assets in the early seventeenth century*

JOSÉ MANUEL DE BERNARDO ARES

I. CONTRACT BETWEEN THE CORDOBA COUNCIL AND THE CROWN COMMISSIONER

By a Royal Warrant, dated in Madrid the 22 April 1629, Don Alonso de Cabrera, lord of the town of Torres Cabrera, was commissioned, in the name of the king and with the full jurisdiction of the Council of the Cámara, to get the city of Cordoba to serve with a donative of 200,000 ducats to help palliate the urgent financial needs of a royal exchequer exhausted by the constant and crushing financial drainage caused by the Italian wars.[1]

The city, in the council meetings of 19 and 24 October 1629, agreed to grant the king a donative in return for a series of exemptions, which were very advantageous to Cordoba and 'which are to remain valid for ever and ever'. A letter of proxy was issued to seven gentlemen councillors and four *jurados*, who in the city's name drew up the deed that was signed in Cordoba on 3 November 1629.[2]

This deed, which was a genuine contract between the central power, represented by the Royal Commissioner, on the one hand, and the local power on the other, has an undeniable importance. Apart from the context of *do ut des* which reveals the close symbiosis between the monarchy and the nobility for the resolution of their reciprocal needs, it enables us to observe one of the most effective mechanisms by which the cities gradually obtained a series of liberties and advantages, benefiting from the ineluctible needs of a

---

[1] The circumstances of the financial crisis in relation to international events is well analysed by A. Domínguez Ortiz, *Política y hacienda de Felipe IV* (Madrid, 1960), pp. 37–50.
[2] AM CO [Archivo Municipal de Córdoba], Contaduría de propios, Sec. XIII, ser. 2°, tomo I: 1492–1773, ff. 20r.–28v. This document is cited, henceforth, as 'Escritura de 1629', together with the number which corresponds to the clause under discussion.

state that was involved in a foreign policy that was draining away its already precarious resources.

Although our first concern here are those prerogatives and powers which enabled the city to increase its assets (*bienes de propios*), the issues will be much better understood if all thirty conditions, or clauses, of the deed are analysed together as a whole. These can be grouped into two main subjects, which in turn can be subdivided, as follows:

A. Special measures or expedients (*arbitrios*) proposed for the payment of the donative.
   (a) Typology of the *arbitrios*
   (b) Administration of the *arbitrios*
B. Privileges granted to the city.
   (c) Exemptions of various kinds
   (d) Increase of assets (*bienes de propios*)

Thirteen of the clauses are devoted to *arbitrios* and twenty to privileges, fourteen of which refer to the improvement or augmentation of assets.[3] In themselves the most numerous of the grants are authorisations, but the conditions established for the administration of the *arbitrios* will be seen to have favoured the interests of the city in general, as a municipal corporation, and of the ruling class in particular (*regidores* and *jurados*), saving any kind of subsidiary responsibility they may have had for the payment and fulfilment of what had been agreed. If the Crown obtained a considerable amount of money to solve its pressing financial problems, the city, in compensation, got notable political-administrative and, above all, economic benefits. The difference lies – and it is essential that this is not overlooked – in that whereas the royal exchequer squandered its revenue at once, the municipal exchequer was endowed with appreciable resources for many years. These resources would have provided a unique and unsurpassable economic spring-board for local development had not an always voracious and pitiless Treasury gradually, over the long term, eaten it away. This is an important point to which I shall return later; but now it is time for a detailed examination of the contents of the clauses.[4]

---

[3] Three clauses are counted twice, because their contents concern both subjects.
[4] The erosion of the municipal treasuries caused by the financial policy of the Habsburgs is brought out by A. Domínguez Ortiz, 'Andalucía en el siglo XVII. Sugerencias sobre algunas líneas de investigación', *Actas del I Congreso de Historia de Andalucía. Andalucía Moderna (siglos XVI–XVII)* (Cordoba, 1978), I, p. 352.

II. THE POLITICAL SUBORDINATION AND ECONOMIC DEPENDENCE OF THE TOWNS AND THE POOR

Under the terms of the aforementioned deed, the city agreed to pay the royal exchequer 200,000 ducats (75,000,000 *maravedís*) over a period of sixteen years, starting from 1 January 1630, in six-monthly instalments of 6,250 ducats, on 25 December and 24 June (San Juan) of every year.[5] To meet the payment of these 12,500 ducats a year, the city adopted the following measures.

(1) The expedients granted to the city in 1614 in order to reduce its debt, by redeeming the annuities (*censos*) it had contracted, produced approximately 8,000 ducats a year, of which 4,000 were earmarked to pay the donative of 1629 during the sixteen years of its concession.[6] These expedients consisted of: a meat tax (*sisa*); two enclosed pastures (*dehesas*) in the district of Almodóvar; stalls leased in squares and streets; three taverns in the areas of La Verdad, San Antón and the Matadero: and three *dehesas* in El Picacho, in the district of Cordoba.[7]

(2) In the districts of Hornachuelos, Montoro and Fuenteovejuna, subject to the authority of the city, the pastures that would best enable each of these towns to contribute 1,000 ducats a year for sixteen years were set aside for that purpose.[8]

(3) Throughout the period of the service the following towns in the jurisdiction of the city were to contribute in accordance with the following schedule:

La Rambla	6,000 ducats
Posadas	5,000
Espiel and Villanueva del Rey	2,000
Obejo	1,500

In order to raise these sums, the towns could impose taxes, although always with the approval of the Cordoba city council; but if they preferred to offer to compound for the service, the city would decide on it at a general meeting.[9]

---

[5] The final half-yearly payment would be due on 24 June 1647.
[6] The other 4,000 ducats were assigned to fund the 1630–4 donative of 20,000 ducats, 5,000 ducats owed to the Cathedral Chapter, and, finally, to redeem the annuities. The 'donative' was a measure much resorted to by the Crown to solve its chronic financial problems.
[7] AM CO. Contaduría, Escritura de 1629, 15.   [8] *Ibid.*, 20.
[9] *Ibid.*, 21–4 and 28.

(4) The *dehesa* of La Jara, which produced acorns and hay, and which was common pasturage for both the city and all the places within its jurisdiction, as well as those exempted from its jurisdiction, was to be fenced and closed off in the months of October, November and December, so that what it produced during those three months could be assigned to the payment of the donative for the sixteen years that it lasted.[10] The annual income expected from each of these special measures was:

1. *Arbitrios* of 1614	4,000
2. *Dehesas* of Hornachuelos, Montoro and Fuenteovejuna	3,000
3. La Rambla, Posadas, Espiel, Obejo and Villanueva	906
4. *Dehesa* of La Jara	4,594
Total	12,500[11]

What does the adoption of these special measures, agreed on by the city for the payment of the donative of 1629, suggest? The very measures chosen reveal the importance of the contribution of the subordinate towns and of the indirect taxes to be paid both by some of the towns and by the city.

Cordoba's contribution was of course by no means insignificant (the leasing of sites in public places, the three taverns, the three *dehesas* of El Picacho and its share of the *dehesa* of La Jara), but it is undeniable that a considerable part of the payment fell on the towns, either because they had to set aside pastures, in the cases of Hornachuelos, Montoro, Fuenteovejuna and Almodóvar, or because they were assigned a specific amount (La Rambla, Posadas, Espiel, Villanueva del Rey and Obejo). This means that, while the city of Cordoba alone was the beneficiary of a variety of privileges in exchange for the donative, the donative itself was provided by virtue of the economic effort which the city in its capacity as 'corporate lord' (*señorío concejil*), in the phrase of Alfonso María Guilarte,[12] demanded from some of the towns of its province. It was the towns,

---

[10] *Ibid.*, 19.

[11] The deed does not specify how the 4,594 ducats needed to make up the annual total of 12,500 ducats were to be obtained. Perhaps from the yield of the *dehesa* of La Jara. Nor is there any mention of where the salaries of the receiver and the clerks were to come from (see below).

[12] A.M. Guilarte, 'Estudio preliminar', in A. Sacristán y Martínez, *Municipalidades de Castilla y León. Estudio Histórico-crítico* (Madrid, 1981), pp. 24–5.

therefore, which did not receive any of the benefits, that contributed most proportionately to the payment of the service.[13]

As well as the income from specific properties (*dehesas*) and services (taverns etc), a series of duties was imposed on basic necessities in order to raise the required funds. The city imposed taxes on meat and the towns were authorised to impose taxes on pigs and sheep, wool, cheese, honey, wax, etc. From the social point of view indirect taxation is regressive because although almost everyone had to pay (keeping in mind the contentious question of refunds), the people seriously disadvantaged were those country or city dwellers with the least purchasing power. With such measures those who paid more were those who had least. A great part of the burden of the payment of the donative fell on the shoulders of the most humble, people who in no way benefited either from the privileges granted to the city, or from the expenditure of a royal exchequer which drained off their financial resources for wars which did not at all serve the interests of the national economy.[14]

Thus the burden of the *arbitrios* established by the Cordoba city council, and in its name by the seven gentlemen *veinticuatros* and four *jurados*, profoundly affected the economic interests of the towns and the humble, rather than those of the city or the powerful. On the contrary, it was the latter who reinforced their economic power at the expense of the former, both protecting the assets they already had and also increasing them substantially, by transforming many of the measures earmarked for the 1629 donative into permanent assets once the 200,000 ducats had been paid in full on 24 June 1647.[15] The monarchy covered its needs and the local magis-

---

[13] This dependency of the towns on the city can be verified in another kind of documentation, see AM CO. Ordenanzas municipales, Sección XIII, serie 10, nos. 5 & 18 (Torremilano), no. 6 (Montoro), no. 15 (Posadas), and no. 21 (Espiel).

[14] According to P. Goubert, *The Ancien Régime. French Society 1600–1750* (London, 1973), pp. 107–13, 217–19, these 'humble' people, the most numerous social group of the *ancien régime*, made up the 'dependent class' – economically, socially, politically and culturally dependent – both in the country and in the city.

[15] We know that in 1647 the measures established for the payment of the donative of 1629 were prolonged and that they were still being collected at the end of the century. In fact they had become so integral a part of the revenue and expenditure of the Cordoba exchequer that they were used to make payments assigned on the city's *bienes de propios*, Cordoba's annual revenues being considerably diminished by the penurious state of the economy in general in those years and totally inadequate for the many pressing needs they had to cover. The *corregidor*'s salary came from donative measures, for example, (AM CO, Actas capitulares, 6 May

tracy, in the name of the city, obtained extra privileges and increased the wealth of the municipality at the expense of third parties – the towns and the majority of the ordinary people, who bore the heaviest burden of the contribution without any positive compensation. As Ramón Carande so rightly reminded us, the detailed analysis of the state's revenues (and 'the donatives', despite the euphemy, were in fact heavy and repeated exactions) directs us to the particular social stratification of a community if we want to see clearly which social groups paid the contributions and which others, from the seats of power in which they were always well represented, decided what those payments were to be.[16] In the case of Cordoba, and from the fiscal perspective, we can see a double binomial whose opposite poles confront each other horizontally and relate vertically, as shown in the following diagram:

EXPLOITED		EXPLOITERS
towns	*confronting*	city
↕		monarchy
the humble	*confronting*	the powerful

In other words, through the action of the state on society, in this case through the fisc, we can understand not only the state's concerns, but also the relationship of political subordination and economic dependence of the towns to the city, and of the humble to the powerful. The political decisions taken in their respective city councils by the latter's representatives – the gentlemen *veinticuatros* and *jurados* – always favoured the economic interests of the dominant social groups in exploiting the towns of their hinterlands and in putting the screws without compunction on the already impoverished economies of the families of ordinary people.[17]

1672, f. 133r), as did the cost of the refreshments and entertainment given to the colonel and soldiers who passed through the city on horseback on 22 June 1674 (*ibid.*, 6 July 1674, f. 166 r.v.), and the cost of the Corpus Christi fiestas in 1679 and 1681 (*ibid.*, 12 Apr. 1679, s.f., and 16 Apr. 1681, ff. 90v. 91r.).

[16] While public spending reveals the structure of the state, the revenue reveals the stratification of society, following R. Carande, *Carlos V y sus banqueros. II. La Hacienda Real de Castilla* (Madrid, 1949).

[17] Power is 'the capacity of a social class to accomplish its specific objective interests', according to N. Poulantzas, *Poder político y clases sociales en el Estado capitalista* (Madrid, 1972), p. 124.

III. THE ADMINISTRATION OF THE *ARBITRIOS* AND EXEMPTION FROM ECONOMIC OBLIGATIONS

The administration of these special measures was the responsibility of a committee named *ad hoc* by the city. It consisted of the *corregidor*, or his deputy, two gentlemen councillors, who had to be elected every year and who under no circumstances could serve for more than two years, the two principal clerks of the city council, who each received 10,000 *maravedís* a year, and a receiver (*receptor*), who got 100 ducats as an annual salary. The money was to be kept in a chest with three locks in the receiver's house, together with the accounts book that he was obliged to keep. The jurisdiction of this committee was exactly the same as that of the *millones* administration. The half-yearly payments to the royal exchequer were to be made punctually with whatever money had entered the coffers. If there was a surplus it could not be used for any other purpose, but had to be kept for the next payment; if there was a deficit, money could be borrowed from the assets of the municipal granary (*pósito*), or a mortgage (*censo*) taken out on the *arbitrios* themselves, by prolonging their term if necessary so as to be able to pay back the money borrowed or to redeem the capital advanced for the *censo*.[18]

The royal commissioner, Don Alonso de Cabrera, undertook that the king would issue all necessary royal warrants. In their clauses it was stated unequivocally that in the event of any lawsuits that might arise in connection with the administration and collection of the *arbitrios*, the only court with cognizance over that litigation would be the Council of Castile, whose prosecutors were to defend and preserve each and every one of the deed's clauses;[19] that, until judgement was passed, the *arbitrios* would remain in effect; and if there were fines to be paid, they would be paid from the *arbitrios* themselves, or from royal taxes, but never from municipal revenues; and, finally, that if any *arbitrio* failed or was unreliable, the city could introduce alternatives, either in the city itself or in its

---

[18] AM CO, Contaduría, Escritura de 1629, 18 and 26.
[19] All matters concerning both jurisdiction and appeal connected with the 1629 donative were to be regulated in accordance with the decrees of Philip II given at Aranjuez and San Lorenzo on 16 May and 15 August 1590, respectively, relating to the service of the *millones*, *Novísima Recopilación*, VII, 16, 9.

subordinate towns, without the need for new authorisation from the crown.[20]

All the costs of the administration of the *arbitrios*, the lawsuits that arose out of them, and the work of marking out the land that had to be enclosed were to come out of the returns from the measures themselves, and it was on those returns alone that the obligation to comply with the terms of the agreement was laid. Neither the revenues of the municipality nor the private property of the *veinticuatros*, *jurados*, or any other citizen were in any way at risk.[21]

On the questions of who was to administer the measures, what jurisdiction the nominated commission had, how the payments were to be made if there was a deficit, and the terms of the royal warrants regulating the matter of appeals and the fixing of new *arbitrios* should that be necessary, it is necessary to make two important observations. The first is that it was essential to issue the city with whatever legal powers it needed so that there would be no obstacles to its management of the *arbitrios* from intermediate courts, and so that it could establish new measures to make up for the inadequacy of those already established, or even to replace them. The second is that to these juridical powers was added the exemption of the municipal exchequer, as well as that of the property of the *veinticuatros*, *jurados* and citizens, from any economic responsibility in the event of non-payment or the non-fulfilment of what had been contracted. That is to say, the city council of Cordoba procured that its administration of the *arbitrios* was to be uninhibited by any legal impediment and that the municipal revenues and those of the local magistrates were to be free of any economic responsibility. Legal facilities on the one hand and the non-contraction of mortgages on the other were the tangible results of a negotiation in which the city council, taking advantage of the royal exchequer's pressing need for funds, obtained for itself the administration of a service with no obligations other than those necessary for the proper management of that service.[22]

[20] AM CO, Contaduría, Escritura de 1629, 25 and 29. [21] *Ibid.*, 30.
[22] This is why in Cordoba there were none of the negative reactions to these 'donatives' that there were in Seville, to which, quoting Guichot, Domínguez Ortiz refers, *Política y hacienda de Felipe IV*, pp. 43–4.

214   JOSÉ MANUEL DE BERNARDO ARES

IV. CONCESSIONS OF PRIVILEGES

In the two preceding sections, dealing with the type and administration of the *arbitrios* chosen to pay for the donative, we have seen how the city of Cordoba came very well out of it. Now, however, in analysing more closely the privileges it was granted by the crown, we shall see that it was the contracting party which got the more substantial benefits. Consequently, the commonplace that fiscal pressure irremediably impoverished local finances has no foundation, at least in the specific case of the service granted by Cordoba to the crown in 1629.[23] It is true that the central treasury found in local resources an inexhaustible vein of funds that the authorities for their part had no objection to mining, because in exchange they increased the assets and revenues of the municipal exchequers which they controlled as they willed. A distinction has to be made, then, between the general resources of a community which the *regidores* had no qualms about disposing of, since they were not their own, and the private resources of the city council, which increased as the former diminished. How could so many public and communal assets have been released from mortgage if they were exhausted? There was certainly a chronic lack of liquidity, but not a reduction in the patrimonial assets of the municipality.[24]

Two other general benefits were conceded in confirmation of earlier grants. One concerned the prohibition of the alienation or new creation of offices, townships and unpopulated jurisdictions as set out in the 'conditions of the *millones*'; the other applied to the two indefeasible requirements for the office of *veinticuatro* of Cordoba: to be a native (by birth) and to be a householder (*vecino*) of the city, in accordance with the ordinances.[25] Two other clauses, of an economic and administrative nature, increased the salaries for *regidores* and *jurados* who were conducting the city's lawsuits to 1,000 *maravedís* a day if they were in Madrid, and 700 if in Granada,

[23] During the course of the century other donatives were granted to the royal exchequer by the city; for those of 1674 and 1676, for example, a third of the tax on wine, vinegar and oil, as well as part of the silk tax, were set aside, AHN Consejos, leg. 42,717, no. 10, and, and no. 9, ff. 1r.–8r., respectively.
[24] On the amortisation of *bienes de propios*, see AM CO, Patrimonio municipal, Sección 5°, serie 72; G. Anes, *El Antiguo Régimen. Los Borbones* (Madrid, 1975), pp. 408–14; F. Tomás y Valiente, *El marco político de la desamortización en España* (Barcelona, 1971), pp. 12–37.
[25] AM CO, Contaduría, Escritura de 1629, 1 and 14.

and forbade the leasing of the office of *escribano mayor de rentas,* which had been going on despite a law passed specifically to prevent it.[26] A fifth concession banned the billeting of soldiers for six years from 1630 in every place under Cordoba's jurisdiction, in view of the peacefulness of the province.[27] And, finally, the way of paying the royal subsidy (*servicio ordinario y extraordinario*) was altered. Hitherto, 2,500 ducats of revenue a year had been collected from excises on fish and soap, but there was so much fraud committed in the payment of rebates that sometimes the money to be refunded exceeded the entire revenue collected. Instead of excises, it was proposed to assign the subsidy to the *arbitrios* of the 1629 donative as soon as this had been paid off.[28]

V. THE IMPROVEMENT AND INCREASE OF THE CITY'S ASSETS

The first four of these privileges fall within the political-administrative sphere, and the last two concern war and public finance. I am now going to concentrate on the rest, which deal with municipal finances, and more specifically with its revenues which basically came from what were known as the *bienes de propios.*[29] Obviously it was not the intention of these fourteen clauses to give a detailed analysis of all the assets that the Cordoba city council possessed, but rather to set out improved terms for those that already existed, add new ones, and define the purposes for which others were to be used. These were royal grants which considerably strengthened the economic position of the city. If this were not important enough, what needs to be emphasised is the way in which the city council went about building up its municipal patrimony as compensation from the crown for a substantial donative, which the city itself administered but did not pay from its own resources, resources

---

[26] *Ibid.,* 12 and 16.   [27] *Ibid.,* 17.   [28] *Ibid.,* 7.
[29] On the basis of the Ensenada *Catastro,* I studied this subject in my 'Hacienda municipal, oficios y jurisdicciones enajenadas. El municipio de Córdoba a mediados del siglo XVIII', *Omeya* (Cordoba) 23 (1976–9), np. At the moment, I have nearly finished another work on a similar subject, to be entitled, 'Los bienes de propios de la ciudad de Córdoba en el último tercio del siglo XVII'. On the nature, types and evolution of the *bienes de propios,* see I. Alvarez de Cienfuegos Campos, 'Notas para el estudio de la formación de las haciendas municipales', in *Homenaje a Don Ramón Carande* (Madrid, 1963), pp. 3–19; and A. Bermúdez Aznar, 'Bienes concejiles de propios en la Castilla bajo medieval', in *Actas del III Symposium de Historia de la Administración* (Madrid, 1974), pp. 829–53.

which remained free from any obligation that had been contracted. The privileges which the city obtained as municipal assets were the following: the farms of Ingenieros, Butaquillos, Virgenes, Paredones, Medina, Perestrella and Las Hazas de Cordoba to be enclosed in such a way that no one could have common rights of pasturage on them, nor any other kind of usage, despite the fact that the existing ordinances had hitherto permitted precisely that. But at the same time that these properties were being enclosed, it was requested that neither the pastures nor the uncultivated land within Cordoba's municipal district or outside it, where the city had common pasturage rights, was to be put under the plough.[30] What is more, no other councils, even those exempt from its jurisdiction, were to be given permission to enclose grass, acorns, grazing, or watering places on their pastures if the city had any rights of pasturage there. If they did get the royal authorisation for such an enclosure, it was not to be put into effect without the city having previously been called to a meeting of the council.[31]

The same did not apply to the Cordoba city council. On the contrary, it looked after its own nest, not hesitating to alter an old bye-law that laid down that the stubble after harvesting was for common use, but not agreeing to the enclosing of pastures where it enjoyed common grazing with other towns. Here is further evidence of the political subordination and economic dependence of the towns on the city of Cordoba, even when they were not under its direct jurisdiction. The city applied the law of the jungle. Its political concerns were only with the interests of those Cordoba residents who were well represented in the municipal micro-state, from which viewpoint they operated as a coercive institution directing the economic activity of the society.[32] The city was not satisfied simply with improvements. It took advantage of the donative of 1629 to increase its assets, not only in real estate, but also in rights and utilities. Seventy *ubadas* (about 1,660 hectares) of uncultivated land (*tierras baldías*) were to be enclosed as reserved pastures on which

---

[30] On this question the city had already won a court order.
[31] AM CO, Contaduría, Escritura de 1629, 3, 5 and 27.
[32] Elsewhere I have emphasised how the *veinticuatros* were not disposed to relinquish their control of the city's economic life which they had enjoyed since time immemorial, as they had the power to appoint the people through whose hands all the strings of the city's economic life passed; see my 'Conflicto entre los regidores y

common grazing would not be permitted, and fifty *ubadas*, leased for the building of a prison, were to pass into the possession of the city once the prison was finished.[33] A weigh-station and market for fresh and dried fruit, commonly known as the 'pesillo', charging dues of 2 *maravedís* per *arroba*, were established as properties of the city, which could administer them directly or farm them out as it chose. The tobacco and mead monopolies could also be farmed out by the city as part of its assets, and a tavern was to be set up in the inn that the city had in the Plaza de la Corredera to sell wine from the Sierra de Cordoba, the leasing of which would be another asset of the city.[34]

Many of the *arbitrios* imposed for the payment of the donative were also scheduled to become the property of the Cordoba city council in 1647, when its contractual obligations would have been fulfilled and the full amount of the 200,000 ducats paid to the royal exchequer. The *dehesa* of La Jara, originally a common pasture, was to be divided into three equal lots, one to be the property of Cordoba, one to go to the seven towns of Los Pedroches, and the last to continue to be common grazing. Of the *dehesas* of the districts of Hornachuelos, Montoro and Fuenteovejuna, half the revenue was to belong to the city of Cordoba, and the other half to the three towns. The three *dehesas* of El Picacho were also to become in their entirety part of the city's properties. From 1647, the three taverns of La Verdad, San Antón and El Matadero, as well as the public stalls leased in the city's squares and streets, were also to be regarded as the city's possessions, to be leased out to the highest bidder.[35]

But not only did the contract sanction the conversion of extra-ordinary measures (the *arbitrios* of 1629) into ordinary revenues (*bienes de propios*), it also assigned from those revenues for twelve years (1647–59) 600 ducats a year for the upkeep of bridges, fountains, prison, roads and paths, and 60 ducats to help with the cleaning of the San Lorenzo stream. Given the pressing needs that were to be met from the proceeds of the city's properties, these *propios* were not to be subject to distraint, and in the official

el corregidor de Córdoba a principios del XVIII', *Revista de estudios de la vida local* 202 (1979), 289–300.
[33] AM CO, Contaduría, Escritura de 1629, 2 and 4.   [34] *Ibid.*, 6, 8 and 9.
[35] *Ibid.*, 15, 19 and 20.

visitations (*residencias*), the judges were to be particularly sure that this was being carried out to the letter.[36] Lastly, the salary of the city's steward (*mayordomo de propios*) was fixed at 200 ducats a year.[37]

VI. CONCLUSION

The conclusion that can be drawn from all this is that the two parties to the contract, formally signed in a public deed, made mutual concessions to each other at the expense of third parties, who, in the present case, were the subordinate towns of the province and the humble folk, both rural and urban, on whose shoulders fell the largest part, in proportion to their resources, of the fiscal burden that was imposed. The donative of 200,000 ducats enabled the Crown to satisfy in part its financial needs; the Cordoba city council reasserted its political-administrative, financial and military powers in general, and its economic power in particular, by the defence and increase of its *bienes de propios*. This analysis confirms that symbiosis between monarchy and nobility, the two keystones on which the arch of the modern state was articulated, that José Antonio Maravall has so often stressed.[38] The monarchy, despite the fact that the winds were blowing against it, was able to continue with a foreign policy that was already in ruins only because in the seventeenth century it could rely on the most absurd and varied ways of raising money, not the least of which were donatives of the kind we are discussing. The nobility of Cordoba, who held the *veinticuatrías* and thus ran the municipality, got additional *bienes de propios*, and improved facilities for their exploitation. As these were among the most important sources of municipal revenue in the *ancien régime*, this meant an extension for the city councillors of their area of economic operation, which made their politico-administrative control of the community even more effective. In other words, the

---

[36] *Ibid.*, 11.   [37] *Ibid.*, 10 and 13.

[38] In *La cultura del Barroco. Análisis de una estructura histórica* (Barcelona, 1975), p. 72 [*Culture of the Baroque. Analysis of a Historical Structure* (Manchester, 1986), p. 28], Maravall describes the symbiosis between the monarchy and the nobility during the *ancien régime* in the lapidary phrase, 'monarchical–seignorial pyramid with a protonational base, which we are calling baroque society'. Within the structure of that society, the relationship between those two forces in the distribution of political power is explained in his other book, *Poder, honor y élites en el siglo XVII* (Madrid, 1979), pp. 173–250.

greater the power of the city council, in effect the local magistrates, the greater the possibilities they had of political action at a local level.[39] Thus, the financial needs of the monarchy and the privileges of the local nobility were the two essential pivots on which the complex structure of the early-modern state gyrated.[40] Each supported the other because the running of the state itself depended on this understanding, easy enough to achieve when it was based on the most generous mutual concessions, made, however, at the expense of the towns and the ordinary people.

The political power – monarchy plus nobility, at the various levels of its public operation, is the result of a socio-economic structure the elements of which become intelligible to the extent that the historian concerns himself not only with the legal-institutional viscera of the state, but also with another perspective which is their necessary complement, the dialectical relationship between those who exercise this power. Their mutual needs are reconciled within the law – though a law that is a legal expression of a specific, socio-economic situation at a particular historical moment[41] – thanks to measures taken *ad hoc* (as with the 1629 donative), but only by circumventing the demands of a less spectacular but more beneficial national policy, in the case of the Crown, and the legitimate desire of the majority of the people to survive, in the case of the nobility.[42]

[39] In my introduction to T. Márquez de Castro, *Compendio histórico y genealógico de los títulos de Castilla y señoríos antiguos y modernos de la ciudad de Córdoba y su reyno* (Cordoba, 1981), pp. 14–15, I proposed that the Cordoban nobility, who had the wealth, dominated the municipality through the possession of all the city councillorships (*veinticuatrías*) and thereby directed local politics in accordance with their interests.

[40] J.A. Maravall, *Estado moderno y mentalidad social (Siglos XV a XVII)*, 2 vols. (Madrid, 1972), I, pp. 300–10.

[41] F. Tomás y Valiente, 'Historia del Derecho e Historia', in his *Once ensayos sobre la Historia* (Madrid, 1976), p. 173.

[42] For the political stance of the upper classes in their urge to control the state apparatus, see G. Durand, *Etats et institutions, XVI–XVIII siècles* (Paris, 1969), pp. 287–93.

11. *Medina del Campo 1500–1800: an historical account of its decline*

ALBERTO MARCOS MARTÍN

If any Spanish city unmistakably typifies the process of decline which affected the interior of the Peninsula in the late sixteenth and early seventeenth centuries, and continued well into the latter period, it is without doubt Medina del Campo.[1] For this reason Medina has become the model for those who attempt to grasp the full dimensions, consequences and significance of this decline. It is true that Medina's decline has its own peculiar characteristics – its scale, its dramatic proportions, its very chronology – but it is no less certain that its particular case coincides in many respects with that of a great number of other Castilian cities which also, after reaching the height of their prosperity in the sixteenth century, entered upon a period of decline and ruin in the following century. Medina thus takes its place in the wider, more relevant context of national and even continental history.

I

Like any other city during the early modern period, Medina del Campo was many things, but above all it was the home of one of the most important fairs in the kingdom of Castile and one of the principal financial exchanges in Europe. Situated as it was in the centre of the northern meseta, which already in the mid-fifteenth century showed signs of becoming the most thriving region in the

---

[1] This contribution is a re-elaboration specially prepared for this volume of the two chapters which I contributed to *Historia de Medina del Campo y su Tierra*, ed. Eufemio Lorenzo Sanz (Valladolid, 1986), II, pp. 481–522 and 523–634. There, as in my *Auge y declive de un núcleo mercantil y financiero de Castilla la Vieja. Evolución demográfica de Medina del Campo en los siglos XVI y XVII* (Valladolid, 1978), fuller reference will be found to matters merely touched on here.

realm in terms of economy and population, Medina del Campo soon benefited from the extensive network of highways which linked the principal urban centres of the Duero basin and which saw the greatest volume of traffic in the whole country during the sixteenth century. The communication factor contributed vitally to the early commercial development of the town. For almost two centuries Medina existed on account of and for its fairs. Its human potential, its employment structures, its physical layout and many other aspects of its everyday life were closely linked to these periodic fairs. This dependence, however, was to prove fatal for the town (it was legally a *villa* and not a *ciudad*) once the fairs began to decline in importance as a result of the royal exchequer's financial difficulties (which had serious, not to say fatal consequences for private business), the continual deferment of payment of royal debts, and the transfer of the centre of gravity to Madrid and the coastal areas.

From this time on, Medina del Campo slowly but surely sank into a decline, the manifestations of which were a sharp drop in population, changes in the social and professional structure, and the physical deterioration of the town itself. As a result of these dramatic changes, an outward-looking, essentially commercial city became a closed unit of property owners, and in the future would survive thanks to the not inconsiderable profits of the agricultural produce of its hinterland.

II

Medina had become an important mercantile centre in the fifteenth century. The fairs, where goods were contracted, had become solidly established by the beginning of the century, and gradually became an occasion for the settling of debts, no longer at a merely local or regional level, but on a national and international scale.[2] The vast range of possibilities which this opened up for the town attracted immigrants from every corner of the Peninsula and from abroad, so that it would be safe to estimate a population of around 20,000 inhabitants in the early years of the sixteenth century, in view of the constant urban expansion and reconstruction which followed

[2] For the origins, still obscure, of Medina's fairs, there are some references in C. Espejo and J. Paz, *Las Antiguas Ferias de Medina del Campo* (Valladolid, 1908), p. 23ff.

the great fire of 1520 and which presupposes the existence of sustained population growth. However, this is no more than a working hypothesis which at present cannot be checked against more definite figures. According to Tomás González, Medina del Campo (including its outskirts) had a total of 3,872 *pecheros* (taxpaying households) in 1530.[3] This figure is not far off the estimates for the beginning of the century, and would indicate, once the corresponding percentages of *hidalgos* and clergy, both regular and secular, who were not included in the census, have been added, a considerable population growth.[4] We should, however, accept with caution the conclusions to which these figures seem to lead us, since the methods employed and the purpose behind the 1528–36 census conditioned the results, and because the calculations and conjectures underlying the 1591 census are unreliable and the figures derived from them obviously too high, especially those for *hidalgos*.[5]

We lack any other census for the first half of the sixteenth century which could shed light on the pattern of population growth in Medina del Campo during this period. However, everything seems to point to a state of equilibrium, which coincides with the period of greatest activity of the fairs. All the same, we should not disregard the possibility that the population had already begun to fall around mid-century, indicating a change in trend which became more pronounced in the following years.

During the second half of the sixteenth century, Medina's popu-

---

[3] Tomás González, *Censo de población de las provincias y partidos de la Corona de Castilla* (Madrid, 1829), p. 22. We do not know where the archivist at Simancas obtained this information since in the summaries of the 1528–36 census, compiled by the Contaduría de Rentas, only the *vecinos* of the province of Valladolid were counted, without specifying the numbers in Valladolid itself, or in Medina del Campo and Medina de Rioseco, where 'it is not known how many *vecinos* there are, since they were unwilling to submit lists (*padrones*)', alleging privileges of exemption which extended to their respective suburbs, AGS Contadurías Generales, leg. 768; and *CODOIN*, XIII, pp. 521–30.

[4] In the 1591 census, *hidalgos* and clergy amounted to 31.8 per cent of the total. If we add this percentage to the 3,872 taxpaying households in 1530, it gives a population of 5,678, that is, 22,712 and 25,551 inhabitants, depending on the *vecino/* population coefficient used.

[5] G. Moraleja, *Historia de Medina del Campo* (Medina del Campo, 1971), p. 137, citing this same source, postulates a total of 4,136 *vecinos*, corresponding exactly to Ramón Carande's calculations, *Carlos V y sus banqueros* (Madrid, 1965 edn), I, p. 60, after adding *hidalgos* and *caballeros*, but not the clergy, to the number of *pecheros*, in accordance with the procedure used for the allocation of the *millones* in 1590.

lation fell sharply, in two clear phases. Up to 1570–5, population loss was slow but constant; from then on, it became more rapid and more pronounced as the fairs declined in importance.

For the year 1561, there exists one of the most reliable population counts of the sixteenth century. It gives a total of 3,297 *vecinos* (householders), which when multiplied by 4.5 amounts to 14,836 inhabitants.[6] We should add to this figure the numerous regular clergy,[7] and the population we must suppose uncounted, such as domestic servants, who are scarcely mentioned in the count. By that date the population clearly no longer matched that of the first half of the century.

According to a letter sent by the town's *corregidor* protesting against the redistribution throughout Castile of the *moriscos* expelled from the kingdom of Granada in 1570, Medina had a population of 3,050 householders,[8] a figure slightly lower than that of the 1561 population count. So the sudden drop in population which took place in the final decades of the sixteenth century had not yet made itself felt. In the next years, Medina was to benefit from the influx of large numbers of *moriscos* from Granada, resettled after the uprising in the Alpujarras (1568–70).[9]

In 1591, according to Tomás González's census, Medina del Campo had a total of 2,760 householders, of whom 1,882 were taxpayers, 700 *hidalgos*, 136 secular clergy, and the rest members of religious orders at a rate of 10 per household (excluding the Franciscans, 50 in all, who were counted separately).[10] However, everything seems to indicate, as in many other cities, that the 1591 figures are too high, and that there were fewer householders than would appear.[11]

In fact, in 1597, six years later, Medina had 1,897 householders, a fairly acceptable figure, considering how scrupulously this census

[6] AGS Expedientes de Hacienda, leg. 125. For the reasons for choosing this particular coefficient, see A. Marcos, *Auge y Declive*, pp. 48–62.

[7] In 1591, the regular clergy – nuns and friars – were 3.8 per cent of the total population, but in reality must have been more, given the inflated number of lay households one detects in this census.

[8] AGS Cámara de Castilla, leg. 2,160, f. 8.   [9] *Ibid.*, f. 6.

[10] AGS DGT, Inventario 24, leg. 1,301.

[11] See, for example, the case of the two neighbouring cities, Palencia and Valladolid, studied by G. Herrero, 'La población palentina en los siglos XVI y XVII', *Publicaciones de la Institución 'Tello Téllez de Meneses'* 21 (1961), pp. 21–2, and B. Bennassar, *Valladolid au siècle d'or* (Paris–The Hague, 1967), pp. 165–9.

was carried out.[12] This represents a total of 8,536 inhabitants. So, in thirty-six years (the 1561 figures, based on the same criteria as in 1597, are a good point of reference) the town's population fell by 42.5 per cent.[13]

Of course, Medina del Campo was no exception to the general trend of population growth during the sixteenth century. From approximately 1570–5 onwards, the majority of urban centres in Castile, in varying degrees of intensity and duration, suffered a considerable reduction in total population by the close of the century. This is in direct contrast to most of the sixteenth century, when Castilian cities enjoyed a splendid era of development thanks to the expansion of economic activity and to the constant influx of immigrants.[14] This deurbanisation was especially serious in the northern meseta, although the southern meseta and Andalusia, where levels of urbanisation in the sixteenth century were even higher than north of the Tagus, were not unaffected. It was, in itself, tangible evidence, of the most significant kind, of economic decline in Castile. Population loss in the cities was accompanied by, if not a direct result of, the progressive slowing down of urban functions and the decline in urban-based trade and crafts, the basic causes of which are difficult to pinpoint and harder still to explain.

III

Medina's peculiarity lies in the precocity of its demographic decline, and that was simply an outward expression of other profound changes. In fact, if we are to believe the 1528–36 census, Medina's population was at that time greater than it had ever been. Even if

---

[12] AGS Expedientes de Hacienda, leg. 125.

[13] Similar losses can be observed in the parish registers. In the parish of Santiago, around 1570, there were 248 parishioners; at the end of the century there were 151, a loss of 39.1 per cent. The parish of San Juan del Azogue had 92 parishioners in mid-century, 36 in 1619, a fall of 60.8 per cent: Archivo Parroquial de Santiago, libro 1 de defunciones; and AP de San Juan del Azogue, libro 1 de bautismos (now in the Archivo Diocesano of Valladolid [ADV]).

[14] These processes are exemplified in A. Marcos, 'La población', in *Historia de Castilla y León*, VI (Ambito, Valladolid, 1985), pp. 40–51, and the same author's 'El declive demográfico', in *Historia de Castilla y León*, VII (Ambito, Valladolid, 1986), pp. 32–43, for Old Castile and León; D. R. Ringrose, 'El desarrollo urbano y la decadencia española', *Revista de Historia Económica* 1: 1 (1983), 37–57, for Castile as a whole; and the chapter by J. E. Gelabert in the present volume.

this cannot be confirmed, since we know nothing for certain of the preceding years nor of the period between the census and the middle of the century, it remains undeniable that at that moment the town possessed more taxpaying inhabitants (excluding *hidalgos* and clergy) than its total population in 1561, thus indicating a clear downward trend in the intervening period. This was due in great measure to the role the town played in the urban system of which it was part. In its essential features that system was fully developed in the northern meseta by the close of the fifteenth or the beginning of the sixteenth century, and was based on the geographical distribution of its various centres according to their different functions. Medina's function within the system was that for which it was, by its central geographical position, most suited. It was a commercial nucleus, a meeting point for merchants and traders who came to buy and sell,[15] which gradually took on the character of a fair at certain times of the year (May and October), coinciding with key periods in the agrarian cycle which was so decisive for economic activity as a whole. These gatherings, which were at first local or regional, from the middle of the fifteenth century, at least, came to take on a national dimension as a result both of the intensification of domestic interchange and also as trade relations with the Atlantic seaboard countries expanded, particularly those with the Low Countries. This traffic required prescribed meeting-points where contracts could be drawn up and fixed dates when debts could be settled, which fitted in to the calendar of existing European fairs.

Thus Medina del Campo's role was distinct from that of Segovia or, on a different level, from that of Palencia or Avila, where wool-related industries flourished and offered a wide variety of job opportunities to immigrants, which made for a stable population. Nor could Medina be compared with Burgos, home of a number of merchant and banking dynasties, which had organised themselves as the *consulado de comercio*, monopolised wool exports and controlled a good part of Castile's trade with the north European seaboard.[16] Neither was it like Valladolid, royal capital until 1561,

---

15 Particularly after Valladolid became the official residence of the Court and its two annual fairs gradually sank into oblivion, A. Rucquoi, *Valladolid en la Edad Media* (Valladolid, 1987), II, pp. 397–403.

16 For the second half of the fifteenth century, see H. Casado, *Señores, mercaderes y campesinos. La comarca de Burgos a fines de la Edad Media* (León, 1987), particularly fig. 14; Carlos Estepa, et al., *Burgos en la Edad Media* (Valladolid, 1984).

or Salamanca, seat of the most important university in the kingdom, both important administrative and judicial centres. Medina could not even boast a cathedral; it was not a provincial capital, and it had no voice in the Cortes. Medina was *solely* the home of one of Castile's most important fairs, and although this meant that for most of the year (the fixed dates of May and October were soon disregarded) it became the financial and commercial capital, it was not enough to attract a permanent population of any size, particularly once the fairs had begun to lose their mercantile character and had become occasions for the payment of debts and exchange, where, apart from the settlement of debts, the business that went on, to judge by the sums of money that were handled, was of a speculative nature.

This gradual change in Medina's fairs was finally consolidated by the lifting, in 1551, of the ban on precious metal exports, which until then, and occasionally thereafter (between 1560 and 1566, for example), had obliged the *asentistas* to buy goods in Castile (chiefly raw materials) for export, in order to recover the money previously lent to the Spanish monarchy in Italy, France and the Low Countries.[17]

Similarly, there is no doubt that the rupture of the Burgos–Bilbao–Antwerp axis, as a result of the rebellion in the Low Countries and the interruption of direct trade with Spain, was also responsible for the decline and fall of Burgos, and affected other cities within the system, amongst them, Medina. As a result, overseas trade shifted to the south and to the Cantabrian, Atlantic and Mediterranean ports. However, the predominance of paper money and letters of credit over merchandise and hard cash was ensured from the moment in the 1520s that the royal exchequer chose Medina's fairs (and to a lesser degree those of Medina de Rioseco and Villalón) as the venue for the negotiation of the advances it needed so desperately for its own payments and to repay its *asentistas*

For the sixteenth century, see the studies by Manuel Basas. A good part of the wool sales were contracted in Medina del Campo, although the corresponding taxes were paid elsewhere. On this point see Falah Hassan Abed Al-Hussein, 'Las Ferias de Medina y el comercio de la lana', in Lorenzo Sanz, *Historia de Medina del Campo*, II, pp. 13–42.

[17] F. Ruiz Martín, *Pequeño capitalismo, gran capitalismo. Simón Ruiz y sus negocios en Florencia* (Barcelona, 1990), pp. 21–7, where he emphasises the boost this gave to Spanish internal trade.

(generally foreigners rather than Spaniards) who, once paid, took the opportunity of settling their own debts with other businessmen.[18] The majority of those debts, however, were owed in other countries, in the exchanges where they had raised the money to lend to the monarchy. So long as the ban on the export of specie was in force, therefore, in order to repatriate their capital, they had to buy at Medina as many letters of exchange on those foreign fairs as possible in return for the bills they had received from the monarchy.

This exchange of one type of credit for another, apart from attracting and neutralising capital, as well as preventing productive investment, had a negative effect on overseas trade. It frequently happened that the full value of Castilian exports was not repatriated, but passed from hand to hand to end up as drafts on one or other of Medina's banking houses, as Ruiz Martín and Lapeyre have noted.[19] From this time on, everything would depend on the speed with which these promissory notes could be turned into ready cash, in other words how promptly the Crown settled its obligations or announced its readiness to do so by a stipulated date. This affected not only the ability to finance imports and to ensure the sustained growth of local merchant capital with repayments from abroad, but also the availability of capital for other commercial or financial operations on the domestic or foreign market, which were closely tied up with the credit system and dependent in the long run on the financial situation of the royal exchequer. The Crown, in turn, relied more and more on the timely arrival of the American treasure ships and on their cargoes living up to expectations. This remained no less true after 1551 or 1566, when the ban on precious metal exports was lifted. With the foreign *asentistas* (almost all of them Genoese by this time) now able to repatriate their capital, they moved away from trade, in the true sense, and by draining the country continuously of gold and silver, raised the price of money, made the promotion of commercial activity very difficult, and left the economy subject to new forms of dependency.

[18] And not only the Spanish Crown. The king of Portugal's agents also negotiated loans and *asientos* there, at least from mid-century, and as well as the merchants and businessmen, the nobility borrowed there short-term before resorting to *censos* against their estates, Al-Hussein, 'El gran crédito' in Lorenzo Sanz, *Historia de Medina del Campo*, II, pp. 93–122.

[19] Ruiz Martín, *Pequeño capitalismo*; and H. Lapeyre, *Une famille de marchands: les Ruiz* (Paris, 1955).

The *desorden de las ferias*, the confusion and uncertainty mentioned in contemporary documents, which historians have described for the period 1559–78, reveals the extent to which the structure of Medina's fairs rested on very shaky foundations. The 'disorder' was in the main due to the constant deferral of payments because of the monarchy's inability (as principal debtor) to meet its obligations within the specified time. This was nothing new,[20] but it became more frequent, and after 1562 of unparalleled proportions, to the extent that it placed in doubt the fundamental norms of credit on which the whole system was based. From that moment on, bankruptcies followed one after the other, the ruin of one dragging down another in a fatal spiral.[21] At the same time, the great international financiers lost confidence in the fairs. In 1567, the Republic of Genoa decided to forbid exchange with Spain except on short dates and at the fairs, and not long afterwards, in 1571, Lyons did the same. By then, however, letters of credit were being issued for payment at a fixed date in Madrid and Alcalá de Henares, outside the fairs, yet another sign of the decadence of Medina's fairs and thus of the town that hosted them.

Yet the worst was still to come. After several years of repeated deferrals of payments, the decree of 1 September 1575, suspending all payments by the Crown and announcing the abrogation of the *asientos* signed after 1560, dealt a death blow to credit and to Medina's fairs. The fairs were not held again until the end of 1580, in consequence of the *medio general* of 9 December 1577 which restored the position of the Genoese.[22] In spite of the success of the reforms of 1578 and 1583 and the relative frequency with which the fairs were held from then on, Medina's fairs never recovered their former splendour. The volume of trade dropped considerably, and

---

[20] In 1551, the prohibition of exchange between Medina del Campo and the rest of the money markets in the Peninsula (except Portugal) and between fairs (except at par) was a severe blow to the system. In a letter of September 1557, the factor López del Campo blamed it for the disruption he had observed in the fairs' normal functioning.

[21] On this point see Al-Hussein's study, 'Las quiebras de los hombres de negocios castellanos', in Lorenzo Sanz, *Historia de Medina del Campo*, II, pp. 221–66, which analyses some of the bankruptcies in Medina's notarial records between 1548 and 1575; in another chapter, at p. 70, he states that of 10,150 letters of credit which were formally contested before Medina's notaries public between 1509 and 1574, 1,985 belonged to the years 1509–50, and the remaining 8,165 to 1551–74, when the economic situation was more precarious.

[22] Ruiz Martín, *Pequeño capitalismo*, pp. 16–30.

the measures taken in 1571 and 1578 could not stem the competition from Madrid and Alcalá de Henares.[23] What is more, a royal decree of 7 July 1583 finally recognised the right of exchange of other cities, outside the hundred days of Medina's fairs. This meant the end of Medina's monopoly, and the establishment of Madrid, where for some time the royal *asientos* had been negotiated, as an important financial market. The monarchy thus gradually ceased to participate in the fairs, and although its withdrawal guaranteed the regularity of settlements, paradoxically it also had fatal consequences for the town. The royal 'bankruptcy' decree of 1596, when Philip II again appropriated the money intended for his creditors, was the *coup de grâce* for Medina's fairs, though they were not legally dissolved until the beginning of the eighteenth century.

IV

But let us return to 1575, for in that year another event took place no less decisive for the future of the fairs. This was the increase in the *alcabala* tax, and with it the withdrawal of the partial exemption which Medina enjoyed during the fairs, measures which provoked the desertion of the town by merchants and traders and the ruin of private commerce.

The *alcabala* was levied in Medina and its jurisdiction by *encabezamiento*, or composition, within a general system for the entire kingdom. An overall amount was voted in the Cortes for the whole of Castile, and local assignments were then subscribed to individually by the separate cities and towns. Beneficial while population remained static or was increasing, it could become an albatross when population fell and the agreed amount to be paid each year had to be borne by fewer tax payers. Medina del Campo is a good example of the extent to which this second eventuality could become a severe handicap, and damaging to the economic welfare of a town.

During the first half of the sixteenth century, the quota for Medina and its district remained almost static at 8,510,000 *maravedís* in 1537–46, and 8,530,000 *maravedís* in 1547–56.[24] However,

---

[23] This refers to the decrees of 28 July 1571 and 7 Dec. 1578, which forbade foreign exchange at any fair other than Medina's.

[24] For what follows, AGS Expedientes de Hacienda, leg. 125; Moraleja, *Historia de Medina del Campo*, pp. 184ff.; M. Ulloa, *La hacienda real de Castilla en el reinado de Felipe II* (Madrid, 1977), pp. 225–7, whose figures for the *alcabalas* and *tercias* collected by the exchequer in Medina differ slightly from those deployed here.

when Philip II succeeded to the throne, the situation changed radically. In 1564, Medina and its district joined in the *encabezamiento general* voted by the Cortes for the period 1562–76. Its contribution was 12,400,000 *maravedís* a year, a substantial but not outrageous increase in view of inflation, which meant that taxation actually fell in real terms during the first half of the century. However, the precarious state of the royal finances forced the king to ask for a three-fold increase in the *encabezamiento* to come into force on 1 January 1575. This huge and sudden increase threatened to bring trade to a standstill. Medina, seriously affected by the royal suspension of payments that same year and by the withdrawal of many of its privileges and tax exemptions, refused to accept the 40,000,000 *maravedís* it had been allocated in the new *encabezamiento*, a sum double what the local authorities had offered.[25] As a result the villages within Medina's jurisdiction made a separate agreement for 3,168,000 *maravedís* in each of the next following ten years,[26] while Medina's own *alcabalas* were administered directly on behalf of the royal exchequer by the *contador* (auditor), Luis de Peralta. In spite of his insistence that the tax be levied at the full rate, Peralta was unable to collect even the 20 million originally proposed by the town.[27] From 1576 to the end of 1580, Medina again compounded, but for sums much below what had been asked for in 1575.[28] In 1582 and 1583 a new *encabezamiento* was agreed at 17,750,000 *maravedís*, and later renewed until 1588, when a reduction to 16,062,365 *maravedís* was accepted. This agreement lasted for only two years. In 1590 the town council refused to renew it, and

[25] This decision was significant since it meant that Medina's town council voluntarily renounced the advantages to be gained from retaining control of tax administration. It emphasises the gravity of the situation.

[26] This meant that Medina forfeited its chance of transferring part of its fiscal burden to other areas within its jurisdiction, something it had doubtless done in previous years and which was the reason why many of those villages, both before and after 1575, paid the king to make them townships and thus exempt them from its jurisdiction.

[27] 'This was done in such a way that instead of compounding, they impounded, and completely confounded Medina [en lugar de encabezar a Medina la descabezaron y totalmente acabaron], for from then on its warehouses shut down, and there was no longer the merchandise that the merchants used to come and buy', López Osorio, 'Principio, grandeza y caída de la noble villa de Medina del Campo', printed in I. Rodríguez y Fernández, *Historia de Medina del Campo* (Madrid, 1903–4), p. 531.

[28] In millions of *maravedís*, the sums collected in the years mentioned were: 20, 17.2, 18.9, 19.7 and 21.6.

again asked that the tax be administered directly by the Crown. Despite the rigour with which the *alcabala* was collected, returns still came to no more than 11,500,000 *maravedís*. The town's *regidores* were thus able to argue for yet another reduction, which was conceded in 1592 and 1593, with a new *encabezamiento* for 12,000,000 *maravedís*. Almost immediately they were forced to withdraw this offer, and the *alcabalas* for 1594 and 1595 were again administered directly. In 1596, the town council once again refused to compound, and the tax continued in direct administration until 1599, when a quota of 6,400,000 *maravedís* was negotiated for the next ten years. This was only half the quota of the town and its district in the period 1562–76, before the 1575 increase, and in real terms, taking account of the inflation of prices, considerably less than that.[29]

V

Emigration was another feature that directly reflected, not just the increased pressure of the fisc, but the decline of the fairs and the loss of employment and business opportunities in the final decades of the sixteenth century, for the fairs had fomented the social division of labour, stimulated the demand for manufactured goods, and laid the basis for the development of a thriving industrial sector. In the register of the parish of Santiago from 1570, the parish priest took the trouble to note in the margin (in different writing) the names of those householders who had left the town after that date. Of the 155 males in the registers, at least 44 (and others may have escaped the priest's keen eye), or 28.4 per cent, are listed as 'absent'. The proportion is considerably lower in the case of widows and unmarried women householders (12.9 per cent), which seems to imply a lesser degree of mobility in females. At the end of the century a new list of a similar kind was compiled. The percentage of 'absentees' was now 15.1 per cent of men and 6.6 per cent of women, though it is likely that these figures are underestimates.[30] However that may be, those figures presuppose a population loss due to emigration, prior to some date around 1600, close to a final figure of 63 per cent.

[29] This would imply, in spite of the creation of new taxes such as the *millones*, which had the opposite effect, that the negative conditions at the root of Medina's demographic decline persisted and cannot entirely be attributed to the fiscal policy of the monarchy.

[30] AP de Santiago, Libro de matrimonios (in ADV).

More than four-fifths of the emigrants registered in that census
(86.4 per cent) were in active employment. Most of them were
employed in the primary sector (44.7 per cent), which probably took
the brunt of taxation, at a moment when the agricultural expansion
of the sixteenth century was beginning to reverse. However, more
than half of this group were simply day labourers (*jornaleros*),
unskilled workers who could be employed in other sectors. Their
participation in the general exodus would therefore indicate the
incapacity of the productive system as a whole to absorb this surplus
labour force. Shrinking demand, a result of the reduced number of
inhabitants and of the dwindling incomes of the majority of the
population, together with the increasing problem of finding a
market for their products at the fairs, also explains the exodus of
craftsmen and other industrial workers (39.4 per cent). Finally, the
departure of merchants and traders (the remaining 15.7 per cent)
was the logical result of the decline in trade in a town which had lost
many of its privileges and tax exemptions, the very factors which
had originally enhanced its development.

The lack of monographic local studies prevents us from establishing either a chronology or a geography of emigration to other
areas from Medina del Campo. However, we can be fairly sure that
emigration was still an important factor up to the middle of the
seventeenth century, when the migratory balance again turned positive. As to its destination, contemporary historians and the town
council's own reports single out Villalón and Medina de Rioseco,
the sites of the two other most important Castilian fairs.[31] Valladolid also seems to have received a large contingent of immigrants

---

[31] The fact that they should have mentioned among the causes of Medina's depopulation the emigration of its inhabitants to these two towns was in keeping with the
reasons alleged by the town council in favour of the restoration of its privileges.
Villalón and Medina de Rioseco were, in fact, seignorial towns whose activities
and prosperity did not, as Medina's authorities were at pains to point out, benefit
the royal exchequer. But behind such arguments, which are symptomatic of the
disputes that were again breaking out among the three towns over what was left of
the commerce of the fairs, it is quite possible that in both Medina de Rioseco and
Villalón the fiscal pressure of the *alcabalas* after 1575 was comparatively less than
in Medina del Campo, part of a carefully planned attempt by their respective lords
to attract population and draw in trade. The available information shows, for
example, that trade conducted from Medina de Rioseco was not completely
interrupted at the critical moment around 1575, and then continued to grow, not
without some difficulty, until the first years of the seventeenth century; see

from Medina. According to data collected by Rodríguez y Fernández, more than 200 *vecinos* headed in that direction shortly after the royal auditor, Luis de Peralta, began his investigations into the increase of the *alcabala*.[32] Proximity and the fact that Valladolid had already agreed its *encabezamiento* and was offering a number of tax concessions and exemptions to immigrants, undoubtedly encouraged the movement of population from one town to the other.[33] The presence of the royal court in Valladolid during the early years of the seventeenth century reinforced this movement. Only more evidence can confirm these suggestions. In reality, the emigrants may have headed for other regions, such as Madrid, whose population already outstripped that of other cities in the centre of the country, while it had begun to take over the financial functions which Medina had previously carried out. Equally, this emigration may have been part of a more general reorientation of population and the economy to the coastal areas of the north and the Mediterranean.

VI

But the clearest evidence of depopulation in Medina are the changes in the physical structure of the town itself. Medina suffered physically, as it were, the consequences of the decline of its fairs and the loss of a considerable part of its human potential. The expansion which had characterised the town from the late middle ages was followed by a progressive abandonment, which resulted in urban decay and the encroachment of the countryside into the town.

In 1597, the census notes the existence of 376 houses 'closed and uninhabited', and another 114 in a state of ruin. The list is, no doubt, incomplete and many of the houses counted in the 1561 census had already disappeared before the later date, but it is interesting to observe that it was not only the poorest areas of the

Bartolomé Yun, *Sobre la transición al capitalismo en Castilla* (Salamanca, 1987), pp. 410–18.

[32] Rodríguez y Fernández, *Historia de Medina del Campo*, p. 626.

[33] 'It is no wonder that Medina del Campo feels this way and with good reason, seeing that her father (since kings are the fathers of their states), treating her sister Valladolid as if she were his favourite daughter, lowered her *encabezamiento* and granted her a free market, exemption for those who went to live there from taxes, and many other privileges besides, to help her recovery.' López Osorio, 'Principio, grandeza y caída', p. 321.

town that had been abandoned. In the Rua Nueva and the Plaza Mayor, in the streets of Cuenca, Torrecilla, Toledo, Segovia and Juan de Alamos, 'where the merchants and bankers used to live', there were fifty-eight houses shut up, 'most of them in ruins and uninhabitable'.[34] In the session held on 20 April 1610, shortly after the expulsion of the *moriscos*, the town council declared that 'all is ruin and decay . . . particularly the fountains and bridges, roads and pavements', and complained of the lack of funds for the necessary repairs.[35] The misery into which the town had sunk and the reduced means of its inhabitants prevented them from undertaking the repair or renovation of those buildings which needed it, many of which lay empty.

The fall in population and thus in the demand for housing damped down the fever of speculation which had gripped the town at the height of its prosperity, and was the direct cause of the bankruptcy of many property owners, such as the *censualistas* for whom housing had been a convenient form of investment.[36] If we are to believe López Osorio, who faithfully recorded Medina's decline, by the beginning of the seventeenth century approximately 2,500 houses had disappeared. Juan Antonio de Montalvo, another eye-witness of the town's tragic decline, put it even more expressively when he claimed that, within the walls alone, the area covered by derelict houses was extensive enough to grow more than 20,000 *fanegas* of wheat.[37] Both accounts are, as one might expect, much exaggerated, but they transmit that same feeling of impotence and desolation that we find in the discussions of the town council. They are nonetheless valuable expressions of the extent of the disaster that was taking place.[38]

---

[34] AGS Expedientes de Hacienda, leg. 125.

[35] Quoted by Moraleja, *Historia de Medina del Campo*, pp. 174–5.

[36] 'Seeing that the owners [of houses] who gained no profit from them for lack of tenants, let them be repossessed by the *censualistas* [that is to say, they were mortgaged, another sign of impoverishment], who, in order to get something back from them, sold them off for building material, and in this way a great number of houses have been pulled down', López Osorio, 'Principio, grandeza y caída', p. 172.

[37] Juan Antonio de Montalvo, 'Memorial histórico de Medina del Campo', in Rodríguez y Fernández, *Historia de Medina del Campo*, p. 416.

[38] The disaster was not to be checked throughout the next two centuries. In 1752, according to the *Respuestas Generales* of the Catastro, Medina del Campo had '600 habitable houses, 100 uninhabited and 300 in ruins' (AGS Dirección General de Rentas, 1 remesa, libro 647), and although our population count, based on the

VII

The final years of the sixteenth century and the beginning of the seventeenth witnessed a widespread outbreak of the plague which had serious effects on an already weakened population, particularly in Castile, where it was most severely felt. In Medina del Campo, however, the disease, to judge from the available data, was less virulent than in neighbouring towns. We cannot, therefore, blame the spread of the disease for the dwindling population, even if the plague did speed up the process; the emigration of a large number of the townspeople was more important.[39] More serious still for the future of Medina were the consequences of the decree of 1609 expelling the *moriscos*, since it meant the loss of more than 100 families from the already reduced population.[40] Shortly afterwards, in the council session held on 20 March 1611 to discuss the latest *encabezamiento*, the *regidores*, after lamenting the 'great decay in the past year', insisted that the town had 'less than 800 families' and refused to accept the quota allotted them, which they said, 'would mean the ruin of the few remaining families, forcing them to leave'.[41] A figure of 800 *vecinos* is much too low, not surprisingly

---

Respuestas Particulares, accounts for 895 houses, some of them uninhabited, apart from those in ruins and uninhabitable (AHP Valladolid, Catastro, libros 139–45), this figure is still far short of the 2,740 houses quoted in the 1561 census, which, as we have seen, is no high point in the demographic history of the sixteenth century. Finally, the 138 *obradas* (the amount of land which could be ploughed by a man in one working day), which made up the total of cultivated land, much of it within the town walls, is another sure sign of the ruralisation of its urban space which was the result of the transformation of the town's economic basis.

[39] The presence of plague, or simply fear of contagion, probably activated some of the factors that led to the exodus, such as fiscal pressure, since the prophylactic measures and controls implanted by the council had to be paid for by new taxation. We know, for example, that at the beginning of 1600, the town applied for permission to recover in *sisas* (direct taxation on consumer goods) the 1,500 ducats which had been spent on warding off contagion, fencing off the town and putting up wicket-gates, setting up a hospital and paying salaries, as well as the purchase of medicines.

[40] We lack accurate figures of the exact number expelled. Parish registers do not refer to *moriscos* and thus do not enable us to make any sort of estimate. The 1597 census notes the presence of 90 *moriscos* (4.7 per cent of the total population), but this does not appear to be very accurate, as according to information passed to the Council of State in 1609, there were 140 *morisco* 'hearths', 15 of them listed as natives [pre-1570]. According to the official lists of those expelled, 123 *moriscos* (the equivalent of 549 individuals) left Medina.

[41] Moraleja, *Historia de Medina del Campo*, p. 175.

given the subject under discussion, but it does allow us to reject the even more inaccurate figure of 600 *vecinos* quoted by Capmany for 1607.[42]

In fact, although baptismal records indicate a constant decrease in population during the first twenty-five years of the century, a new census drawn up in 1625, in response to the 'donative' demanded by Philip IV, gave a total of 870 *vecinos*, excluding the clergy, both secular and regular, and the *hidalgos*, whose proportion to the total population must still have been high. Mention was made only of thirty-nine *hacendados* and twelve noble widows. Furthermore, only *vecinos* with some trade or profession were counted, perhaps because the census was made by guilds and not by streets, thus omitting dependants and the unemployed.[43] It does not seem possible, therefore, that the population could have fallen below 1,000 families at this period, and Moraleja's figure of 1,194 *vecinos* for 1626 coincides well enough with our own estimate. However, Medina's population had not yet reached the bottom of its slide. The disaster which struck the convent of San Agustín in 1629, causing a death toll which, though accidental, was nonetheless catastrophic in its effects, and the crisis of 1628–32, in which disease and famine combined, reduced still further the town's population and hampered the possibilities of growth in the following years.[44] According to Juan Antonio de Montalvo, who lived through this period, Medina had under 1,000 households at the beginning of 1631, and by 1633, only 700, some 350 families having died out in the meantime.[45] Though not very reliable, the 1646 census is one of the few that exist for the seventeenth century. The report sent in by

---

[42] A. de Capmany, *Memorias Históricas de Barcelona* (Barcelona, 1961), I, p. 905.

[43] AP de la Antigua, Libro de defunciones (in ADV).

[44] For these events, see Marcos, *Auge y declive*, pp. 225–37, correcting what is said there about the nature of the disease, which was not plague but typhus, unrelated to the plague which swept through Catalonia at about the same time, V. Pérez Moreda, *Las crisis de mortalidad en la España interior* (Madrid, 1980).

[45] Montalvo, 'Memorial histórico', p. 416. The registers of several parishes corroborate the extent of this population loss. La Antigua, outside the town walls, in 1594 had a total of fifty-seven parishioners who were heads of families, not counting widows, and in 1617, a total of forty, a reduction of at least 29.8 per cent in only twenty-three years (AP de la Antigua, Libro de defunciones [in ADV]); San Miguel in 1602 had eighty parishioners and in 1639 only fifty-seven, despite having merged with the parish of San Juan del Azogue, a loss of 28.7 per cent, undoubtedly a minimum figure as the final pages of the 1602 register have been lost (AP de San Miguel, Libro de matrimonios [ADV]).

the town council gives a total of 2,383 *vecinos* within its jurisdiction, of whom 650 correspond to the town itself.[46] About this time, baptismal records also reach their lowest point for the whole of the period under study. Nevertheless, this total must be rejected as far too low. The figure of 818 *vecinos* that Moraleja cites for 1648, just two years later, based on a population count carried out street by street, deserves much more credence.[47]

In the second half of the seventeenth century, Medina's population again began to increase as immigration recommenced.[48] In the parishes of Santo Tomás and San Martín, for example, the number of parishioners rose from an index of 100 in 1626–9, to 106 in 1674–8, 121 in 1683–4, and 138 in 1690.[49] Similarly, baptisms in five parishes (San Miguel, San Martín, Santo Tomás, Santiago and San Facundo) rose by something more than 50 per cent in the second half of the century, although most of the rise was limited to the final decade when the positive results of earlier immigration were reflected in the birth rate.

The evolution of Medina's population is in keeping with the general recovery of Castile, noted some years ago by Domínguez Ortiz, and since confirmed by other authors using more precise data.[50] One of them, Henry Kamen, has used Medina as a model for the cities in the northern meseta whose population showed a net increase from mid-century onwards.[51] He gives a figure of 990 householders for 1683, a good deal smaller than the 1,200 inhabitants which Ortega Rubio claims for 1672.[52] These figures can be compared with the 942 *vecinos* of the general census of 1694, and, despite the many deliberate omissions, are indicative of the extent of the growth of population during the second half of the seventeenth

46 AGS Diversos de Castilla, leg. 23.
47 Moraleja, *Historia de Medina del Campo*, p. 233. The figure of 600 *vecinos* given by Artero Moyano for this same year is obviously too low, 'La Guía de Medina', in Rodríguez y Fernández, *Historia de Medina del Campo*, p. 990.
48 The extent and nature of this emigration have been reconstructed from information on the origin of couples named in marriage registers, Marcos, 'El declive demográfico', pp. 274–96.
49 AP de Santo Tomás, Libro 2 de bautismos; AP de San Martín, Libro 1 de matrimonios (in ADV).
50 A. Domínguez Ortiz, *La sociedad española en el siglo XVII* (Madrid, 1963), p. 113.
51 Henry Kamen, *Spain in the Later Seventeenth Century, 1665–1700* (London, 1980), pp. 42–6.
52 J. Ortega Rubio, *Los pueblos de la provincia de Valladolid* (Valladolid [1895] edn 1979), p. 238.

century – 45 per cent more in 1694 than in the no less inaccurate 1646 census.[53] As a result, it is not unlikely, given the necessary corrections, that Medina's population had once again surpassed the 1,000 *vecino* mark by the end of the century.[54]

There was, however, nothing definitive about the process of demographic recovery, nor did it guarantee constant and sustained growth throughout the following century. In other words, Medina del Campo did not share in the general growth of population which was characteristic of the eighteenth century. In common with other cities in the same area, it could not even maintain the population level it reached after the boom of the second half of the seventeenth century. Prosperity, and with it population, had abandoned Castile for good at the end of the sixteenth century. Thereafter, the ruralisation of the northern meseta would intensify during 'the crisis of the seventeenth century', evidence of the steady 'peripheralisation' of the region within the Peninsula and of the persistence of the factors which had originally contributed to its urban decline. The changing economic structures of its cities and the dismantling of the Castilian urban network are the most obvious symptoms of this process. The recovery which took place in Old Castile and León in the eighteenth century was essentially agrarian in nature. It was the countryside which played the principal role in this new phase of growth, which followed the same channels as previous periods of expansion, but this time without any economic stimulus from the cities. From now on, they would live at the expense of the relative prosperity of the rural areas. The lands of the Duero basin would remain trapped by the weight of outdated structures, accentuating their differentiation from other parts of the country where a new economic order was beginning to bear fruit, or, at least, where they were more able to take the opportunities still offered by the old structures. Medina del Campo, in the very heart of the meseta, typifies, we might say dramatically, the development of many Castilian cities and, indeed, of the interior of Spain as a whole, during the eighteenth century.[55]

---

[53] *Ibid.*   [54] Tomás González, *Censo de población*, p. 22.

[55] Birth rate figures back up this statement, since at no time during the eighteenth century did baptisms equal those of the last thirty years or so of the seventeenth. This is confirmed by the general censuses made in the eighteenth century, in none of which does Medina's population number more than 1,000 *vecinos*. Thus, although the *Respuestas Generales* of Ensenada's Catastro in 1752 speak of a population of 'about 1,000 *vecinos*' (AGS Dirección General de Rentas, 1 remesa,

A good many years were to pass before Medina would succeed in emerging from its long-term collapse. Seriously affected by the widespread crisis at the beginning of the nineteenth century, when to the effects of a severe food shortage were added those of a malaria epidemic and the events of the War of Independence, in which the town was painfully involved, Medina's population was to fall still further. In 1810, there were only 681 householders. In 1838, four years after cholera had decimated the population, the total number of inhabitants was 3,274,[56] fewer than in 1752 or 1787. Medina had become, demographically speaking, little more than a village, in sharp dissonance with the large number of churches, convents and mansions within its walls. These buildings were material evidence of a social and economic domination in the past which showed no signs of diminishing. In this respect, the dissolution of the property of the regular clergy, and similar measures taken later by Madoz, solved nothing, at least, in the short term. In 1848, Medina had, according to figures quoted by Madoz in his *Diccionario Geográfico*, 730 households with a total of 2,760 inhabitants. In 1855 there were 3,174. Only the construction of the railway through Medina to the north in the 1860s would arouse the town from its centuries-long lethargy. Benefiting once more from its advantageous geographical position, Medina became, from that time on, a railway hub and a major communications centre, essential prerequisites for its development as an important regional base for the distribution of

libro 647), the number of 'families' (probably not the same as *vecinos*) registered in the *Respuestas Particulares* totals 929, the equivalent of 3,441 inhabitants, at a rate of 3.7 persons per family (AHP Valladolid, Catastro, libro 142). To this total should be added the families of approximately 50 members of the secular clergy, which still leaves us below the 1,000 mark. There are good reasons to suspect that Medina's population fell below even these levels in the second half of the eighteenth century. This can be deduced from the 9 per cent decrease in baptisms from the first half of the century, although we cannot accept a corresponding reduction in the birth rate. This hypothesis is supported by the results of the *Comprobaciones* of the Catastro carried out in 1761 (743 *vecinos*) and of the census of 1765 (671 *vecinos*). These figures should not be taken too literally, since they obviously do not include the entire population. Unfortunately, the data contained in Aranda's census of 1768 is incomplete – figures for three parishes are missing (Biblioteca de la Real Academia de la Historia, leg. 9/6.176); but the 3,454 inhabitants, including members of the regular and secular clergy, noted in Floridablanca's census of 1787 (Bibl. RAH, leg. 9/6.253), are proof that Medina did not participate in the general population growth which other areas of the country were experiencing at this very period.

[56] Moraleja, *Historia de Medina del Campo*, pp. 337, 311.

produce and an incipient industrial nucleus. Needless to say, it had gone a long way round to reach this point and, in the meantime, had let many opportunities pass it by. The single fact that it was not until the 1870s, and without any great change in its demographic structures, that Medina surpassed its baptism figures for the final years of the seventeenth century, to say nothing of earlier periods when the town's population was four or five times greater, is revealing enough.

VIII

Medina del Campo thus constitutes an illuminating example of resistance to social and economic change. It indicates just how slowly the transition to capitalism took place in Castile. Commerce and the fairs had put life into the town during the fifteenth and sixteenth centuries and had given it a preeminent place in the incipient capitalism which was developing at home and abroad. But with economic activity limited to the circulation of money and financial speculation, the traditional structures hardly changed. Indeed, when economic activity declined, they emerged even stronger. Medina survived during the centuries that followed essentially as a rentier town, the seat of a few religious institutions and the residence of a privileged minority, who appropriated to itself a substantial part of the product of the labour of the majority, over an area which extended well beyond the limits of the town. The underlying logic of the socio-economic system in which it was embedded would finally triumph and determine the subsequent development of the town, not only preventing its recovery after the decline of the fairs, but also limiting the possibilities of growth in the future.

Let us examine, therefore, this other reality, since it lies behind the demographic changes we have been describing. Some of the censuses we have used provide full information about the economic activities carried on by the people of Medina and make it possible to calculate the proportion of productive and non-productive residents, and the relationship between them, and between the various types of economic activity and the different occupations. The population counts of 1561 and 1597, the list of householders in 1625, and the Catastro of 1752 make it possible to sketch over the long term a reasonably accurate picture of the division of labour at each of these dates, and, more interestingly, to compare them.

In 1561, the predominance of industrial activities over the primary sector was total, with, respectively, 47.3 and 19.1 per cent of all those with an occupation. The growth of the tertiary sector, with 33.5 per cent, despite the diversity of its trades and professions, underlines the eminently urban character of the town, and bears testimony to its commercial orientation. The fairs, still thriving at this date, undoubtably account for this distribution, bringing together as they did, merchants and other businessmen, whilst creating employment linked to those commercial activities, and constituting an excellent market for the sale of local manufactures.

By the end of the sixteenth century, the situation had changed considerably. While the proportion of those employed in industry was still more or less the same at 44.8 per cent, the decline in the fairs had created a slump in commercial activities and consequently in the tertiary sector, down to 27.5 per cent. Most of the trades linked to large-scale commercial activities had disappeared. Meanwhile the ruralisation that was to become established in the early years of the next century, was getting under way, a process which the growth of employment in the primary sector to 27.6 percent of those with occupations fully confirms. Once the fairs disappeared and economic depression had set in, Medina, like other cities in the meseta, returned to the soil as the only, however uncertain, means of survival.

In 1625 the structure of employment that was to be characteristic of the town until the advent of the railway was clearly in place. This was defined primarily by the overwhelming predominance of agriculture (43.5 per cent), at the expense of manufacturing (27.3 per cent); the composition of the service sector (29.1 per cent), made up mainly of small-scale trades, if we exclude those activities connected with the wine trade, underlines the residual and unproductive nature of this sector. Thus, in little less than fifty years, Medina's economic life had undergone drastic transformation.

During the eighteenth century this occupational structure persisted, only accentuating those elements most directly linked with the agrarian economy. By 1752, agriculture gave employment to practically half the work-force (48.2 per cent), a figure which would be higher if we included those who combined agriculture with other occupations. On the other hand, the manufacturing sector fell to 26.1 per cent of the active population, the lowest figure for the whole period. Finally, the tertiary sector suffered a corresponding reduction (25.6 per cent), despite the town's continuing to be the centre of administration and other services for its district.[57]

A more detailed analysis reveals that more than two-thirds of those employed in agriculture at these four dates were day labourers (*jornaleros*), unskilled workers with no land of their own. On the other hand, the proportion of husbandmen – *labradores* (not necessarily peasant proprietors), was little more than one-tenth of those employed in agricultural activities in 1561 and 1597, 18.2 per cent in 1625, and 17.9 per cent in 1752, figures which indicate the existence of a very polarised structure of landownership. Also notable is the existence in 1561 of a substantial number of market-gardeners, indicating a growing diversification of demand for foodstuffs and, consequently, a higher standard of living. In subsequent listings their number shrinks markedly, and in 1625 there are none at all. Cattle and sheep farming gained in importance, in both absolute and relative terms, rising in the first three censuses from 6.4 per cent, to 9.5 per cent and 12 per cent of all primary activities, paralleling the process of ruralisation that dominated the town once the fairs had begun to decline. By 1752, these activities had decreased, although there was still an excessive number of shepherds for a town whose flocks were not at all numerous.

As for craftsmen, in every case the textile and leather industries absorbed more than half of those employed in manufacturing. Nevertheless, the make-up of the various trades does not suggest the existence of any large industries. They are, in the main, one-man activities (tailors, shoemakers, stocking-makers, tanners, saddlemakers, etc.), with no more help than that of a journeyman or an apprentice. The craftsmen connected with the different production processes of large-scale industries (weavers, carders, cloth-shearers, dyers, etc.) are few. What we have then is a second-order manufacturing activity of re-elaboration, geared to the making-up of consumer goods (clothes and shoes). The rest of manufacturing activity depended even more on the vicissitudes of the economy. Thus,

[57] These percentages largely tally with those for the sectoral distribution of the net domestic product of the town (53.1 per cent, 18.4 per cent and 28.4 per cent respectively), which can be accurately estimated by aggregating the monetary values (or net family incomes) established in the Catastro. Attention should be drawn to the importance of agriculture-related production, despite the output of this particular sector being the most undervalued, and of the tertiary sector compared to that of craft manufactures.

whereas in 1561 and 1597 the percentage of the active population employed in the timber, metal and building industries comprised 12.5 and 11.8 per cent of the total, and 8.2 per cent in 1752, it was a mere 1.6 per cent in 1625, when, in keeping with what we have said about the physical decay of the town, no building activity of any kind is recorded. The same can be said of the decorative and the book industries (silversmiths, jewellers, engravers, gilders, painters, printers and bookbinders), which were closely connected with the fairs and almost non-existent once they had ended. On the other hand, the proportion of workers in the food trade kept up throughout the period, though not without fluctuations. Nonetheless, the rich variety of food-related trades in 1561, pastry-cooks, confectioners, marzipan-makers, nougat-makers, as well as bakers and millers, gives the impression of a considerable diversification of demand at this date.

The tertiary sector includes representatives of wholesale and retail businesses, the professions, and even the small, marginal trades. Amongst the former, the 1561 census counts thirty-eight merchants, four of them dealing in cloth, and three in iron, four representatives of foreign firms, six traders, three money-changers or bankers, and a considerable number of subsidiary agents connected with commerce and finance (sixty-two brokers, fourteen contractors and four cashiers). Together they made up 6.4 per cent of the active population. By 1597, big business employed only twenty-two persons, most of them brokers and contractors, clear proof that the decline of the fairs was a reality before the end of the century. Ten brokers and four contractors, all involved in the wine trade, were, by 1625, all that remained of business on a large scale, and by 1752 there is no one at all who fits into this category. The celebration every Wednesday of a free market, and that of no great size, was by then all that was left of the town's once brilliant mercantile past.[58]

The decline in small businesses – particularly food supply and clothing – was less spectacular, although the variety of trades in this category by 1752 in no way compares with that in 1561. Indeed, certain activities, such as book-selling (there were fourteen

---

[58] A privilege, granted by Charles II to Medina for a 'service' of 2,000 ducats, permitted the celebration of weekly markets. By the mid-eighteenth century, however, according to the *Respuestas Generales* of Ensenada's Catastro, the market had become so reduced that there was 'very little trade, few wares for sale, and so it was of neither use nor profit'.

booksellers in 1561, nine in 1597, and only one in 1625), had disappeared totally by 1752.

The decline which took place in Medina from the end of the sixteenth century was felt also in local administration and in the organisation of the life of the community. Thus, whereas in 1561 there was a remarkable variety of services and public officials, by 1597 their number had fallen considerably, although the proportion of the active population employed in this sector had actually increased. In 1625, the only representatives of this branch of activity were the town councillors (*regidores*), their numbers having increased, by virtue of the sale of offices by the Crown, to twenty-eight, from sixteen in 1561, and twenty-five in 1597. Meanwhile, other responsibilities of municipal government were neglected. By 1752, there were only seven *regidores*, one office being vacant, but other public offices had been revived, some of which no doubt existed in 1625 without being listed. The liberal professions and personal services (cleaners, notaries, schoolmasters, treasurers, etc.) suffered a reduction in numbers, matching the decline of population, but remaining at about 5 per cent of the total, only rising to 7.6 per cent in 1752. Finally, the existence of nine couriers in 1561, but only two, plus a postmaster and one postman, in 1597, is indicative of Medina's growing isolation from the rest of the world. Neither in 1625 nor in 1752 did anyone involved with the transmission of news and letters, services which had once functioned actively and efficiently, as Simón Ruiz's rich archives show, appear in the censuses.

This occupational structure is an inverse image of the structure of demand. In other words, it corresponds to a relationship between needs and purchasing power which was realised in the market. Furthermore, in view of our analysis so far, it would not be too rash to claim that Medina's income was, on the whole, higher in the sixteenth century than in the seventeenth or in the eighteenth, as the nature of the various activities and the greater diversity of output and demand would suggest.

In fact, while at any of the four dates in question more than half of those in employment carried out activities related to the production of staples and necessities (clothing, food, housing), items which absorbed practically the entire disposable income of the majority of the population, it is equally true that this proportion varied markedly from one period to another. In 1561, those employed in the food, clothing and housing sectors comprised 58.1 per cent of the total, but only 21.4 per cent of them were employed in food production (primary activities as well as the food industries), whereas clothing-related crafts and shoe-making accounted for 26.6 per cent. At a time when the demand for food was naturally greater than the demand for textile goods or footwear, such proportions reflect the dominance of secondary and tertiary activities in urban centres, leaving those activities directly concerned with food production to a more or less extensive rural hinterland upon which the towns depended for their provisioning. Moreover, through the fairs, industrial activity in Medina at this time satisfied a much wider demand than the merely local.

The diversity of demand in 1561 reflects this penetration. The book and the art industries gave employment to 4.6 per cent of the active population; the timber, leather or metal industries, together, employed only 16 per cent. The demand for services, from both the public and the private sectors, contributed in turn to increasing the relative weight of the tertiary sector and lent a more modern and diversified tone to the social and professional structure of the town. Alongside the demand for domestic and religious services, hard to estimate from the 1561 census, but to judge by the other sources very large, there existed a considerable demand for notarial, legal and medical services, which employed ninety-eight persons (4.8 per cent of the active population). Another sixty-five individuals (3.2 per cent) were directly involved in the demand created by the local authorities. There still remains a group ranging from inn-keepers to large-scale businessmen, and including the small tradesmen, who totalled in all 13.1 per cent of the active population.

By 1597, the situation had changed substantially. To begin with, the food/clothing/housing group employed 64 per cent of the active population, although the most noteworthy change is the increase of those employed directly in the production and distribution of food, a third of the total (36.6 per cent, to be exact). These proportions – 77.4 (excluding housing which had no representatives) and 58.4 per cent respectively – were even higher in 1625, when the process of ruralisation which had begun at the close of the sixteenth century was reaching its peak. The decline of the fairs, on the one hand, and almost certainly the fall in income levels, on the other, shifted the pattern of demand for the majority of Medina's inhabitants and, therefore, the structure of production towards the satisfaction of primary needs, and reinforced the movement towards the consolidation of a predominantly agrarian economy, with a high degree of autarky.

Things do not seem to have changed much in the years that followed. In 1752, 66.7 per cent of the active population was still employed in food production and distribution, clothing and housing. With these should be included thirty retailers (4.4 per cent of the total), who were simply shop-keepers selling food and clothing. The occupational classification of the rest of the active population fully confirms this stasis. The timber, leather and metal trades employed 13.2 per cent of the active population in 1597, 5.4 per cent in 1625, and 6.5 per cent in 1752, revealing the continuing weakness of these genuinely industrial sectors. At the same time, the demand for luxury or art goods reached rock bottom. Only the demand for personal services remained stable, or even rose somewhat, with 5.4 per cent of the active population in 1597; 5.7 per cent in 1625; and 7.6 per cent in 1752. This was caused by the demand for services from certain specific individuals and institutions, some of whom were non-resident landowners whose rents were managed by a local steward or administrator. But what most reveals the changes in the town's economic structure, once the irrevocable decline of its fairs had set in, is the reduction of those occupations directly related to commercial activity. Indeed, by the middle of the eighteenth century, Medino del Campo was no different from any other Castilian city of a similar size and category. It had even fallen behind, in wealth and manpower, other towns formerly under its jurisdiction, such as La Nava, and to a lesser degree, Rueda, La Seca or Sieteiglesias, all of which had emerged from the crisis of the seventeenth century relatively better off.

IX

The reason for this is to be sought in the consolidation in the old fairs town of Medina of social relations of a feudal type, typified by an extremely unequal distribution of property, which not only determined the forms of exploitation of the land and the distribution of agricultural surpluses, but also effectively blocked the development of productive forces once they had passed a certain limit. In fact, only 24.6 per cent of unirrigated arable land was owned by *vecinos* of Medina. The bulk of it was in the hands of religious institutions

(46.4 per cent), or of clergymen in a private capacity (4.6 per cent). The remaining 24.3 per cent belonged to residents of other towns of the district (3.2 per cent), or to others who lived further afield, mostly members of the nobility (21.2 per cent). Medina's laity owned rather more of the vines (28.9 per cent), which, though occupying almost a quarter of all cultivated land, had shrunk significantly since the sixteenth century. Their ownership was very fragmented, as was that of the orchards and allotments, which were in any case little more than 1 per cent of the total arable area.[59]

But it was not only in the ownership of the land and in the resulting appropriation of a substantial proportion of the surplus product of the soil that the dominance of the privileged classes, especially of certain religious institutions, was felt.[60] As beneficiaries of the tithes and recipients of incomes from perpetual leases of lands, including those pertaining to other towns of the province, their position was reinforced within the complex mechanism of the distribution of production.[61] Not only that, the Church, in general, and some noble landowners and local oligarchs, in particular, were also the principal holders of government bonds and private annuities (*juros* and *censos*). The amount of capital placed in these forms of debt is clear proof of the power of these *rentistas*, who, in this way, extended their involvement in the product of the land, both

[59] AHP Valladolid, Catastro, libros 139–45. These figures should be analysed from two points of view. In the first place, because land ownership was very concentrated, many of Medina's *labradores* were merely tenants. The marquis of Tejada, for example, owned a third of all the arable and a fifth of the vineyards held by the *labradores* listed, who themselves owned only 6.1 per cent of the arable and 13.6 per cent of vineyards within the *término* of the town. Secondly, a good deal of the land considered by the Catastro to be the property of those directly working it, was in actual fact held on hereditary or perpetual leases (*foro* or *censo enfitéutico*) from one of the many religious institutions or private individuals. Furthermore, much of the land owned by residents of Medina was mortgaged against *censos*, with the loss of certain property rights to the benefit of their creditors or *censualistas*.

[60] For 72.4 per cent of rented lands in Medina's jurisdiction in 1752, this represented 15.8 per cent of the gross product obtained from them in an average year, a figure which automatically increased when harvests were poor. The burden of this should be calculated against net income rather than the gross product, that is, what was left of the harvest once the farmer had put aside the amount necessary for the following year's sowing and for other production costs.

[61] The income from *foros* and *censos perpetuos*, and there were as many as 1,858 contracts of this type registered in the Catastro, of which more than two-thirds were held by the clergy, exceeded in monetary value all the rent from land in the district of Medina, although covering a much wider area.

around the town itself and further away from it.[62] The same is true of the numerous legacies, masses, chaplaincies, charities, etc., with which certain estates and rents were burdened (when they were not themselves endowments), and from which the Church benefited as patron, and/or supplier, of the perpetual religious services stipulated in these bequests.

These were, in effect, further means for the extraction of profit which, together with state and municipal taxation, made for a new redistribution of income, accentuating even more the inequalities between the few who benefited from this flow of wealth, and who were at the same time the beneficiaries of the unequal distribution of landownership, and the great majority of the population. The effect on the ordinary household was to depress still further the disposable incomes of a wide range of social groups, with negative results for patterns of spending and production. That in turn reduced the capacity for saving and investment of the population as a whole. The privileged groups and institutions who monopolised a great part of the wealth and income were practically the only ones able to save and invest. It is clear, however, that they were not at all disposed to alter a system of which they were the greatest beneficiaries, and naturally tended rather to its perpetuation, by putting capital into the very forms of investment (land, mortgages, etc.) which enabled them to extend the means of extraction available to them and, consequently, their share of agricultural production.

This was the outcome to which Medina del Campo was destined once its fairs went into decline at the end of the sixteenth century. The 'crisis of the seventeenth century' played a crucial role in the consolidation of the economic and social order which the Ensenada *Catastro* describes in the mid-eighteenth century, and which, in turn, explains both the dimensions of the 'crisis' in Medina and the difficulties the town was to face in the future in maintaining a continuing and self-sustaining growth of its economy on the basis of the only alternative left to it – agriculture.

---

[62] The nominal value alone of the *censos consignativos* held by townsmen and religious institutions in Medina, in 1752, amounted to 6,084,346 *reales*, equivalent to a sum five times greater than the entire net product of the town, although the geographic area from which they were drawn was not limited to Medina, but extended throughout the whole province of Valladolid, and even further afield.

12. 'Refeudalisation' in Castile during the seventeenth century: a cliché?

IGNACIO ATIENZA HERNÁNDEZ

To respond coherently to the question in the title and to enter into a serious discussion of refeudalisation would require the prior definition of what we understand by feudalism – given the rather ambiguous nature of the term, which, like other terms, has changed over time,[1] – in order then to explain which structures were preserved in full vigour, or indeed resuscitated in this period. The limited length of this chapter makes this task impossible and the nature of its readers renders it unnecessary.

Fortunately, we seem to have left behind the less than purely scientific confrontations between institutionalists and historical materialists when it comes to defining the historical construct of feudalism.[2] The brick walls between those who try to classify it in exclusively juridico-political terms and those who want to reduce everything, dogmatically and mechanistically, to the development

Although some of the ideas expressed here have been refined in later works, especially in 'El Señor avisado: programas paternalistas y control social en la Castilla del siglo XVII', *Manuscripts* 9 (1991), 155–207, and 'Consenso, solidaridad vertical e integración versus violencia en los señoríos castellanos del siglo XVII y la crisis del Antiguo Régimen', in *Señorío y feudalismo en la Peninsula Ibérica. Siglos XII–XIX* (Zaragoza, 1991), I remain convinced of the essential validity of my arguments written nearly eight years ago. Following a great deal of thought, my conviction that history as a discipline must preserve the historiographical records which reveal the degree of knowledge and the state of research in specific fields at all times, leads me, despite generous invitations from the editors, to repeat intact what I wrote so long ago, except for including in the bibliography works which at that time were in the process of being published.

[1] M. Foucault, *Archéologie du Savoir* (Paris 1969), and *Le Mots et les choses* (Paris, 1966).

[2] A good summary of the various stances is found in John E. Martin, *Feudalism to Capitalism. Peasant and Landlord in English Agrarian Development* (London, 1983), pp. 1–57.

of the productive forces, the relations of production and the appropriation of surplus value seem to be crumbling, and for the better, allowing some communication between the two sides.

We say for the better, not because we want to defend an eclecticism that in general is unsustainable, but rather because we agree that a socio-economic formation is something unitary, though consisting of multiple variables and parts with their own (variable) hierarchy of importance, and that the totality can only be comprehended by taking into account all its constituent parts.[3]

In the limited space available I shall concentrate on two elements that seem to me especially important in the definition of feudalism, naturally without discounting other possibilities; on the one hand the existence of the *señorío* (lordship), and on the other the influence of the *nobleza* (nobility) as a hegemonic class (a term I believe it is legitimate to use for this period)[4] in the political sphere.[5] This is understood in the Weberian sense of the 'privatisation' of the use of military violence, and in the corporate appropriation of the means of administration. Thus I believe we must analyse the material means of political power in the same way as the means of production. Political and economic structures cannot be analysed independently, but only symbiotically, to use a biological term, or bijugatively, to use a mathematical one.

We believe that during the seventeenth century, at least in the Crown of Castile, the quantitative and qualitative development of the *señorío* is unquestionable, as is the increase in the effective power of the nobility. It would, therefore, be correct to speak of refeudalisation as we conceive it. To this we should add the existence of some intermediate powers of increasing importance, the municipalities, which have prompted an excellent English historian, I. A. A. Thompson, to refer, perhaps not entirely exactly, to a period of

[3] P. Vilar, *Iniciación al vocabulario del análisis histórico* (Barcelona, 1980), pp. 67–70; see also the argument of Reyna Pastor in the collective work *Estructuras feudales y feudalismo en el mundo mediterráneo* (Barcelona, 1984). There is a review of the problem in Ignacio Atienza Hernández, 'El "revival" de la feudalidad y la búsqueda de las "entidades nacionales"', *Revista Internacional de Sociología* 43 (1985), 529–32.

[4] Its theoretical basis is in Vilar, *Iniciación al vocabulario del análisis histórico*, pp. 107–41.

[5] Javier Gil Pujol, 'Notas sobre el estudio del poder como nueva valoración de la historia política', *Pedralbes. Revista de Historia Moderna* 3 (1983).

'decentralisation', 'provincialisation . . . of power' and 'debureau-
cratisation'.[6]
With this approach we move away from the under-substantiated
and over-categorised definition of refeudalisation, employed by
such an eminent historian as Hobsbawm, who, referring to the
Italian model, speaks of a 'parasitical capitalism in a feudal world',[7]
and closer to Rosario Villari when, in analysing the Italian case, he
believes it important to emphasise that refeudalisation

> is not only observed in an accentuated redeployment of capital
> and initiatives from the manufacturing and mercantile sectors
> into agriculture or into privileged rentier investment, but also in a
> kind of secular paralysis that affects the entirety of human
> activity, economic and political. It is something like the triumph
> of a social mechanism that prevents the formation and develop-
> ment of any force tending to act with independence of the feudal
> structures.[8]

The existence of a refeudalisation during the seventeenth century
will mean breaking with the unidirectional analysis often applied to
the evolution of European history, a slanted approach, given that
rather than a march towards what the defenders of this option call
progress or, what is synonymous, capitalism, historical reality is
dialectical. It is a process of push and pull, of advance and regression, always, of course, more or less in agreement with our own
convictions which lead us to subscribe to one or other historiographic model.[9]
After this preamble, necessary to explain the methodological
coordinates from which we are starting, it is time to embark on a
critical and empirical examination of the problem, without forgetting that it must necessarily be set within the context of the so-called

[6] I. A. A. Thompson, *War and Government in Habsburg Spain 1560–1620* (London, 1976). Note the critique and comments on the opinions of the above in Pablo Fernández Albaladejo, 'La decadencia española a través de los historiadores anglosajones', *Libros* 12 (Dec. 1982), 9–11.
[7] E. Hobsbawm, 'The Overall Crisis of the European Economy in the Seventeenth Century', *Past and Present* 5 and 6 (1954).
[8] R. Villari, *La revuelta antiespañola en Nápoles* (Madrid, 1979), p. 15. By the same author, *Rebeldes y reformadores del siglo XVI al XVIII* (Barcelona, 1981). There are three interesting articles on the topic in this book.
[9] J. Fontana, *Historia. Análisis del pasado y proyecto social* (Barcelona, 1982). Ignacio Atienza Hernández, '¡Temblad, temblad, Neorrankianos y otras hierbas académicas!', *Revista Internacional de Sociología* 48 (1983), 691–4.

'crisis of the seventeenth century' that has spilt rivers of ink.[10] It was a crisis that had its effect on a royal fiscal policy which had already suspended payments in 1557, and that cannot be unconnected with the bankruptcies of 1575, 1596 and 1607[11] and the introduction of a new system of taxation (the service of the *millones*) in 1590 and 1600, which meant the victory of a medieval fiscality over a modern fiscal regime,[12] and, by permitting the intervention of the Cortes, opened the way to constitutional dysfunctions.[13]

The pressure on the royal finances was derived in the first instance from military expenditure. Thus it was war that was largely responsible for provoking specific changes in the structures of the seventeenth century, in line with the well-known arguments of Sombart (1913) and Nef (1942), as refined by Theda Scockpol's view that European history was determined by the conflicts generated between its political components, and as applied to the early modern Castilian case by Thompson.[14]

In the desperate search to obtain hard cash the monarchy attempted a series of solutions, symptoms of the crisis, that were in addition an unquestionable sign of this refeudalisation. I refer to the sale of titles and the misnamed sale of vassals, or 'seignorialisation'.

The social organisation of the *ancien régime* was based on orders. In fact some authors, Artola amongst them,[15] characterise the

---

[10] For reasons of space only we select the debates in *Past and Present* assembled by Trevor Aston in *Crisis in Europe 1560–1660* (London, 1965). For a commentary on and a summary of the latest opinions of Morineau, Wallerstein, Italian historians and others, see P. Fernández Albaladejo, 'Veinticinco años de debate sobre la crisis del siglo XVII', pp. 368–89. Regarding the Castilian example, one of the latest contributions is that of Angel García Sanz, 'Auge y decadencia en España en los siglos XVI y XVII: Economía y sociedad en Castilla', *Revista de Historia Económica* 1 (1985), 11–27.

[11] Felipe Ruiz Martín, 'Las finanzas españolas durante el reinado de Felipe II', *Cuadernos de Historia* 2 (1968), 109–73; David Ringrose, 'El desarrollo urbano y la decadencia española', *Revista de Historia Económica* 1 (1983), 37–41.

[12] Ignacio Atienza Hernández and Beatriz Cárceles de Gea, 'El gobierno político de la monarquía (1577). II. La Hacienda Real. Ingresos y gastos', in papers of the conference, *Hernán Cortés y su tiempo* (Cáceres, 25–30 Nov., 1985), Mérida, Junta de Andalucía, 1987, pp. 558–68.

[13] Pablo Fernández Albaladejo, 'Monarquía, Cortes, y "cuestión constitucional" en Castilla durante le Edad Moderna", *Revista de las Cortes Generales* 1 (1984), 11–34.

[14] Thompson, *War and Government in Habsburg Spain.*

[15] 'El Antiguo Régimen', in *Estudios sobre Historia de España. (Homenaje a Tuñón de Lara)*, I (Madrid, 1981), pp. 149–66; Introduction to *La Hacienda del Antiguo*

ancien régime in terms of its juridical hierarchisation and grouping of men, together with the existence of an absolute monarchy at the summit. Closely connected to rank, order or estate – terms found repeatedly in the literature of the time and, naturally, in the historiography – is the notion of privilege. As opposed to the concept of legal equality consolidated in the liberal-bourgeois revolution, the previous period established inequalities of status in various spheres, amongst the most important of which were legal and fiscal inequalities,[16] without forgetting those involving the exercise of power, which will be discussed later.[17] By their different treatment in these areas, the privileged (nobility and clergy) were differentiated from the non-privileged (the Third Estate, the excluded).[18]

The privileged orders maintained horizontal solidarity, arising from their common membership of the group and their unity of interests. But naturally there were also vertical differences derived from hierarchical distinctions and personal disparities inside that class. These dissimilarities – we are talking now only about the nobility – had their origin in the way nobility had been acquired as well as the rank occupied within it. The former remained important, not because of any differences in legal privileges, but rather for reasons to do with psychology and custom, or social acceptance, given that nobility by definition springs from birth. *Nobilis* is to be *ortus parentibus nobilis, ex nobili genere, ex nobili prosapia*. The material essence of the nobility, according to theory, is blood, and it is precisely for this reason that genealogical texts systematically distinguished between nobility of the blood (*nobleza de sangre*) and nobility by patent (*nobleza de privilegio*).

The forms of access to the latter were very varied. Amongst them was purchase from the monarch in times of financial difficulty (we

Régimen (Madrid, 1982), pp. 9–11; Introduction to *La economía española al final del Antiguo Régimen. IV. Instituciones* (Madrid, 1982), esp. pp. xv–xvi.
[16] B. Clavero, 'Derecho y privilegio', *Materiales* 4 (1977), 19–32.
[17] M. Artola, *Los Orígenes de la España Contemporánea*, I (Madrid, 1975), pp. 13–15; J. A. Maravall, *Poder, honor y élites en el siglo XVII* (Madrid, 1979), pp. 11ff.
[18] Professor Domínguez Ortiz continues to be the greatest authority on the history of the privileged classes in Spain. His classic study, *Las clases privilegiadas en la España del Antiguo Régimen* (Madrid, 1973), is the best synthesis of this subject. We should also mention Ignacio Atienza Hernández, 'La nobleza en el Antiguo Régimen: Clase dominante, grupo dirigente', *Estudios de Historia Social* 36–7 (1986), 465–95, and *Aristocracia, poder y riqueza en la España Moderna: La Casa de Osuna (siglos XV–XIX)* (Madrid, 1987), pp. 9–70.

must not forget that only the king could confer a patent of nobility), which is what happened in the seventeenth century. It was, as Stone has called it, a period of inflation of honours that provoked a series of conflicts, sometimes quite bitter, between the traditional nobility and the newcomers.

To give some examples: the number of grandees, approximately 100 at the end of the sixteenth century, had tripled by 1700. Charles II alone created 12 viscounts, 80 counts and 236 marquises, while 26 titled nobles received the distinction of grandee.[19] Those numbers cast into shade the already inflated figures of the reign of Philip III, who ennobled 46 new marquises and 32 counts in the kingdom of Castile alone (see Appendix 12.1). This was not, of course, a practice unique to the Spanish monarchy, but a phenomenon general in western Europe, the prime example being the Stuarts in England, under James I and his favourite, the duke of Buckingham.[20]

During the seventeenth century titles acquired an exchange value. Thus, in 1623, a royal decree granted the monastery of Guadalupe a title of marquis in Italy for it to sell.[21] We do not know if in fact the receipts from the sale of the title allowed the works it was intended to finance to be completed. This is likely to have been difficult, given that at the end of the reign of Charles II, in 1700, the convent of Santa Juana de la Cruz stated that it had at its disposal a title for which it had hoped to obtain 22,000 ducats, but 'despite considerable efforts it had not even had an offer of 7,000, and it believed the expected figure would be impossible to achieve'.[22] In effect, as a result of their 'generous' concession by the crown, especially

---

[19] A. Domínguez Ortiz, *La sociedad española del siglo XVII*, I (Madrid, 1963); H. Kamen, *Spain in the Later Seventeenth Century, 1665–1700* (London, 1980), p. 249. A quantification and interpretation of the phenomenon can be found in I. A. A. Thompson, 'The Purchase of Nobility in Castile, 1552–1700', *The Journal of European Economic History* 8 (1979), 313–60; in a Comment in the same publication, 11 (1982), 219–26, James Amelang criticised the latter's figures.

[20] Roger Lockyer, *Buckingham. The Life and Political Career of George Villiers, First Duke of Buckingham, 1592–1628* (London, 1981); Linda Levy Peck, *Northampton. Patronage and Policy at the Court of James I* (London, 1982); G.F. Lytle and Stephen Orgel (eds.), *Patronage in the Renaissance* (Princeton, 1981), especially the articles by L. Levy, 'Court Patronage and Government Policy: The Jacobean dilemma', pp. 27ff., and R. Harding, 'Corruption and the moral boundaries of patronage in the Renaissance', pp. 47ff.

[21] British Library, Egerton 335, f. 455.

[22] Archivo Histórico Nacional (AHN) Consejos, legajo 7259 (*consulta* of 28 June 1700).

Table 12.1. *Noble titles, 1520–1700*

Year	No. of noble titles	Rate of annual increase
1520	60	
1554	68	0.24
1581	100	1.19
1597	124	1.5
1631	241	3.44
1700	533	4.2

in the seventeenth century, titles had lost their value, as Table 12.1 shows:[23]

When Charles I created the honour of 'grandee', there existed about 60 noble titles,[24] and that number doubled during the sixteenth century.[25] However, the annual increase was slow compared with the seventeenth century. Between 1597 and 1631 the number of noble titles doubled yet again.[26] Berní y Catalá claims that 66 new titles were created during the reign of Philip III, and 184 under Philip IV,[27] although this figure is improbable, since a more reliable

[23] Unfortunately the data is only an estimate since as far as we know there exists no source that brings together on an annual basis all the titles granted. Indirect sources, with their inherent problems of reliability, have to be used, Ignacio Atienza Hernández and Mina Simón López, 'Patronazgo real, renta, patrimonio y nobleza en el siglo XVI y XVII: Algunas notas para un análisis político y socioeconómico', *Revista Internacional de Sociología* 45 (1987), 25–75.

[24] Fernand Braudel, *The Mediterranean and the Mediterranean World in the Age of Philip II*, trans. S. Reynolds, 2 vols. (London, 1972), II, p. 715; Domínguez Ortiz, *Clases privilegiadas*, p. 71, gives a figure for that year of twenty grandees and thirty-five titles. Marie-Claude Gerbet has studied the number of *hidalgos* and *caballeros* in the early sixteenth century, 'La population noble dans le Royaume de Castille vers 1500. La répartition géographique de ses différentes composantes', *Anales de Historia Antigua y Medieval*, University of Buenos Aires, 1977–9, pp. 78–99.

[25] The figure for 1581 is also Braudel's; that of 1554 appears in AHN Consejos Suprimidos 4430, Cámara de Castilla, 1646, no. 120, 12 July 1646. The figure for 1597 differs somewhat from that offered by Domínguez Ortiz, who says that at the end of the reign of Philip II there were nearly 100: 18 dukes, 38 marquises and 25 counts.

[26] Archivo General de Simancas (AGS), Guerra Antigua 1035, 'Papel del Consejo de Castilla', 1631.

[27] José Berní y Catalá, *Creación, Antigüedad y Privilegios de los Títulos de Castilla* (Madrid, 1763). Domínguez Ortiz states that Philip III created 20 marquises and 25 counts; Philip IV, 67 marquises and 25 counts; and Charles II, 5 viscounts, 78 counts and 209 marquises.

document reveals the appearance of 133 new titles between 1621 and 1635.[28] Thus we can speak of a 'bastardisation' of nobility, a process that disturbed the Cámara de Castilla, which in 1647 warned the king that many claimants could neither prove their purity of blood nor possessed the personal qualities required for war (the defining function of the nobility), and that titles were being granted without adequate vetting.[29] Nevertheless, wealth counted for more than 'supposed purity'. Jewish families, like the banker Manuel de Paz, obtained the title of count on paying 1,500,000 *maravedís*. Something similar occurred in the case of the Cortizo family, and others.[30]

As the titled nobility withdrew more and more from its primal function, war, there began a desire for public offices, most notably at Court, in other words, for direct participation in power. This process came to be quantitatively important from the reign of Philip III, when the upper and middle-ranking, titled nobility became definitively a court-nobility, following the path of their European counterparts, as Norbert Elias has pointed out.[31] Their unfavourable economic situation, the fruit of inadequate estate administration and an imbalance between expenditure and income, largely due to excessive sybaritic consumption that caused indebtedness through recourse to the consignatory mortgage (*censo*),[32] did not prevent an increasing exodus to the Court of Philip III, where they built their mansions. This is not a merely antiquarian matter, but the sign of an important political process, as Tomás y Valiente once noted with reference to the *valimiento*.[33] The aim was to be able to influence the king either directly, or institutionally, through the royal councils. These, especially the Council of War and the Council of State, were filled with grandees, greatly influencing Spanish

---

[28] Biblioteca Nacional, Madrid (BN) Ms. 11077, ff. 55–8, 'Títulos de Duques, Marqueses, Condes y Vizcondes que ha dado el Rey Don Phelippe quarto ... hasta 1635'.

[29] AHN Consejos Suprimidos 4430, Cámara de Castilla, 1646, no. 34, 12 Apr. 1647.

[30] Quoted by Julio Caro Baroja, *La sociedad criptojudía en la Corte de Felipe IV* (Madrid, 1963), p. 58.

[31] Norbert Elias, *The Court Society* (Oxford, 1983).

[32] Ignacio Atienza Hernández, 'La "quiebra" de la nobleza castellana en el siglo XVII. Autoridad real y poder señorial: El secuestro de los bienes de la Casa de Osuna', *Hispania* 156 (1984), 49–81.

[33] F. Tomás y Valiente, *Los validos en la Monarquía española del siglo XVII* (Madrid, 1982), esp. pp. 117–22.

Table 12.2. *Members of the Council of State in the reign of Philip IV*

Year	Grandees	Titúlos	Others	Total	% of titled nobles
1623	2	8	7	17	58.8
1643	4	6	1	11	90
1649	6	5	1	12	91.6

Table 12.3. *Representative offices in Italy*

Offices	Grandees	Titúlos	Others	Total	% of titled nobles
Viceroy of Naples	7	2	6	15	60
Viceroy of Sicily	7	3	7	17	58.8
Governor of Milan	4	8	6	18	66.6

foreign policy. Of the forty individuals occupying posts in the Council of State under Philip III, twenty-eight were from the higher titled nobility,[34] and there was no diminution of their influence under his successor (see Table 12.2).[35]

No less desirable than posts in the Council of State were the viceroyalties, especially the Italian ones, that guaranteed power and prestige, and sometimes substantial income, more or less legitimate.[36] Eleven of the twenty-eight noble members of the Council of State during the period 1595–1621 had been viceroys, three had been ambassadors, and ten army commanders, as Batista i Roca has

[34] J. M. Batista i Roca, Foreword to Helmut G. Koenigsberger, *The Government of Sicily under Philip II of Spain* (London, 1951), p. 34. There is a monograph by Feliciano Barrios on *El Consejo de Estado de la Monarquía española: 1521–1812* (Madrid, 1984).

[35] J. H. Elliott, *The Revolt of the Catalans* (Cambridge, 1963); F. Bertaut, *Journal du Voyage d'Espagne* (Paris, 1669); Gil González de Avila, *Teatro de las Grandezas de la Villa de Madrid, Corte de los Reyes Católicos de España* (Madrid, 1623). The data has been analysed by C. J. Jago, 'Aristocracy, war and finance in Castile, 1621–1665: The titled nobility and the house of Béjar during the reign of Philip IV', PhD thesis, University of Cambridge, 1969, p. 32. My thanks to the author for permitting me access to it.

[36] In 1682 Cornaro, the Venetian ambassador, confirmed that the palace being built by the duke of Osuna in Madrid was the product of his time in Milan; the riches of the palace of the marquis of Astorga stemmed from his forebears' posts in Naples, etc., cited by Domínguez Ortiz, *Las clases privilegiadas*, pp. 15–16.

also indicated. Their influence in these occupations remained undiminished throughout the seventeenth century[37]

Thus, in the seventeenth century the titled nobility attained important positions in the institutional apparatus of the monarchy, above all in the fields of military and foreign affairs. Recruitment to other councils, finance, the Indies, Castile, etc., and thus to other duties, was different, for they inevitably required a more technical background. Thus most of them were lawyers, experts in the law,[38] graduates of the *colegios mayores*, in contrast to the titled nobility who usually had their own private tutors, or who were taught in the recently formed Jesuit institutions, such as the Imperial College of Madrid for nobles, run by the followers of Ignatius of Loyola, and opened under the auspices of Olivares in 1625. Its function, until its closure under the liberal regime at the beginning of the nineteenth century for its denial of the principle of equality by not admitting commoners, was to give the young a highly vocational training in languages, both ancient and modern, dance, sport, the military arts, history and geography,[39] in order to equip them for the diplomatic and military roles that were by birthright theirs.[40]

The interests as well as the education of the nobility were often different from those of the other councillors. In the nobility's bankrupt economic situation during the seventeenth century, a substantial proportion of its creditors were either councillors of this sort, or members of the social group to which they belonged. Thus conflicts between them were numerous and important, for the motivations of the two groups did not generally coincide.

It was this crisis of the nobility in the seventeenth century that led them to turn to the king in search of favours. The monarch himself was in a precarious economic situation, and his aid to the titled

[37] Batista i Roca, Foreword to Koenigsberger, *The Government of Sicily*, p. 28; *Cambridge Modern History*, XIII (Cambridge, 1911), Tables 137 and 138.
[38] J. M. Pelorson, *Les "letrados" juristes castillans sous Philippe III* (Poitiers, 1980); J. Fayard, *Les Membres du Conseil de Castille à l'époque moderne (1621–1746)* (Geneva–Paris, 1979); R.L. Kagan, *Students and Society in Early Modern Spain* (Baltimore, 1974), especially pp. 82–7.
[39] Thompson, *War and Government*, pp. 146–59, on the role of the nobility. By the same author, 'The Armada and administrative reform: the Spanish Council of War in the reign of Philip II', *English Historical Review* 82 (1967), 698–725.
[40] J. Varela, *Modos de educación en la España de la Contrarreforma* (Madrid, 1983), pp. 58–126; José Simón Diaz, *Historia del Colegio Imperial de Madrid*, 2 vols. (Madrid, 1951).

nobility came in driblets. Indeed, it was he who often 'ransacked' them.[41] They were like two blind men trying to find their way together. Their mutual assistance was at times at the expense of other social groups, like the town councils, whose assets were to a great extent expropriated and redistributed.[42] Furthermore, the monarch's will was fickle and even had he wanted to satisfy the needs of all the privileged he would have found it impossible. Thus were formed factions and groupings of nobles who tried to dominate and monopolise the monarch, resulting in inter-noble conflicts as they fell in and out of favour.

The involvement of the nobility in public office in no way signified a lessening of the so-called absolutism that has caused so much ink to flow. In fact, it made them more dependent on the monarch, since it was the king who could alleviate the heavy burden of the crisis by grace of a policy of grants, concessions, appointments to office, and so on. It was necessary to keep in favour with the king.[43]

Despite what is commonly believed, Spain was not exceptional. As elsewhere in Europe, the Court was an arena of political competition and power struggles where the patron-client relationship ruled and shaped the fight to secure the favours of the supreme patron, the king.[44] It was a case of overcoming the conflict between

[41] In 1639 the duke of Osuna provided the king with 250 soldiers, AHN Osuna, legajo 15, no. 20; 'Valor de las lanzas años 1738, 1739 y 1743', AHN Osuna, legajo 23, no. 10; commutation of lance tax in exchange for arming twenty soldiers, AHN Osuna, legajo 15, no. 25 (1639); 'Pago de lanzas y media annata, 1748', AHN Osuna, legajo 24, no. 5.

[42] In exchange for military services the king sometimes authorised the ploughing of municipal land; for example, licences for 3,068 *fanegas* to the duke of Osuna in September 1639 and 600 in December, AHN Osuna, legajo 15, no. 19. On other occasions it was the duke's creditors who were hit. In the seventeenth century, as with many other houses, the Osuna fortune was confiscated or 'secuestrado', in the terminology of the epoch, which meant that the assets of noble estates were not administered by their owners, but by a Crown agent, or a board of creditors. Thus, Philip IV allowed Juan Téllez Girón to take from his sequestrated assets 5,000 ducats 'for the expenses of the troops with which he had undertaken to serve His Majesty', AHN Osuna, legajo 15, no. 21. In 1641 this was repeated to pay 400 infantry, legajo 15, no. 23. Obviously the burden fell on the lenders, who were, of course, not nobles like him, but in general ecclesiastical institutions, guilds, and the urban bourgeoisie.

[43] We must still make use of Jules Gounon-Loubens, *Essais sur l'administration de la Castille aux XVIe siècle* (Paris, 1860).

[44] G. R. Elton, 'Tudor Government: The points of contact: the Court', in *Studies in Tudor and Stuart Politics and Government. Papers and Reviews* (Cambridge, 1983); Lytle and Orgel, *Patronage in the Renaissance*; Lockyer, *Buckingham*; Levy Peck,

the various factions, as occurred in Elizabethan England or in Philip's Spain, by the creation of a single faction. That was what Olivares attempted,[45] trying to govern through his creatures, through the favourite's favourites, and keeping other patrons or factions outside the circle of power. Clearly this institutional approach could not succeed, among many other reasons, such as the failure of his Catalan and Portuguese policies, because of the reaction of the grandees and titled nobility against those attempting to keep them from power.[46]

In conclusion, the failure of the nobility's income and wealth to increase in proportion to the near quadrupling of prices in the sixteenth century (see Appendix 12.2) provides one possible explanation of its hunger for public office and for a share of political power. This critical economic situation had become particularly conflict prone around 1580. A year earlier, of the 20,000 ducats distributed by the royal alms office a large part was doled out to help the nobility. That was why no account of its distribution had to be submitted, 'so that honourable persons be not deterred from requesting it, lest afterwards they have to put it down on paper'. The method of distribution was 'that the almoner send a very reliable and diligent assistant to visit the homes of those requesting charity, and give aid in accordance with the need and quality of the person'.[47]

At this point, we need to mention, albeit briefly, another of the manifestations of this process of refeudalisation, the extension of seignorialisation. This began in a significant way in the reigns of Charles V and Philip II.[48] A large part of the assets – including baronies – of the Military Orders sold by Charles V and Philip II,

---

Northampton. There is a study of the question in Julio A. Pardos and Antonio Feros, 'Todos los hombre del valido', *Libros*, 33–4 (1984), 3–7.

[45] John H. Elliott, *Richelieu and Olivares* (Cambridge, 1984).

[46] Gregorio Marañón, *El Conde-Duque de Olivares* (Madrid, 1985), pp. 74–80; Beatriz Cárceles de Gea, 'Valoraciones y controversias en el conflicto político de la España de 1621 a 1643', Memoria de Licenciatura, Universidad Autónoma de Madrid, July 1983.

[47] 'Salarios que el Rey de España da en su Casa Real, Consejos y Chancillerías y Audiencias y Inquisición y guarda de su persona', British Library, Harleian Ms. 6,275; further information in B. Cárceles de Gea and I. Atienza Hernández, 'El gobierno político de la monarquía (1577). I. Instituciones y Casa Real', in papers of the conference, *Hernán Cortés y su tiempo* (Cáceres, 25–30 Nov. 1985), Mérida, Junta de Extremadura, 1987.

[48] S. de Moxó, 'Las desamortizaciones eclesiásticas del siglo XVI', *Anuario de Historia del Derecho Español* 31 (1961), 327–61; J. Cepeda Adán, 'Desamortiza-

and of the churches, bishoprics and monasteries sold by Philip, were purchased by the bankers and financiers of the royal treasury, particularly the Genoese (the Centurions, Spinolas, Lomellinis and Cataneos), who had eclipsed the Germans under Philip II, and by royal councillors and secretaries. In this way Cobos, Eraso, Gaspar Ramírez de Vargas, Secretary of the Royal Council and of the Cortes of 1535, the Treasurer Melchor de Herrera, named marquis of Auñón, and others acquired their ancestral seats.

This phenomenon reached its peak in the seventeenth century when a critical conjuncture provoked a series of financial disasters in the monarchy which, together with a militaristic policy designed as a desperate attempt to preserve the Empire, forced it to alienate a great part of the territory within the royal jurisdiction (*realengo*), so creating pockets of seignorial power, and offices that encouraged the development and reinforcement of municipal oligarchies, and the formation of an urban patriciate.[49]

One of the clearest manifestations of the process of refeudalisation is to be seen in one of the most fundamental elements of the nobility's authority, that which derived from the exercise of jurisdiction as a function of the *señorío*. In this way there took place a 'privatisation' of public functions, including governmental and judicial functions, though naturally within the framework of a unitary authority.[50]

ción de tierras de las órdenes militares en el reinado de Carlos V', *Hispania* 146 (1980).

[49] Relevant studies, among others are: Antonio Domínguez Ortiz, 'Ventas y exenciones de lugares durante el reinado de Felipe IV', *Anuario de Historia del Derecho Español* 34 (1964), 163 207; by the same author, 'Ventas de tierras y oficios públicos en la España de los Austrias', *Troisième Conférence Internationale d'Histoire Economique* (Munich, 1965); in the same publication, the article by Felipe Ruiz Martín, 'El fisco y la economía de Castilla en los siglos XVI y XVII'; Francisco Tomás y Valiente, 'Las ventas de oficios de regidores y la formación de oligarquías urbanas en Castilla (siglos XVII y XVIII)', *Historia. Instituciones. Documentos* 2 (1976), 525–47, and by the same author, 'Venta de oficios públicos en Castilla durante los siglos XVII y XVIII', in his *Gobierno e instituciones en la España del Antiguo Régimen* (Madrid, 1982), pp. 151–77; a general survey in 'La Hacienda Real', by Alvaro Castillo Pintado and Juan Ignacio Gutiérrez Nieto, in *La España de Felipe IV, El Gobierno de la Monarquía. La crisis de 1640 y el fracaso de la hegemonía europea*, vol. XXV of *La Historia de España* founded by Ramón Menéndez Pidal and directed by José María Jover Zamora (Madrid, 1982), pp. 215–332.

[50] See in particular the debate between A. Gallego Anabitarte, 'Administración y jueces: gubernativo y contencioso', *Revista general de legislación y jurisprudencia* 23 (1971), 235–48, and García de Enterría, 'La formación histórica del principio de autotutela de la Administración', *Moneda y Crédito* 128 (1974), 58–87.

The agglomeration of different baronies, a seignorial or, if it carried a title, a noble estate, can be seen as a 'juridical-political-administrative unit', located within another, larger entity, the noble House. The seignorial estate is a power centre, in the Weberian sense, since from it were issued specific orders, with a great likelihood that they would be obeyed by a given number of persons.[51] This power was, on the other hand, subordinate to higher authorities, in this case to the Crown, the residence of sovereignty.[52] The monarchy, despite being an ally of the nobility, on occasion confronted it when their interests appeared antagonistic. It was power also in terms of the lord's capacity for the appropriation and/or management of the surplus product and certain assets – rivers, scrubland, forests, etc. – for himself, and the exclusion of the rest of the community from their use.

This power was developed and channelled through certain institutions and individuals; the judicial path, local ordinances, regulatory rather than legislative; the ideological, by means of the right of patronage in education and the church; and through the control and nomination of officials who maintained the public order, jailing, watching over and defending the lord's interests.

For all these reasons, it seems appropriate to use the term 'non-economic coercion' to describe the actions of the lords in the Crown of Castile under the *ancien régime*. There existed 'subterranean' black holes of power, where at times even the orders and legal/judicial procedures of the king were ignored, that need to be studied and known about. This would necessitate studying the seignorial estates from a perspective of the microphysics of power,[53] in order, as Professor González Alonso has repeatedly and correctly emphasised, to describe and enumerate in specific detail the powers of the lords and to show how they were exercised.[54] It is obvious that a

---

[51] Max Weber, *The Theory of Economic and Social Organizations* (Glencoe, IL, 1947).

[52] Atienza Hernández, *Aristocracia, poder y riqueza* esp. ch. 3, 'El Estado de Osuna, El Señorío', pp. 113–96.

[53] We acknowledge the methodological debt owed to Michel Foucault and his 'genealogy of power', especially with regard to his works: *Histoire de la folie à l'âge classique; Archéologie du savoir* (Paris, 1969); *Surveiller et punir. Naissance de la prison* (Paris, 1975); *A verdaderas formàs jurídicas* (Rio de Janeiro, 1978); *Microfísica del poder* (Madrid, 1978), and *Diálogo sobre el poder* (Marid, 1981).

[54] Atienza Hernández, in 'Corona y señorío', *Aristocracia, poder y riqueza*, ch. 4, pp. 114–233.

seignorial estate should not be categorised and studied in isolation but within the wider institutional context of royal administration, municipalities, corporations, and Church, in order to determine their multiple interactions.

The critical economic situation of the Castilian nobility in the seventeenth century caused it to attempt a number of solutions, in addition to its resort to access to political power, which we have already dealt with, measures such as mortgaging entailed properties, deferring repayment to their creditors with the acquiescence of the Crown,[55] selling municipal offices in a similar way to the Crown, etc.[56]

But what we now need to see is how this state of penury went hand in hand with an *intensification of seignorial power*, as Jago has shown,[57] and I believe my own doctoral thesis also demonstrates.[58]

With such a large topic, we can only make some general points concerning the way the lords embarked upon a systematic usurpation of wastelands and commons,[59] and increased the pressures exercised by their justices, in ways not entirely lawful,[60] in defence of their 'private interests', notably where it concerned the repayment of debts,[61] or the protection of their forests. One case in point was the protest of the vassals of the duke of Osuna that 'he has taken part of the land of Osuna and joined it to his forest in Puebla

55 Atienza Hernández, 'La "quiebra" de la nobleza castellana'; Charles Jago, 'The Influence of debt on the relations between crown and aristocracy in seventeenth century Castile', *Economic History Review*, 2nd series, 26 (1973), 218–36.
56 AHN Osuna, legajo 11, no. 7 (1598–9); legajo 3509, 'Arrendamiento, cuentas y ventas de oficios en Arahal (1592–1687)'; and legajos 33, no. 3; 2047; 1511; 98, no. 15 (1638); 15, no. 24; 67, no. 15 (1638); 15, nos. 24, 28 and 29; 66, no. 2 (1645).
57 C. J. Jago, 'The "Crisis of the Aristocracy" in seventeenth century Castile', *Past and Present* 84 (1979), 60–90.
58 'Una casa nobiliaria: Osuna (1450–1900)', Universidad Autónoma de Madrid, Apr. 1985.
59 AHN Osuna, legajo 15, no. 19 (1639), no. 21 (1635), no. 23 (1641).
60 For example, the decree of the Chancillería of Granada which ordered 'that the Justices of Arahal, Marchena and other seignorial villages observe the Royal Order that the peasants are not to be arrested or otherwise molested for their debts, nor to be forced to pay for the wheat given to them in kind', AHN Osuna, legajo 60, no. 21 (1641).
61 In contrast to the documents cited in note 60, the same monarch issued writs to the justices ordering them to be especially hard with the farmers of the lords' revenues and with their debtors, AHN Osuna, legajo 15, no. 23 (1641). He went so far as to permit the lords' officials to pronounce sentence, in the first instance, in this type of dispute, AHN Osuna, legajo 19, no. 7 (1708); legajo 19, no. 10 (1709).

de Cazalla and prohibited hunting'.[62] Another complaint was against his use of force to impose illegal monopolies: 'he monopolizes the bakeries, prohibiting ovens in private houses, . . . the oil presses (no citizen may have one), . . . and the tanneries . . . and if people bring partly tanned hides in from outside, he makes them pay a tanning fee as if they had been tanned in the town'.[63] To this was added the imposition of certain dues by the lord on the processing of grapes: 'the grapes have to be brought in through one gate (presumably to control the payment of the tithe, weighing charges, etc.) even though it is a long way round from where the vineyards are situated, and they lose half their value in the extra transport costs because of this long detour'. Or they denounced his usurpation of the utilisation of certain communal rights, such as grazing the stubble, 'which is the town's own property, but the count has seized half of it and charges 70,000 *maravedís* a year for its use'.

These and other protests by vassals against their lords were relatively frequent in the seventeenth century, palpable proof of our case for the intensification of feudal burdens. They would have been even more numerous had the clear subordination of lordly authority to the Crown, at least from the fifteenth century,[64] promoted in two key ways, by royal laws binding in both royal and seignorial jurisdictions and by the right of appeal to the royal courts against the sentences of seignorial tribunals, not been ignored and such general legislation by-passed by the lords' own ordinances and by-laws.[65] Furthermore, the cost in time and money of litigation under the *ancien régime* reduced the number of appeals and limited them to collectives (town councils, monasteries, universities, etc.),[66] or to

---

[62] AHN Osuna, legajo 9, no. 13. The prohibiting of hunting or felling in the pastures of Alcalá, property of the duke of Osuna, allowing him to mount a guard to arrest anyone entering 'without permission of His Excellency or his Governors, and the ordinary justice shall punish and sentence them', AHN Osuna, legajo 16, no. 20 (1661).

[63] AHN Osuna, legajo 9, no. 13 (1661).

[64] Ignacio Atienza Hernández, 'El poder real en el siglo XV: lectura crítica de los documentos de donación de villas y lugares. La formación de los Estados de Osuna', *Revista Internacional de Sociología* 1 (1983), 557–91.

[65] Amongst others; AHN Osuna, legajos 60, no. 10; 82, no. 3; 93, no. 11; 94¹; 95, no. 7; 102, no. 3.

[66] Francisco Tomás y Valiente, *El derecho penal de la monarquía absoluta (siglos XVI–XVII–XVIII)* (Madrid, 1969); Richard L. Kagan, 'Pleitos y poder real. La Chancillería de Valladolid (1500–1700)', *Cuadernos de Investigación Histórica* 3 (1978), 291–316, and *Lawsuits and Litigants in Castile (1500–1700)* (Chapel Hill,

individuals of a certain social status, generally *hidalgos* suing over the control of half the local offices,[67] or to titled nobles. Another factor restricting appeals was that sentences were statistically biased in favour of the lord's interests.[68] If that did not happen on the second appeal in the Audiencias or Chancillerías, given that the first appeal was an attribute of the lord's own jurisdiction, the lord would appeal repeatedly against an unfavourable sentence even up to the Council, so exhausting his opponents economically.[69]

At the same time, it was obvious that in structural terms, and leaving aside for the moment the small and unimportant breaches that could occur from time to time, the Crown protected its leading vassals, the nobility, especially at times when they were in difficulties.[70] Its response to the protests of the aristocracy's creditors leaves no room for doubt. It blocked action in the lower courts, and in the Audiencias and Chancillerías, had the matter dealt with by the Council and reduced the rate of interest in the nobility's favour. It is true that on occasion the property and estates of the titled nobility were sequestrated and taken into administration, but in the long run this worked to their benefit. They did not forfeit the exercise of jurisdiction, and at a time they were short of liquidity they were guaranteed a considerable annual income.

There is no doubt that the monarchy had established mechanisms of institutional control, inspections and judicial visitations (*residencias*), not only in royal but also in seignorial jurisdictions,[71] but how effective were they? In the first place, as Professor González Alonso has stated, neither inspections nor judicial visitations penetrated noble estates before the second half of the sixteenth century.[72]

NC, 1981); María Paz Alonso, *El proceso penal en Castilla (siglos XIII–XVIII)* (Salamanca, 1982).
[67] AHN Osuna, legajos 94¹ (1638); 67²; 84, no. 2 (1607); 29, no. 13; 15, no. 3 (1617–34); 103².
[68] For example this appears clearly in the AHN Osuna, legajo 9, no. 13.
[69] AHN Osuna, legajos 16, no. 9 (1653–5); stack 22, no. 10⁴; stack 83, no. 6 (1579), no. 7 (1580), no. 8 (1595), no. 9 (1601).
[70] Atienza Hernández, 'La "quiebra" de la nobleza en el siglo XVII'.
[71] A resumé of the problem is contained in B. González Alonso, 'Control y responsabilidad de los oficiales reales: notas en torno a una pesquisa del siglo XVIII', in his *Sobre el estado y la administración de la Corona de Castilla en el Antiguo Régimen* (Madrid, 1981).
[72] B. González Alonso, 'Notas sobre relaciones del Estado con la administración señorial en la Castilla Moderna', *Anuario de Historia del Derecho Español* 53 (1983), 387.

But more than that, at the same time that seignorialism was in full expansion in the seventeenth century, the monarch commonly delegated the execution of both forms of control and the inspection of officials, institutions, etc., to the lords themselves,[73] though it is true that the possibility of appealing to the Chancillerías against unacceptable judgements still existed. In this way both the institutional and the direct mechanisms of supervision by the Crown were short-circuited and a separate system began to develop in seignorial jurisdictions, where the action was initiated by lords who only occasionally had to account to royal institutions.

The development of inspections and/or visitations in the seventeenth century

	at times	
Chancillería or Audiencia	←	intermediate lord
directly ↓	→	↓
royal lands		señorío

What is more, a series of 'legal' obstacles were established to prevent the 'visited' in dispute with the lord from having access to royal justice. For example, the house of Osuna protested to Charles II in 1696 that the Chancillería of Granada was intervening overmuch in its judicial visitations and accepting without discrimination every appeal sent up to it, which, in the words of its agent, 'was causing the duke grave and notorious damage'.[74] The monarch's reply was categorically supportive of ducal interests. A Royal Warrant was issued on 16 February determining that

henceforth the visitations conducted in the aforementioned towns and villages of the said duke of Osuna may not be appealed nor sent up to that Chancillería [of Granada], except in cases where there be a formal personal complaint, or where our procurator fiscal denounce the offences committed, in which case documented proof of the charges contained in the complaint, or of the offences in the denunciation, will be required, and in no other circumstance.[75]

[73] AHN Osuna, legajos 18, no. 1; 10, no. 2; 17, no. 12 and 19 a–c; Archivo de la Real Chancillería de Granada, cabina 508, legajo 205, pieza 7, and Sala 3ª, legajo 985, pieza 3.
[74] AHN Osuna, legajo 18², no. 8.   [75] *Ibid.*

The conclusion is clear: in moments of financial crisis for the Crown and also for the landed nobility, the latter closed ranks and turned in upon itself. Manifest proof of this from the point of view of the history of mentalities was the increasing complication and complexity of its ceremonies and forms of address, and its predilection for baroque festivities inaccessible to and often isolated from the rest of society.[76]

In that way an ontologically necessary relationship between king and nobility of a symbiotic character, articulated along the patron/client axis and crystallised into what we might call accepted relations of authority, came to be formed.

The king was the repository of sovereignty, absolute and above the law by virtue of precepts like *An Princeps sit legibus solutus*, and others of a similar nature, or by the inclusion in legal documents of clauses such as *ex certa scientia, motu propio*, or *plenitudo potestatis*, which denoted the dispensable or revocable nature of any precept that contradicted the new norms allowing the king to impose his will, *non obstante aliena lege*, by use of his *potestas absoluta*. This is apparent to us, as is the fact that in exchange for 'bleeding' his nobility by means of 'gracious and voluntary' grants, such as the equipping of soldiers, the concession of donatives, and so on, he left them a free rein on their estates and acquiesced in their appropriation of waste and common lands, their control over their municipalities, and, in particular, the utilisation of their jurisdictional authority to defend, preserve and increase their privileges, as we have tried to show on the basis of the archival material we have cited.

It is precisely this situation, and its intensification in the seventeenth century, that allows us to speak unambiguously of 'refeudalisation'. It is this which has kept alive a historical debate about the value of using the concept of the state prior to the liberal-bourgeois revolutions, and of applying instead the term 'pre-state political

---

[76] See, BN Ms. 6494, f. 62, 'Tratamiento a los títulos'; Real Academia de la Historia, F-11 (9-419), ff. 64 et seqq., 'La ordenanza en la Capilla Real'; British Library, Egerton Ms. 332, f. 297, 'Copia de consulta, en que responde el Consejo de Castilla a una orden, que embió su Magd sobre el punto de tratamiento de cortesias'. N. Elias, *The Court Society* (Oxford, 1983); Pilar Pedraza, *Barroco efímero en Valencia* (Valencia, 1982); L. Clare, *La quitaine, la course de bague et le jeu des têtes* (Paris, 1983), in which are analysed the equestrian sports of the Court. For codes of etiquette for the use of the nobility, AHN Osuna, legajo 1537; on bullfights, BN Raros 31633.

formations' to characterise the political structure of the *ancien régime*.[77]

In relation to this phenomenon of reseignorialisation or, more broadly, refeudalisation, one of the problems currently preoccupying early modern historians is to understand the relationship between jurisdiction and popular migration during the *ancien régime*, and more specifically in the seventeenth century, within the possible combinations of royal and seignorial jurisdiction.

We have to admit that the current state of research does not allow conclusive answers to be given, nor is it likely they will be furnished. To do so we would first need to establish regional differences, for example between the kingdoms of Castile and Aragon. In the latter, seignorial pressure was intense and, more for reasons of custom than law, so was their jurisdictional power, allowing them to prohibit and punish attempts to move into royal jurisdictions.[78]

In Castile the situation was different. Here, and especially in Andalusia, the lords had tried to repopulate their lands, and thus in the fifteenth and sixteenth centuries they had granted a series of privileges giving fiscal exemptions (freedom from certain taxes) and judicial rights (non-custodial sentences for certain crimes), or had redistributed the lord's lands to the new settlers.[79] This had encouraged a migration from royal to seignorial domains.[80] There were, of

---

[77] B. Clavero, 'Institución política y derecho: Acerca del concepto historiográfico de "Estado Moderno"', *Revista de Estudios Políticos* 19 (1981), 43–57, and, 'Señoríos y hacienda a finales del Antiguo Régimen en Castilla', *Moneda y Crédito* 135 (1975); Carlos Martínez Shaw, 'Sobre el feudalismo tardío en España; algunas acotaciones a Bartolomé Clavero', *En Teoría* 4 (1980), 163–86; Pablo Fernández Albaladejo, 'La transición política y la instauración del absolutismo', *Zona Abierta* 30 (1984), 63–75; González Alonso, *Sobre el estado y la administración*; J. A. Maravall, *Estado moderno y mentalidad social. Siglos XV a XVII*, 2 vols. (Madrid, 1972); F. Tomás y Valiente, 'El gobierno de la monarquía y la administración de los reinos en la España del siglo XVII' in *La España de Felipe IV* (Madrid, 1982), pp. 30–43. On this subject the bibliography is exhaustive, so I shall confine myself to recommending the excellent article by Salustiano de Dios, 'Sobre la génesis y los caracteres del estado absolutista en Castilla', *Studia Histórica* 3: 3 (1985), 11–45.

[78] Gregorio Colás Latorre and José Antonio Salas Ausens, *Aragón en el siglo XVI. Alteraciones sociales y conflictos políticos* (Zaragoza, 1982).

[79] AHN Osuna, legajo 3497. An extract from the document was published by Juan Moreno de Guerra y Alonso in the *Boletín de la Real Academia de la Historia* 62 (1913), pp. 418ff. AHN Osuna, legajos 1, no. 12; 93, no. 11; 61, no. 6; 5, no. 3.

[80] Manuel González Jiménez, *La repoblación de la zona de Sevilla durante el siglo XIV. Estudio y documentación* (Sevilla, 1975); Antonio Collantes de Terán

course, exceptions, and Valentina Fernández Vargas has demonstrated that, in León at least, there was a migration of seignorial vassals to America, which obviously did not please their lords who put all kinds of obstacles in its way. Thus when Padre Las Casas began recruiting, the inhabitants of Berlanga, whose lord was the Constable of Castile, joined up in secret, not because they hoped to make their fortunes from the venture, but because they wanted greater liberty: 'more than seventy of the 200 inhabitants enrolled, and to do so entered the *cabildo* in secret, for fear of the Constable, . . . (and some said) . . . Sir, none of us wants to go to the Indies out of necessity, as we each have an income of 400,000 *maravedís* or more, but we are going in order to raise our children in free and royal lands.'[81] This is the same argument for liberty that is repeated in the Comunero movement, when the inhabitants of Dueñas justified their participation, 'because they are under the jurisdiction of the count of Buendía, and those under royal jurisdiction, in comparison with the rest, are thought to be freer'.[82]

This could, of course, be thought to be a form of ideological legitimation and therefore to give a false impression of reality, an imaginary ideology as Duby said. The truth is that the studies mentioned above, other research, and my own doctoral thesis have noted a major increase in the seignorial population in Castile in the fifteenth and sixteenth centuries that cannot be explained by natural growth alone, but only as the result of migration.[83] This increase of population has also been shown in seignorial enclaves in the eighteenth century.[84] What happened in the seventeenth century is

Sánchez, 'Nuevas poblaciones del siglo XV en el Reino de Sevilla', *Cuadernos de Historia. Anexos de la Revista Hispania* 7 (1977), 283–336.

[81] Fray Bartolomé de Las Casas, *Historia de las Indias*, quoted by Valentina Fernández Vargas, 'El control señorial en España y la emigración a las Indias. Una aproximación al tema' in *América y la España del siglo XVI*, Instituto 'Gonzálo Fernández de Oviedo' (Madrid, 1983), II, p. 35.

[82] J. Maldonado, *La revolución comunera* (Madrid, 1975), p. 124, quoted in Fernández Vargas, 'El control señorial', p. 35. An approach to the possible connections between the War of the Comunidades and the anti-seignorial movement is to be found in Juan Ignacio Gutiérrez Nieto, *Las comunidades como movimiento antiseñorial* (Barcelona, 1973).

[83] Valentina Fernández Vargas, 'Población urbana y población rural en León en el siglo XVI', in *La Ciudad Hispánica* (Madrid, 1985), pp. 617–23.

[84] Juan Manuel Guisado López, 'La propiedad de la tierra y su jurisdicción en el Reino de Granada hacia 1750. Un ensayo de cuantificación de la magnitud del régimen señorial', *Congreso de Historia Rural, Siglos XV al XIX* (Madrid, 1984), pp. 599–612; Valentina Fernández Vargas, Juan Llaneras Leal, et al., 'Despoblados

still to be discovered, although there is nothing to indicate a change in tendency. Our case study, the estates of the house of Osuna, points in this direction. It is true that both seignorial income and pressure increased during the process of refeudalisation we have described, but it is also true that royal taxation in non-seignorial jurisdictions became intolerable compared with its relative mildness prior to the reign of Philip II.[85]

These are questions, not answers, and they need to be answered by regional case studies that can establish both similarities and differences.

y nuevas poblaciones en Andalucía durante el Antiguo Régimen. Hipótesis y líneas de investigación', *Actas del I Congreso de Historia de Andalucía. Andalucía Moderna (siglo XVIII)*, (Cordoba, 1978), I, pp. 173–7.
[85] Atienza Hernández and Cárceles de Gea, 'El gobierno político de la monarquía (1577). II. La Hacienda Real'.

Appendix 12.1

Creation of titles during the reign of Philip III: lineages and incomes
(A) Marquises

Title	Lineage	Income in 1617	Income in 1620
Laguna	Cerda	10	2 (without free assets)
Malagón	Pedro y Tabera		30
Cca	Sandoval [assimilated to the title of duke of Lerma]		
Malpica	Ribera	30	30
Coriana	Dávila y Mejía		12
Fuentes	Guzmán	12	10
Tarandilla	Toledo [incorporated into the title of count of Oropesa]		
Orellana	Fonseca y Figueroa	10	12
Caracena	Carrillo, Pacheco y Toledo	12	16
Guadalcázar	Córdoba	10	20
Povar	Avila y Guzmán	12	12
Valle de Zarato	Acuña	12	11
Belmonte	Rojas y Sandoval		20
Floresdavila	Zúñiga	6	10
Hinojosa	Guzmán y Mendoza	8	25
Salinas	Velasco	16	20
Toral	Guzmán		2
Eliseda	Silva		4
Siete Iglesias	Calderón y Vargas		
	[withdrawn by judicial order from Rodrigo de Calderón]		
Viso	[incorporated into title of marquis of Santa Cruz]		
Montalbán	[incorporated into the title of marquis of Priego]		
Bedmar	Cueva y Mendoza		12
Valderrábano	Enríquez de Almansa		30
Villar	Requesens y Zúñiga		40
Celada	Cardona y Aguilar	8	6
San Román	[incorporated into the title of marquis of Velada]		
Valdefuentes	Sandi		5
Villamayor	Pacheco y Córdoba		14
Jabalquinto	Benavides		12

271

Appendix 12.1 (cont.)

Title	Lineage	Income in 1617	Income in 1620
Jodar	Carvajal		10
Gelves	Portugal		15
Baides	Zúñiga		8
Belmonte	Cárdenas y Manrique		12
Heliche	Guzmán el Bueno	6	
Lisala	Gómez de Lisón	6	
Villamilar	Sandoval	10	
Aldeanueva	Fonseca	13	
Fuentes	Fuentes y Guzmán	12	
Pozuelo	Sandoval	10	
Oropesa	Enrique de Borja	24	
Loriana	Avila	14	
Armunia	Córdoba	14	
Terranova	Mazaladrón de Ribera	14	
Avila	Lafoz	12	
Castelrodrigo	Mora	30	
Cadrete	Almendares		
Zamudio	Guzmán		

(B) Counts

Title	Lineage	Income 1620
Caracena	Carrillo de Toledo	[changed to marquis]
Los Arcos	Laso de Vega	20
Fuentidueña	Luna	16
Villalonso	Ulloa	8
Grajal	Vega	8
Villa Mediana	Tassis y Peralta	12
Torrejón	Carvajal	6
Villamor	Albarado	12
Casa Rubios	Chacón	8
Villaverde	Guzmán	4
Peñaranda	Bracamonte y Pacheco	16
Aramajona	Idiáquez y Mújica (included in the title of duke of Villareal)
Ayala y Salvatierra	Fonseca	20
Salazar	Velasco	12
Castrillo	Delgadillo y Abellaneda	4
Cantillana	Vicentelo	20
Ampudia	Sandoval [united with the House of Lerma]
Saltes	Silva	4
Oliva	Vargas	8

Appendix 12.1 (cont.)

Title	Lineage	Income 1620
Fuente el Zauco	Deza	10
Mora	Rojas y Guevara	8
Salvatierra	Ayala, Sotomayor y Sarmiento	9
Montijo	Portocarrero [united with title of marquis of Valderrábano]	
Tripiana	Guevara	30
Torre	Sandoval y Ribera	8
Gondomar	Sarmiento, Acuña, Ribadavia y Mendoza	3
Mejorada	Padilla, Cerda y Mendoza	16
Villalba	Ayala	3
Mondova	Portocarnero	10
Bentosa	Sandoval	2
Revilla	Velasco	4
Peñaflor	Villacis	14

Note: Incomes are expressed in 1000s of ducats.
Source: Pérez Carrillo, *Diálogo de las virtudes cardinales.*
1617: Biblioteca Nacional, Madrid, Manuscript 6,494.
1620: Biblioteca Nacional, Madrid, Manuscript 1,254.

Appendix 12.2

Annual revenues of Dukes (sixteenth and seventeenth centuries) (1000s of ducats)

Titles	(I) 1520	(II) 1539	(III) 1577	(IV) 1580	(V) 1597	(VI) 1610	(VII) 1615	(VIII) 1616	(IX) 1617	(X) 1620	(XI) 1630	(XII) (1)	(XIII) (2)	Totals
Alba	30	50	60	100	120	70	90	90	90	120	100	90	100	1,110
Alburquerque	20	25	50	100	50	50	50	50	50	50	50	40	50	635
Alcalá de los Gazules	—	30	100	100	100	90	100	100	100	100	80	50	80	1,030
Arcos	30	25	70	80	80	90	80	80	70	80	50	50	50	835
Béjar	24	40	50	75	80	90	75	75	90	80	70	70	70	889
Cea	—	—	—	—	—	—	11	—	80	40	—	—	40	171
Escalona	—	60	82	100	100	100	100	100	100	100	100	100	90	1,132
Feria	—	—	30	40	75	40	65	65	56	70	50	40	50	581
Frías	50	60	—	70	60	70	90	90	70	80	80	70	70	860
Infantado	30	60	100	120	120	100	100	100	90	120	100	100	120	1,260
Lerma	—	50	—	—	—	60	150	150	84	24	340	60	180	1,098
Maqueda	—	—	40	40	50	50	50	50	50	60	90	50	90	620
Medina de Rioseco	32	50	100	120	130	100	150	150	150	130	120	120	140	1,492
Medina Sidonia	50	55	150	200	170	200	160	160	160	170	300	140	200	2,115
Medinaceli	24	30	28	50	60	50	55	55	50	80	44	46	40	612
Nájera	16	39	50	40	50	56	60	60	50	50	—	40	—	502
Osuna	22	20	112	100	150	130	140	140	140	150	140	100	150	1,494
Pastrana	—	—	32	90	80	80	70	60	70	80	40	50	60	712
Sessa	16	60	34	70	100	—	70	70	—	50	120	70	120	780
Annual totals	344	645	1,088	1,495	1,575	1,426	1,716	1,645	1,590	1,654	2,034	1,036	1,700	18,218

Sources: (I) Karl Otto Muller, *Quellen zur Handelsgeschichte der Paumgartner von Augsburg (1480–1570)* (Wiesbaden, 1955), pp. 113–17. (II) Lucio Marineo Siculo, *Las cosas memorables de España* (Alcalá, 1539). (III) British Library, Ms. Harl. 6,275: Ps/5, 633. Estado de España. (IV) Biblioteca Nacional, Madrid, Ms. 18.731 (26), 'Relación de las rentas que tienen los duques, marqueses y condes de España'. (V) Núñez de Salcedo, 'Relación de los títulos que hay en España, sus rentas. solares, linajes . . .', *Boletín de la Real Academia de la Historia* 73 (1918), 468–91. (VI) Biblioteca Nacional, Ms. 1.610, fols. 149–71, 'Sumario de los Señores, assi eclesiásticos como seglares de España con las rentas que tienen hecho por el licenciado Bartolomé Niño Belasques, vecino de Sevilla'. (VII) British Library, Sloane Ms, 1.573. (VIII) Biblioteca Nacional, Ms. 7.423, fols. 127ff., 'Arçobispados y Obispados, . . . duques, condes, marqueses, y algunos señores de vasallos de España . . .'. (IX) Biblioteca Nacional, Ms. 6.494. Gabriel de Lobo Lasso de la Vega, 'Relación de todos los títulos de España, así las Casas . . . como las rentas', fols. 44v and ff. (X) Biblioteca Nacional, Ms. 1.254, Pérez Carrillo, 'Diágolo de las dos virtudes cardinales . . .', fols. 185v and ff. (XI) James Wadsworth, *The Present Estate of Spayne* (London, 1630). (XII) Real Academia de la Historia, Papeles de Jesuitas, vol. 182, 'Relación de todos los titulados de España y de sus Casas y Linaxes y de las rentas que tienen y . . .' (XIII) Real Academia de la Historia. Colección Salazar, vol. 20, no. 32.733. F/11, 'Relación de todos lcs títulos de España . . . e de la renta de cada uno'.

Appendix 12.3

The top ten ducal revenues (sixteenth–seventeenth centuries)

Title	1520	1539	1577	1580	1597	1610	1615	1616	1617	1620	1630	(1)	(2)
Alba	6	5	6	6	4	7	5	5	5	5	4	5	5
Alburquerque	10	10	7	5	—	9	9	10	8	10	7	9	7
Alcalá de los Gazules	—	—	—	—	—	—	—	—	—	—	—	—	—
Arcos	5	—	5	—	8	5	6	6	7	7	8	7	6
Béjar	8	7	9	7	7	6	7	7	4	8	6	6	8
Cea	—	—	—	—	—	—	—	—	—	—	—	—	—
Escalona	—	—	—	—	—	—	—	—	—	—	—	—	—
Feria	—	—	—	—	—	—	—	—	—	—	—	—	—
Frias	2	3	—	—	—	—	—	—	—	—	—	—	—
Infantado	4	2	4	2	5	3	4	4	6	4	5	4	4
Lerma	—	—	—	—	—	—	—	—	—	—	—	—	—
Maqueda	3	6	3	3	3	4	3	2	2	3	3	2	3
Medina de Rioseco	1	4	1	1	1	1	1	1	1	1	1	1	1
Medina Sidonia	7	9	—	9	9	10	10	9	9	6	9	8	9
Medinaceli	—	—	—	—	—	8	8	8	10	9	10	10	10
Nájera	—	8	8	10	10	—	—	—	—	—	—	—	—
Osuna	9	—	2	4	2	2	2	3	3	2	2	3	2
Pastrana	—	—	—	—	—	—	—	—	—	—	—	—	—
Peñaranda	—	—	—	—	—	—	—	—	—	—	—	—	—
San Lúcar la Real	—	—	—	—	—	—	—	—	—	—	—	—	—
Sessa	—	1	10	8	6	—	—	—	—	—	—	—	—

13. The Castilian aristocracy in the seventeenth century: crisis, refeudalisation, or political offensive?

BARTOLOMÉ YUN CASALILLA

Contrary to what might be assumed from the title of this chapter, it is not my intention to embark upon a terminological debate in the way that, unfortunately, has been so common among historians. It is far more profitable to pose a series of questions relating to the specific situation of the Castilian aristocracy in the seventeenth century and its possible relevance to the general historical process. The precise position of the aristocracy among the range of forces within the state and the degree of its identification with it, the room for manoeuvre it had with respect to institutions and society in general, its financial and economic situation, and the juridical context in which it was created, constitute some of the basic explanations of the problems of the epoch and of the way historical change occurred, not only in Castile, but in the monarchy as a whole.

The aim of this chapter is not to publicise the final results of original research but, by stating precisely what should be understood by these terms and by considering to what extent each part explains the whole, to indicate methods of analysis and research rather better than those currently in use. At the same time we can highlight a series of topics that need the prompt attention of specialists if we are to understand better the concepts of 'crisis', 'refeudalisation' and 'political offensive' as applied to the seventeenth-century aristocracy.

This chapter is concerned primarily with the Castilian aristocracy of medieval origin, and in particular with those families which rose in the fourteenth and fifteenth centuries. We leave on one side, therefore, the new aristocracy that, thanks above all to state service, was given titles and grandeeship in the early modern period, but which could, nonetheless, be included in some of the statements that follow.

I. 'CRISIS OF THE ARISTOCRACY' AND 'REFEUDALISATION'

These two concepts are without doubt the best known and most commonly used of the three we are discussing. In reality they are the hub around which have revolved a series of recent investigations which to a great extent have developed along lines initiated some time ago by A. Domínguez Ortiz.[1]

According to current general opinion, the old Castilian aristocracy of medieval origin was faced from the sixteenth century onwards with a series of financial difficulties, caused by price inflation and the high costs of court life, which brought about a 'seignorial reaction', especially after 1600, when its ordinary revenues began to decline. This reaction, often encapsulated in the concept of 'refeudalisation', was directed to the resuscitation of old rights which had lapsed and operated through the extension of seignorialism and a general increase in seignorial pressure. This phenomenon, which was also advanced both by the grant of jurisdictions and titles by the state and by the incorporation of fresh blood into the baronial class, has been regarded as a return to the past and an increase in the power of the lords. It was, at the same time, a general process that affected in various ways all the countries of Europe.

[1] In reality the term 'crisis of the aristocracy' is a transposition from Anglo-Saxon historiography, best represented in L. Stone, *The Crisis of the Aristocracy, 1558–1641* (Oxford, 1965). The situation in Spain was described some time ago, but without using the label, by A. Domínguez Ortiz, especially in *Las clases privilegiadas en el Antiguo Régimen* (3rd edn, Madrid, 1983). It is perhaps significant that it should have been an Anglo-Saxon historian, C. J. Jago, who used the term with reference to Spain, in an essay of 1979, 'The "Crisis of the Aristocracy" in seventeenth-century Castile', *Past and Present* 84 (1979), 60–90, which was translated into Spanish in 1982. It was later used, sometimes with variations, by other authors, such as I. Atienza Hernández, 'La quiebra de la nobleza castellana en el siglo XVII. Autoridad real y poder señorial: el secuestro de los bienes de la casa de Osuna', *Hispania* 44: 156 (1984), 49–81, and by the present author, in 'Aristocracia, señorío y crecimiento económico en Castilla: reflexiones a partir de los Pimentel y los Enríquez', *Revista de Historia Económica* 3 (1986), 443–71. 'Refeudalisation', which has a much older place in our conceptual baggage, has recently been taken up again by I. A. A. Thompson, *War and Government in Habsburg Spain, 1560–1620* (London, 1976). Even more recently, I. Atienza, 'Refeudalización en Castilla durante el siglo XVII: ¿Un tópico?', *Anuario de Historia del Derecho Español* 56 (1986), 889–920, has mounted a brilliant and wholehearted defence of the utility of the concept [See chapter 12 above.] Though less enthusiastically, I also had something to say in *Sobre la transición al capitalismo en Castilla. Economía y Sociedad en Tierra de Campos, 1500–1830* (Salamanca, 1987).

It must be admitted, however, that we cannot be entirely satisfied with the knowledge we have. We need to define further in what form this 'crisis of the aristocracy' and this 'refeudalisation' came about and how we should interpret their long-term historical significance. Concerning the so-called 'crisis of the aristocracy', we have suggested elsewhere that it should be viewed as an episode in the development and, therefore, in the crisis and transformation of feudalism, not merely as a question of court expenses and price movements.[2] Although the latter are important, given the widespread nature of the *señorío* and the financial value of its political and military powers, at the root of this 'crisis' is the contradiction created within the feudal economy by the monopolisation of power by the state. From an early date the aristocracy had sought to alleviate this problem by increasing the share it got of the royal revenues from alienated rents and payments for its services to the Crown.[3] However, the result of this tacit pact was to increase tension with the monarchy, in addition to the tensions already existing for purely political reasons. The Crown's increasing financial needs meant that this bleeding of its resources could only be overcome by switching the ever-growing burden of taxation onto other groups in society. These contradictions, which had become apparent between 1504 and 1522, were resolved in the Comunero Revolt in a way favourable to the central authority. Although it was not the lords who emerged defeated from the conflict, their long-cherished hopes for a strengthened role in the kingdom *vis-à-vis* the Crown were left disappointed,[4] and, after 1522, a return to the past was unthinkable.

[2] 'Aristocracia, señorío', pp. 453 and 454.
[3] The phenomenon has been drawn attention to in other regions by G. Bois, *Crise du feudalisme* (Paris, 1976), and is clearly represented in Castile in the importance assumed by the *tercias* and *alcabalas* in scigniorial revenues from the fourteenth and fifteenth centuries onwards; see, for example, the case of the counts of Benavente in I. Beceiro Pita, 'El señorío de los Benavente en el siglo XV', doctoral thesis presented in the University of Valladolid, 1980; or the importance they assumed, from the very beginning, in the estate of the Enríquez, Admirals of Castile, P. Martínez Sopena, *El estado señorial de Medina de Rioseco* (Valladolid, 1979). From the point of view of the royal treasury the phenomenon can be followed in various studies by M. A. Ladero Quesada, in particular, *La Hacienda real de Castilla en el siglo XV* (La Laguna, 1973), p. 75. Pioneering work on this topic has been done by S. de Moxó, of which I shall mention only his *La alcabala. Sus orígenes, concepto y naturaleza* (Madrid, 1963).
[4] For an exposition of this aspect of the problem, B. González Alonso, 'Las Comunidades de Castilla y la formación del Estado Absoluto', in his *Sobre el Estado y la Administración de la Corona de Castilla en el Antiguo Régimen* (Madrid,

If this argument is accepted, the 'crisis of the aristocracy' acquires a political dimension. Alongside the problems of prices and dispendiousness, there is a problem of power which is directly related to the structural development of the absolutist state. There are unfortunately many unresolved questions concerning the situation of the Castilian upper nobility during the reign of Charles V and the early years of Philip II. It seems clear that this was the key phase in the penetration of mercantile capital into seignorial economies through loans at high rates of interest which, by means of the *censo*, were transformed into a consolidated debt.[5] Thus, at the same time that they were being excluded more from central power,[6] the lords watched helplessly the real depreciation of

---

1981), pp. 7–56. The problem can be pursued further in S. Haliczer, *The Comuneros of Castile. The forging of a revolution* (Madison, Wisc., 1981), which analyses the crisis of the Comuneros in the light of earlier tensions.

[5] The subject still awaits in-depth study by specialists in the period and has great explanatory potential, above all if we bear in mind its relevance to the mechanisms of distribution and transfer of the social product between the two groups and to the study of the means by which mercantile capital had the capacity to effect the dissolution of the feudal system, and of the legal barriers which in the Spanish case acted to slow it down. We should bear in mind that consignatory *censos* were not, in the sixteenth century, the immediate cause of debt, which consisted rather of loans from the great bankers at high rates of interest – often up to 20 per cent – employing the exchange operations of the great Castilian fairs. There are references in various studies to the many *censos* established with the sole purpose of substituting existing floating debt with a less burdensome, consolidated debt; see, for example, the case of the marquis of Priego, who fell into debt in order to purchase the *alcabalas* of Castro del Río, for which he borrowed 100,000 ducats from Nicolo Grimaldo, in J. Aranda Doncel, 'Castro del Río en el último tercio del siglo XVI', in *Castro del Río. Bosquejo histórico de una villa andaluza* (Cordoba, 1986), p. 135; the loan obtained from Italian bankers by the counts of Benavente is described by Yun Casalilla, 'Aristocracia, señorío', p. 454. All this information should be added to that provided in the detailed study by F. H. Abed Al-Hussein, 'Trade and the business community in Old Castile: Medina del Campo 1500–1575', PhD thesis, University of East Anglia, 1982. (I am grateful to the author for allowing me to read the unpublished text.) The question possesses especial interest in that the chronology of indebtedness revealed by these studies suggests an earlier start for this phenomenon than has commonly been accepted.

[6] As is well known, the upper nobility were more or less cut out of politics by Charles V, made suspicious by what had happened at the beginning of the Comunero movement. The most striking case is that of the Admirals of Castile, whose complaints are listed in the texts cited and analysed by J. Perez, *La révolution des 'Comunidades' de Castille (1520–1521)* (Bordeaux, 1970), pp. 674–81. However, perhaps this is something that should not be exaggerated since, even during his reign, there were cases of grandees who were forced into debt in an attempt to satisfy the monarch's demands; such was the case, for example, of the counts of Benavente. But what does seem clear, at least until there are more solid studies on

their incomes, which were based to a large degree on alienated royal rents, which did not keep pace with price inflation, or on fixed sources, derived from their eminent lordship of the land or from seignorial rights. Only the legal mechanism of entailment (*mayorazgo*) and the permission to fund *censos* on income from their *mayorazgos* which only the king could grant, prevented the most precocious price revolution in Europe from totally undermining their economic foundations. What needs to be stressed is that part of their indebtedness was caused by the need to buy land or alienated royal revenues. This confirms the belief that the crucial activity for the aristocracy at this time was to continue the expansion of seignorialism, and for that, given the absence of the alternative means that had been available in the Middle Ages, it was essential to spend. Furthermore, because of the entail, the financial difficulties of the aristocracy had become transformed into a crisis of liquidity which, at worst, could lead to the 'sequestration' and administration of their estates by the Crown or by private individuals.

This political aspect of the 'crisis of the aristocracy' and its concrete expression on the financial plane seem to me fundamental to the understanding of the extent of the phenomenon and the capacity for resistance and reaction in these families after the second half of the sixteenth century. 'Refeudalisation' has to be located in a concrete political framework, and, contradictory as it may seem, that framework was the absolutist state.

It is necessary, however, before advancing conclusions, to consider the second aspect of the matter. I want to show that the events of the seventeenth century that are usually included within the rubric of 'refeudalisation', because the expression is both clastic and precise at the same time, raise a number of questions concerning how and in what sense their significance should be understood.

One dimension of the term involves the creation of titles and the alienation of royal jurisdictions. It needs to be emphasised from the outset that this process was not a consequence of an institutional weakness of the state, but only of its financial needs, and that, as we shall see, is of importance when we come to interpret these events.

the subject, is that the ability to take advantage of these services to get their way at Court was less than it was to be in the seventeenth century, as we shall see. The phenomenon of the political displacement of one specific family, related this time to the ascendancy of the lawyers from the time of the Catholic Kings, is described by H. Nader, *The Mendoza Family in the Spanish Renaissance* (New Brunswick, 1979), pp. 155–208.

However, for the proper understanding of the place this issue should be accorded in the process of 'refeudalisation', it is vital first of all to undertake a series of regional studies to establish to what extent there were areas where class relations and the social distribution of production remained largely unaffected by this process. The reason is that, although there is no shortage of examples of new lords adopting a policy of increasing pressure upon their vassals, nor of jurisdictional authority ensuring the better collection of revenues,[7] it is likely that, as occurred in many parts of Italy, what we are seeing is simply the selling of lordships or titles, significant only juridically or for the social prestige of the purchaser.[8] We also need to know to what extent these jurisdictions were acquired by non-aristocratic noble families, or by the newer aristocracy. If they were, we would have to modify the idea, sometimes implicit in the concept of 'refeudalisation', that we are dealing with a 'feudal' or 'seigniorial' reaction, and instead regard the acquisition of jurisdictions as a form of social and economic advance for a group born and raised under the wing of the state, something which would make the state's attitude towards such acquisitions understandable.[9]

It is equally evident that this 'refeudalisation' took the form of an increasing seigniorial pressure on their vassals and on society at large. But given the limitations of our current knowledge this is still an open and imprecise question, imprecise because it is difficult to

[7] See, for example, the case study by A. García Sanz, *Desarrollo y crisis del Antiguo Régimen en Castilla la Vieja: economía y sociedad en tierras de Segovia de 1500 a 1814* (2nd edn, Madrid, 1986), pp. 371–4; however, the author himself thinks this is not generalisable.

[8] See the stimulating observations of G. Muto, 'La feudalità meridionale tra crisi economica e ripresa politica' in *Studi Storici Luigi Simeoni* 46 (1986), 29–55, in which he collates testimonies to this effect, amongst others those of E. Sereni, *Storia del paesagio agrario italiano* (Bari, 1961). It seems that this occurred in Castile in those municipalities whose jurisdiction only had been acquired, and not the income from *tercias* and *alcabalas*, where the interests of the new owners were limited to jurisdictional lordship.

[9] This is what happened, for example, in many places north of the Duero; see L. Fernández Martín, 'Las ventas de las villas y lugares de behetría y su repercusión en la vida económica y social de los pueblos de Castilla', *Anuario de historia económica y social* 1 (1968), 261–80. There, with the exception of the purchases, subsequently blocked, of the duke of Lerma, the majority of acquisitions were made by this type of individual or by the older aristocracy of second rank. Something similar is found in J. Aranda Doncel, *Historia de Córdoba en la Edad Moderna* (Cordoba, 1983), pp. 160–4; he has further information in 'La villa de Santaella en la Edad Moderna, 1569–1733' in *Santaella, Estudios históricos de una villa cordobesa* (Montilla, 1986), p. 153.

establish an exact chronology and, consequently, to decide if it was a universal phenomenon or a structural feature of feudalism.[10] Moreover, we need to differentiate between what was really a seignorial offensive and what should strictly be considered as resistance by their vassals.[11] It is an open question because there are reasons for believing that this pressure was exercised selectively from district to district and was a function of specific concerns and situations, whether the lord did or did not have rights to the *alcabalas*, for instance, and, therefore, whether he was or was not interested in the total or partial depopulation of those districts. Furthermore, given the legal differences created during the Reconquest, we might suspect that it was also related to the possibilities of success of an action that would be certain to unleash a chain of extremely expensive lawsuits.

But, above all, there are two aspects crucial to an adequate understanding of the events of the seventeenth century which lead us automatically to consider the problem of 'refeudalisation' as a facet of a much wider question concerning the general strength of the aristocracy within the state, to which we shall refer in the following section.

I refer, firstly, to the fact that this seignorial reaction as it is usually defined does not encompass all aspects of the aristocracy's struggle to overcome its difficulties. In the cases known to us, it seems clear that their 'refeudalising' offensive and the direct pressure they put on their vassals to draw off a greater share of the social product were much less effective than other measures made possible because of their influence at Court, such as the reduction of the interest rate on *censos* on the revenues of their entails, or the

[10] There is no shortage of examples to show that many such conflicts, which lasted throughout the early modern period and into the eighteenth century, started much earlier.
[11] This happened with many of the lawsuits about seignorial monopolies in Andalusia and which, in reality, seem to have derived from the wishes of the vassals to get rid of some privileges that restricted the productive process in the period of demographic and economic expansion during the sixteenth century. This can be inferred from the judgement favourable to the marquis of Priego over the oil presses of Montilla, where, nevertheless, the increase of seigniorial pressure in other respects is patent, see J. Aranda Doncel, 'La oposición a los monopolios e imposiciones señoriales en Montilla durante los siglos XVI y XVII' in *Montilla, aportaciones para su historia* (Montilla, 1982), pp. 237–64. Many more cases, capable of being interpreted in both ways, are found in J. Calvo Poyato, *Del siglo XVII al XVIII en los señoríos del Sur de Córdoba* (Cordoba, 1986), pp. 503–6.

ratification of special arrangements they might have made with their creditors.

Furthermore, this 'refeudalisation' did not mean any decrease in the institutional power of the state, nor *a fortiori* any political independence for the *señor*, nor any fragmentation of the political system as a whole. The work of legal historians in this respect is particularly revealing.[12] In addition, even when the military role of the lord and of the *señorío* was reinforced, it is not right to speak of a loss of the power of decision by the king, since the *señores* were operating as instruments of a superior military and political organisation.[13]

This question is important, not only from the perspective of historians of law, but also from that of historians in general, and of economic historians in particular. This is because if we accept, as now is accepted even by Marxist historians (despite their supposed resistance to this sort of approach), that the legal-political dimension is a material consideration in the distribution of the social product in feudalism, it is obvious that changes occurring within that dimension must have had a direct influence on economic processes.

We should add that, although the lords gained in decision-making capacity and extended their seignorial jurisdiction, their general support for the Crown did not disappear, for the Crown was, after all, the mainstay of a system of wealth distribution of which they were the beneficiaries and of which the monarchy's fiscal apparatus was one of the most important pillars. That support persisted not least because as, or even more, important than the sale of jurisdic-

---

[12] B. González Alonso, 'Notas sobre las relaciones del Estado con la administración señorial en la Castilla Moderna', *Anuario de Historia del Derecho Español* 53 (1983), 365–94. In the same vein are the later remarks of S. de Dios, 'Sobre la génesis y los caracteres del Estado Absolutista en Castilla', *Studia Histórica (Historia Moderna)* 3: 3 (1985), 11–46. Here the author reaches conclusions similar to those expressed by the present author concerning the aristocracy's need for a strong monarchical power, and the complementarity in practice between the state and the *señorío*.

[13] This is one of the conclusions that can be extracted from the work of L. G. White, 'War and government in a Castilian province: Extremadura, 1640–1668', PhD thesis, University of East Anglia, 1985, pp. 268–324 (I should like to thank the author for allowing me to consult her manuscript.) It should not be forgotten, however, that the ability of the lords to recruit was very important for the system of military mobilization in the period, see Thompson, *War and Government*, ch. 4,

tions, which at the end of the day was by itself of no decisive consequence for the distribution of surplus product, was the alienation of royal revenues (*alcabalas, tercias, cientos*), which increased the lords' interest in the maintenance and perpetuation of the most unpopular and controversial aspect of the seventeenth century, the tax system, which at times they seemed to defend even against the desires for reform of the Crown itself.

It seems clear, therefore, that 'refeudalisation' must be understood not as a process prejudicial to the absolute power of the king, but rather as something internal to it, even though it involved the extension of seignorial competence within the legal framework that the king had established. In this sense it is inappropriate to speak of regression. Long gone were those attempts at a 'rectification' of the legal-political organisation of the kingdom which, according to B. González Alonso, had suffered such a severe set-back in 1521.[14] And this without forgetting that, as the same writer later recognised, referring to the state and seignorialism, we still lack an explanation of the 'internal mechanisms that facilitated their harmonious integration'.

2. 'POLITICAL OFFENSIVE'

At this point, we need to consider how far 'refeudalisation' was related to the broader spectrum of relations between the aristocracy and the state. Such a perspective, not always adopted in the analysis of this subject, could be of great help in clarifying the way in which the 'crisis of the aristocracy' was overcome, and has the advantage of allowing the formulation of new hypotheses of undeniable importance.

The most recent studies have confirmed the idea that from the final decades of the sixteenth century the presence of the aristocracy, in particular houses of medieval origin, in politics, administration and the military increased markedly. Parker and Thompson have proved this in respect of the military, both inside and outside the Peninsula.[15] A glance at the list of the viceroys of Naples and Sicily

---

pp. 103–45. It is very possible that it all depended on the degree of control and the concrete situation in which it took place.

[14] González Alonso, 'Las Comunidades de Castilla', pp. 7–56.

[15] G. Parker, *The Army of Flanders and the Spanish Road, 1567–1659* (Cambridge, 1972); Thompson, *War and Government*, pp. 146–59.

or the governors general of Milan shows that, although some branches of the upper aristocracy had already played a distinguished role in earlier years, it was from this time that their presence became the norm. Something similar occurred in the other peninsular kingdoms. Moreover, we know that these posts were steps on a longer career path leading to the Councils of State and War, bodies apparently very much under the control of the Castilian aristocracy during the seventeenth century, and whose importance within the monarchy needs no restatement.[16] The very institution of the *valido* has been considered by Tomás y Valiente as the expression of an aristocratic movement,[17] already perceived by J. A. Maravall, for whom the nobility moved from 'social order to power elite'.[18] Maravall also has the merit of having furnished an account of some of these issues and of the general trajectory of the problem from the fifteenth century from a socio-political perspective.

Nevertheless, we still lack a satisfactory explanation of how this situation came about and the concrete positions from which it began, as well as of the nature of its causes and the historical conjuncture behind it. Because the history of the aristocracy in the sixteenth century is less understood than that of the seventeenth, what has been overlooked is that this process of *rapprochement* became increasingly evident precisely when military and public expenditure in general were rocketing,[19] and when Philip II was searching for new ways of financing his military enterprises and his political apparatus. It is understandable, therefore, that the king should have favoured a compromise with the aristocracy beneficial to both sides, the full working-out of which remains, I think, still somewhat unclear.

With regard to the traditional military function of the aristocracy, it is now accepted that the summonses to suppress the Moorish uprisings, as well as that of 1590, cannot be categorised as

---

[16] See the foreword by J. M. Batista i Roca to the study by H. G. Koenigsberger, *The Government of Sicily under Philip II of Spain* (London, 1951), p. 28.

[17] F. Tomás y Valiente, *Los validos en la Monarquía española del siglo XVII* (Madrid, 1982), p. 56.

[18] J. A. Maravall, *Poder, honor y élites en el siglo XVII* (Madrid, 1984), p. 56.

[19] Thompson, *War and Government*, pp. 67–100, for a description of the difficulties of financing the army and the various operations put into practice by Philip II to improve it. See also the Appendix on p. 288.

successes.[20] But these episodes demonstrate rather the financial incapacity of the aristocracy than the impossibility for the Crown to employ them. Events show that, amongst other things, the grandees could provide the monarch with the political presence necessary for the government of the 'empire' and (although it might seem paradoxical given their crisis of liquidity) the credit and ready cash to undertake the duties entrusted to them. To make this possible, all that was needed was to generalise the practice of imposing *censos* on the revenues of entailed estates, not solely for the benefit of their owners, but increasingly for the service of the state. The ploy, which had begun to be used earlier, was to appoint for some mission a lord with sufficient credit to draw on the savings of private investors by mortgaging the revenues of his entail in order to enable him to embark on his commission. The frequent concessions for the imposition of *censos* in the last decades of the sixteenth century, even to the point of allowing them to be underwritten by the lord's towns, some of which came to act not only as guarantors but as suppliers of the initial capital, is proof enough of this. It is not surprising, then, that more than 60 per cent of such grants by the Crown were generated for these reasons,[21] nor that the selection of various great nobles for high military office owed more to their disposable funds than to their talents. As a specialist on the subject has said, 'Wealth had become a prime military asset.'[22]

In this way the king was able to draw upon private savings indirectly and with no economic commitments of his own, whilst at the same time exhibiting the duty of the grandees and titled nobility to serve the Crown and the legal function of the *mayorazgo* in the fulfilment of that service. This was done knowing full well that, like so many of the financial expedients of the state, it did not represent a long-term economy, since in one way or other the redemption of that mortgage would have to be paid for.

---

[20] On this point see Domínguez Ortiz, *Las clases privilegiadas*, pp. 97–9, and Thompson, *War and Government*, p. 147.
[21] According to C. J. Jago, 'The Influence of Debt on the Relations between Crown and Aristocracy in Seventeenth-Century Castile', *Economic History Review*, 2nd series, 26 (1973), p. 224, 59.1 per cent of the licences for *censos* granted up to the beginning of the seventeenth century were intended to finance the costs of embassies, viceroyalties, military levies, etc. I have subsequently introduced some modifications in 'La situación económica de la aristocracia castellana durante el reinado de Felipe III y Felipe IV', in J. H. Elliott and A. García Sanz (eds.), *La España del Conde Duque de Olivares* (Valladolid, 1990), pp. 517–51.
[22] Parker, *Army of Flanders*, p. 119.

However, looked at in this way, the granting of licences to raise *censos* acquires a dimension that has not always been considered in recent studies. They were not only a way for the higher nobility to overcome its crisis, but also a royal expedient to meet its own needs quickly without prior or immediate expenditure, without direct commitments to the lenders, and without increasing the swollen floating debt of the Treasury.

This practice, that in form brings to mind the operations of 'administrative fragmentation' expounded in magisterial fashion by Thompson,[23] seems to me to be also a source of compromise between state and *mayorazgo* that, together with the increasing military usefulness of the *señorío* emphasised by the above-mentioned author, is one of the keys to the explanation of that 'integration' between state and seignorial organisation addressed by González Alonso. Furthermore, this mutual relationship strengthened the Crown's interest in the maintenance of the *mayorazgos* (sometimes even at the expense of their actual holders) and in their rehabilitation, by inserting clauses in some licences for *censos* (applied for for private ends) which required the redemption of other loans at higher interest rates, or by decreeing a general reduction of interest rates on *censos*, for the benefit not only of the lords, but also, ultimately, of the state itself.[24]

Of course, it is unwise to attribute all the responsibility for this *rapprochement* to the needs of the Crown, or to forget the advantages obtained by the lords. Many of these families pressed hard at Court in search of a more prominent place, and there is no doubt that they knew how to take advantage of the roles they were being asked to take on within the state. This occurred as much in the economic as in the political field, if these can be separated in a society in which, in many ways, public service and power were forms of private profit.

As far as the particular issue of their indebtedness is concerned, available studies have drawn attention to the way in which that was

[23] *War and Government*, p. 275, though the theme is developed throughout the study.
[24] We should not lose sight of the fact that the royal treasury itself also benefited from this type of measure, on the one hand, because this was the only way to reduce the interest rates on *juros* without savings in Castile being diverted towards *censos*, but also because this was a very effective way of reducing the debts of the cities and *mayorazgos*, some of which were already unsecured, and thus also increasing the possibility of continuing to intensify the tax burden on both.

exploited, and thus there is no need to return to the subject.[25] We know that, in many cases, licences to raise *censos* were a pretext to obtain capital far in excess of what their services to the monarchy actually justified.[26] In addition, as the influence of these families increased at Court, the possibility of obtaining royal grants for their private ends also increased. Among the most important of these were dowries, an apparently trivial matter from the social point of view, but extraordinarily important if we remember that marriage was one of the most effective methods of acquiring and preserving the primary 'commodity' that these families had, their social and political position.[27]

In a different vein, attention has often been drawn to the political role of the aristocracy in the seventeenth century; less often highlighted has been the importance of public office and the delegation of military and civil functions as sources of irregular income, which we sometimes forget to include in the revenue figures most frequently cited. It is precisely this lack of proper estimates which stimulates me to say something about this matter in advance of the more accurate information I intend to publish in the near future.

Posts abroad, for example, carried far from negligible 'official' salaries. The salary of the viceroy of Naples at the end of the sixteenth century varied between 10,000 and 18,000 ducats, and in 1610 it reached 29,700 a year, always, of course, paid in coin. Nor was this all. Apart from the salary, there was a variety of other payments, such as help with expenses, remuneration for related

---

[25] There are references in many of the studies referred to above. However, the most complete and exhaustive account is Jago's 'The influence of debt'.

[26] Domínguez Ortiz, *Las clases privilegiadas*, pp. 97–9.

[27] For the well-known example of the Count-Duke of Olivares, whose marriage to the *camarera* of the Queen, Doña Inés de Zúñiga, was thought even at the time to be designed to increase his influence over the entire royal family, see the 'Relación política de las más particulares acciones del Conde-Duque de Olivares . . . escrita . . . en Nápoles a primero de Julio de 1661', I.F. 51, Mss, Biblioteca Nazionale di Napoli, restated by G. Marañón, *El Conde-Duque de Olivares* (14th edn, Madrid, 1975), p. 34. Other marriages had a more economic purpose. Juan de Zúñiga, marquis of Villar, son of the count of Benavente, married the eldest daughter of the count of Alcaudete, whose estate was worth 'twenty-four thousand ducats in income, and that free of debt', according to L. Cabrera de Córdoba, *Relaciones de las cosas sucedidas en la Corte de España desde 1599 a 1614* (Madrid, 1857), p. 444. On other occasions the aim was to resolve differences, as in the case of the marriage between the eldest son of that same count of Benavente, the count of Luna, and the eldest daughter of the marquis of Los Vélez, 'to resolve the law suit that the latter had filed against the estate of Luna', *ibid.*, p. 161.

military duties, and a range of tips, bonuses and rewards that could bring the total up to nearly 60,000 ducats.[28] If we bear in mind that the ordinary income of the count of Benavente in 1638 was about 60,000 ducats a year, we can see that the seven years he served as viceroy were, on this level alone, of considerable economic importance for him, even at a time when the custom of giving the viceroys of Naples and Sicily a share of the 'donative', which at the beginning of the seventeenth century was worth about 75,000 ducats in the former case, and in 1610 reached the scandalous sum of 300,000, had already been abolished.[29]

To all this we must add many other benefits obtained from this type of post which because of their unofficial (if not fraudulent) nature are difficult to quantify. A letter written by the Jesuit, Father Mendoza, to the count of Lemos before he took up his post as viceroy of Naples, is a clear testament to the many opportunities available, as well as to the legal and moral dubiety of each of them, all the more interesting in that it demonstrates that many operations that today would be considered venal, were then justifiable.[30] Thus, although the scrupulous Jesuit was doubtful about the viceroy's exploitation of the pardons granted to criminals for a cash settlement, he recognised that 'it was customary for past viceroys to take

[28] R. Mantelli, *Il pubblico impiego nell'economia del Regno di Napoli: retribuzioni, reclutamento e ricambio sociali nell'epoca spagnola (sec. XVI–XVII)* (Naples, 1986), pp. 104–5. We do not mention here the highly lucrative posts of viceroys in the Indies. A brief account can be found in Domínguez Ortiz, *Las clases privilegiadas*, pp. 112–13.

[29] Some evidence, perhaps inaccurate due to its 'antifeudal' bias, typical of its 'national-liberal' tendency, but reliable in general terms, is to be found in D. Winspeare, *Storia degli abusi feudali* (2nd edn, Naples, 1883), p. 182. The same phenomenon involving similar features and sums occurred in Sicily, see G. Blasi, *Storia cronologica dei viceré, luogotenenti e presidenti del Regno di Sicilia* (Palermo, 1842). According to the author, the custom became widespread following the government of Colonna, p. 250. For one illustration, the duke of Osuna was awarded a private donation of 50,000 florins in 1611, the year in which such private practices were prohibited, *ibid.*, p. 286.

[30] P. Hernando de Mendoza, 'Tres tratados compuestos por el P. Hernando de Mendoza, de la Compañia de Jesus para el muy Excellentisimo señor Conde de Lemos, virrey de Nápoles, y Mandados imprimir por el señor Don Francisco de Castro, su hijo y sucesor en el cargo' (Naples, 1602), manuscript in Biblioteca Nacional de Madrid (my thanks to Roberto Mantelli for referring me to this text, which he also used in *Il pubblico impiego*, pp. 105ff). For the moral criteria of the epoch and the manoeuvring made possible by the control of public offices, see J. C. Waquet, *La corruzione. Morale e potere a Firenze nel XVII e XVIII secolo* (Milan, 1986).

money for these pardons without scruple'.[31] Still greater could be
the profits derived from trading licences that some viceroys issued to
themselves, or sold to others. Apparently these could yield up to
15,000 ducats.[32]

These posts in government also brought great power which, with
the control they had over appointments to public offices and
employment, was the basis for the widening of one's clientele and
patronage. The *protegés* (among them such prominent names as
Francisco de Quevedo y Villegas, in Italy at the orders of the restless
duke of Osuna) formed a faction whose loyalty matched the opportunities for profit that could be expected from the office.[33]
Moreover, we can be absolutely certain, because the various official
inspections confirmed it, that the economic beneficiaries of this type
of post were numerous, even if the means they employed were often
illegal.[34] No less valuable were the opportunities for these clients in
a political career. It is enough to glance at a list of the Secretaries of
State and War of the Army of Flanders to see how often the
appointment went to the men closest to the top brass.[35]

There are reasons for believing – despite the lack of hard evidence
– that the viceroys themselves found in the performance of their
offices ways of enriching themselves which were also of questionable
legality. It depended very much on their individual moral standards.

31 Hernando de Mendoza, 'Tres tratados', p. 120.
32 *Ibid.*, p. 150. The author states that this was the opinion of 'several persons of
authority and experience who advised His Excellency on what to do, and that it
would be a great mistake to do the opposite, and that all other viceroys have done
the same'. It seems to be the case that 'one of His Majesty's important ministers'
and an 'experienced and learned cleric' thought similarly.
33 The three treatises of P. Mendoza refer to the legality of and the opportunities for
enrichment by the servants and officials appointed by the viceroy. It is curious that
on some points the Jesuit father is more flexible in these matters, and recognises
that 'all the viceroys have done it', *ibid.*, p. 122. In the 'Relación del Conde de
Olivares sobre el gobierno de Sicilia', Biblioteca Communale di Palermo (BCP),
Qq E 23, p. 67, the father of the future Count-Duke related how the viceroys could
dispose of saleable offices from the time they became vacant until they were sold,
and how they were offered *mediante pecunia*. An equally rich source of information of this kind is 'Breve resumen del Gobierno de Sicilia', BCP, Qq E 63,
p. 39. Here are detailed all the offices at his disposal, like the posts belonging to the
militia, the naming of six judges to the supreme court, with a list of salaries of
ministers and permanent officials, of non-venal offices, etc.
34 There is much information in P. Burgarella and G. Fallico, *L'archivio dei visitatori
generali di Sicilia* (Rome, 1977), and G. Coniglio, *Visitatori dei vicerregno di
Napoli* (Bari, 1974).
35 Parker, *Army of Flanders*, Appendix E, pp. 285–6.

Our ignorance in this area should perhaps be imputed to the total inability of the inspectors to carry out personal investigations of the viceroys in the seventeenth century, but there are plenty of details to support reasonable suspicion.[36] The opportunities were, of course, numerous. They had at their disposal, for example, the so-called 'spese segrete' fund, which in 1681–3 could amount to 90,000 ducats a year. In theory it was earmarked for secret official expenses, but because it was secret and because the inspectors were prohibited from looking into it, it could be spent at the viceroy's discretion. Furthermore, the extraordinary power of the viceroy made him the continuous object of donations, private gifts and so on.[37]

A question often ignored that nevertheless offers interesting possibilities concerns the extent to which these families, assisted by the power they wielded, found in the territories subject to the monarchy a new space in which to extend their possessions and continue the dynamic growth of their economies thanks to the fiefdoms they were granted by the monarchy as a reward for their services. A simple glance at the Neapolitan documentation that records the payment of the levy for the enjoyment of fiefs and seignorial revenues immediately reveals the presence of families as important as the Ponce de León, Zúñiga, Requesens, Alvarez de Toledo y Enríquez de Rivera (dukes of Alba), Toledo y Osorio (marquis of Villafranca), Pimentel (counts of Benavente), Hurtado de Mendoza (dukes of Infantado) etc. To judge by the amount of tax

---

[36] Apart from well-known cases like that of the duke of Osuna, further evidence is available. Thus, the count of Benavente, viceroy at the time of the *visita* of Juan Bautista de la Cueva in 1607, was involved in grain speculation with a Portuguese named Miguel Vaaz, see Coniglio, *Visitatori*, pp. 32ff. Much earlier, the Viceroy Colonna had been involved in a similar situation, see Burgarella and Fallico, *L'archivio dei visitatori*, p. 47.

[37] Despite the prohibitions of private donations to the viceroys, they continued to receive presents. In Naples, Doña Catalina de la Cerda y Sandoval, wife of the count of Lemos, received 30,000 ducats from the nobility, which she dedicated to charitable foundations, see D. A. Parrino, *Teatro eroico, e politico de' governi de' vicere del Regno di Napoli* (Naples, 1770), p. 312. In Sicily, the traditional struggle for the status of capital between Palermo and Messina was another motive for favouring the viceroys, who decided where the government should be located. In 1606, the duke of Feria received from the people of Messina the present of a large silver figure of Messina. Shortly afterwards, the inhabitants of Palermo offered the marquis of Villena 60,000 *escudos* to pay the ransom of his son; apparently he did not accept, but the shadow of doubt fell on him since shortly afterwards he decided that their city should again be the capital. We also know of presents to the

they paid, which should have been a tenth of total income, but which, without any doubt, was under-assessed, they were drawing revenues of up to 20,000 ducats a year.[38] In addition, part of Crown revenue in those kingdoms was alienated to the benefit of those families, or was used for the assignment of grants for which there was insufficient revenue free in Castile. In both cases the question becomes even more important if we remember that via this expedient not only was their income guaranteed, but the Crown also evaded the commitment, repeatedly made to the Cortes of Castile, not to alienate its revenues.[39]

If the fringe benefits, economic as well as social and political, that could be obtained in posts abroad were large, no less were those derived from influence at Court and from high politics in Madrid. This was the goal to which many dedicated themselves once they had achieved a position in the Council of State or War, or once they managed, after sordid palace intrigues, to get their leaders into the royal favour. So varied were the possibilities that we shall not

count of Castro and the duke of Alburquerque in 1618 and 1630 respectively, see G. di Blasi, *Storia cronologica*, pp. 271, 279 and 309.

[38] This documentary material is not in reality a first-hand source, since what it lists is the payment of the *relevo* and we do not always know, except when we have information of the first payment made, who was the original beneficiary of the seignorial rights for which it was paid. Nevertheless, for present purposes, the source is entirely satisfactory since the appearance of these notables paying the tax means that some member of the family had received the fief earlier. My evidence, which relates to the Toledo y Osorio, marquises of Villafranca and dukes of Ferrandina, the counts of Lemos, the Zúñiga y Requesens, the Alvarez de Toledo, dukes of Alba, the Pimentel, counts of Benavente, the dukes of Infantado and Pastrana, and others, is extracted from the index volumes conserved in the 'Elenco dei feudatari tratto dai volumini dello "Spoglio delle Significatore dei relevi, anni 1509–1768"', in the Archivio Storico di Napoli (ASN).

[39] There are abundant references in Collaterale, Mercedum, ASN. Examples include the transfer of 12,000 ducats a year of revenues the count of Fuentes, councillor of state, had in the Canary Islands to import dues in the Kingdom of Naples and the state of Milan, to which was added another 6,000 as compensation for his services as governor of Milan in 1606 (vol. I, ff. 151–5). Juan Alfonso Pimentel de Herrera, count of Benavente, was given, in 1607, another 4,000 from the same revenue of the treasury of the Kingdom of Naples for his services to Philip II and Philip III (vol. I, ff. 156–9). An identical sum was assigned to the count of Oñate in 1625 for his embassies in Rome and Alexandria (vol. VI, ff. 25–8). Similar grants were made to the marquis of Leganés in 1639 (vol. VI, ff. 191–9 and 213–16), to the count of Monterrey in 1641 (vol. VI, ff. 171–4), to the marquis of Salinas in 1658 (vol. I, ff. 25–8), and others, for services to the Crown in the central organs of the Monarchy or in Italy. I would like to thank Imma Ascione, archivist of the Archivio di Stato di Napoli, for allowing me to consult her files on the subject, which greatly facilitated my research.

attempt to describe or evaluate them at the moment. It is enough to remember the Sicilian wheat export permits which gave the duke of Lerma profits of 81,051,000 *maravedís* between 2 October 1601 and 3 July 1603,[40] or the concession to the Count-Duke of Olivares to charter a ship of up to 150 tons to trade between the Philippines and New Spain with goods to the value of 150,000 *pesos*. Moreover, with access to the Court and with the entrée it allowed into politics in general, the aristocracy were able to participate in the decisions of 'the greatest lord in the world', the king of Spain, of whom a Venetian ambassador said that:

> not to speak of his finances, he has much to give . . . He can appoint twenty or more viceroys, forty-six captains general . . . He distributes masterships (of the Military Orders) . . . more than five hundred commanderies, some worth twenty thousand ducats and the least of them five hundred . . . eight or more Archbishoprics, the meanest of five thousand ducats; seventy-three bishoprics . . . most of twenty thousand ducats, and none less than three thousand.

A quick glance through the work of Cabrera de Córdoba shows that an important part of what the king had to give, ended up in the hands of the court aristocracy.[41]

The insertion of the aristocracy into the heart of the state is, I believe, a process the importance of which it would be hard to exaggerate for its political and social, and for its economic significance. As for the latter, I believe that the figures given in the examples above speak for themselves, and we must bear in mind that they are incomplete since, as J. C. Waquet has shown for Florence, in a case-study that has general validity, corruption, in the widest sense of the term, was a decisive component.[42]

What this means, of course, is that estate revenues had become for some houses no more than just another element in their total incomes. On the other hand, it was the only element subject to the

[40] Archivo General de Simancas (AGS), Cámara de Castilla, legajo 1190, exp. 43.

[41] The quotation of the ambassador is from the 'Relación que hizo a la República de Venecia, Simón de Contarini, al fin del año 1605 de la Embajada que había hecho en España', in Cabrera de Córdoba, *Relaciones*. Both Cabrera's *Relaciones* and his *Historia de Felipe II, Rey de España* (Madrid, 1877), contain numerous references to the majority of the great families present at Court and the favours they received from the king.

[42] Waquet, *Corruzione*.

burden of mortgage. It remains to be discovered which families achieved a positive balance in this service–benefit relationship with the Crown, and by how much. Similarly, we need to know what contribution this benefit made to their threadbare economies, which cannot be studied solely at the level of the *señorío*. It seems clear that the aristocracy's expenditure as a whole (and not only that caused by obligations and costs borne on their estate incomes) must be a priority for analysis, as must be the extent to which these supplementary resources affected family politics. In this sense, we still need to study the budgetary bases and the objective reasons for an 'economic ethos' that made expenditure, and not revenue and savings, the fundamental independent variable in the management of their patrimonies.

The overall process implied a notable capacity on the part of the aristocracy to use the institutions of the state for its own economic and political ends, not only at the level of Court politics, but also in the application of power and influence at more concrete, local levels, including the *señorío*. This is what Waquet has called, in an exaggerated but graphic expression, 'the appropriation of the state', characterised by a 'nebula of autonomous elements, more or less independent of the central power'.[43]

3. PROPOSALS FOR A REFORMULATION OF THE PROBLEM

The preceding exposition leads me to put forward a number of propositions that I regard as entirely open to debate, but which do have the virtue of suggesting points for further discussion.

Seen in perspective, the evolution of the aristocracy in the sixteenth and seventeenth centuries can be considered as the history of the overcoming by that group of the difficulties posed for its social and economic survival by the emergence of the absolutist state, on the one hand, and by the development of a merchant class, on the other. Caught between the former's hold on power and its own indebtedness to the latter, resulting from its needs for funds to attend to the exigencies of seignorial expansion, the Castilian aristocracy had at its disposal a number of weapons of undoubted efficacy. One of these was the legislation relating to entails; another was the legal chicanery which, by permitting the imposition of

---

[43] *Ibid.*, ch. 3, pp. 86–109, particularly p. 107.

censos on the revenues of entailed estates, converted their floating debt, raised on the open money market, into a consolidated debt, underwritten by mortgages on their entails and thus subject to 'political' rates of interest, regulated by royal decree. In this way the capacity of commercial capital to break down existing economic and social structures, at least in this area, was notably reduced. As has been well said, it moved in the 'pores of the system', whilst the essentials of that system were preserved, jealously defended by a series of legal and institutional measures. Against this background, the needs of the monarchy, on the one hand, and the interests of the aristocracy, on the other, explain how the aristocracy was integrated into the bosom of the state and permitted, even at some obvious cost, not only a place in the general political life of the monarchy, but also a considerable ability to exploit particular institutions to reinforce its own direct power within the social fabric. This strengthening of its power was, however, firmly channelled by the king, the source of power, and by the existence of an operational and relatively effective judicial system, which in the last instance was not under the control of the lords.

This process of adaptation by which the aristocracy, continuously rejuvenated as a group by the entry into its ranks of new families, came to be a key element within the absolutist state, is essential for a correct evaluation of the so-called 'refeudalisation'. In effect, the influence of the aristocracy within the state was at the root of many processes, usually held to be involved in the concept of 'refeudalisation', which were only made possible by the exploitation of absolute power for private ends. This was the case with operations such as the king's ratification of the settlement between the counts of Benavente and their creditors in 1650;[44] or the usurpation of wastelands by the dukes of Osuna, also ratified by the king;[45] or, to cite another well-known case, the licences to enclose communal land, sell municipal offices and dispose of knighthoods of the Military Orders given to the dukes of Béjar in compensation for their donatives and military levies.[46] Something similar can be said

---

[44] Yun Casalilla, 'Aristocracia, señorío', pp. 464–5.

[45] Atienza Hernández, 'Refeudalización en Castilla'.

[46] Jago, 'Crisis of the aristocracy', p. 84. Something similar to what has been said about these three families could be said about the marquis of Priego, whose actions to the detriment of the municipality of Montilla were performed with royal

of the grants made to the Count-Duke of Olivares and other nobles, like the count of Castrillo, who were given both economic and political favours by virtue of the king's suspension of 'any laws and pragmatics of these kingdoms whether made in the Cortes or not', that is to say, by the specific evasion of that legal principle which, paradoxically, in the fifteenth century, the nobles had been defending.[47]

In this sense, 'refeudalisation' (if, given these remarks, we should continue to use the term) should be seen as one facet of a process operating within the heart of the state. Moreover, it could be said that, with this cession of powers and with their access to the channels through which the power of the monarchy flowed, the lords enjoyed in certain spheres a *de facto* autonomy that, without a doubt, was greatest in the government of their own jurisdictions. Although it was a precarious balance, it is clear that some parcels of lordly power can only be understood as an instrumentalisation of the state; and that was possible, as Albaladejo has pointed out, because the antithesis between state and society did not exist in the same manner or degree as it was to later in the liberal state.[48]

All these were elements in the 'integration' of state and *señorío*, but, clearly, it was not a 'harmonious' integration. Indeed, friction must have been frequent and, of course, the lords, in their struggle with their vassals, repeatedly came up against a legal and judicial system that, despite being amenable to their wishes, did not always rule in their favour. In any case, that struggle often generated lengthy litigation that was costly for everybody.

Nor was the relationship between the aristocracy and the Crown perfect or free from conflict. The convergence of basic interests was a factor for stability, but the sort of tacit pact we have described, and about which we have still a lot to learn, contained a number of conditions that, if breached, could lead to serious tension and even to conflict. This happened on various occasions in the reign of Philip IV, notably after 1640, when a series of mild fiscal reforms were

acquiescence and licence in return for a donative. On this see J. Aranda Doncel, 'Oposición a los monopolios', p. 225.

[47] Note that one of the questions that the nobles hoped to resolve in 1464 was the non-observance of the laws by the monarchy itself, in disregard of the law that applied in the kingdom, González Alonso, 'Las comunidades', p. 22.

[48] P. Fernández Albaladejo, 'El absolutismo y la transición política', *Zona Abierta* 30 (January–March 1984), 68.

introduced, aimed at the substitution of the 'lance' tax, the standard pretext for the imposition of *censos*, by an annual cash payment, a hearth tax, and other taxes on leasable properties and seignorial rights, all at the same time that a programme to recover alienated revenues, by reselling them, was being initiated. This obviously upset that equilibrium and affected the 'centralized feudal rent' that was the cornerstone of the community of interests they both had in the distribution of the social product. The reaction of the aristocracy is not clear, but it is obvious that there is a connection with the palace intrigues and with the revolts of the duke of Medina Sidonia, the marquis of Ayamonte and the duke of Híjar, which took place in these years, although it is apparent that other factors also played a part. The simple fact that these proposals were dropped and a revolt of the privileged was aborted before it materialised, is sufficient for the phenomenon not to be ignored. It is not irrelevant to remember that in England, at the same time, similar circumstances were giving rise to the onset of a revolutionary process in which the fact that, despite their common features, the relations between aristocracy and Crown were very different from those in Spain was undeniably decisive. For all these reasons, the binomial reform-reaction, so obvious during the seventeenth century, constitutes a plane of intersection with our subject without which some crucial nuances could be missed.

In addition, the approach to the topic we have just outlined raises a number of questions and issues for study which are of the greatest interest. Given that the aristocracy's access to and participation in power took place at Court, and given that their tactics could be extremely diverse, ranging from political marriages to palace alliances, we need to reexamine family and Court history, seemingly now reduced to matters of purely social resonance, and think of them as an integral part of a tactic of economic management and political advance. This is especially important in the case of family and matrimonial policy, which is of the very greatest interest from the economic and social point of view.

Equally interesting, it seems to me, is to consider the many and varied reasons why the aristocracy should have wanted the monarchy, upon which it based its expectations, to have an international dimension. It is evident that this was crucial for the great Castilian (and some non-Castilian) families. The information presented above, which was chosen precisely for its relevance on this point, shows that from the Pacific to the Mediterranean there was an abundance of opportunities both for those sent out with governmental functions and for those who exercised their influence in Madrid. Given this, it is obligatory to pose questions which go beyond the limits of this study. Can we retain, for example, the deeply ingrained idea that the wars in which the monarchy was engaged in the seventeenth century were pursued exclusively in the king's own interests or for dynastic reasons? What were the interests of the aristocracy in this respect, and how far did they influence, at various stages, the formation of pro- and anti-war parties at Court? What influence could they have, if indeed they had any, in the maintenance of a foreign policy that had little or no support in the Cortes of Castile, where even the important *millones* tax was established on the express condition that it was to be solely for the defence of the kingdom's frontiers?

I believe that what has been said above also poses interesting questions concerning the aristocracies of what we might call the 'peripheries' in the state. It is vital to advance our knowledge of the fusion between them and the Castilian aristocracy, as well as of the way that affected the history of each of them and of the whole complex of the territories, especially the peninsular kingdoms.[49] As far as 'refeudalisation' is concerned, it is clear it took a different form in each of them, and we need to study to what extent the greater or lesser capacity to use the state to overcome the crisis was at the root of that difference.[50] As can be seen, these reflections pose more questions than they answer. It seems clear that answers will have to come from the parallel analysis of the three concepts that we have been discussing. Starting from this point, a useful approach

[49] This topic is vital if we are to understand and date the formation of a state-wide upper aristocracy, wider than that of the old kingdoms. It ties up with the integration of the higher and lower nobility and with the emergence of the new aristocracy of business or service to the state. In this connection, it seems to me of the greatest interest to continue, from the Castilian perspective, the line of argument initiated by P. Ruiz Torres, 'La nobleza del País Valenciano durante la transición al capitalismo', *Revista d'historia moderna. Manuscrits (Transició del feudalisme al capitalisme: noves reflexios per à un debat necesari)*, 4/5 (April 1987), 91–106.

[50] For some brief reflections on the Catalan case in the light of recent studies, E. Serra y Puig, 'Tensions i ruptures de la società catalana en el procès de formació de l'Estat Modern. Una reflexió', *ibid.*, 71–9. There are also some interesting observations in R. García Cárcel, *Historia de Cataluña. Siglos XVI–XVII*, (Barcelona, 1985), I, pp. 227ff.

would be to consider the aristocracy as part of an equilibrium of forces involving several elements, with the Crown on the one side (given the political and financial concerns it had at any particular moment) and a variety of pressure groups, including the Cortes, the financial consortia, and the different factions of which the aristocracy was composed, on the other.

14. Spain and the seventeenth-century crisis in Europe: some final considerations[1]

BARTOLOMÉ YUN CASALILLA

'Lively', 'durable', 'diffuse and inconclusive' are some of the descriptions of the so-called 'debate on the crisis of the seventeenth century'.[2] The studies presented in this volume are evidence that the same things could be said about the debate in Castile, and more generally in Spain. A consideration of the case studies of the regions that we have omitted from this collection would be enough to make it necessary to qualify the general nature of the 'crisis'.[3] But the purpose of this conclusion is not to take up all the loose ends the debate has left: was the 'crisis' *general*? was it a recession? was it merely a series of problems? Nor is its purpose to provide answers to questions, but rather to reflect on the current state of our knowledge about Spain and its implications for the history of Europe.

I

As if trying to fulfil all the requirements of the 'general crisis' model, Castile in this period experienced organisational and institutional rigidities powerful enough to have an impact upon demographic, agrarian and industrial growth.[4] It had to bear the burden of the

[1] Much of the reading for these pages was made possible thanks to a year spent at the Institute for Advanced Study in Princeton (USA), during the 1990–1 session. I should like to express most sincerely my gratitude to that Institution.
[2] J. H. Elliott, 'Revolution and Continuity in Early Modern Europe' in G. Parker and L. Smith, *The General Crisis of the Seventeenth Century* (London, 1978), p. 110. And more recently the editor's Introduction to P. Clark, ed., *The European Crisis of the 1590s. Essays in Comparative History* (London, 1985), p. 3.
[3] 'Crisis' and recession take very different forms within the same kingdom. See, J. M. Pérez García, 'Economía y sociedad' in A. Domínguez Ortíz, ed., *Historia de España*, VI, *La crisis del siglo XVII* (Barcelona, 1988), pp. 325–33.
[4] See the studies of A. García Sanz, V. Pérez Moreda, J. E. Gelabert, G. Anes, E. Llopis and García-Baquero González included in the present volume.

political and financial costs of defending a limitless empire, in the
'supreme stage of the development of feudalism',[5] and experienced
difficulties of 'distribution' of the sort that Steensgaard has established as a component of the crisis.[6] The 'crisis' which, from the
perspective of E. J. Hobsbawm's seminal study, can be seen in
theoretical terms as a manifestation of the 'obstacles which still
stood in the way of the full development of capitalism',[7] initiated a
deep and prolonged process of deurbanisation[8] that was strong
enough, in the opinion of some, to interrupt earlier expectations of
promise,[9] and is evidence of a 'peripheralisation'[10] that was
manifested in the continued weakness of the textile sector even in
1700, when agricultural revival was again making itself felt in the
countryside.[11]

Whatever theory one adopts, whether one talks of a crisis of the
colonial economy, of a greater retention of treasure in America
itself, of a decline in receipts of precious metals, or of an increasing
diversion of bullion to other countries, as far as Castile was concerned everything seems to indicate that the flow of silver coming
into Seville stagnated, at best. That had an impact upon trade and
production that was all the greater in that, as seems likely, a larger
and larger proportion of manufactured goods exported to the

[5] The characterization of 'old colonial system' that E. J. Hobsbawm applies to the Spanish empire ('The Crisis of the Seventeenth Century' in T. Aston, ed., *Crisis in Europe, 1560–1660* [London, 1965], p. 23) was stressed in 1956 in a suggestive article by P. Vilar, available in English as 'The Age of Don Quixote', in Peter Earle, ed., *Essays in European Economic History 1500–1800* (Oxford, 1974), pp. 100–12.
[6] N. Steensgaard, 'The Seventeenth-century Crisis' in Parker and Smith, *The General Crisis of the Seventeenth Century*, pp. 26–56.
[7] Hobsbawm, 'Crisis of the Seventeenth Century', p. 29.
[8] In addition to the essay by J. E. Gelabert included above, see D. Ringrose, *Madrid and the Spanish Economy, 1560–1850* (Berkeley, 1983) and, more recently, D. S. Reher, *Town and Country in Pre-industrial Spain. Cuenca, 1550–1870* (Cambridge, 1990), especially pp. 33–67.
[9] J. Casey, 'Spain: A Failed Transition', in Clark, *European Crisis of the 1590s*, pp. 209–28.
[10] See the study by J. I. Fortea above. On the wool trade with Europe, the positions set out in the present volume by E. Fernández de Pinedo and L. M. Bilbao can be complemented by other studies which deal also with the sixteenth-century situation: H. Lapeyre, 'Les Exportations de laine de Castille sous le règne de Philippe II' in *La lana come materia prima. Atti della seconda settimana di studio di Prato*, II (Florence, 1978), pp. 221–40; C. Rahn Phillips, 'The Spanish Wool Trade, 1500–1780', *Journal of Economic History* 42 (1982), 775–95, and J. Israel, 'Spanish Wool Exports and the European Economy, 1610–1640' in *Economic History Review*, 2nd series, 33 (1980), pp. 193–211.
[11] See Fortea Pérez, ch. 7 of this vol.

Americas came from other countries.[12] At the same time, the growing power of the aristocracy ('refeudalisation'?)[13] was associated with indications of a dangerous polarisation of wealth to the benefit of nobles, clergy and the urban patriciate, a polarisation that seems to have been at the root of a contraction of the market similar to that noted by Romano, and by Hobsbawm himself.[14]

It would probably not be possible to draw up a balance that could fully match all the various elements of the seventeenth century crisis to the Spanish situation. But the history of Spain, and in particular that of Castile, can be both a confirmation and a challenge to more general explanatory models.

On this assumption of the 'prevalence' of feudal structures, writers like Wallerstein have constructed the image of a country that 'already suffered from some underlying faults of economic structure as she entered the sixteenth century' and that, after the bankruptcy of 1557, began to be transformed into a 'semi-peripheric' economy

---

[12] On these questions which cannot be discussed here, see J. TePaske and H. S. Klein, 'The Seventeenth-Century Crisis in New Spain: Myth or Reality?', *Past and Present* 90 (1981), 116–35; H. Kamen and J. Israel, 'The Seventeenth-Century Crisis in New Spain: Myth or Reality?' and J. TePaske and H. Klein, 'A Rejoinder', both in *Past and Present* 97 (1982), 144–61.
The debate to which the chapter in this volume by A. García-Baquero is contributing, has as obligatory starting-points the studies of H. and P. Chaunu, *Séville et l'Atlantique (1504–1650)* (Paris, 1955), and M. Morineau, *Incroyables Gazettes et Fabuleux Métaux. Les retours des trésors américaines d'après les gazettes hollandaises (XVIe–XVIIIe siècles)* (Cambridge, 1985).

[13] Apart from the essays by Atienza and Yun included above, see Charles Jago, 'The influence of debt on the relations between crown and aristocracy in seventeenth-century Castile', *Economic History Review*, 2nd series, 26 (1973), 218–36, and the same author's 'The "Crisis of the Aristocracy" in Seventeenth-Century Castile', *Past and Present* 84 (1979), 60–90. I. A. A. Thompson, *War and Government in Habsburg Spain 1560–1620* (London, 1976) and 'Aspectos de la organización naval y militar durante el Ministerio de Olivares' in J. H. Elliott and A. García Sanz, eds., *La España del Conde-Duque de Olivares* (Valladolid, 1990) pp. 249–74, especially, 266–9. The concept has been criticised by A. Domínguez Ortíz, 'Algunas consideraciones sobre la refeudalización del siglo XVII' in M. del C. Iglesias, C. Moya and L. Rodríguez Zúñiga, eds., *Homenaje a José Antonio Maravall* (Madrid, 1985), I, pp. 499–507.

[14] R. Romano, 'Tra XVI et XVII secolo. Una crisi economica: 1619–1622', *Rivista Storica Italiana* 74 (1962), 480–531, at p. 518, available in English as 'Between the sixteenth and seventeenth centuries: the economic crisis of 1619–22' in Parker and Smith, *The General Crisis of the Seventeenth Century* 165–225, at p. 202], and the opinion of Hobsbawm, somewhat reluctant to accept the thesis of 'refeudalisation' as part of the explanation of the crisis, in his 'Crisis of the Seventeenth Century', p. 69. A recent view from a Ricardian perspective is P. Malanima, 'Espansione e declino: economia e società fra Cinque e Seicento', *Studi Storici* 20 (1979), 287–316.

dependent on the export of primary materials.[15] Others, like Kamen, who also supports the 'schema of dependence', have regarded economic decline as a historical myth, simply because 'Spain never rose'.[16] Cipolla, more subtly, claims, 'The decline of Spain in the seventeenth century is not difficult to understand . . . Spain never developed to begin with.'[17]

But some of these views, especially in their more extreme forms, now appear exaggerated. That the Castilian economy did not grow is not easily tenable, although the phase of expansion was not sudden and had its roots in the first half of the fifteenth century.[18] Nevertheless, local studies show that population, agricultural and industrial production, and commerce grew, with the inevitable fluctuations, at least until the 1560s.[19] This wave of expansion weakened between 1560 and 1580. The bankruptcy of 1557, the increased

---

[15] I. Wallerstein, *The Modern World-System. Capitalist Agriculture and the Origins of the European World-Economy in the Sixteenth Century* (New York and London, 1974), I, especially pp. 181, 184; the quotation on p. 191.

[16] H. Kamen, 'The Decline of Spain: a Historical Myth?', *Past and Present* 81 (1978), 24–50; see, for example, p. 25.

[17] C. Cipolla, *Before the Industrial Revolution: European Society and Economy, 1000–1700* (London, 1976), p. 233. The distinction between growth and development might be crucial here in that an economic expansion is conceivable without major changes in the productive base. However, Cipolla's assertion does not seem to go that far since for him the concept of 'decline' contrasts not with change but with expansion.

[18] In line with his denial of growth in the sixteenth century and his emphasis on the subsequent idealisation of the reign of the Catholic Kings, Henry Kamen took up the idea – now obvious – that growth originated much further back. What perhaps requires modification is the view that contemporaries were correct in believing 'it was at the beginning of the sixteenth century that the great opportunity had been missed', from the economic point of view at least. The relevant bibliography on the fifteenth century is abundant. A recent survey of agriculture can be found in J. A. García de Cortázar, *La sociedad rural en la España medieval* (Madrid, 1988). At the local level, there are estimates of output based on fairly detailed tithe sources, see M. A. Ladero and M. González, *Diezmos eclesiásticos y producción de cereales en el reino de Sevilla (1408–1503)* (Seville, 1979). A similar growth of manufacturing and commercial activity in the towns is apparent from works such as P. Iradiel Murugarren, *Evolución de la industria textil castellana en los siglos XIII–XVI. Factores de desarrollo, organización y costes de producción manufacturera en Cuenca* (Salamanca 1974), and A. Collantes de Terán, *Sevilla en la Baja Edad Media. La ciudad y sus hombres* (Seville, 1977). But examples are too numerous to mention. For a recent update see, P. Iradiel Murugarren, 'La crisis medieval' in A. Domínguez Ortíz, ed., *Historia de España*, IV, *De la crisis medieval al Renacimiento* (Barcelona, 1988), pp. 81–125.

[19] For a recent survey, J. E. Gelabert, 'Economía y sociedad' in A. Domínguez Ortíz, ed., *Historia de España*, V, *El siglo de oro (Siglo XVI)* (Barcelona, 1988), pp. 207–400. Gelabert shows that expansion encompassed the non-Castilian territories as well, and that to distinguish between Castile and the rest of Spain in that respect is not tenable.

fiscal pressure that followed from it and the rupture of the axis of
wool exports between Burgos and Antwerp damaged the financial
and commercial networks. But in the short term this neither disrupted the forces of production nor undermined the vitality of an
agrarian sector which depended more on population pressure and
the continuance of urban networks, which in many areas of the
country were still bullish, than on the export of raw materials.[20]

Some of the data used to emphasise the dependent nature of the
sixteenth-century economy can also be called into question. Contrary to what has been imagined,[21] the Mesta was not the biggest
problem nor the principal reason for the persistence of property
rights little conducive to capitalist development. Its expansion
peaked around 1520–30, and then gave way before non-transhu-
mant sheep-herding which, although extensive, was very much in
tune with the interests of the urban patriciate and the middling
nobility,[22] and which allowed precisely that kind of mixed growth of
agriculture and pastoralism that Wallerstein thought was lacking.[23]
If sheep-raising was an obstacle to agricultural expansion, it was so
in a different way. More important than the privileges of the Mesta
was the survival of 'public' properties, the use of which was more
and more being monopolised by the rulers of the cities. We know
now that the Castilian textile industry, far from being static, tried to
adapt – and in some centres with success – to changes in demand,
shifting its activity towards the production of better quality cloths.[24]

[20] See Gelabert, 'Economía y sociedad'. I have tried to explain the reasons for that
complex development in the northern meseta in B. Yun, 'Estado y estructuras
sociales en Castilla. Reflexiones para el estudio de la "crisis del siglo XVII" en el
Valle del Duero (1550–1630)', *Revista de Historia Económica* 3 (1990), 449–574.
[21] See D. North, *Structure and change in Economic History* (New York and London,
1981), p. 150.
[22] Kamen himself develops this idea, 'The Decline of Spain', pp. 37–9. In more detail,
see J. P. Le Flem, 'Las cuentas de la Mesta (1510–1709)', *Moneda y Crédito* 121
(1972), 68–9. The evolution of the pastoral sector is studied in F. Ruiz Martín,
'Pastos y ganaderos en Castilla. La Mesta, 1450–1600' in *La lana come materia
prima. Atti della seconda settimana di studio di Prato* (Florence, 1978), II,
pp. 271–90.
[23] Wallerstein makes the activities of the Mesta chiefly responsible for the absence of
enclosures in Castile, blaming this for restricting agricultural expansion as against
an alternative model of mixed pastoral and agricultural growth more concordant
with the interests of the cities, 'The modern world system', p. 191, note 128.
[24] Iradiel Murugarren, *Evolución de la industria textil castellana*, pp. 215ff.; J. I.
Fortea, *Córdoba en el siglo XVI: las bases demográficas y económicas de una
expansión urbana* (Cordoba, 1981), pp. 289–312. A. García Sanz, 'Mercaderes
hacedores de paños en Segovia en la época de Carlos V: organización del proceso
productivo y estructura del capital industrial', *Hacienda Pública Española* 108–9
(1987), 65–79.

If its productive capacity did not reach the levels of Italy, the 16,000 pieces of cloth produced in Segovia and the 18,000 in Cordoba (in addition to another 7,000 in the surrounding district) was by no means insignificant. Compared with the 20,000 of Venice or the 30,000 that Florence produced at its peak, the least that can be said is that it was not the level of output of a dependent economy.[25] Recent studies of the sixteenth century reveal high proportions of the urban population occupied in the secondary and tertiary sectors and urban networks with a high degree of hierarchalisation. That does not conform with what can be expected of a country whose economy depended solely on the export of wool and precious metals.[26] In

[25] The comparison is no more than suggestive and concerns woollen cloths alone. The figures for Segovia, where the piece was some 30 metres in length, refer to 1579–84 and come from F. Ruíz Martín, 'Un testimonio literario sobre las manufacturas de paños en Segovia' in *Homenaje al Profesor Alarcos García* (Valladolid, 1965–1967), II, pp. 787–807. The Cordoba figures are for 1580–1 and refer to smaller pieces of perhaps 25 metres; they come from Fortea Pérez, *Córdoba en el siglo XVI*, pp. 311–12 and 389. For Florence and Venice respectively, see P. Malanima, *La decadenza di un'economia cittadina. L'industria di Firenze nei secoli XVI–XVIII* (Bologna, 1982), p. 295 and D. Sella, 'Les Mouvements longs de l'industrie lainière à Venise aux XVIe et XVIIe siècles', *Annales ESC* 12 (1957), 30ff. The Venetian cloth measured some 38 metres, p. 29, note 1. Account needs also to be taken of the fact that the Italian cloth was of better quality and thus more expensive. Nevertheless, the figures point to the reservations to be made in applying the term 'dependent economy' to sixteenth-century Castile.

[26] That does not support the view that growth occurred only 'in those sectors that serve the demands of the dominant market', Kamen, 'The Decline of Spain', pp. 47–8. Studies of interest on the occupational structure of the towns are B. Bennassar, *Valladolid au siècle d'Or; une ville de Castille et sa campagne au XVIe siècle* (Paris, 1967); J. Vela, 'Salamanca en la época de Felipe II' in *El pasado histórico de Castilla y León* (Salamanca, 1984), II, pp. 281–322; S. Tapia, 'La población de Avila en el siglo XVI', *ibid.* pp. 201–24; A. Marcos Martín, *Auge y declive de un núcleo mercantil y financiero de Castilla la Vieja. Evolución demográfica de Medina del Campo en los siglos XVI y XVII* (Valladolid, 1978); for the southern half of Spain see, among others, Fortea, *Córdoba en el siglo XVI*, pp. 223–66; A. M. Bernal, A. Collantes, A. García Baquero, 'Sevilla: de los gremios a la industrialización', *Estudios de Historia Social* 5–6 (1978), 7–307; F. Chacón, *Murcia en la centuria del Quinientos* (Murcia, 1979). On the urban networks in the sixteenth century see, Reher, *Town and Country*, pp. 33–57; J. Vela, 'La red urbana de la meseta norte en la segunda mitad del siglo XVI', typescript. The latter author also makes interesting evaluations to show the importance of agriculture in the great urban centres of Andalusia in contrast to the importance of the secondary and tertiary sectors in the northern meseta, in 'Sobre el carácter de la formación social bética en la segunda mitad del siglo XVI' in *Actas II Coloquios de Historia de Andalucía. Andalucía Moderna* (Cordoba, 1983), I, pp. 377–411.

sectors such as mining, the adoption of the advances made by the Germans at the end of the fifteenth century and the discovery of more effective processes confirm a technological progress that some recent studies have stressed in other sectors also, such as hydraulic engineering and its application to public works, the extent and nature of which is at present difficult to assess.[27]

In short, the growth that has been denied in order to simplify or confute the concept of crisis, not only took place, within, of course, the possibilities of a pre-industrial age, it also was concordant with a much more complex model.[28] The export of raw materials played an important role in the Castilian economy and growth should not be regarded as involving development in the way it would be defined today. Indeed, if this is what Cipolla means, then he does not seem to be wide of the mark. However, the system as a whole did not react solely to the demands of the international market, but also to a rather more complex set of relationships within which the domestic market and the pressures of economic and social change were of importance.

This brings us to the question of the implications of that growth for the qualitative changes which took place within the social structure and thence to the other great problem inherent in the 'crisis' theme, the problem of the transition to a capitalist economy. Everything leads us to believe that in the sixteenth century as well as in the seventeenth those changes were of a much more limited nature than in countries like Holland and England where the 'crisis of the seventeenth century' was to take on a different character. But it is not enough to admit that 'the scope of capitalist expansion will be limited by the general prevalence of the feudal structure of

---

[27] J. Sánchez, *De minería, metalúrgica y comercio de metales. La minería no férrica en el reino de Castilla 1450–1610* (Salamanca, 1989); D. C. Goodman, *Power and Penury. Government, Technology and Science in Philip II's Spain* (Cambridge, 1988); N. García Tapia, *Técnica y poder en Castilla durante los siglos XVI y XVII* (Salamanca, 1989).

[28] It could not really be otherwise, keeping in mind that the 'schema of dependence' did not only mean that there had to be relatively developed export sectors, but that they had to be of such a form and extent as to reflect the 'logic' that determined the general operation of the economic system. That would have been difficult in an economy with a necessarily small market sector. On this point, C. R. Phillips, 'The growth and composition of trade in the Iberian empires, 1450–1750' in J. D. Tracy, ed., *The Rise of Merchant Empires. Long-Distance Trade in the Early Modern World, 1350–1750* (Cambridge, 1990), pp. 34–101.

society'.[29] The danger is that those 'structures' will be regarded as excessively static and lacking in tensions, as givens which were not themselves affected by the development of the forms of production.[30] What the Castilian example actually shows is that the development of commerce and the economic growth of the sixteenth century generated serious and very complex problems for the maintenance of the social framework, including the financial difficulties of the aristocracy, the multiplication of paupers, and the growing power of a patriciate who were the beneficiaries of expansion. For that reason the question is not resolved by explaining the 'crisis' in terms of 'feudal obstacles'. The key lies in explaining how the *evolution* of the institutions upon which privilege and social dominance rested was able to absorb competing lines of development and to reproduce, in Brenner's words, that '*new* crystallization of social relations [which] were to be disastrous for economic development'.[31]

In this sense, and without having to enter into all the issues raised by Brenner concerning the origins of capitalism, the example of Castile can also be revealing. The very variety of different agrarian structures it embraced suggests a more open and flexible relationship between capitalist development and 'property relationships'.[32] It also provides a useful contrast on account of the importance in Castile of factors not otherwise considered: the development of institutions and their impact on economic changes and continuity; the market, understood not only in terms of the degree of its development, but also in terms of its structure and of the particular aspects which were dependent on factors like the configuration of the urban network; the function of the state, both in its capacity to generate and redistribute a centralised feudal rent, and as a point of

[29] Hobsbawm, 'Crisis of the seventeenth century', p. 15.
[30] See the criticisms of Brenner by Malanima, 'Espansione e declino' and J. Torras, 'Class struggle in Catalonia. A note on Brenner', *Review* 4:2 (Autumn, 1980), 253–65.
[31] R. Brenner, 'The Agrarian Roots of European Capitalism' in T. S. Aston and C. H. E. Philpin, *The Brenner Debate. Agrarian Class Structure and Economic Development in Pre-Industrial Europe* (Cambridge, 1985), p. 290. Italics are mine.
[32] Despite also being the case in England and France as J. P. Cooper once pointed out ('In Search of Agrarian Capitalism' in Aston and Philpin, *The Brenner Debate*, pp. 138–91, especially pp. 141ff.), it is even more suggestive in the case of Castile where a strong tendency to the concentration of land, particularly though not exclusively in Andalusia, coexisted with a tendency for the settlement of more flexible and market-orientated peasant holdings.

convergence for interests attracted by a fiscal system whose incidence was both socially and sectorally unequal.

On the level of institutions and the state, the Castilian case can throw considerable light on a classic explanation such as that of Niels Steensgaard. It would be difficult to find anywhere in Europe where the strengthening of the 'public sector' at the expense of the private was more apparent or where the crisis of redistribution that resulted from it was more acute.[33] But it is also difficult to find a country where that feature was combined with the absence of another key element in the concept of 'crisis', generalised outbursts of political conflict.

Perhaps this seeming paradox can be explained by applying to cases like that of Castile Steensgaard's observations upon the theories of Lane and Van Klaveren regarding, respectively, the function of the state as a supplier of 'protection' and 'the part played by corruption in the pre-industrial socioeconomic system'.[34] Moreover, these theories might well oblige us to modify the methodological divide between 'public' and 'private' sectors which Steensgaard himself employs.

Today we know that the needs of the Crown also bore upon the nobility, the clergy and the cities in the form of 'services'. Indeed, the demands of the state were one reason for their economic difficulties.[35] Yet, at the same time, the Crown was not only incapable of breaching the complex of fiscal privileges in any definitive way,[36] but it never succeeded in its attempt to impose a fiscal system that could by-pass the need for the mediation of the urban patriciates

---

[33] Steensgaard himself pointed to the high levels of fiscal pressure in Castile in support of his thesis, taking up Domínguez Ortiz's belief that taxation must have amounted to some 11 per cent of the gross national product, 'Seventeenth-century crisis', p. 38. See A. Domínguez Ortiz, *Política y Hacienda de Felipe IV* (Madrid, 1960), pp. 180–5, a figure not substantially modified by later research, I. A. A. Thompson, 'Taxation, military spending and the domestic economy in Castile in the later sixteenth century' in *War and Society in Habsburg Spain* (Aldershot, 1992).

[34] Steensgaard, 'Seventeenth-century crisis', p. 47.

[35] A. Domínguez Ortiz, *Política fiscal y cambio social en la España del siglo XVII* (Madrid, 1984), pp. 86ff.

[36] The resort to a 'service' was usually the result of a clash between fiscal privilege and attempts at fiscal reform. The outcome was a system maintained by the grant of *auxilium* by the subject on the one hand, and the recognition of extensive powers over the administration of that *auxilium* to the subject, as well as rewards given in compensation for the grant, on the other.

and the nobility.[37] In the view of some authors, it was even forced to a 'devolution of functions' such that 'Each contractor, each province, lord or city was in its own way a separate administrative and jurisdictional unit.'[38]

The outcome was a complex situation in which these elements took advantage of the powers attributed to them for their own benefit. The nobility, sustained by their borrowing against their *mayorazgos*, which underwrote the 'aids' they provided to the king, utilised service to the Crown to supplement their extraordinary incomes and to reinforce their freedom to act against their vassals.[39] The patriciate of the cities and the clergy profited from the collection of the *millones*, from the local administration of the *alcabalas*, and from the sale of commons and wastes.[40]

Thus, the 'redistribution' of wealth effected by the state through the extraction of resources directed to increasing 'protection services' at the expense of disposable private wealth was, in reality, a rather more complex operation. It was not only a flow of wealth extraction by the 'public sector' in response to 'the wish of the masses',[41] but also a mechanism for the preservation and consolidation of economic and social differences which left the dominant

---

[37] P. Fernández Albaladejo, 'Monarquía, Cortes y "cuestión constitucional" en Castilla durante la Edad Moderna', *Revista de la Cortes Generales* 1 (1984), 11–34; I. A. A. Thompson, 'Crown and Cortes in Castile, 1590–1665', *Parliaments, Estates and Representation* 2 (1982), 29–45; C. Jago, 'Habsburg absolutism and the Cortes of Castile', *American Historical Review* 86 (1981), 307–26; J. I. Fortea, *Monarquía y Cortes en la Corona de Castilla. Las ciudades ante la política fiscal de Felipe II* (Salamanca, 1990). The study in the present volume by Bernardo Ares is illustrative of the *do ut des* that was the outcome of this complex balance.

[38] Thompson, *War and Government*, p. 275. This devolution has been identified as a constant going back much further than the reign of Philip II by H. Nader, *Liberty in Absolutist Spain. The Habsburg Sale of Towns, 1516–1700* (Baltimore, 1990).

[39] See the chapters in the present volume by Atienza and Yun.

[40] The case of Cordoba, studied here by J. M. de Bernardo Ares, is followed up in some aspects by J. Aranda, 'Crisis de la Hacienda Real y contribuciones de los municipios en el siglo XVII: la ayuda económica ofrecida por la ciudad de Córdoba', *Notas para la Historia de Córdoba y su provincia* (Cordoba, 1986), pp. 5–16, and the same author's 'El Municipio de Córdoba y la crisis de la Hacienda Real en el siglo XVII a través de un cabildo abierto', *Axerquía* 14 (1985), 127–44. The complex politics and the opportunities this created for the oligarchies of the cities are discussed in my 'Introducción' to J. Ruiz de Celada, *Estado de la bolsa de Valladolid. Examen de sus tributos, cargas y medios de su extinción. De su gobierno y reforma* (Valladolid, 1775), ed. B. Yun (Valladolid, 1990).

[41] The words are Mousnier's taken up by Steensgaard, 'Seventeenth-century crisis', p. 45.

groups advantaged in their private capacity, at the same time that it propagated rules of behaviour which received a fundamental support from 'political revenues' and created complex situations for the aristocracy, for example, by combining their economic problems and their difficulties in maintaining liquidity with important sources of non-recurrent income. Moreover, whether it is true or not that the kingdom had never been 'so thoroughly protected as under Philip IV',[42] it is clear that a good part of the 'public' revenues were not targeted to that end but to the maintenance of the delicate social compromises of the absolutist regime. That had its repercussions on the economy because, looked at in that light, Castile's 'crisis' and decadence appear to be not only (or not so much) the consequences of overtaxation, but also the corollaries of a political system whose social implications generated an administrative apparatus incapable of dealing with the enormous costs of an empire much more difficult to defend than that of any other state. It is obvious, therefore, why it was the very people who were 'privatising' a good part of the 'public sector' who were opposed to any attempt at reform,[43] and also why Castile remained relatively quiescent despite the growing fiscal pressures. The really decisive reform projects were frustrated in their essentials and brought the rapid downfall of their promoters.[44] All this not only helps us understand, more than the polemics of Mousnier and Porchnev, the complexity of the 'nature of exploitation during the later stages of feudalism',[45] it also shows that the analytical polarity Lane–Van Klaveren proposed by Steensgaard calls for a productive modification of his own theories.

[42] Steensgaard, 'Seventeenth-century crisis', p. 41.
[43] The subject has been studied for the time of Olivares, undoubtedly the most intense moment of reforming ideas, in the various works of J. H. Elliott, notably *Richelieu and Olivares* (Cambridge, 1984), pp. 64ff., and *The Count-Duke of Olivares. The Statesman in an Age of Decline* (New Haven and London, 1986), pp. 146ff.
[44] J. H. Elliott, 'Una sociedad no revolucionaria: Castilla en la década de 1640', *1640: La Monarquía hispánica en crisis* (Barcelona, 1992), pp. 102–22. [There is an English version 'A Non-revolutionary society: Castile in the 1640s', in Jean de Viguerie (ed.), *Etudes d'histoire européenne. Mélanges offerts à René et Suzanne Pillorget* (Angers, 1990), pp. 253–69.] B. Yun, 'Aristocracia, Corona y oligarquías urbanas en Castilla ante el problema fiscal, 1450–1600. (Una reflexión en el largo plazo)', *Hacienda Pública Española*, 2nd series, 1 (1991), 25–41, especially pp. 36–41.
[45] Steensgaard, 'Seventeenth-century crisis', p. 46.

II

Until about thirty years ago there was an 'excessive concentration on the *external* influences on the Spanish economy' and a tendency to 'an overwhelmingly economic interpretation of Spain's decline'.[46] Since then the picture has changed greatly and to that extent the history of Castile is assisting with the understanding of that of Europe at the same time as it is developing its own lines of renewal.

As to the former, if Theodore Rabb said that the 'crisis' of the seventeenth century was the culmination of a 'mounting tension and conflict' since the fifteenth century,[47] how has the entity which, within a wide and varied network of power, most influenced the political life of the continent prior to 1648 been left out?

In this sense it is important to consider both the destructive effects of war and the positive impact that the military spending of the Spanish monarchy in Europe could have had. There is room to believe that the powerful system created by the Habsburgs around Castile acted as a pump redistributing resources from some regions to others.[48] Moreover, it is evident that the operations of the money market in Castile and the payments to financiers affected European commerce in the sixteenth century.[49] But the question cannot be reduced to those aspects, which are in any case difficult to evaluate.[50]

---

[46] J. H. Elliott, 'The Decline of Spain' in Aston, *Crisis in Europe 1560–1660*, pp. 170, 171.

[47] T. K. Rabb, *The Struggle for Stability in Early Modern Europe* (Oxford, 1975), *passim* and pp. 62ff.

[48] Some figures on costs in the arena of greatest conflict from the later sixteenth century are available in G. Parker, *The Army of Flanders and the Spanish Road, 1567–1659. The Logistics of Spanish Victory and Defeat in the Low Countries' Wars* (Cambridge, 1972), pp. 231–68. The same author examined the economic consequences of the conflict in 'War and economic change: the economic costs of the Dutch Revolt', *Spain and The Netherlands, 1559–1659* (London, 1979), pp. 178–203. There is a general discussion of the subject in I. A. A. Thompson, 'The impact of war' in Clark, *European Crisis of the 1590s*, pp. 261–84.

[49] F. Ruiz Martín, *Lettres marchandes échangées entre Florence et Medina del Campo* (Paris, 1965), pp. xxix et seqq.

[50] Regardless of their exactness, the figures in F. Braudel, *The Mediterranean and the Mediterranean World in the Age of Philip II* (London,1972), I, pp. 587–91, 637–40, would seem to support those who have drawn attention to the need to study the impact of war in Spain not only from the perspective of taxation, but also taking into account the fact that, after the Low Countries, it was the region that most benefited from government spending, see Thompson, 'Taxation, military spending and the domestic economy in Castile in the later sixteenth century', *passim*. The question clearly calls for more detailed study given that the impact of taxation and

Castile played a role even more important in the complicated tensions which affected the economic development of many regions. Italy is one of the best studied cases. Rightly or wrongly, G. Galasso has emphasised that the Spanish presence in Naples contributed to the blocking of industrial development, ruptured the 'retrenchment and renewal' derived from a policy more in accordance with the interests of the kingdom and led to an economy based on agricultural expansion and the production of primary materials.[51] And very recently it has been claimed that Spanish rule helped 'undermine the basis of Naples' great fifteenth-century achievements'.[52] Similar arguments could be presented, though in a contrary sense, for Genoa, where the institutional structure and the uneasy balance between the *nobili vecchi* and the *nobili novi*, underwritten by the Habsburgs in 1528 and 1575,[53] reinforced the flow of capital in speculative directions which dragged this 'feudal capitalist' polity, nourished by its special relationship with the Habsburgs, towards the problems it was to meet in the seventeenth century.[54] Furthermore, both in this case as in that of Naples, the mopping up of private savings, made possible by the financial needs of the Spanish monarchy, contributed to the subsequent economic recession.[55] The very movement of the Italian economy and the disparate evolution of north and south were also conditioned by Spanish influence.[56]

In some areas outside the Spanish sphere, Spanish influence was

expenditure depends on many related issues, not only the sums themselves but the ways they were collected or disbursed, their sectoral incidence and the multiplier effect of each of them, etc.

[51] G. Galasso, 'Momenti e problemi di storia napoletana nell'età di Carlo V', *Archivio Storico per le Provincie Napoletana* 80 (1961), 47–110, and *Dal Comune medievale all'Unità. Lineamenti di storia meridionale* (Bari, 1969), p. 117.

[52] A. Calabria, *The Cost of Empire. The Finances of the Kingdom of Naples in the Time of Spanish Rule* (Cambridge, 1991), p. 4.

[53] R. Savelli, *La Repubblica oligarguica. Legislazione, istituzioni e ceti a Genova nel Cinquecento* (Milan, 1981).

[54] Hobsbawm, 'Crisis of the seventeenth century', p. 18.

[55] Calabria, *Cost of Empire*, pp. 5–6.

[56] G. Galasso argued that the penetration of Genoese into Naples by means of the purchase of baronies and rural properties with the intention of controlling the wheat growing areas, and its effects on agricultural specialisation in the south of Italy, was very much tied up with the alliance of the Genoese with Charles V, 'Momenti e problemi di storia napoletana'. A. Calabria has emphasised how the fiscal pressure of the Habsburgs in the Italian Peninsula shifted at the end of the

no less decisive. The early financial revolution in Holland was connected with resistance to pressure from the Habsburgs,[57] and that pressure cannot be disassociated from the changing economic circumstances and the freedom of action available to them in Castile.[58] We also know that Holland's industrial foundations – particularly emphasised in recent work – were, in part, the indirect consequence of Philip II's religious policy and the emigration of craftsmen from the south with their knowledge of the techniques of the 'new draperies' which they established.[59]

All that argues for the very obvious and significant role of Spain in seventeenth-century Europe. But it also shows the need to follow the course of the internal history of Castile in order better to comprehend the European economy. A dimension implicit in the original presentation of the 'crisis' problem, namely the displacement of Europe's centre of gravity to the north[60] and the changes in the development of industry in the various regions, is revealing in the same way.

The diffusion of English textiles into the Mediterranean, and into the Iberian Peninsula in particular, from the end of the sixteenth century, something well known to English historians for some time now,[61] is even better understood if the explanation goes beyond the effectiveness of English and Dutch textile manufacturing to a consideration of the difficulties through which the Castilian urban

century from Lombardy to Naples with much greater negative consequences for the latter kingdom, *Cost of Empire*, p. 4.

[57] J. Tracy, *A Financial Revolution in the Habsburg Netherlands* (Berkeley, 1985).
[58] It is not surprising that these pressures should have become particularly acute in the 1530s, after the failure of the 'general excise' scheme proposed by Charles V and the petrification of the composition of the *alcabalas* until 1561, when the *encabezamiento* was raised; see R. Carande, *Carlos V y sus banqueros*, new edn (Barcelona, 1987) II, pp. 230–8 and 508–22.
[59] This fact has been recently stressed by J. Israel, *Dutch Primacy in World Trade, 1585–1740* (Oxford, 1989), pp. 54ff. and 187–96.
[60] Hobsbawm, 'Crisis of the seventeenth century', p. 7. The idea, emphasised some time ago in the writings of F. Braudel, has been given renewed interest with Israel's discussion of the mechanisms which operated on the process, J. Israel, 'The phases of the Dutch *Straatvaart*, 1590–1713: a Chapter in the Economic History of the Mediterranean', *Empires and Entrepôts. The Dutch, the Spanish Monarchy and the Jews, 1585–1713* (London and Ronceverte, 1990), pp. 133–62.
[61] B. Supple, *Commercial Crisis and Change in England, 1600–1642* (Cambridge, 1964); F. J. Fisher, 'London's export trade in the early Seventeenth Century', *Economic History Review* 2nd series, 2 (1950), 151–61; D. C. Coleman, 'An innovation and its diffusion: the "New Draperies"', *Economic History Review* 2nd series, 22 (1969), 417–29.

economy was passing as a result of increasing fiscal pressure, rising subsistence costs, insuperable organisational rigidities imposed by the guilds, and the retreat of business capital from the investments which could have set in train the qualitative developments which were beginning to take place in northern Europe.[62]

The more qualified version we now have of Italian industrial decline, a crucial element in that displacement of the European centre of gravity northwards, might perhaps be better understood in the light of the role Castile played in the Mediterranean economy. From the 1560s the fiscal exertions of Castile were serving to transfer resources which were effectively dynamising the economy of the state of Milan, through which the Spanish Road passed. It was Milan where the arms industry and the manufacture of quality textiles responded with redoubled vigour to the demands of the market.[63] At the same time, the redirection of the wool trade towards the Mediterranean, following the rupture of the Burgos–Antwerp axis, and the problems suffered by the industries of the Low Countries as a result of the conflict there, had similar consequences.[64] Simultaneously, the Italian grain supply networks, working at full power in an environment of decisive constraints, absorbed a commodity in great shortage in the more inland and less viable cities of Castile.[65]

---

[62] Apart from the general overview presented by Gelabert in this volume, see the analysis of a specific example, like that of Cordoba (Fortea, *Córdoba en el siglo XVI*, pp. 413–70).

[63] D. Sella and F. Capra, 'Il Ducato di Milano, 1535 al 1796', in G. Galasso, ed., *Storia di Italia* (Turin, 1984), pp. 107ff. A. Calabria refers to the way Lombardy was transformed into a fortress that had to be maintained, whereas fiscal pressure shifted towards Naples, *Cost of Empire*, pp. 4–5.

[64] H. Lapeyre, *El comercio exterior de Castilla a través de las aduanas en tiempos de Felipe II* (Valladolid, 1981), pp. 187–96; and Ruiz Martín, *Lettres marchandes échangées entre Florence et Medina del Campo*, pp. civ–cxx. More recently, and from the Italian perspective, P. Malanima. 'An example of industrial reconversion: Tuscany in the sixteenth and seventeenth centuries' in H. Van der Wee, ed., *The Rise and Decline of Urban Industries in Italy and in the Low Countries* (Leuven, 1988), p. 65, and the same author's *La decadenza di un'economia cittadina*, pp. 259, 263.

[65] J. Israel has noted a phenomenon that would have been difficult for Castilian merchant capital to have managed, at least on the same scale, the bulk of the wheat from the north brought into the Mediterranean was controlled by Italian capital, 'The Phases of the Dutch *Straatvaart*', pp. 137, 139. The constriction of the grain market at the end of the sixteenth century can be seen even in regions, such as the Spanish Levant, traditionally well supplied from Sicily and Sardinia;

In a subsequent phase, when the output of woollens was falling, industries like that of Florence began a process of reconversion to the manufacture of silk and, as the problems of the Spanish manufacturing centres of Cordoba, Toledo and Granada worsened, found in the Spanish Court an important market.[66] Cipolla, who suggested this line of argument, spoke of an Indian Summer for the Italian economy.[67] Cannot everything be better explained in view of the fact that the Castilian economy was very much weaker than the Italian in a world with a far narrower margin for action, as the Mediterranean was becoming from 1560 to 1620?

And as for Castile itself? To what extent has the pattern of research altered and what are the prospects for the future? Greatly influenced by the *Annales*, Spanish historiography has been absorbed with regional and local studies which have concentrated on the internal dimension.[68] That has made possible a fairly precise know-

---

see T. Halperín Donghi, *Un conflicto nacional en el siglo de oro. Moriscos y cristianos viejos en Valencia* (Valencia, 1980), pp. 28–9.

[66] J. Goodman, 'Tuscan commercial relations with Europe, 1550–1620: Florence and the European textile market', *Firenze e la Toscana dei Medici nell'europa del '500*, (Florence, 1983), VII, pp. 328–41; Malanima, 'An Example of Industrial Reconversion', *passim*. The greater resistance of the silk sector in Toledo has been attributed to the proximity of the Court in Madrid, J. Montemayor, *Tolède entre fortune et déclin (1530–1640)*, 2 vols. (Toulouse, 1991), II, pp. 435–6.

[67] Cipolla, *Before the Industrial Revolution*, p. 239. The question squares with the vision of the general European situation presented by R. Romano on the basis of what happened in Italy. For Romano commerce held up, despite the weakening of agrarian growth, until the decisive crisis of 1619–21, 'Between the sixteenth and seventeenth centuries', and 'Encore la crise de 1619–1622', *Annales ESC* 19 (1964), 31–7.

[68] Even limiting ourselves to the basic monographs and studies the examples are innumerable. But for rural history mention must be made of P. Saavedra, *Economía, política y sociedad en Galicia: la provincia de Mondoñedo, 1480–1830* (Madrid, 1985); E. Fernández de Pinedo, *Crecimiento económico y transformaciones sociales del País Vasco* (Madrid, 1974); F. Brumont, *Campo y campesinos de Castilla la Vieja en tiempos de Felipe II* (Madrid, 1984); B. Yun, *Sobre la transición al capitalismo en Castilla. Economía y sociedad en Tierra de Campos (1500–1830)* (Salamanca, 1987); A. García Sanz, *Desarrollo y crisis del Antiguo Régimen en Castilla la Vieja: economía y sociedad en tierras de Segovia de 1500 a 1814* (Madrid, 2nd edn, 1986); J. M. López García, *La transición del feudalismo al capitalismo en un señorío monástico castellano. El Abadengo de la Santa Espina (1147–1835)* (Valladolid, 1990); J. López-Salazar Pérez, *Estructuras agrarias y sociedad rural en la Mancha (siglos XVI–XVII)* (Ciudad Real, 1986); M. Weisser, *Peasants of the Montes: the Roots of Rural Rebellion in Spain* (Chicago, 1976). For urban history, in addition to the works cited in note 25, see A. Rodríguez Sánchez, *Cáceres: población y comportamientos demográficos en el siglo XVI* (Cáceres, 1977); J. E. Gelabert, *Santiago y la tierra de Santiago de 1500 a 1640* (Santiago, 1982); J. I.

ledge of the movement of population and production[69] and has portrayed a 'crisis' of receding perspectives. Regional differences have been noted and general overviews have been undertaken.[70] Moreover, and without implying that this line of work should be abandoned, the problem at the moment is to integrate these regional and local studies into a general interpretation, now that some of these syntheses have pioneered the description of regions in their entirety, combining one with another in an overall reinterpretation of the Castilian economy. In this sense, it is necessary to continue along the lines that start from supra-regional analytical concepts, such as urban networks,[71] and move out towards the scarcely considered issue of the external connections of the Spanish economy starting from the influence of changes taking place at the global level, a question which has scarcely been looked into.[72]

An explanation of decline that, without ignoring the economic dimension, tends to see it as a consequence of the working of the political and institutional systems, perhaps has something to contribute to the history of the economy. On the one hand, the reexamination of the nature of the state and the role of the Cortes, cities, aristocracy and Church in the evolution of the fiscal and social framework is opening up a much more comprehensive view of the subject.

Fortea, *Córdoba en el siglo XVI*; A. Marcos Martín, *Economía, sociedad, pobreza en Castilla: Palencia 1500–1814* (Palencia, 1985); A. Gutiérrez Alonso, *Estudio sobre la decadencia de Castilla. La ciudad de Valladolid en el siglo XVII* (Valladolid, 1989); C. R. Phillips, *Ciudad Real, 1500–1750: Growth, Crisis and Readjustment in the Spanish Economy* (Cambridge, MA, 1979).

[69] Two of the pillars of Castilian power about which, according to Elliott, little was known in 1961, 'Decline of Spain', p. 171.

[70] Apart from the great number of regional histories, usually collective works, this approach can be found in chapters of the most up to date general histories of Spain, as for example the previously cited J. M. Pérez García, 'Economía y sociedad', or A. García Sanz, 'El sector agrario durante el siglo XVII: depresión y reajustes' in A. Domínguez Ortiz, ed., *La crisis del siglo XVII: Historia de España dirigida por D. Ramón Menéndez Pidal* (Madrid, 1989), XXIII, pp. 161–235.

[71] See, in particular, the previously cited studies of Ringrose, Reher and Vela.

[72] Some of the studies that have concerned themselves with such crucial issues as the blockades and embargoes in the war with the Dutch have scarcely considered investigating the evolution of the manufacturing activities, like textiles, associated with them. On the former, see above all A. Domínguez Ortiz, 'Guerra económica y comercio extranjero en el reinado de Felipe IV', *Hispania* 23 (1962); J. Israel, *The Dutch Republic and the Hispanic World 1606–1661* (Oxford, 1982), and the same author's 'Spanish wool exports and the European economy', 'A conflict of empires: Spain and the Netherlands, 1618–1648', and 'Spain, the Spanish embar-

It is to be hoped that those aspects relating to the evolution of production and population will be filled out and even modified by taking into account the means, the extent and the implications of the redistribution of wealth in which power and privilege had such a crucial part to play. It is also likely that we shall gain a more subtle and complex view of the intensity and weight of the state and of privilege on the productive base. Research is revealing the limits of the effectiveness of the fiscal system, the importance of fraud and the extent to which that pressure was mediated through local power structures.[73] Whether all that will force us to abandon the explanation of the crisis as a crisis of distribution is still debatable insofar as the sectoral distribution of taxation was very uneven and tax evasion was inherently a distortion of certain economic activities.

Moreover, in view of the great adaptability which we now recognise in peasant economies, we might arrive at a more qualified view of the economic implications of the so-called 'refeudalisation'. One is beginning to suspect that, after the huge demands that coincided with the most acute moments of the financial crisis, the competition between Crown and aristocracy for control of the country's wealth as well as the perception of social relations as relationships of patronage induced the aristocracy to adopt less rigorous policies towards their vassals in certain areas.[74]

Issues like industrial backwardness, the difficulties of employing a large and impoverished population of rural origin, or the restraints

---

goes, and the struggle for mastery of world trade, 1621–1643', the last two repub lished in *Empires and Entrepôts*, pp. 1–42 and 189–212.

[73] Some relevant observations in J. E. Gelabert, 'El impacto de la guerra y del fiscalismo en Castilla' in Elliott and García Sanz, *La España del Conde-Duque de Olivares*, 556–73; Yun, 'Introducción' to *Estado de la Bolsa de Valladolid*, pp. 27–32; F. Ruiz Martín, 'Palencia en el siglo XVII', *Actas del I Congreso de Historia de Palencia* (Palencia, 1987), pp. 18–19.

[74] I. Atienza, 'El señor avisado: programas paternalistas y control social en la Castilla del siglo XVII', *Manuscripts* 9 (1991), 155–207, and 'Consenso, solidaridad vertical e integración versus violencia en los señoríos castellanos del siglo XVII y la crisis del Antiguo Régimen', *Señorío y feudalismo en la Península Ibérica* (Zaragoza, 1991). On the tendency of some lords to relax demands on their estates in order to attract population, see B. Yun, 'Aristocracia, señorío y crecimiento económico: algunas reflexiones a partir de los Pimentel y los Enríquez (siglos XVI y XVII)', *Revista de Historia Económica* 3 (1985), 461–2; and I. Atienza, *Aristocracia, poder y riqueza en la España moderna. La Casa de Osuna. Siglos XV–XIX* (Madrid, 1987), pp. 307–13.

on the spread of technology, too often forgotten,[75] are finding in the social implications of the institutional framework a new field of analysis. Thus, few historians now occupy themselves with E. J. Hamilton's old thesis concerning the relationship between prices and wages.[76] Instead, more to the fore is the extent to which the impact of fiscal pressure in the form of excises on foodstuffs reduced demand for manufactured goods and increased the costs of the upkeep of apprentices in the craft shops. From that we perhaps should take up again more strongly the subject of guild organisation and the interests they represented.[77]

That analytical viewpoint serves also to bring together the achievements in the fields of internal history and international relations. Perhaps the weakness of a colonial empire that had depended in the sixteenth century on a bureaucracy generated by the most remarkable educational revolution in Europe,[78] can be explained by the inability to maintain that effectiveness in the seventeenth. Issues that have been stressed for some time, such as the importance of fraud and corruption,[79] need to be related to the whole institutional complex referred to above and to the confusion of public and private accentuated in the 'devolution of functions'.[80]

[75] It is interesting, for example, that Spanish historians of the textile industry have not raised the question of its decline, not only in terms of its failure, but even to consider why it did not prove possible in the seventeenth century to establish techniques like those of the New Draperies.

[76] E. J. Hamilton, 'Wages and subsistence on Spanish treasure ships, 1503–1660', *Journal of Political Economy* 37 (1929) and 'American treasure and the rise of capitalism (1500–1700)', *Economica* 9 (1929), 338–57.

[77] This has been done in Fortea, *Córdoba en el siglo XVI*, pp. 378–88, and also in Bernal, Collantes and García-Baquero, 'Sevilla: de los gremios a la industrialización', pp. 76–273, and Montemayor, *Tolède entre fortune et déclin*, pp. 318–27.

[78] J. H. Elliott, *Spain and its World 1500–1700: Selected Essays* (Yale, 1989), pp. 14–18.

[79] J. Lynch, *Spain under the Habsburgs* (Oxford, 1969), II, pp. 163–9, and H. Pietschman, *El Estado y su evolución al principio de la colonización española de América* (Mexico, 1989), pp. 173–82, and the same author's 'Les Indes de Castille' in C. Hermann, ed., *Le Premier Âge de l'État en Espagne (1450–1700)* (Paris, 1989), pp. 147–88, especially 116–17, and 'Burocracia y corrupción en Hispanoamérica colonial. Una aproximación tentativa', *Nova Americana* 5 (1982), 11–37.

[80] J. Vicens Vives, following Van Klaveren, developed the idea that corruption was transformed into a system from the second half of the sixteenth century and that the sale of offices in the Indies can be regarded as a 'defence against corruption', 'The administrative structure of the state in the sixteenth and seventeenth centuries' in H. J. Cohn (ed.), *Government in Reformation Europe 1520–1560* (London, 1971), pp. 83–7. See also, J. Van Klaveren, 'Die historische Erscheinung

And that not only for the administration of the Americas, where the ability of the fiscal apparatus to penetrate the colonial economy has been the focus, but also for that of the other territories, like Italy, where that cancer seems to have spread so far as to have blocked the functioning of the whole system.[81] Was it possible to carry out a mercantilist colonial policy on those administrative foundations? Were contemporaries like the Count-Duke of Olivares right when they envisaged 'reform' as something that would have to have an economic pay-off but which would have to be effected by means of political and social reform? Have we here one of the keys to the failure of Spain and the stagnation of her economy compared with those of other countries, such as Holland, which were then demonstrating to Europe the benefits of creating a very different sort of 'anti-state'?[82] Even accepting that we have elements here common to other monarchies of the time, how far was it possible to maintain the effectiveness of that system while facing the huge costs of a vast imperial machine?

A consideration of the institutional and social structure can raise wider questions for economic history. Despite the presence of powerful internal tensions, political stability served to perpetuate a situation hardly conducive to long-term improvements in production. That calls for some reflection. It is evident that in future we shall have to try to assess how far the capacity to generate growth in such a system was a function of that fact. Many questions remain to be raised at the level of pure economic analysis: techniques of production and marketing, the geography of the market for manufactures, questions relating to the movement of capital, to living standards and the composition of consumption and demand, and so on. Many of these questions will be clarified as we consider the ways in which the state conditions the functioning and the development of

der Korruption in ihrem Zusammenhang mit der Staats- und Gesellschaftsstruktur betrachtet', *Vierteljahrschrift für Sozial- und Wirtschaftsgeschichte* 44 (1957) and 45 (1958), and also his *Europäische Wirtschaftsgeschichte Spaniens im 16. und 17. Jahrhundert* (Stuttgart, 1960). Cf. R. Carande, 'Zum Problem einer Wirtschaftsgeschichte Spaniens', *Historische Zeitschrift* 193 (1961), and R. Konetzke, 'La literatura económica. Así se escribe la historia', *Moneda y Crédito* 81 (1962).

[81] R. Mantelli, *Il pubblico impiego nell'economia del regno di Napoli: retribuzioni, reclutamento e ricambio sociale nell'epoca spagnuola (sec. XVI–XVII)* (Naples, 1986), pp. 288ff.

[82] J. H. Elliott, 'Yet another crisis?', in Clark, *European Crisis of the 1590s*, p. 31.

the financial system and investments.[83] In addition, a perspective of this sort will serve to construct a 'social history of the economy' that will be concerned with the way in which the continuation of the institutional and political superstructure frustrated alternative modes of economic development. In this way economic history has much to hope for from progress in other fields, from the history of belief to the analysis of the forms of social legitimation which are helping us understand the reasons for the absence of revolutionary change.

[83] A good starting point is A. Domínguez Ortiz, *Política y Hacienda de Felipe IV* (Madrid, 1960), and, more recently, J. C. Boyajian, *Portuguese Bankers at the Court of Spain, 1626–1650* (New Brunswick, 1983), and F. Ruiz Martín, *Las finanzas de la Monarquía Hispánica en tiempos de Felipe IV (1621–1665)* (Madrid, 1991).

Index

agriculture, output, 15, 17, 22, 29, 30, 60, 75–6, 79–82, 87, 111; in Andalusia 65, 130–4, 138
arable farming 30, 67, 76, 79–82, 94, 95, 111
livestock 15, 22, 66, 68, 83–6, 93, 111
market, deficiencies of 67, 69, 86–7
agronomy 72–3
Alava 204
Albacete, province, plague in 36
alcabalas 170–3, 175, 192–4, 195, 229
Alcalá de Henares 196, 228–9
Alcalá Zamora, José 11
Alcaracejos, Los 159
Alcudia 162
Algés (Toledo) 64
Alicante 34, 183–4
Almagro 196
Alpujarras 137, 223
Alvarez Santaló, L.C. 125, 127
American trade, movement of, 2, 4, 8, 61, 115–18; measurement of 118–22; contraband 123
changing structure of 122–4
impact on Andalusia 115–35
demand from 60; and Cordoba textile exports 138, 152, 165–6
bullion returns from 118–24, 147, 227, 302
Andalusia, population of 75, 125–7; plague in 34, 46
economic situation of 131–5; agriculture in 65, 130–4, 138
Andújar 152, 187
Anes, Gonzalo 7, 77, 78, 84, 86, 89, 132
Annales school 4, 316
Appleby, Andrew B. 40, 41
arable land 30, 67, 76, 79–82, 94, 95, 111

extension of 60, 62, 65, 66; retreat of 24, 31, 74
balance arable/pasture 62–3, 65–7, 75, 83–6, 110, 111
Aragon 5, 7, 203; plague in 43, 45
Aranda de Duero 33, 37
arbitrios 207, 212–13
arbitristas, arbitrismo 4, 13, 28, 71
Arévalo 37, 200
Artola, Miguel 252
asientos, asentistas 172–3, 227
Astorga, diocese of 69, 70
Asturias 33, 74
Avila, city 176, 197, 201, 225; population of 188, 189; plague in 37
Avila, province, plague in 33, 45
Ayamonte, marquis of 298

Badajoz 111
Baena 137, 138
Baeza 187
'bankruptcy', of Crown 191, 193, 221, 228–9, 252, 304
Barcelona, wages in 202
barley 80–1, 93
Basque region 5, 14, 74, 203; plague in 33
Batista i Roca, J.M. 257
Baza 137
Béjar, dukes of 296
Benavente, counts of 289–90, 292, 293, 296
Benítez Sánchez-Blanco, Rafael 132
Bennassar, Bartolomé 33, 36, 37, 40, 41, 44, 55, 56
Berlanga 269
Bernal, A.M. 130–1
bienes de propios, of Cordoba, 207, 208, 215

Bilbao 113
Bilbao, L.M. 83
birth control 51
bourgeoisie in Spain 170
Brenner, Robert 1, 308
Buendía 269
Bujalance 137, 138, 139, 144
bullion returns 118–24, 147, 227, 302
Bureba, La, population 185
Burgo de Osma, plague in 49
Burgos, city 197, 201; population of 28, 184, 185; plague in 37, 47; commerce of 27, 225–6; decline 191
 consulado 225
Burgos, province, population of 185; plague in 33, 44

Cabrera, Don Alonso de 206, 212
Cabrera de Córdoba, Luis 294
Cáceres, city 113
Cáceres, province 80, 85; plague in 45
Cadiz 122, 123, 129–30, 190; population 126; plague in 47
Canary Islands 122
Cañete de las Torres 137, 138
Cano, Rodrigo 72
Cantabria 5, 11, 14, 63, 106; plague in 33, 39, 42
Carande, Ramón 170, 211
Carmona 187
Cartagena 190
Carvajal, Don Antonio de 199
Castrillo, count of 297
Castro del Río 132, 137, 138, 146
Catastro 111, 234, 238–9, 240, 248
Caxa de Leruela, Miguel 24, 31, 63, 85
censos 178–80, 208, 212, 247–8, 280, 287–8
Chaunu, P. 4, 115, 116, 122
Chiloeches, plague in 48, 49, 54
Chueca 64
Cipolla, Carlo M. 304, 307, 316
Ciruelos 64
city development in Spain 70, 169, 182–90
 differential growth of town and country 184–9, 205
 decline of urban network 169, 175, 187–8, 189–90, 203, 220, 224, 238; impact of taxation 191, 194–205, 214

ruralisation of cities 203–4, 238, 241
Ciudad Real, city 186, 202; province 186
Ciudad Rodrigo, plague in 42, 43, 45, 51
Cobos 162
Coca 90
Colbert, J.-B. 108
Colchester 141, 161
Collado de Contreras, plague in 41
Colmenares, Diego de 38
Colón de Larreátegui, José 180–1
common lands 83; privatisation of 22, 84, 88–92, 259, 305
communitarian system 88–9
Comunero Revolt 113, 269, 279, 285
Constable of Castile 269
Cordoba, city 2, 199, 200, 206–19; population 187; silk guild 153, 157, 163–4, 166; cloth output of 306
 municipal authorities 207, collusion with Crown 218–19, relationship with *tierra* 209, 211
 municipal finances 21, *sisas* 208, 210, *arbitrios* 207; *bienes de propios* 207, 208, 215
 taxes in 194
 campiña 75, 141
Cordoba, kingdom of 187; population 125–7; manufacturing in 128–30; agriculture in 132; alienations in 196–7
 see also textile industry
Cortado, Esteban 151, 152, 154, 159, 160
Cortes of Castile 4, 13, 24, 28, 66, 172–3, 293, 299, 300, 317
Council of State 256, 257, 286, 288, 293
Council of War 256, 286, 293
Court 27, 259, 288–9, 293, 298–9
crop specialisation 70; rotation 64
Crusade Bulls 57
Cruz, Francisco de la 165
Cuenca, city 186, 189, 199; taxes in 194
Cuenca, province 65, 186; plague in 36, 45
Cuevas 64

debasement of coinage 22, 147–8
decline, decadence of Spain 3, 13, 14, 71
 historiography of 6
 representation in art 72

demand, foreign, for agricultural
    produce 60–4, for wool 101,
    103–13; internal, for wool 110;
    from cities 65, 68, 70, 75, 85
'dependence' 5, 8, 101, 114, 304–7
deurbanisation 5, 9, 224
Deza, Lope de 56
disentailment, *desamortización* 170, 180,
    239
Domínguez Ortiz, A. 33, 57, 91, 131,
    237, 253, 278
Doña Mencia 201
donatives 206, 208, 213, 214
Dueñas 269
Dutch Revolt, economic and financial
    impact of 28, 226

Ecija 164, 187
Elias, Norbert 256
elites, patriciates, *poderosos* 210–11,
    218–19, 247–8, 309–10
Elliott, J.H. 2, 4
encabezamiento 170–5, 176, 192–4, 195,
    229–31
Ensenada, marquis of La 41, 111
Escorial, monastery of El, 87
Espejo 132, 137, 138
Esquivias 64
Estrella, monastery of La 83
Estremera 64
Expedientes de Hacienda 173
Extremadura 17, population 186;
    plague in 36, 43, 64
    agriculture in 85–6, 111; pastures
    110, 112–3

fairs, in Castile 220–1; of Medina del
    Campo 225–9
Fernández de Navarrete, Pedro 56
Fernández Vargas, Valentina 269
fiscal expedients 207, 212–13, 287
fiscal privileges, of nobility 175–6, 195,
    198–200, 253; of provinces 203
fiscalism 29–31
Flinn, M.W. 43
Floridablanca census of 1787 169
forests, afforestation 66, 94
Fortea Pérez, José Ignacio 126, 129
Foucault, Michel 262
Fuenterrabía, plague in 40

Galasso, G. 313
Galicia 5, 14, 74; plague in 33, 34

García Fuentes, L. 116, 122, 123, 124
García Sanz, Angel 4, 5–6
Garzón Pareja, M. 11
Genoese 173, 228, 261
Góngora y Argote, Luis de 72
González, Tomás 222, 223
González Alonso, Benjamín 262, 265,
    285, 288
grain, price of 67, 68; trade 69; export
    policy 148–9
Granada 2, 11, 153; *moriscos* of 187,
    223
granaries, see *pósitos*
grazing, shortage of 66–7, 84, 93
Guadalajara 202; province 64, 186,
    plague in 36, 43, 45
Guadalupe, monastery of, 84, 254
Guadix 137
Guilarte, Alfonso María 209
guilds 6, 171, 179
Guipúzcoa 74, 204

Hamilton, E.J. 4, 11, 17, 39, 118, 134,
    319
Haro 203
Herrera, Melchor de, marquis of
    Auñón 261
hidalgo values 3, 6
Híjar, duke of 298
historiography in Spain, 4, 5, 11, 13–15,
    131, 316–17
Hobsbawm, E.J. 1, 251, 302, 303
Hollingsworth, T.H. 43, 46
horticulture 65, 138
Huelva 129, 132; population 126–7
Huete 196

infanticide 51
Inquisition 3
Israel, J.I. 84, 315

Jaén 34, 164
Jago, C.J. 263
Jerez de la Frontera 187, 190
Junta de Comercio 136, 152
Junta de Población 56
Junta de Reformación 28
juros 170, 180, 194, 221, 226–7, 247

Kamen, Henry 8, 123, 237, 304
Klaveren, J. van 309
Klein, Julius 74, 102
Kriedte, Peter 1

labour productivity 74–5
labour shortages 65–6, 74
Laguna, Andrés 51
lance tax 298
land, rents 15, 22, 70, 87, 92; shortage
    of 67; changes in use of 93
landownership 15, 22, 247;
    concentration of 6, 15, 22
    in Medina del Campo 247–8
Lane, F.C. 309
Lapeyre, H. 227
Larreta, Enrique, *La gloria de Don
    Ramiro* 176
Las Casas, Fr Bartolomé de 269
Le Flem, J.-P. 11, 83, 102
legal system 265–6
Lemos, count of 290
León, population 105; plague in 44
Lerma, duke of 177, 294
Lisón y Viedma, Mateo de 72, 204
livestock, farming 22–4, 62–3, 67, 83–6,
    111
Llopis Agelán, Enrique 7
Logroño 33
López, Francisca 165
López Osorio, 234
Lucena 201

Madoz, Pascual de 180, 239,
    Diccionario geográfico 239
Madrid, capital, 64, 186, 187, 189, 190,
    228–9, 232
    population of 17, 27, 75; plague in 47
    as financial market 228–9, 233
    wages in 202
Madrid, province 186; plague in 37, 43,
    45
Madrid, Colegio Imperial 258
maize 14, 74
Malaga, plague in 47
Malthusian model 7–8, 88
Mancha, La 64; pastures 110;
    population 186, 187
manufacturing, in Seville 128–30; in
    Cordoba 128–30
Maravall, José Antonio 70, 72, 286
Mariana, Juan de, SJ 37
Marín, Fermín 92
market, for agricultural produce 67, 69,
    86–7, 149
Martínez de Mata, Francisco 73
Mateo Alemán 39
Medina del Campo, population 28, 185,

189, 221–4, 235–8; infanticide in
    51; emigration from 231–3
fairs of 27; financial and commercial
    role 225–7
taxes in 193, 229–31
topography, dereliction 233–4;
    ruralisation of 235, 238, 241
socio-economic structure 240–6;
    social stasis 240, 246–8
church in 239, 246–8
Medina de Rioseco 185, 189, 226, 232
Medina Sidonia, duke of 298
medio general of 1577 228
Mendizábal, J.A. 180
Mendoza, P. Hernando de, SJ 290–1
Mercado, Luis 51
Mercado, Tomás de 38
merchants, abandonment of
    manufacturing 27
Mérida 11, 196
Mesa, Antonio de 139, 142, 144, 154
Mesta 24, 31, 66, 73–4, 84, 92, 103, 109,
    110, 305
    privileges of 6, 7, 31, 101
migration 16, 17, 54–5, 56, 57–8, 61, 65,
    76, 78
millones 90, 170, 171, 175–7, 192,
    194–5, 198, 252
Molinié-Bertrand, A. 184, 190
Mondéjar 64
Montalvo, Juan Antonio de 234, 236
Montaña 33, 74
Montes de Toledo 186
Montilla 137, 138, 201
Montoro 137, 139
Moraleja, G. 236
Morineau, M. 118–23, 124
moriscos, expulsion of 6, 7, 76
mules, replace oxen, 63, 66, 67, 74, 80,
    88, 93
municipal authorities 173–7
municipal debts 90, 170, 178–81, 194;
    administration of 212–15
Muñoz de Velasco, Don Rodrigo 154
Murcia 199; population 187, 190; silk
    production in 143–5, 152, 156
mutton prices 24, 68, 84

Nadal, Jordi 2, 15
Navalcarnero, plague in 46, 49
Navarre 33
Nef, J.U. 252
New Draperies 104–5, 140–1

Niebla 137
nobility 250; access to 253, 282;
    devaluation of 256
  inflation of honours 254–5, 281–2
  'Crisis of' 258–9, 278; economic
    situation of 256, 258, 260, 263,
    278, 280–1; indebtedness 259,
    280
  mayorazgo 281, 287–8
  fiscal privileges of 175–6, 195,
    198–200, 253
  education of 258
  and Court 256, 259–60, 283, 293; and
    office 257–8, 259, 285–6, income
    from 289–95; and Crown
    258–60, 262, 265, 266–7, 286,
    297–300; and state 279–80, 284,
    294–5
  increase of authority and economic
    control 263–5; access to social
    product 284–5
North, D.C. 1

Ocaña 190
oil, olive cultivation 64, 83, 138
oligarchisation 7, 8, 10
Olivares, count-duke of 258, 260, 289,
    294, 297; policies of 28, 320
Orihuela, population 183–4
Ortega Rubio, J. 237
Osuna, dukes of 259, 263, 264, 266,
    270, 296
Otero de Herreros 50, 52

Palencia 225
  province, population 185; plague in
    33; agriculture in 81
Pamplona, plague in 40, 47
Parker, Geoffrey 285
partido 172
pasturage, cost and supply of 74, 86,
    92, 103, 109, 110–11;
  shortage of 66–7, 84, 93
  regimes, ownership of 110, 111–13;
    enclosure of 92
Paular, monastery of Santa María del,
    pastures 112–13; wool 109
Paz, Manuel de 256
peasantry, differentiation 91;
    indebtedness 70
Pedro Abad 160
Pedroches, Los 137, 139, 141, 143, 144,
    159, 160, 161

Peralta, Luis de 230, 232
Pérez de Herrera, C. 38
Pérez Moreda, Vicente 6, 15, 78, 86
peripheralisation 5, 302, 303–4
Philip II 173
Pineda, Don Bernardo de 142
plague in 1596–1602 16; chronology of
    41–3; geography and extent of
    33–6, 43–5; intensity of 43–7;
    seasonality 37–8
  medical response to 47
  and famine 36–9
  social incidence of 38, 39
  urban-rural incidence 37–8
  incidence by age and gender 40–1
  demographic and economic impact of
    6, 15, 16, 47–59
poderosos, increase control of agrarian
    resources 8, 10, 91, 113
polarisation of society 170, 303
Ponce Cordones, F. 126
Ponsot, Pierre 75, 132–4
population 15, 60, 61, 71
  movement and statistics 15, 16, 61,
    78, 110, 184, 189, 204
  baptisms 15, 16, 52–3, 58, 61;
    depopulation 71, 78; mortality
    15; migration 15, 54, 56–7, 65,
    188, 198–9, 205, 231–3
Porquicho Moya, I. 126
pósitos, public granaries 69, 149–50, 171
Posthumus, N.W. 105
Pozoblanco 159
prices, general movement of 22, 29, 60,
    65, 68–9, 83–6
  agricultural 22, 30, 67–8, 83–6, 134;
    cloth 144; wool 24, 105, 109;
    wine 83; mutton 24, 68, 84
Priego 137, 138, 147, 164
privatisation of commons 7, 8, 22, 84,
    88–94
privileges, regional *fueros* 6
Puebla de Cazalla 263
Puente Genil 137, 138
Pulido Bueno, I. 126, 129

Quevedo y Villegas, Francisco de 291

Rabb, Theodore K. 312
Rambla, La 137, 139
readjustment, concept of 7, 15, 24, 73,
    76, 78
refeudalisation 5, 10, 250, 267, 278, 296–7

reform policies 28–31, 72–3
Reglá, Joan 2
Reina, Francisco de 155, 159, 160
rents, of land, 15, 70, 87, 89, 92; in
    Andalusia 134–5
revolts, in Andalusia 1647–52 131, 148;
    political acquiescence in Castile
    309, 311
Ringrose, David R. 7, 191
Rodríguez y Fernández, I. 233
Romano, Ruggiero 303, 316
Romero, Ignacio 165
Ronquillo Briceño, Don Francisco 136,
    151
rotation of crops 64
Roxas, Fr Don Pedro de, bishop of
    Astorga, 69
Ruiz, Simón 244
Ruiz Martín, Felipe 227
Ruiz de Zelada, José, *Estado de la
    Bolsa de Valladolid* 179–80
rural manufactures 70; shift of
    manufacturing from towns
    202–3
ruralisation 9, 203–5
Rute 137, 138, 201
rye, 80–1, 93

Salamanca, city, population 185
Salamanca, province, 199, 201, 226;
    plague in 36, 45
    alienations in 197
Salazar y Torres, 72
sale of *alcabalas* 195, 197–200, 285; in
    Cordoba 198; in Valladolid 198
sale of titles 252, 253, 254–6
sale of townships and exemptions 196–7
sale of vassals 252, 261, 281
Salomon, Noël 73
Sánchez, Tomás, SJ 51
Sánchez Salazar, Felipe 94
Sandoval monastery, León, land rents
    87
Santander 33
Santiago de Compostela 189, 190
Sayatón 64
Scockpol, Theda 252
Segovia, city 197, 201, 202, 225
    population 27, 184, 185, 189; plague
        in 37, 47
    textile manufactures in 2, 10, 24, 27,
        29, 306
    diocese of 17, 24, 87

Segovia, province, population of 52–3;
    plague in 43, 45
    agriculture in 75, 81–2, 86
    wool production 109
seignorialism 15, 76, 91, 198–201, 252,
    260–1, 263, 278, 281
    increase seignorial and ecclesiastical
        authority 15, 76
    jurisdiction of lords 261, 265–6
    intensification of seignorial burdens
        282–3, 318
    complaints of vassals against lords
        264, 283; migration from *señorío*
        268–70
señorío 250, 262–3; military role of 288
servicios 192, 215
Seville 64, 106, 122, 196; population
    125–7, 187, 190; plague in 34;
    manufacturing in 128–30; guilds in
    128
    taxes 194, 195
Seville, archdiocese of 132
sheep herding, sedentary flocks 74,
    84–5, 88, 106, 110; increase of
    24, 74, 75, 84–5, 107
    transhumant flocks 84, 102–3,
        109–10; decrease of 24, 84, 102,
        106, 109
silk industry 137, 139, 145; in Cordoba
    129–30
silver imports 118–24, 147, 227, 302
sisas, excise taxes, 177–80, 195
    impact on cost of living 179, 180,
        195, 201
    impact on labour costs 180, 202
Sobradillo 50
social factors in agrarian depression
    22
Sombart, Werner 252
Soria, city 199, 201, 203
    province, plague in 36, 43, 45; wool
        production 109; alienations in
        196–7
specialisation of crops 64, 70
state, institutions, role of in crisis
    308–11, 317, 320–1
state debts 9; *juros* 170, 180, 194, 221,
    226–7, 247
Steensgaard, Niels 302, 309, 311

Talavera de la Reina 186, plague in 34,
    49
tasa, grain price maxima, 30, 70, 148–9

328   *Index*

taxation 28, 93, 107, 193–5
  administrative procedures 173–9,
    191–2, 195–200, 215, 229
  differences royal and seigniorial areas
    198–200, 232, 269–70
  privileges, foral 203–4, social 175–6,
    195, 198–200, 253
  impact on economy 6, 7, 9, 22, 28,
    66, 88–91, 194, 200–4
  on urban network 191–205
Tendilla 64
tercias 172–3
tercio de frutos 125, 130, 132
textile industry 10, 11, 15, 24, 27, 29,
    103, 105, 128–30, 305–6
  in Cordoba, 136–68
  organisation and mercantile
    activity 144–6, 159–60
  capital and credit 145–7, 159–60;
    merchants 165–6
  regulations 151, 162–4;
    protectionism 152
  guilds, attitudes, policies of 153,
    157, 162–5; hostility to
    merchants 163
  rural manufactures 137, 139–40,
    151, 159–60, 167
  foreign competition 140, 151, 161;
    quality of 140–2, 164; imitation
    of 161–2; importation of foreign
    craftsmen 151–2
  product development, silk 155–7
  raw materials, supply of 143, 151, 156
  taxation 158
  reform projects 148, 150–4; failure
    of 158; outcome of, wool 154–5,
    silk 153, 155–8
Thomas, R.P. 1
Thompson, I.A.A. 250, 252, 285, 288
Tierra de Campos 22, 81, 82, 89, 90,
    149, 185; population 187
tithes, as sources 12, 17, 60, 75, 79
Toledo, city 64, 186, 188, 189, 153, 162,
    196, 197, 202
  population 27; plague in 40, 47;
    textile manufactures 2, 10, 24
Toledo, archdiocese 17, 79–80, 82
Toledo, province, population 65, 186;
    plague in 45
Tomás y Valiente, Francisco 256, 286
Topographical Relations 60, 64, 71, 186
Torrecampo 159
towns, sale of jurisdictions 195, 196–7

relations with *tierras* 196–7, 206–19
Trujillo 80–1, 110, 111, 186
typhus in plague of 1596–1602, 36–7, 38

Ubeda 187
urban demand for agricultural products
    60, 62, 65, 66

Valencia, city, hospital deaths 47
  kingdom, plague in 33
  silk production 143–5, 152, 153, 156,
    167
Valencia, Pedro de 73
Valladolid, city 27, 169–81, 201, 202,
    225, 232
  plague in 47; population 185
  guilds 179
Valladolid, province, population 185;
    plague in 37, 44
  alienations in 197
Vassberg, David E. 88, 93
Vega, Lope de 72
vellón, debasement 22
Vicens Vives, Jaime 2, 6, 319
Vilar, Pierre 202
Villacastín, plague in 38, 49
Villafranca, marquises of 292, 293
Villalba, Joaquín de 33, 34
Villalón 185, 226, 232
Villari, Rosario 251
Vincent, Bernard 34, 46, 127
viticulture 63, 64, 68, 75, 83, 133, 138
Vitigudino, plague in 40, 42
Vries, Jan de 1, 182

Wallerstein, I. 1, 8, 303, 305
Waquet, J.C. 294, 295
war, impact on economy 84, 312, on
    Italy 313, 315; on expenditure and
    political structure 252, 308, 309–11
weather 69, 131, 138
woodland, ploughing up of 62–3, 65,
    66; reforestation 66–7
wool exports 2, 8, 27, 83–4, 101–2,
    105–110, 143
  qualities of Spanish wool 103–4
  prices 24, 105, 109

yields, 62, 68, 74–5, 94
Yun, Bartolomé, 89, 90

Zamora, population 184, 185
Zaragoza, hospital deaths 47

Past and Present Publications

General Editor: PAUL SLACK, *Exeter College, Oxford*

Family and Inheritance: Rural Society in Western Europe 1200–1800, edited by Jack Goody, Joan Thirsk and E. P. Thompson*

French Society and the Revolution, edited by Douglas Johnson

Peasants, Knights and Heretics: Studies in Medieval English Social History, edited by R. H. Hilton*

Town in Societies: Essays in Economic History and Historical Sociology, edited by Philip Abrams and E. A. Wrigley*

Desolation of a City: Coventry and the Urban Crisis of the Late Middle Ages, Charles Phythian-Adams

Puritanism and Theatre: Thomas Middleton and Opposition Drama under the Early Stuarts, Margot Heinemann*

Lords and Peasants in a Changing Society: The Estates of the Bishopric of Worcester 680–1540, Christopher Dyer

Life, Marriage and Death in a Medieval Parish: Economy, Society and Demography in Halesowen 1270–1400, Zvi Razi

Biology, Medicine and Society 1840–1940, edited by Charles Webster

The Invention of Tradition, edited by Eric Hobsbawm and Terence Ranger*

Industrialization before Industrialization: Rural Industry and the Genesis of Capitalism, Peter Kriedte, Hans Medick and Jürgen Schlumbohm*

The Republic in the Village: The People of the Var from the French Revolution to the Second Republic, Maurice Agulhon

Social Relations and Ideas: Essays in Honour of R. H. Hilton, edited by T. H. Aston, P. R. Coss, Christopher Dyer and Joan Thirsk

A Medieval Society: The West Midlands at the End of the Thirteenth Century, R. H. Hilton

Winstanley: 'The Law of Freedom' and Other Writings, edited by Christopher Hill

Crime in Seventeenth-Century England: A County Study, J.A. Sharpe†

The Crisis of Feudalism: Economy and Society in Eastern Normandy c. 1300–1500, Guy Bois†

The Development of the Family and Marriage in Europe, Jack Goody*

Disputes and Settlements: Law and Human Relations in the West, edited by John Bossy

Rebellion, Popular Protest and the Social Order in Early Modern England, edited by Paul Slack

Studies on Byzantine Literature of the Eleventh and Twelfth Centuries, Alexander Kazhdan in collaboration with Simon Franklin†

The English Rising of 1381, edited by R. H. Hilton and T. H. Aston*

Praise and Paradox: Merchants and Craftsmen in Elizabethan Popular Literature, Laura Caroline Stevenson

The Brenner Debate: Agrarian Class Structure and Economic Development in Pre-Industrial Europe, edited by T. H. Aston and C. H. E. Philpin*

Eternal Victory: Triumphal Rulership in Late Antiquity, Byzantium, and the Early Medieval West, Michael McCormick†*

East-Central Europe in Transition: From the Fourteenth to the Seventeenth Century, edited by Antoni Mączak, Henryk Samsonowicz and Peter Burke†

Small Books and Pleasant Histories: Popular Fiction and its Readership in Seventeenth-Century England, Margaret Spufford*

Society: Politics and Culture: Studies in Early Modern England, Mervyn James*

Horses, Oxen and Technological Innovation: The Use of Draught Animals in English Farming 1066–1500, John Langdon

Nationalism and Popular Protest in Ireland, edited by C. H. E. Philpin

Rituals of Royalty: Power and Ceremonial in Traditional Societies, edited by David Cannadine and Simon Price*

The Margins of Society in Late Medieval Paris, Bronisław Geremek†

Landlords, Peasants and Politics in Medieval England, edited by T. H. Aston

Geography, Technology, and War: Studies in the Maritime History of the Mediterranean, 649–1571, John H. Pryor*

Church Courts, Sex and Marriage in England, 1570–1640, Martin Ingram*

Searches for an Imaginary Kingdom: The Legend of the Kingdom of Prester John, L. N. Gumilev

Crowds and History: Mass Phenomena in English Towns, 1780–1835, Mark Harrison

Concepts of Cleanliness: Changing Attitudes in France since the Middle Ages, Georges Vigarello†

The First Modern Society: Essays in English History in Honour of Lawrence Stone, edited by A. L. Beier, David Cannadine and James M. Rosenheim

The Europe of the Devout: The Catholic Reformation and the Formation of a New Society, Louis Châtellier†

English Rural Society, 1500–1800: Essays in Honour of Joan Thirsk, edited by John Chartres and David Hey

From Slavery to Feudalism in South-Western Europe, Pierre Bonnassie†

Lordship, Knighthood and Locality: A Study in English Society c. 1180–c. 1280, P. R. Coss

English and French Towns in Feudal Society: A Comparative Study, R. H. Hilton

An Island for Itself: Economic Development and Social Change in Late Medieval Sicily, Stephan R. Epstein

Epidemics and Ideas: Essays on the Historical Perception of Pestilence, edited by Terence Ranger and Paul Slack

The Political Economy of Shopkeeping in Milan, 1886–1922, Jonathan Morris

After Chartism: Class and Nation in English Radical Politics, 1848–1874, Margot C. Finn

Commoners: Common Right, Enclosure and Social Change in England, 1700–1820, J.M. Nelson

Land and Popular Politics in Ireland: County Mayo from the Plantation to the Land War, Donald E. Jordan Jr*
The Castilian Crisis of the Seventeenth Century: New Perspectives on the Economic and Social History of Seventeenth-Century Spain, edited by I. A. A. Thompson and Bartolomé Yun Casalilla

* Published also as a paperback
† Co-published with the Maison des Sciences de L'Homme, Paris